TOEFL®
TEST STRATEGIES

Third Edition

Eli Hinkel, Ph.D.
Seattle University

WITHDRAWAL  **BARRON'S**

All inquiries should be addressed to:
Barron's Educational Series, Inc.
250 Wireless Boulevard
Hauppauge, New York 11788
http://www.barronseduc.com

TOEFL answer sheets are reprinted by permission of
Educational Testing Service, the copyright owner. No
endorsement of this publication by Educational Testing
Service should be inferred.

Library of Congress Catalog Card No.: 2003060506

ISBN-13: 978-0-7641-7745-3 (Book and 5 CDs Package)
ISBN-10: 0-7641-7745-1 (Book and 5 CDs Package)
ISBN-13: 978-0-7641-2342-9 (Book only)
ISBN-10: 0-7641-2342-4 (Book only)

Library of Congress Cataloging-in-Publication Data

Hinkel, Eli.
    TOEFL strategies / Eli Hinkel. — 3rd ed.
       p. cm.
    ISBN 0-7641-2342-4 — ISBN 0-7641-7745-1 (book with Audio CDs)
     1. Test of English as a Foreign Language—Study guides. 2. English language—Textbooks
for foreign speakers. 3. English language—Examinations—Study guides. I. Title.

    PE1128.H46 2004
    428'.0076—dc22

                                                                                    2003060506

PRINTED IN THE UNITED STATES OF AMERICA

9 8 7 6

Contents

Preface   v

1   About the TOEFL   1

2   About the Computer TOEFL   5

3   Strategies for Listening Comprehension   15

4   Practice for Listening Comprehension   35
    Supplement to Listening Practice   43
        Idioms in Daily Conversation   43
        List of Idioms and Two- or Three-Word Verbs Frequently Used on the
            TOEFL   43

5   Strategies for Structure and Written Expression   51

6   Practice for Structure and Written Expression   71

7   Strategies for Reading Comprehension   103

8   Practice for Reading Comprehension   117

9   Test of Written English   143

Practice TOEFL 1   165

Practice TOEFL 2   191

Practice TOEFL 3   215

Practice TOEFL 4   239

Practice TOEFL 5   263

Practice TOEFL 6   287

Practice TOEFL 7   313

Practice TOEFL 8   339

Appendix

    A. Tapescript for Chapter 4:
            Listening Comprehension   365
    B. Tapescripts for Practice TOEFL Tests 1–8   375
    C. Scoring Practice Tests   435
    D. Answer Keys   440
    E. Answer Sheets   455

Preface

TOEFL Strategies is intended for students who are preparing for the TOEFL as it is administered in the United States or at international sites. Teachers of TOEFL preparation courses will also find this book an invaluable asset in addressing students' needs and providing realistic exercises for practice.

This book is based on research on the TOEFL between 1980 and 2003. It provides the most up-to-date test information available on the market today. The questions, sentences, vocabulary, and texts from dozens of tests were classified according to the linguistic categories the questions were designed to test, the correct responses, the distractors, and the topics. Most TOEFL technical reports and other materials published by Educational Testing Service (ETS) were examined and applied to the research. *TOEFL Strategies* provides updated information on these changes as well as computations of the frequency with which certain structures and reading selections appear on the test.

Furthermore, this book includes strategies and practice for all three required TOEFL sections: Listening Comprehension, Structure and Written Expression, and Reading Comprehension.

The exercises differ from the practice tests in an important way. The exercises contain TOEFL-like questions focusing on one structure or question type at a time. For example, one exercise centers on sentences that test active/passive voice discrimination. On the other hand, in the practice tests all structures tested on the TOEFL are included in the same proportions as on the actual test.

In addition to the computed frequencies of the various TOEFL questions, Chapter 5, "Strategies for Structure and Written Expression," also incorporates a linguistic sentence analysis that allows both students and teachers to utilize the regularities of English syntax to their best advantage. The long-term benefits of sentence and phrase analysis can extend beyond preparation for the TOEFL. Heightened awareness of English syntax and phrase structure can raise students' overall proficiency in reading, writing, and aural comprehension.

Chapter 1, "About the TOEFL," provides a brief description of the test and general strategies for taking the TOEFL. Chapter 2 provides a tutorial with strategies specifically for the Computer-Based Test (CBT). Chapters 3 and 7, "Strategies for Listening Comprehension" and "Strategies for Reading Comprehension," include both TOEFL-specific tasks and methods of sentence and text analysis to improve aural comprehension and reading skills. The text analysis method of preparing for the TOEFL relies on discrimination between the primary and secondary information contained in a text, and the ways in which such elements as negations, comparisons, and conditionals affect the meaning of a sentence or passage.

The book contains a strategies and a practice chapter for each of the TOEFL sections: Listening Comprehension, Structure and Written Expression, and Reading Comprehension. As for the Test of Written English (TWE), Chapter 9 includes an analysis of topics used on the TWE in the past, examples of good and poor essays, and strategies for obtaining the best possible score on this portion of the test.

The eight practice tests provide students with ample test-taking and learning experience. The exercises for the three TOEFL sections and the sizable number of model tests allow the students and/or the teacher to choose the particular types of work that can best meet diverse student training needs and expectations. If the teacher wishes, some of the exercises and practice tests can be assigned as homework or as independent study to supplement the course text.

This resource of sufficient training materials offers teachers flexibility in meeting the test preparation requirements of a student audience whose test-preparation and language learning needs are seldom uniform. The strategies in this book have been classroom-tested for several years in four universities. In addition, the texts included in this book and the practice materials for each section have been administered to students in TOEFL preparation courses in four universities in the United States. The manuscript was reviewed by over a dozen professional English as a Second Language (ESL) instructors, whose suggestions were incorporated.

Acknowledgments

For providing me with their valuable comments, I appreciate the help of Pam Lovern, Deborah Schiavo, and Julianne Taaffe, teachers at the American Language Program, and Ian Balmer and Bruce Rogers, teaching associates at the ESL Composition Program at The Ohio State University. Mary Sheridan and Lara Dorger, instructors in the ESL Program at Xavier University, contributed much to the quality of this text. I am grateful to them for their meticulous analysis of items and for their cheerful support. Above all, I would like to express my gratitude to Rodney Hill, a technical writer, who painstakingly read every word in this book and performed each task. Without his assistance and advice, my job would have been immeasurably more difficult. His help and comments were invaluable.

About the TOEFL

The TOEFL is prepared and administered by the Educational Testing Service (ETS), a private company located in Princeton, New Jersey. ETS handles all activities related to the TOEFL, but it does not establish the scores necessary for admission to particular universities, colleges, schools, or departments. These decisions are made by the individual educational institutions. You can obtain information about the TOEFL or about any related matters by visiting the web site at http://www.toefl.org or by writing to:

> TOEFL Services
> Educational Testing Service
> Princeton, NJ 08541-0001
> USA

Structure of the TOEFL

Most TOEFL tests consist of three sections and 150 questions. Each test begins with the Listening Comprehension section, followed by the Structure and Written Expression section and, finally, the Reading Comprehension section. These sections are further divided into parts. Listening Comprehension contains Part A, Part B, and Part C; Structure and Written Expression includes Part A and Part B. Although the parts of the sections primarily test the skills described in the title of the section, each part approaches the testing of these skills differently. The specific differences between the parts are described in the corresponding chapters of this book.

The Test of Written English (TWE), required by many universities, is administered at specified times. Detailed information about this test is given in Chapter 9.

What You Should Know About TOEFL

Students who are planning to take the TOEFL should be aware of certain specific features of the test.

First, the writers of the test frequently use distractors (tricks), which make wrong answers to questions seem correct. There is only one way to deal with these distractors: you need to know English. Many students believe that studying TOEFL preparation textbooks is all they need to do to obtain a high score on the test. Although such textbooks can provide practice opportunities and a review of listening, grammar, and reading skills, it is not sufficient simply to concentrate on these texts. There is no substitute for studying English in a systematic way.

Second, although many topics are based on U.S. history and social situations, most of these materials are presented in a way that does not require prior familiarity with them. All materials and questions that involve American topics require only the ability to comprehend oral and written English and a knowledge of English grammar.

Third, such controversial issues as religion, death, political disagreements, historical disputes, violent crime, and topics that some ethnic groups may find objectionable do not appear on the test. The writers attempt to make the test materials as neutral as possible.

Skills Tested on the TOEFL

Being able to speak English well does not mean that you are assured of a high score on the test. The TOEFL tests the language skills appropriate in academic and professional settings. In addition to good listening skills, you need to have solid skills in grammar, vocabulary, and reading. In fact, generally it is not those who speak English well who receive high scores on the test, but rather those who write well. The reason is that writing requires strong skills in grammar, vocabulary, and reading comprehension, which constitute two of the three TOEFL sections.

Budgeting and managing your time is another skill that is very important for TOEFL-takers. When you are working on the Structure and Written Expression section or the Reading Comprehension section, you should try to work as fast as you can. When you are preparing for the test, use your watch to time yourself and figure out which aspects of the test take more time than you can spend. The chapters on the individual sections tell you how much time each question should take in order for you to complete the section within the time allotted.

General Strategies for Taking the Paper TOEFL

WHAT NOT TO DO ON THE TOEFL

1. Do not mark two answers on the answer sheet. If you do, both will be counted wrong even if one of them is correct.
2. If you change an answer, do not leave any pencil marks on the sheet except in the answer you have chosen. Erase your first answer completely.
3. Do not leave any answers blank. There is no penalty for guessing.
4. Do not write anything on the answer sheet except what is required on the test. TOEFL answer sheets are graded by a machine that can "see" only dark or light circles. If you write on your answer sheet, the machine may "confuse" your writing with your answers and not give you credit for a correct answer.
5. Do not get distracted, or stop for a little rest.
6. When answering the questions in sections 2 and 3, do not think that you have to do the questions in order. First, work with the questions that are easy for you; then return and do the difficult ones.
7. Do not attempt to cheat. ETS has taken steps to make cheating difficult. In order to stop people from copying answers from others, ETS may administer several forms of the same test at the same time. In such forms, the questions are printed in a different order, or an extra question may be added at the beginning of a section (or a part) and the last question omitted. This organization makes all the questions "slide down" one row.

In the past few years, test-takers have had to provide identification with a photograph during registration for the test. The college or university to which the student is eventually admitted can compare the appearance of the person who took the test with that of the person who submitted the score. If the two individuals are clearly different, the student can be expelled from the college or university and may have to return to his or her country.

WHAT TO DO ON THE TOEFL

1. When you do not know the correct answer to a particular question in the Listening Comprehension section, you should mark an answer anyway and not spend too much

time thinking about it. Many students who take the TOEFL lose time on questions in the Listening Comprehension section and do not finish their Structure and Written Expression and Reading Comprehension sections.

2. Use your knowledge of English and your understanding of the TOEFL to make the best guesses possible. It is very important to remember that in all three sections the choices (B) and (C) are correct 60–65 percent of the time. Answer (A) is correct only about 15–20 percent of the time and (D) about 20–25 percent. This book provides you with many effective strategies for guessing the answers on the test.

Test Differences

Although the TOEFL designers try to make all tests of equal difficulty, this is not always possible. However, differences in test difficulty are eliminated statistically by means of complicated mathematical operations, so that a given test score indicates a specific level of proficiency regardless of the difficulty of the test.

Tests can differ in length, as well. Some contain 150 questions, and others 200 questions. For all tests, only 150 questions count in the score. The other 50 questions are administered by ETS to try out new materials before including them in future tests. However, since test-takers do not know which questions count and which do not, they have to try their best on all of them. The disadvantage of taking a 200-question test is that test-takers tend to get tired during a longer test and may not do as well as on the shorter version. The 150-question tests take approximately 3 hours; the 200-question tests take about 4 hours.

The TOEFL Now and in the Future

Currently, the TOEFL is required by almost all colleges and universities in the United States and some Canadian institutions. In addition, the TOEFL is required by many state and government agencies that license foreign professionals, such as medical doctors, dentists, and nurses. These institutions use TOEFL scores to evaluate your English language proficiency and to determine whether your language skills are sufficient for you to do well in American academic and professional settings.

In the past few years, many professionals in American education have expressed concerns as to whether a TOEFL score can provide a good indication of one's success in academic institutions in the United States. To deal with these concerns, ETS has added another section to the traditional TOEFL format: the Test of Written English. Although the TWE is not included as a part of every TOEFL administration, the number of tests that include the TWE has been increasing over the years. Chapter 9 explains how the TWE is administered. It also suggests strategies for successful preparation for this part of the TOEFL, analyzes good and poor sample essays, and offers writing topics for practice.

Because simply adding the TWE to the basic TOEFL did not satisfy a large number of professionals in the teaching of English as a Second Language (ESL) and in universities where many foreign students pursue their studies, ETS has initiated a program to revise the test. The goal of this program, which is called New Generation TOEFL, is to change the test layout and the materials included in the test by the end of the year 2005.

ETS plans to continue to make changes in the TOEFL in the next few years. Beginning in 2001, ETS introduced computer-based TOEFL tests. These tests are currently offered in North America, some countries in Latin America and Europe, some centers in Australia, and a few Asian countries. By the year 2005, ETS plans for most TOEFL testing to be computer-based. The New Generation TOEFL will continue to test Listening Comprehension, Structure and Written Expression, and Reading Comprehension, although the form of the questions may change. The new TOEFL will also require test-takers to write an essay and add a speaking component. For those who are not familiar with the use of computers, ETS already provides computer training for one and a half hours before the actual test.

This book has been prepared for your practice for the paper test as it exists now. However, in the future, when the TOEFL changes, later editions of this book will change with it so as to continue to provide you with the best up-to-date preparation for the test.

About the Computer TOEFL

The computer version of the TOEFL test includes the same four sections that the paper version of the test includes: Listening Comprehension, Structure[1], Reading Comprehension, and Writing. The same language skills are tested on both the computer and the paper tests, so if you have prepared for and are able to do well on the paper test, you should also do well on the computer test. There are some differences between the computer test and the paper test, especially in the Listening and Reading Comprehension areas, which include new question types.

When the computer test is offered at a given location, you do not have the option to take the ETS-scored paper test instead. In most locations, however, institutional TOEFL tests in the paper version are also offered.

The advantages to taking the computer test are that you can easily see how much time remains in a section, you do not have to worry about completely filling the circles for the correct answer in a selection, and you can get your scores more quickly than when you take the paper test.

On the other hand, some of the tips that work well for the paper test do not work on the computer test. While listening to a speaker in the Listening Comprehension section of the computer TOEFL, you cannot scan ahead to see what questions will be asked because the questions are not displayed on the computer until after the dialog or lecture has been played. Also, you cannot skip questions you do not know the answer to and come back to them later on the Listening Comprehension and Structure sections because the computer TOEFL will not let you go on to the next question until you have answered the current question. When you are taking the computer TOEFL, you cannot go back and change any of your answers except in the Reading Comprehension section.

STUDY TIP

Despite the new appearance of the computer test and basic computer skills that are required for CBT TOEFLs, the language skills tested on both the computer and paper versions largely remain the same. The test tasks you need to perform on both versions of the TOEFL are also very similar. Thus, to do well on the test you need to concentrate on largely the same types of questions found in both types of the test.

---

[1] The Structure section on the computer TOEFL corresponds to the Structure and Written Comprehension section on the paper-based TOEFL.

Starting the Computer Test

When you start a section of the computer test, the screen displays the instructions for that section. You must click the **Dismiss Directions** button to move to the first question. You should be familiar with the instructions for the various sections from the text and practice tests in this book.

Do not waste time reading the instructions again, but click **Dismiss Directions** immediately.

Here is the basic appearance of the screen you will see when you are taking the computer TOEFL. The upper-left corner displays the time remaining in the section. In this case, there are six minutes remaining. The upper-right corner displays the number of the question you are answering and the total number of questions for the section. In this example, question 11 out of a total of 20 questions is displayed.

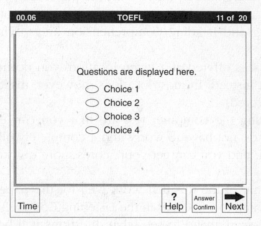

STUDY TIP

You must use the computer mouse to answer questions and move to new questions. Unlike with most computer programs, with the computer TOEFL you cannot use the keyboard to answer questions or move from option to option.

Time

Each section has a time limit, which is roughly similar to those on the paper test and which is displayed in the upper-left-hand corner of the screen. The **Time** button in the lower-left-hand corner of the screen allows you to turn off the time display if you want. It is better, however, to leave the remaining time displayed so that you can easily glance up and see how much time you have left.

Help

The **Help** button is available when the directions are displayed and when you are answering questions. Clicking the **Help** button will open a screen with the directions for the section you are taking at that time, as well as general instructions for using the computer TOEFL program. You should understand the various sections and how to use the program before you get started on the actual test because the time is continuing to be counted when you are looking up instructions in the Help file. Do not click the **Help** button. It will waste time that you need to spend actually answering the questions.

Answering Questions

To answer each question, you must click the mouse *at least three times* on each screen.

1. Click to select the answer in the question area. This may mean clicking an oval, an underlined word or phrase that is incorrect, a small picture that answers the question, or several words or pictures to place them in the proper sequence or category.

2. Click the **Next** button. When you click the **Next** button, the **Answer Confirm** button will be slightly darker than before, indicating that you can choose it. You cannot click the **Answer Confirm** button until have you clicked the **Next** button.

3. Click the **Answer Confirm** button. Until you click the **Answer Confirm** button, *you cannot see the next question.*

STUDY TIP

A common mistake is to click just the Next button and wait for the next question to be displayed. This can cost you precious seconds and much time throughout the test. Remember to click the Answer Confirm button immediately after you click the Next button.

In addition to the question types described throughout this book, the Listening and Reading Comprehension sections also include new question types that test essentially the same language skills that are tested on the paper test.

Listening Comprehension

Before the actual test begins, you can adjust the volume of the headset only at the start of the test during the directions. *After the test begins, you cannot adjust the volume.* To adjust the volume, click the **Volume** button to the left of the **Help** button. In the volume adjustment screen, click the up arrow to increase the volume or the down arrow to decrease the volume.

When a dialogue or lecture is played, pictures are displayed on the screen. If the pictures are only of people talking or sitting in a lecture room, do not focus on the pictures. Studies have shown that focusing on the pictures can marginally reduce your ability to answer the questions correctly because pictures are distracting. Just concentrate on what is said. On the other hand, some of the pictures illustrate content to go with a lecture (for example, pictures of paintings by particular artists in a lecture on art styles), and you must pay attention to this type of picture.

If you know the answer, choose it quickly and move on. The time you save on the easy questions can be used on the harder questions. On average, budget your time so that you spend about 12 seconds on a question.

In the listening section of the paper TOEFL, the questions require you to select one and only one answer. There is only one right answer to the questions on the paper TOEFL. In the computer version of the TOEFL, there are additional types of questions. Instructions for a question are presented with a gray background.

In some questions with one right answer, you are instructed to click on the correct letter. In the following example, the question is "Which section of the page is the footnote?" You must click on the letter on the correct portion of the page to give your answer. In this question, the correct answer is **C**.

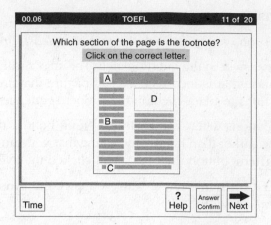

In some questions, you will be asked to click on a picture instead of a letter, oval, or check-box. A dark border will surround the picture you choose. In this example, the question is "Which shape is the cylinder?" You must click on the correct picture to give your answer. In this example, the correct answer to the question is the round shape in the lower right among the four shapes.

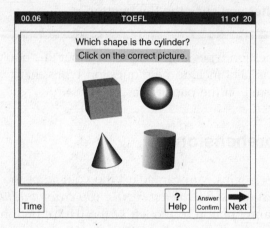

Some questions have more than one correct answer. Instead of ovals in front of your choic-es, these questions have little squares, or checkboxes, and the instructions clearly state how many answers you are to choose. In this example, the question is "Which of the following ver-tebrates are mammals?" The instructions specify that you need to give *two* correct answers to get the full score, and you will not be able to move to the next question if you click only on one correct answer. In this question, the correct answers are *squirrels* and *beavers*.

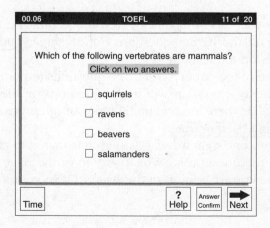

Some questions will ask you to make matches among sets of words. For example, the question in the following illustration asks you to sort words by categories. In the example below, these categories are:

animal plant mineral

You need to fill each box with the word that best goes with the word below the box. In the following example, "raven" goes into the "animal" box, "quartz" goes into the "mineral" box, and "fern" goes into the "plant" box.

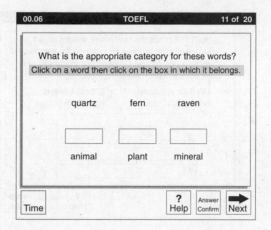

When you click on the word, it is highlighted in black, as is the word "raven" in the following illustration.

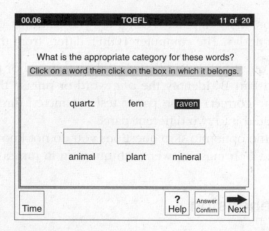

After you have clicked and highlighted a word, click the box you want to put it in. The word then appears in the box, as in the following illustration.

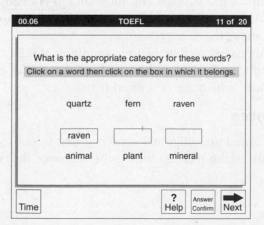

If you want to change your answer, you can click another word, and click on the same box to put the new word in the box. Make sure you use each word only one time.

Another type of computer TOEFL Listening question requires you to order items in a sequence. You need to click on the sentence or phrase that comes first, then click on the first box. In the following example, you would click on "Mix flour and water." and then click on the first box. Next, you would click on the sentence or phrase that comes second ("Knead the dough.") and then on the second box, and so on until you have used each item once and have them in the correct order.

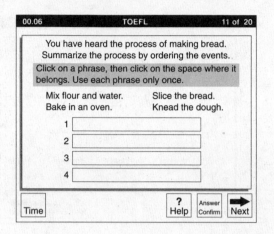

Structure

Structure questions on the computer TOEFL are the same as on the paper test and are described in Chapters 4 and 5. The computer TOEFL differs from the paper test in two ways.

- The two types of questions in Part A (Select the *one* word or phrase that best completes the sentence) and Part B (Identify the *one* word or phrase that should be changed for the sentence to be correct) of the paper test are mixed throughout the computer test rather than separated into two different parts.
- You do not have the option to skip questions you do not know the answer to and come back to them later. You must answer each question in turn as it is displayed.

Reading Comprehension

Each passage in the Reading Comprehension section is displayed before the questions are displayed. *Do not read the whole text at first.* Move the scroll bar on the right side of the reading passage to the bottom of the passage and then click **Proceed**. You'll be able to read the passage when the questions are displayed, plus you'll be able to see what the questions are that you are reading to answer.

The Reading Comprehension section of the computer TOEFL contains the same types of questions as described in Chapter 7 of this book. In addition, the computer TOEFL includes a few new types of question, which are described here.

Inserting New Sentences

You may be asked to read an additional sentence that is not included in the original passage and select a location in the passage where the sentence fits best.

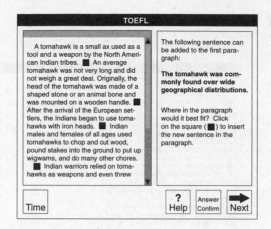

In this example, you would click the first black square in the passage. The new sentence would then be automatically inserted in that location.

You need to check the context of each square in the passage to determine if the new sentence should go there. In this example, the very first sentence in front of the first black square—"A tomahawk is a small ax used as a tool and a weapon by the North American Indian tribes."—suggests a large geographic space because of the phrase "North American Indian tribes." The sentence to be inserted also mentions a wide geographical area.

The sentence in front of the second black square describes the construction of tomahawks before Europeans arrived on the North American continent, and the sentence after the second black square describes a change in the construction of tomahawks after European arrival. The sentence to be inserted does not talk about materials used for making tomahawks. Therefore, if the sentence is inserted after the second black square, it would break up/separate the two sentences about materials already in place, so the second black square would be the wrong place to insert the additional sentence.

The sentence in front of the third black square talks about materials of the tomahawk and the sentence after it talks about uses of tomahawks. Although you could insert the new sentence here, nothing in either sentence deals with the geographical area where tomahawks were used mentioned in the additional sentence.

The sentences before and after the fourth black square talk about uses of the tomahawk (and not the area) and inserting the new sentence here would break up the information about tomahawk uses with unrelated information, so this is not a good place to put the additional sentence. The first black square is the place to insert the added sentence.

Different Wording for Questions

Some questions on the computer TOEFL are essentially the same as questions on the paper TOEFL but are worded differently and answered differently on the computer TOEFL.

Vocabulary

Some vocabulary questions ask you to click on a word in a portion of the reading passage that is close in meaning to another highlighted word in the text. The language skill tested is identical to the skill required for vocabulary questions on the paper TOEFL and described in Chapter 7. You just need to click the mouse on the word you want to choose as the correct answer to the question. On the paper TOEFL, you need to eliminate three wrong answers to vocabulary questions, but on the computer TOEFL, you need to eliminate many more. If the word you are trying to match is a verb, in the selection of possible answers, concentrate only on the verbs for words with similar meaning. If the word is a noun, only look at nouns.

In the following example, the word "split" is closest in meaning to the word "cut," so you would click on the word "split."

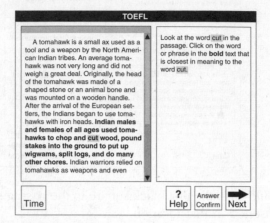

Locating Information in the Passage

Some questions ask you to click on the sentence in the passage that provides certain information. The language skill tested is identical to the skill required for vocabulary questions on the paper TOEFL and described in Chapter 7, such as "Where in the passage does the author describe/discuss xxx?"

The question in the following example asks you to click on the sentence that describes what tomahawks were constructed of before the arrival of the European settlers. You would click on the following sentence: "Originally, the head of the tomahawk was made of a shaped stone or an animal bone and was mounted on a wooden handle."

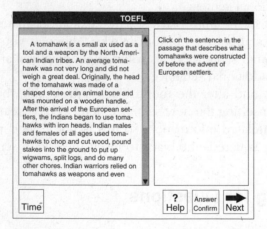

The Reading Comprehension Section is the only one on the computer TOEFL where you can skip questions without answering them.

Writing

On the computer TOEFL, you have the option of typing your essay response into the computer or writing your essay by hand on a piece of paper. If you choose to write your essay by hand, however, it will take you longer to get your TOEFL score report than if you type your essay on the word processor because TOEFL essays are scored by a computer, instead of real readers.

The computer program allows simple cut, copy, and paste operations, as well as one "undo" operation that allows you to go back only one step. Unless you are quite comfortable typing and composing with a word processor, or unless your handwriting is very hard to read, you are probably better off using pencil and paper. On the other hand, if you are used to working on a word processor, you should type your essay. As always, do not forget to proofread and check your essay before submitting it. It is important to remember that the TOEFL word processor is very simple compared to common word processing programs, and it has no spell-checker.

Originally, when the computer TOEFL first appeared, the plan was to eliminate the paper TOEFL completely and require all test-takers to take CBT. Since then, however, it became clear that so many test-takers have avoided the computer test that between 2002 and 2003 more than a hundred computer TOEFL centers were closed. If in your country or city it is possible for you to take the paper test instead of the computer test, you should attempt to take the paper test because it allows greater flexibility in strategy use than the computer test.

CHAPTER 3

Strategies for Listening Comprehension

About the Listening Comprehension Section of the Test

The Listening Comprehension section of the test consists of three parts with a total of 50 questions: 30 in Part A, between 7 and 9 in Part B, and between 11 and 13 in Part C. The time is controlled by the tape and you have between 45 and 47 minutes to complete the entire section—approximately 12–15 seconds to answer each question. Headphones are not provided for test-takers. Instead, the listening selections are channeled through speakers, and the quality of the sound may vary.

It is important to note that no prior knowledge of the topics covered in any part of the TOEFL test is necessary for a successful test score.

The speakers on the tape use American English with American pronunciation. They frequently use common American expressions. In all three parts of the Listening Comprehension section, the speakers talk at a speed that the designers of the test consider usual in American English. However, test-takers whose listening comprehension skills are not very good may think that the rate of speech on the tape is a little too fast for comfort.

There are three parts in the Listening Comprehension section of the test, and you are faced with three different listening tasks:

1. Responding to one question that follows a short exchange between two speakers (Part A).
2. Answering several questions about a longer conversation between two speakers (Part B).
3. Answering specific questions about information contained in a short lecture, which is similar to the task you have to perform when listening to a professor in a lecture class (Part C).

STUDY TIP

There is no penalty for wrong answers on the TOEFL. Even if you are not sure what the correct answer is, try to select the answer that you think is best and fill in the corresponding circle on your answer sheet. If you have no idea which answer is correct, guess. Remember that responses (B) and (C) are most often correct. In the computer version of the test, you cannot leave a question unanswered.

When working with the listening comprehension tasks on the paper-based TOEFL, you should try to figure out what the next listening selection will be about. To do this, you need to look at the multiple-choice responses to the next question in your test booklet before the speakers begin that selection.

Example of a short dialogue in Part A:

In Part A, you will hear 30 short dialogues between two speakers. The purpose in Part A is to test your ability to understand conversations on common, everyday topics. Academic topics seldom appear in this part of the TOEFL. Because exchanges between the two speakers are very informal and social, in Part A you will hear many contractions and idioms.

First example of a dialogue in Part A:

> Man: I think Sue knows how to get to the bus terminal.
> Woman: I've been trying to get hold of her for half an hour.

In the test, this dialogue will be followed by a question:

QUESTION: What does the woman mean?

This second sentence in the dialogue contains a contraction *I've* and an idiom ("frozen expression"), *to get hold of someone*. The contraction indicates the conversational style of this statement. The idiom can mean *to talk to someone, to reach someone, to get in touch with someone,* or *to contact someone.* Therefore, the statement means I *have been trying to contact Sue for half an hour.* The meaning of the verb *try* implies that the speaker has not been successful.
The multiple choice selection for this statement might be:

(A) Sue's been holding it for half an hour.
(B) Sue's been here for thirty minutes.
(C) I've been talking to Sue for half an hour.
(D) I haven't been able to contact Sue.

(A) is not correct; it states *Sue has been holding it,* but the second speaker states *I've been trying to get hold of Sue.* (B) is not correct: it states *Sue's been here* but the speaker does not really state where Sue is. (C) says *I've been talking to Sue,* but the speaker has been *trying* to reach Sue. (D) is correct: *I haven't been able to contact Sue* restates the meaning of the sentence in different words.

Second example of a short dialogue in Part A:

> Woman: Could you tell me what time the next train is due to arrive?
> Man: At six. I think it's a little behind schedule.

QUESTION: What does the man mean?

The conversationally polite expression *Could you* and the contraction *it's* again indicate the conversational style of this exchange. The phrase *due to arrive* in the woman's question means *is supposed to arrive.* In the man's response, the most important information is *behind schedule* meaning *the train is late.*
The multiple choice items for this short dialogue might be:

(A) The train is behind the station.
(B) The next train is due in six hours.
(C) The train may arrive late.
(D) The schedule is wrong.

(A) is not correct because the man said *behind schedule,* not *behind the station;* (B) is also wrong because nothing was said about the train being *due in six hours.* (C) is correct. (D) is not correct because the man did not say anything about the schedule being wrong.
In Part B, you will hear two types of listening tasks: long dialogues between two (and sometimes three) speakers, and short lectures given by one speaker.

Example of a longer dialogue in Part B:

Man: This beach is really dirty. Look at all these pieces of plastic and litter everywhere.

Woman: It's terrible. I'm sure some of it has washed up from the ocean. Plastic trash from ships has been dumped into the ocean for years.

Man: I'm surprised that waste can just be dumped into the ocean. Essentially, the ocean has become a receptacle for both industrial and city garbage. It is a disaster for sea birds and all forms of marine life.

Woman: You can say that again. Birds get caught in the plastic bags and packing materials that are dumped in the water. Why is such pollution allowed to happen?

Man: You should have seen what the sea water looked like just five years ago. The pumping of waste water into the ocean had continued for decades. Finally, new laws prohibit dumping industrial or city waste in the ocean. So, hopefully, over time, both the water and the beaches will become cleaner.

Woman: It's a good thing. Who knows, the entire marine environment could have been spoiled by garbage.

The dialogue is followed by several questions, each spoken only once. In your test booklet or computer screen, you will see the multiple-choice selections for each question.

The questions and answer choices for the preceding dialogue might be:

QUESTION 1:   Where does this conversation take place?

        (A) At a garbage dump.
        (B) In the city.
        (C) On the seashore.
        (D) In a marine lab.

The first sentence in the conversation is "This beach is really dirty." A beach is a sandy section of the seashore that gently slopes into the water. (A) is not correct because the speaker said "This beach." This means that the conversation is taking place at the beach. For this reason, (B) and (D) are also not correct. The correct answer is (C).

QUESTION 2:   What is said about the condition of the ocean waters?

        (A) They are stormy.
        (B) They are unpopulated.
        (C) They are polluted.
        (D) They are deep.

(A) is not correct because neither speaker mentioned stormy weather or waters. (B) is not correct because "sea birds and all forms of marine life" were mentioned. (C) is a possible answer; (D) is clearly incorrect because the dialogue does not discuss the ocean depth. Therefore, the correct answer is (C).

QUESTION 3:   According to the dialogue, why is waste dumping dangerous for sea birds?

        (A) They lose their habitats.
        (B) They become entangled in waste products.
        (C) They seek shelter on the shore.
        (D) They are being dumped into the ocean.

The speakers in the dialogue do not mention birds' habitats; therefore (A) is incorrect. (B) is possible because the woman in the dialogue noted that birds can become caught in plastic materials dumped into the ocean. (C) is incorrect because no mention is made of the birds seeking shelter anywhere. In (D), *they* refers to birds since *birds* is the only plural noun in the question, but "trash from ships" (trash is not plural) was mentioned as being "dumped into the ocean." The correct answer is (B).

QUESTION 4:   How does the law protect the ocean from pollution?

        (A) The beaches are cleaned regularly.
        (B) Marine life lost to pollution has to be restored.
        (C) Disposing of waste in the ocean is forbidden.
        (D) Garbage must be retrieved from the ocean.

The man in the dialogue said: "New laws prohibit dumping industrial or city waste in the ocean." The word *dumping* is synonymous with *throwing out* or *disposing of*. Therefore, the sentence means that new laws no longer allow disposal of waste in ocean waters. The speaker did not mention that the law requires cleaning the beaches, so (A) is incorrect. Similarly, he did not indicate that the law is concerned with the loss of sea animals and birds; (B) is also incorrect. (C) is the correct answer because it is simply a restatement of a sentence in the dialogue. In (D), *retrieved* means *taken out*. The speakers did not say that the new laws require taking the garbage out of the ocean. (D) is incorrect.

In Part C, you will hear several short lectures. As in Part B, they will be followed by questions. Both the lectures and the questions will be spoken only one time. The multiple choice selections will not be heard. Instead, you will find them printed in your test booklet or displayed on the computer screen.

Example of a short lecture in Part C:

If you need to buy a good lock, there are several things you should keep in mind. Locks differ in price and quality. You can make a decision about which lock you want to buy if you know how they work. Let me show you what we have here and quickly explain how basic locks work. When the correct key is inserted into the door lock, the notches on the key make metal plates align. Once the plates are aligned, the key pushes the bolt inside the lock between the door and the frame. Spring bolts are considered more convenient because you don't need to use a key to lock them. When the door closes, they snap into the door frame and stay locked until a key is used to open them. However, spring locks are not as secure as dead bolts because they can be easily picked or pried open. It's not hard to do; you can see for yourself. On the other hand, dead bolts work from inside the door, and they need a key to unlock them. Dead bolts are called "dead" because they don't move until you move them with a key. Spring locks and dead bolts are the two types of locks we sell most.

QUESTION 1:   What is the main topic of this talk?

        (A) The uses of doors
        (B) Why a lock is essential
        (C) How locks operate
        (D) How to install a lock

Although doors are mentioned in the lecture, the uses of doors are not discussed. (A) is incorrect. The lecture does not discuss why locks are essential; therefore, (B) is incorrect. The main topic of the talk is how basic locks work. (C) is the correct answer. Installing a lock is also not discussed, so (D) is a wrong answer.

QUESTION 2:   Why are dead bolts called "dead"?

> (A) They are no longer used.
> (B) They are poorly designed.
> (C) They are difficult to maintain.
> (D) They require a key to open them.

(A) is not correct because the speaker said that spring locks and dead bolts are commonly used. Nothing was mentioned regarding the design of dead bolts or their maintenance, so both (B) and (C) are wrong. (D) is the correct answer.

QUESTION 3:   What are the disadvantages of spring locks?

> (A) They are not convenient.
> (B) They are not common.
> (C) They are not secure.
> (D) They are not cheap.

(A) is not correct because the speaker said, "Spring bolts are considered more convenient...." The last sentence in the talk states, "Spring locks and dead bolts are the two types of locks we sell most," so (B) is also incorrect. (C) is a possible answer. Because the text does not mention the price of locks, (D) is incorrect. The correct answer is (C).

What the Listening Comprehension Section Is Designed to Test

The topics in the Listening Comprehension section do not require special knowledge of any specific subject. They are based on daily activities that can occur in most public places, such as libraries, schools/colleges/universities, banks, offices, shops, and parks. Some statements or portions of conversations might be made over the telephone. Many of them refer to basic cultural aspects of life in the United States. The main purpose of the Listening Comprehension section of the TOEFL is to measure how well you can function in the daily life and activities in the country.

The Listening Comprehension section tests a wide variety of grammatical structures, including affirmative and negative sentences, questions, and commands. Almost all verb tenses (including conditionals), active and passive voice, two-word verbs, prepositions, words with several meanings, personal names, nicknames, family names, forms of address, comparisons, numerals, and simple computations can appear in conversations and lectures in this section. When listening to the tape, you need to notice contractions *(I'm, you're, he's)*, contractions with negations *(don't, isn't)*, and final sounds and combinations of sounds *(-ed, -ing, -s)*. All sentences in the Listening Comprehension section are grammatical, and most are complete. They are spoken mostly in conversational English and only occasionally involve academic topics.

Since most topics in this section are not academic, the vocabulary tested in Section 1 is seldom very complicated. However, because idioms are frequently used in American conversational speech, you will find many idioms in the Listening Comprehension section.

Since 1986, the three most frequent listening tasks on the TOEFL have been:

(1) understanding idioms, conversational expressions, and two- or three-word verbs;
(2) discerning implied meanings; and
(3) answering questions about the specific content of a conversation or a short talk.

Other frequent test tasks include:

(4) interpreting emphasis, stress, and tone;
(5) sound discrimination; and
(6) understanding comparisons.

Each of these areas is explained below, with examples.

Examples of the frequently tested listening tasks

On the test, you will not see the text that is spoken on the tape. Only the directions and the multiple-choice answers for each short dialogue, extended dialogue, or short lecture will appear in your test booklet or on the computer screen. Directions and examples are given in the practice tests in this book.

TASK 1:   Idioms, conversational expressions, and two- or three-word verbs

An idiom is a group of words, used mostly in conversational English, that has a meaning different from the meanings of the individual words included in the group. For example, the expressions *to lose one's cool, to fly off the handle,* and *to blow one's stack* mean *to get angry.* If the words in any of these expressions are replaced by other words, the expression loses its meaning.

A two- or three-word verb usually consists of a verb and another word, such as a particle *(down, off, up, after),* that together have a meaning different from that of the main verb. For example, *to take off* means *to remove (clothing)* or *to depart (for an airplane),* and *to take after* means *to look or act like.*

Idioms or two- or three-word verbs may appear in a short dialogue, as in Part A:

You will hear:
      Woman: Was the math test difficult?
         Man: The teacher put the test off because she ran out of time.

QUESTION: What did the man say about the test?

You will read:

      (A) The test is canceled.
      (B) The test is postponed.
      (C) The teacher took off her coat.
      (D) The teacher ran outside.

The answer is (B). One of the meanings of *put off* is *postpone.*

Idioms or two- or three-word verbs may also appear in short dialogues.

You will hear:
         Man: We haven't seen Larry in a while.
      Woman: Why not have him over this weekend?

QUESTION: What does the woman mean?

      (A) She saw Larry for a while during the weekend.
      (B) She thinks they should invite Larry for a visit.
      (C) She doesn't like it when Larry comes over.
      (D) She sees Larry every day during the week.

The answer is (B). *Have (someone) over* means *invite for a visit.*

Idioms or two- or three-word verbs may appear in a long dialogue, as in Part B:
You will hear:

Man:	Hello, Betty. I didn't know you come here for lunch. Do you mind if I join you?
Woman:	Hello, Rick. No, I don't mind at all. I like the food here. In fact, I come here for lunch at least once a week.
Man:	I like their salad bar. I think it's the best in town. Actually, it's surprising we haven't met here before.
Woman:	Oh, usually I have my lunch break between 11 and 12. But today our secretary is out sick, and I had to answer the office phone.
Man:	So, if I come here between 11 and 12, chances are we'll have lunch together more often.
Woman:	In that case, I'm sure we'll run into one another again.

QUESTION 1: Where does this conversation take place?

You will read:

(A) On the street
(B) In a phone booth
(C) In a restaurant
(D) In a bar

The answer is (C). The man said "lunch," and the woman said, "I like the food here."

QUESTION 2: What does the man say he likes?

You will read:

(A) The town
(B) The sandwiches
(C) The drinks
(D) The salad

The answer is (D). You can often get salads at a *salad bar*.

QUESTION 3: What did the woman do in the morning?

You will read:

(A) She performed her usual job assignments.
(B) She visited the secretary who was sick.
(C) She did the secretary's job.
(D) She interviewed the office manager.

The answer is (C). The woman said "… today our secretary is out sick, and I had to answer the office phone."

QUESTION 4: What do the man and the woman say about meeting again?

You will read:

(A) They agree to meet in another place.
(B) They decide to go out between 11 and 12 o'clock.
(C) They plan to see one another later in the day.
(D) They hope to meet again in the future.

The answer is (D). The man said, "… chances are we'll have lunch together more often." The expression *chances are* means *possibly* or *probably;* the man and the woman did not schedule or plan another meeting.

TASK 2:   Implied meanings (not directly stated)

Here is a short dialogue, as in Part A:

You will hear:

> Woman: This suitcase is as heavy as the box was. I can't even lift it to put it
> into the trunk.
>
> Man: Should I do it for you?

QUESTION: What did the man offer to do?

You will read:

> (A) Put the box into the suitcase.
> (B) Carry the box and the trunk out to the car.
> (C) Put the suitcase into the car.
> (D) Carry the box and the suitcase to the car.

The answer is (C). *It* in the man's question, "Should I do it for you?," refers to the woman's statement about putting the suitcase "into the trunk" (of a car).

Here is a short lecture about the Loch Ness monster, as in Part C:

You will hear:

> The Loch Ness monster is a huge animal or aquatic creature that, according
> to the local residents, lives in a lake in northern Scotland. If this animal really
> exists, it avoids contact with humans. However, hundreds of those who lived in the
> area in the past or live there now have reported seeing it.
>
> The first descriptions of the animal date back to A.D. 565. In the 1930s, a high-
> way was constructed in the area, and the lake became more accessible to
> tourists. Since then, reports of sightings have risen dramatically. In the past 40
> years, several scientific expeditions have attempted to detect the presence of
> large objects in the lake. Their results indicate that large moving objects indeed
> exist. Unfortunately, to date there has been no consensus among the experts as
> to what these objects actually are.

QUESTION 1:   What is the main topic of this lecture?

> (A) Scientific research on life forms in a lake.
> (B) Attempts to detect the Loch Ness monster.
> (C) Legends about lake monsters in Scotland.
> (D) The shape of the Loch Ness monster.

The answer is (B). The speaker mentioned only one animal and said "If the animal really exists, …" *implying that it is not known whether it actually does.*

QUESTION 2:   What can be said about the monster?

> (A) It is possible that it really exists.
> (B) Its value to science is high.
> (C) It frightens people to drive them away.
> (D) Its specific characteristics attract people.

The answer is (A). It is not known whether the animal exists, but it is possible.

QUESTION 3:   Why have the reports of sightings become more frequent?

> (A) The highway traffic bothers the monster.
> (B) More people travel in the area.
> (C) Tourists who go to the lake disturbed the animal.
> (D) Scientists are able to reach the lake.

The answer is (B). The passage mentions that reports of sighting increased after the area became more accessible.

QUESTION 4:   How long ago were the first sightings of the animal reported?

> (A) 65 years
> (B) 500 years
> (C) In the 1930s
> (D) Nearly 1,500 years

The answer is (D). First descriptions date back to A.D. 565.

TASK 3:   Specific content questions (tested in Parts B and C of the Listening Comprehension section)

Here is an example of an extended dialogue about a course attendance policy, as in Part B. You will hear:

> Man: I am a little surprised that the psychology instructor has such a strict attendance policy. Missing seven class meetings would result in a lower grade.
>
> Woman: Don't you think that college students should be expected to attend their classes regularly?
>
> Man: College students are adults, and they don't need to be told to come to class. In addition, the instructor said that if a student submits an assignment one day late, she will lower the grade one whole point. And if the assignment is three days late, the student receives a failing grade. I don't understand why she is so strict.
>
> Woman: Well, some students may lack the self-discipline to turn in assignments on time. In my economics class, the professor also requires that students call her if they are going to miss a class, and she refuses to accept late assignments.
>
> Man: Really? I am glad I am not taking her class.
>
> Woman: Also, in the economics class, if a student misses just five classes, his or her grade will be lowered. So, I don't think that our psychology instructor is strict.
>
> Man: Well, I see your point. However, I still think that in college classes an attendance policy is not necessary.

QUESTION 1:   How many classes is a student allowed to miss in the psychology class without getting a lower grade?

> (A) One
> (B) Five
> (C) Six
> (D) Seven

The answer is (C). The man said, "Missing seven class meetings would result in a lower grade."

QUESTION 2: What do students in the economics course need to do if they cannot attend a class meeting?

> (A) Submit an assignment late.
> (B) Inform the professor.
> (C) Come to class anyway.
> (D) Go to the psychology class.

The answer is (B). The woman said, "The professor also requires that students call her if they are going to miss a class."

QUESTION 3. What would happen in the economics course if the student's assignment is late?

> (A) It won't be accepted.
> (B) It won't be missed.
> (C) The grade will be lowered.
> (D) The student will be called.

The answer is (A). The woman said that the economics professor refuses to accept late assignments.

QUESTION 4. In the economics course, a student's grade will be lowered if the student misses how many classes?

> (A) Two
> (B) Three
> (C) Five
> (D) Six

The answer is (C). One of the speakers said, "If a student misses just five classes, his or her grade will be lowered."

Here is a short lecture about air, as in Part C:

> Air consists of a mixture of gases and extends from the surface of the earth to outer space. The principal gases of the air are nitrogen and oxygen. Nitrogen accounts for about 78% of dry air, that is, the air from which all water vapor has been removed. Oxygen makes up approximately 21% of dry air. Other gases, mainly argon, make up the remaining 1%. Water vapor and carbon dioxide serve as an insulator and prevent the earth's surface heat from escaping into space. In addition, water vapor yields precipitation in the form of rain and snow.
>
> The amount of water vapor in the air, known as humidity, depends, among other things, on the air temperature. Warm air can hold more water vapor than cold air, and the air is usually less humid on clear days than on cloudy days. When the air becomes sufficiently cold, the water vapor condenses to form water droplets. The temperature at which water vapor starts to condense is called the dew point.

QUESTION 1: How much oxygen does dry air contain?

> (A) 1%
> (B) 21%
> (C) 78%
> (D) 100%

The answer is (B). The speaker said, "Oxygen makes up approximately 21% of dry air."

QUESTION 2:   How do water vapor and carbon dioxide help the earth to retain its heat?

>   (A) They produce precipitation.
>   (B) They insulate it.
>   (C) They help the snow melt.
>   (D) They condense the air gases.

The answer is (B). The lecture states, "Water vapor and carbon dioxide serve as an insulator and prevent the earth's surface heat from escaping into space."

QUESTION 3:   What causes water vapor to condense?

>   (A) Water droplets
>   (B) High humidity
>   (C) Low temperature
>   (D) The earth's cloud cover

The answer is (C). The lecture says that condensation occurs "when the air becomes sufficiently cold...."

TASK 4:   Emphasis, stress, and tone (tested only in Part A of the Listening Comprehension section)

Here is a short dialogue, as in Part A:

>   Man: Did you use my umbrella again?
> Woman: *Your* umbrella?

QUESTION: What does the woman mean?

>   (A) She doesn't have an umbrella.
>   (B) She doesn't think the umbrella is his.
>   (C) The man doesn't like to use umbrellas.
>   (D) The man has lost his umbrella.

The answer is (B). The woman puts emphasis on the word *Your,* meaning that she doesn't realize that the umbrella is his.

TASK 5:   Sound discrimination (tested in Part A of the Listening Comprehension section)

Here is a short dialogue, as in Part A:

>   Man: Do you know what the director said during the meeting yesterday?
> Woman: Yes, that Arnold lacks the funds to complete his project.

QUESTION: What can be said about Arnold?

>   (A) He has been lucky with his work.
>   (B) He is fond of his project.
>   (C) He has no money to finish the job.
>   (D) He has fun with the completed project.

The answer is (C). The woman said "lacks funds," meaning *has no money*.

TASK 6:   Comparisons (tested in Parts A and B of the Listening Comprehension section)

Here is a short dialogue, as in Part A:

Woman: How long does your commute take you?
Man: It takes me longer to drive five miles through the city than it takes to drive twenty miles on the highway.

QUESTION: What does the man mean?

(A) He likes to drive both in the city and on the highway.
(B) Driving on the highway and in the city takes a long time.
(C) A 20-mile drive on the highway does not take as long as a 5-mile drive in the city.
(D) A 25-mile drive in the city takes a shorter time than a 5-mile drive on the highway.

The answer is (C). The man said that the drive on the highway doesn't take as long as the shorter drive in the city.

Here is a long dialogue, as in Part B.

You will hear:

Woman: I learned some pretty interesting things in my sociology lecture today. It turns out that how people shop depends not only on their incomes, but also on their education.
Man: Really? I wouldn't think that people's shopping habits are at all related to their education.
Woman: Actually, there are things that all people need to buy, such as food, clothing, and items for the home. But what specific products they buy depends on their jobs and professions. For example, professional men and women are more interested in fashion than people who do not have a college education. Another example is how people buy furniture. Those with more education buy stylish furniture, and those with less tend to purchase more traditional items.
Man: How about cars? I think that how people buy cars would be similar to how they buy furniture.
Woman: You're right. More than half of the people with higher levels of education, such as college or professional training, own a foreign car. On the other hand, only one fifth of those with only high school education do. In the past, the majority of people who bought trucks were those with a high school education, but today, even college graduates own them. And, of course, people with more education usually earn more than those with less education. For this reason, those who are better educated also travel more.
Man: You must learn a lot in this class. I should probably take it next term.

QUESTION 1.   What is the main topic of this conversation?

(A) A connection between people's education and their habits.
(B) The shopping habits of people with college education.
(C) The influence of people's education on their shopping preferences.
(D) The shopping preferences of people with high school education.

The answer is (C). The conversation describes shopping preferences of two groups of people.

QUESTION 2.   What types of clothing do people with college education tend to buy, compared to those with lower levels of education?

(A) More fashionable
(B) Less stylish
(C) More traditional
(D) Less interesting

The answer is (A). The woman said that professional people are more interested in fashion.

QUESTION 3.   What group of people owns the larger proportion of foreign cars?

(A) Those with high school education.
(B) Those with college education.
(C) Those who work as professors.
(D) Those who also own trucks.

The answer is (B). The information in the dialogue states that more than half of the people with higher levels of education, such as college or professional training, own a foreign car.

QUESTION 4.   Why do people with college education tend to travel more?

(A) Their jobs require more travel.
(B) They own more cars and trucks.
(C) They have higher incomes.
(D) Their education is better.

The answer is (C). The woman said that people with more education usually earn more than those with less education.

Strategies for Guessing the Answer

The skills and strategies that you need when working with the Listening Comprehension section of the TOEFL are different from those necessary for obtaining a good score on the other sections. In the paper version of the TOEFL test, on the Structure and Written Expression and the Reading Comprehension sections, you can first answer the questions that are easy for you and then return to those that you were not sure about. However, you cannot use this strategy with the listening tasks.

In the computer version of the TOEFL test, you will not see any questions until after you have heard the selection. Instead, you will see photographs of speakers or scenes of the conversation. Pay attention to what is said, NOT the pictures. Pictures have been shown to distract test-takers, and the questions all have to do with what is said—not with what you see on the picture.

If you have time, when taking the paper version of the test, quickly look over the answers for a selection before it begins. When listening to a selection, concentrate on its meaning, make your best choice from the ones given, and then focus fully on the next selection. Remember that you have only a few seconds to answer each question. There is no connection between questions, even those that are based on the same dialogue or lecture. Therefore, thinking about the question that was spoken a few seconds ago while another one is being read will distract you from choosing the correct answer.

Another faulty strategy is trying to read the possible answers while listening to a selection. This approach will also divide your attention and distract you from listening to the speakers. In actuality, the Listening Comprehension section is as much a test of concentration as it is of comprehension. For this reason, you should not allow yourself to be distracted by other students taking the test or by noise in the testing room. You need to concentrate on each question to the best of your ability.

STUDY TIP

In Part A, words from the statement may be used in the correct answer. Watch out for similar-sounding words or words containing sound combinations similar to those in the statement. Similar sounds are frequently used in incorrect responses.

Part A: Short Dialogues

Part A includes 30 very short dialogues between two (or sometimes three) speakers. In most of these exchanges, each speaker speaks one time. On very rare occasions, you will hear three turns, two for the first speaker and one for the second. In conversations between two speakers, the most important information is usually stated by the second speaker. For this reason, you should pay more attention to the second speaker's turn than to the first.

After the short dialogue, you will hear a question. The four possible answers to the question are listed in your test booklet or on the computer screen. While all answers are grammatical and each one **appears** to be appropriate, only one of them is correct. You have approximately 10–12 seconds to answer each question. Every question begins with a question word, such as *What, When, Where,* and more rarely *Why, Which, Who, How.* The questions most frequently asked are:

What does the man/woman mean?

Where does this conversation take place/occur?

What can be said about the man/woman?

What is the man's/woman's occupation/profession?

Idioms and two- and three-word verbs are often included. Because all dialogues are limited to the kinds of conversations that people have daily in common places (stores, restaurants, etc.), academic vocabulary is rarely found in this part.

The distractors (tricks) used in Part A can be based on:

1. Similarities in the vocabulary used in the sentence and in one or more multiple-choice items.
2. Similarities in the sounds used in the sentence and in the multiple-choice items.
3. Similarities in the grammatical structures of the sentence and the multiple-choice items.

STUDY TIP

The multiple-choice selections can be similar to the sentence in vocabulary, grammar, and/or sound. In Part A, you need to look only for similarity in meaning.

On the actual test, you will not be able to see the sentence. All you will have to work with are the multiple-choice items given in your booklet or on the computer screen. **Contractions and complex grammatical structures such as questions, negatives, comparisons, and conditional tenses are common in Part A.**

Conversational expressions are used to communicate certain special meanings in American English, that is, they serve as a signal. For example, Americans can say "Good morning" or "Good evening" to signal a greeting or to begin a conversation. On the other hand, "Have a nice day" and "Good day" mean *Good-bye* and are used to finish a conversation. To someone who does not know the difference between these expressions, those that serve as greetings and those that signal good-byes may appear similar in meaning, as both are used to wish someone to have a good day or a good part of a day.

People who have never been in the United States or have never paid attention to how Americans use their conversational expressions may have difficulty with some of the TOEFL listening selections. Research has shown that American conversations contain a great number of patterned expressions that are used as formulas. For example, "Can I help you?" spoken by a salesperson is not a real question. This expression means *Tell me what you want*. In response, one might say: "Do you have envelopes? I can't find them," or "I can't find post-cards" (meaning *Tell me or show me where the envelopes or the postcards are*). Similarly, the response to the salesperson could also be "Not yet" or "No, thank you."

In American English, patterned expressions are used in many everyday situations. It is frequently impossible to tell the meaning of a conversational expression from the meanings of the words in the expression. For example, "I'm afraid we are all out" does not mean that the speaker is afraid of something or that the speaker is outside. *I'm afraid* is a polite expression that usually begins a negative response, and *to be out* is used by store clerks to mean that the store does not have the item requested. The expression actually means *I am sorry that we don't have what you need* or, simply, *We don't have it*.

To improve your Listening Comprehension score, you must be familiar with American conversational expressions. Practice tapes, radio shows, TV shows, and, best of all, conversations with Americans can do a great deal to improve your listening comprehension. When you are watching TV or listening to the radio, pay attention to the expressions that you hear. When talking to Americans, do not hesitate to ask what a particular expression means if you do not understand it. Most Americans would be happy to explain and will not be offended at all. Make note of the expressions you hear and of the explanations.

Sometimes, the information necessary to answer a question is not openly stated in a dialogue in Part A. You need to figure it out from other information contained in the conversation. Such questions are based on inference, that is, the ability to make a conclusion based on information not stated directly. For example:

You will hear:
          Man: Can I help you?
    Woman: I need new soles and heels.

QUESTION: Where does this conversation take place?

The four possible answers for this question might be:

         (A) In a church
         (B) In a hotel lounge
         (C) In a dining hall
         (D) In a shoe-repair shop

The first speaker uses a traditional expression for addressing customers. You already know that the conversation takes place in a business setting, so (A) is probably wrong. The second speaker mentions "soles and heels," parts of a shoe. Therefore, you can tell that both (B) and (C) are wrong because only (D) mentions a place that has anything to do with shoes.

In some other types of questions, you need to notice the speaker's emphasis on a particular word or phrase. Such emphasis usually implies that it is not the meanings of the actual words that are important but other meanings conveyed in the speaker's tone. For example:

Man: The children are being so loud today.
Woman: You should have heard them *yesterday!*

QUESTION: What does the woman mean?

The four possible answers for this short dialogue might be:

(A) The children weren't there yesterday.
(B) The children were louder yesterday than they are today.
(C) The man heard the children yesterday and today.
(D) The man thinks the children were loud yesterday.

In this dialogue, you need to focus on the tone and/or the word stress used by the second speaker. Usually, a word, phrase, or statement spoken with a falling or a rising tone has a special meaning. In the example above, the clue is the tone the speaker uses when saying the word *yesterday*. This is the key word in the second statement.

(A) is wrong because the children were there yesterday, that is, the man could have heard them if he had been there. The second speaker says, "… you should have heard them *yesterday*" with a special stress on *yesterday* implying that the children were even louder yesterday than they are today. Therefore, (B) is correct. Because we already know that the man was not there yesterday, (C) is not correct. The second speaker's "you should have heard them *yesterday*" means that the man wasn't there yesterday; therefore, (D) is also incorrect.

Another purpose that an emphatic tone can serve is to mean the opposite of what is said. For example,

Woman: Can you have this report written, typed, copied, and mailed before the post office closes today?
Man: *Today?*

QUESTION: What does the man mean?

(A) The post office is already closed.
(B) The report is due tomorrow.
(C) He can't finish all these tasks today.
(D) He will be able to mail the report today.

The answer is (C). In this example, the man's emphatic tone signals that he cannot complete all the tasks in the time mentioned by the woman. In the man's response, the rising tone is higher than it would be if he were simply looking for clarification. What the man's response means is *All this cannot be done today.*

> ### STUDY TIP
>
> **In Part A, you should pay special attention to word stress and to the rising and falling tone of the statements by the second speaker. Very often, such tones indicate the opposite meaning of what is said or a meaning different from the obvious one.**

Part B: Long Dialogues

Part B consists of two types of listening selections: long dialogues between two speakers and short lectures. Usually on the TOEFL, you will hear two dialogues with three or four questions each. On rare occasions, you will hear only one listening selection, with seven or eight questions.

Each listening selection usually consists of 140–290 words and lasts about 40–80 seconds. The topics are somewhat more academic than in Part A and can include history, science, or university organization. Numerical information is frequently contained in the passages. No knowledge of the subject matter is required to understand the material in the dialogues.

While you are listening to the selection, you are not allowed to take notes. You should concentrate on the information in the selection. On the paper version of the test, if you can answer a question quickly and have a few seconds left before the next one is spoken, you should look over the multiple-choice answers for the next question.

At the beginning of each selection, you will be told the number of questions that will be asked on that selection, for example: "Questions 42–47 refer to the following conversation." Then you will hear the long dialogue. After the dialogue, each question will be spoken only once, with a 12-second pause for you to select your answer before the next question is asked. The questions will usually begin with question words: *What, How, Where, Why, Who,* and *Whom.* For example:

What is the main topic of this conversation?

Where does this conversation take place?

What will the man/woman probably do next?

> ### STUDY TIP
>
> **In Part B, the questions always follow the order in which information is presented in the long dialogue or the lecture. To answer most of the questions following the text, you need to understand the overall meaning of what the speakers said.**

Frequently, you will be asked a question about the specific information in the listening selection. To answer these content questions you have to concentrate on the facts contained in the selection. For example,

Man: The other day, my son and I went to the store to buy him a bicycle. I had never imagined how many types of bicycles they make today.

Woman: I know what you mean. To begin with, there are 6 bicycle wheel sizes, then there are 8 frame sizes for riders of different heights, and finally, there are 7 main styles of bicycles.

Man: Not just that—bicycles also vary in the number of speeds they can have. You can buy a bicycle with 3, 5, 10, 12, or even 18 speeds. Until yesterday, I had never heard of an 18-speed bicycle.

Woman: Those are used by touring cyclists who travel great distances. Because they are made from special alloys, they are very light, and sometimes weigh only 20 to 25 pounds.

Man: I'll tell you frankly, I would have had a hard time deciding which bike would be best for my son. Fortunately, he knew exactly what he wanted, so we were able to choose which one to get. Otherwise, I'd probably still be standing there trying to make up my mind.

QUESTION 1:   How many bicycle wheel sizes are currently on the market?

    (A) 3
    (B) 6
    (C) 12
    (D) 16

The answer is (B). The woman said, "… there are 6 bicycle wheel sizes."

QUESTION 2:   What type of bicycle is specially designed for touring cyclists?

    (A) 10-speed
    (B) 12-speed
    (C) 18-speed
    (D) 25-speed

The answer is (C). The man said, "Until yesterday, I had never heard of an 18-speed bicycle." The woman responded, "Those are used by touring cyclists …".

QUESTION 3:   How did the man decide which bicycle to purchase?

    (A) He chose the lightest bicycle.
    (B) His son helped him choose a bicycle.
    (C) He hasn't made up his mind yet.
    (D) He chose an 18-speed bicycle.

The answer is (B) because the man states that his son "knew exactly what he wanted, so we were able to choose which one to get."

STUDY TIP

For long dialogues, you need to use your knowledge of idioms, as well as your ability to infer (figure out) meanings that are not directly stated. You need to concentrate on the numbers and comparisons used in a dialogue.

Part C: Short Lectures

In Part C you will hear short lectures that are usually called "talks." Many of the talks often contain information presented in university orientation sessions for new students, descriptions of course and attendance policies, or academic lectures. Talks are almost never longer than two minutes. Vocabulary is more specialized and therefore may be more difficult to understand. The emphasis of the talks is to test oral comprehension of academic presentations. Occasionally, talks include the material found in radio programs or news reports, but this material is of general interest and does not require listeners to be familiar with the subject matter. A good vocabulary is necessary for the talks in Part C because speakers frequently use different words and phrases to express similar meanings.

After each talk, questions follow that frequently require you to infer information not directly explicitly stated. In many cases, the first question that follows the listening selection is: What is the main idea/topic of this talk? Because the topic of a dialogue or lecture is rarely stated directly, you need to rely on the information presented to determine the main idea.

In addition to such general questions, specific inference questions may also appear:

Who is the speaker?

What is the speaker's occupation?

Where does this talk/lecture probably take place?

To answer such questions, you need to gather information from the selection, analyze it, and come to correct conclusions. (On the paper version of the test, it is particularly helpful to look ahead at the multiple-choice responses to the questions so as to limit your choices while you are listening to the lecture.) Many of the strategies needed to answer questions in Part B are also useful for correct answers in Part C.

Here is an example of a short talk, as in Part C.

You will hear:

> Instructor: In research, conclusions are based on findings and data analysis that the researcher has collected. Research or scientific data consist of the observations, facts, measurements, and information that is necessary to test the hypotheses. After the data is gathered, researchers examine it to find patterns that can help them test their hypotheses or objectives. Then the researcher considers the findings or the results of measurements and attempts to figure out what they mean.
>
> In most cases, research does not end when the gathering of data or making conclusions ends. In fact, research is a never-ending process of collecting additional or new data. Another important characteristic of the research process is identifying new problems that require future investigation. Each research project is simply a step toward the next study, and scientific investigation is a dynamic process of discovery.

QUESTION 1. Who is the speaker?

(A) A radio announcer
(B) A statistician
(C) A computer operator
(D) A scientist

The answer is (D). The talk does not seem to be of general interest and appears to be more appropriate for university students. Therefore, (A) is not a good choice. Neither statistical analyses nor computers are mentioned in the talk, and (B) and (C) are not likely answers.

QUESTION 2. After the data is collected, why is it examined?

(A) To measure its results.
(B) To figure out if it has patterns.
(C) To find out if it has features.
(D) To prove its advantages.

The answer is (B). The speaker said, "After the data is gathered, researchers examine it to find patterns …"

QUESTION 3. According to the speaker, what can be said about research in general?

(A) It is an ongoing process.
(B) It ends when conclusions are made.
(C) It improves in the future.
(D) It is an exciting adventure.

The answer is (A). The speaker said that research is "a never-ending process." *Never-ending* can have meanings similar to *ongoing*.

QUESTION 4. What did the speaker mention as another important characteristic of research?

(A) Identifying areas that need further investigation.
(B) Developing new data collection procedures.
(C) Creating information for the next generation.
(D) Asserting the validity of the current data.

The answer is (A). The speaker states that "Another important characteristic of the research process is identifying new problems that require future investigation."

CHAPTER 4

Practice for Listening Comprehension

Exercise 1: Idioms

Part A

DIRECTIONS: Choose the one phrase or sentence that is the best answer to the question you heard on the tape.

1. (A) Brian's mother doesn't hear well.
   (B) Brian's mother hasn't been in touch.
   (C) Brian heard his mother's voice.
   (D) Brian and his mother are close.

2. (A) Professor White is less likely to forget the data analysis.
   (B) Professor White pointed to the persistent data shortage.
   (C) Professor White called attention to the flaws in the data.
   (D) Professor White showed us a shortcut for the data analysis.

3. (A) Students should study all the time.
   (B) Exams can be written in advance.
   (C) Usually, we are busy and have little time.
   (D) The written exam was finished on time.

4. (A) The man can take his time next week.
   (B) The man needs to change planes.
   (C) She'd like to know if the man changes his plans.
   (D) She'd like to help the man with the changes.

5. (A) Ann was picked up near the florist's.
   (B) The florist dropped the flowers.
   (C) Ann was choosing the flowers for the wedding.
   (D) The florist arranged the flowers as Ann wanted.

6. (A) He wandered around and got on the wrong bus.
   (B) He had to walk because he made a mistake.
   (C) He was surprised that he had to walk.
   (D) He was wondering where to get off.

7. (A) Jane stopped by the school.
   (B) Jane stopped attending school.
   (C) Jane's grades are down.
   (D) Jane posted the grades downstairs.

8. (A) She finally got used to her new car.
   (B) She usually uses her new car.
   (C) She drives her new car only on campus.
   (D) She doesn't use her new car daily.

9. (A) Mr. Winters is at the insurance office.
   (B) In winter, lunch can be ordered in.
   (C) Mr. Winters can't look into the woman's policy right now.
   (D) Insurance coverage doesn't apply during the winter.

10. (A) He left the first sentence alone.
    (B) He made two different errors.
    (C) He teaches during the first period.
    (D) He put away his second article.

11. (A) Go on a diet.
    (B) Go to the movies.
    (C) Reduce expenses.
    (D) Take a cut in pay.

12. (A) The meeting place will be announced tomorrow.
    (B) The choice of books should be discussed.
    (C) We'll find a place for you at the book fair.
    (D) We should bring the book to the meeting.

13. (A) At the store
    (B) At the school
    (C) On Main Street
    (D) On the running path

14. (A) Come up with another idea.
    (B) Think about the offer.
    (C) Travel to the coast.
    (D) Drive to Kansas.

15. (A) The man should work hard.
    (B) The man needs to look up.
    (C) The man will find another job.
    (D) The man can wait for his turn.

16. (A) He paid his brothers for their time.
    (B) He wanted his brothers out of the way.
    (C) His brothers helped him.
    (D) His brothers had other things to do.

17. (A) She'd rather sort out her mail.
    (B) She doesn't like sunsets.
    (C) She doesn't feel well.
    (D) She doesn't like the man.

18. (A) He is hard to understand.
    (B) He likes to talk about himself.
    (C) He talks about important things.
    (D) He makes a lot of difference.

19. (A) Chuck spends his money unwisely.
    (B) Chuck supports his family.
    (C) Chuck should work harder.
    (D) Chuck should look more carefully.

20. (A) She will drop by the library on her way downtown.
    (B) She will return to the dentist after going to the library.
    (C) The man could take the children to the dentist.
    (D) The man could go to the library for her.

Part B

Directions: Choose the one phrase or sentence that is the best answer to the questions you heard on the tape. Answer the questions on the basis of what is stated or implied by the speakers.

21. (A) At a party
    (B) In the street
    (C) In the library
    (D) On a ship

22. (A) He has fallen behind in his work.
    (B) He has changed residences.
    (C) He made house alterations.
    (D) He is coming around for a visit.

23. (A) She doesn't like the weather.
    (B) She is moving to San Diego.
    (C) She's been taking care of her sister.
    (D) She hasn't been feeling well.

24. (A) 5 years
    (B) 15 months
    (C) 5 months
    (D) 25 years

25. (A) Keep up with her homework.
    (B) Tell the truth about her skills.
    (C) Make an appointment.
    (D) Return to her studies.

26. (A) He doesn't believe the woman.
    (B) He doesn't like the idea.
    (C) He is greatly confused.
    (D) He is pleasantly surprised.

27. (A) During the semester
    (B) In the autumn
    (C) As soon as she can
    (D) Before you know it

28. (A) She is in good shape for her age.
    (B) She will soon master the subject.
    (C) She can visit him any time.
    (D) She should be positive in her thinking.

Exercise 2: Implied Meanings

Part A

<u>DIRECTIONS</u>: Choose the one phrase or sentence that is the best answer to the question you heard on the tape.

1. (A) She thinks that Friday is not a good day.
   (B) It's too early to make a reservation.
   (C) Window seats won't be available until Monday.
   (D) Reservations for seats are not accepted here.

2. (A) Molly has surely called.
   (B) Molly can't call you.
   (C) You shouldn't call Molly.
   (D) You can't rely on Molly.

3. (A) Harold is moving on Thursday.
   (B) Harold picked up the truck.
   (C) Packing is as important as renting a truck.
   (D) Friends are going to Harold's on Tuesday.

4. (A) The course has been discontinued.
   (B) The course won't be taught this term.
   (C) The composition of the course has been changed.
   (D) A cut in class size will take place.

5. (A) Karen's new skirt didn't fit well.
   (B) Karen should buy a matching blouse.
   (C) The skirt didn't match the blouse.
   (D) The birthday gift was inappropriate.

6. (A) Was Nancy asked to come to the club?
   (B) Why isn't Nancy at the Athletic Club?
   (C) Isn't Nancy a receptionist at the club?
   (D) Only athletes are invited to the reception.

7. (A) It was hard to give up swimming and taking walks.
   (B) She can't believe that the man didn't go swimming for a week.
   (C) The man hardly ever went swimming and walking.
   (D) Their vacation has been over for a week now.

8. (A) Cooking meals takes a lot of time.
   (B) I like cooking every day.
   (C) I'm not a very good cook.
   (D) Cooking is enjoyable for me.

9. (A) Students should hold onto Dr. Collins.
   (B) Students should make appointments to see Dr. Collins.
   (C) Dr. Collins refuses to see students during the summer.
   (D) Dr. Collins has a regular appointment.

10. (A) The kitchen hasn't been cleaned in a long time.
    (B) They can play after we finish cleaning the kitchen.
    (C) He hates cleaning the kitchen and the living room on the same day.
    (D) Together, they can finish cleaning up quicker than if one of them did it alone.

11. (A) Fred is not very good with faucets.
    (B) Fred is handy when it comes to faucets.
    (C) Fred doesn't like to ask for help.
    (D) Fred is faced with several problems.

12. (A) A carpenter's shop
    (B) An automobile repair shop
    (C) A clothing store
    (D) A construction site

13. (A) He wants to know if the woman eats breakfast.
    (B) He disagrees with the woman.
    (C) He is too busy to eat breakfast.
    (D) He thinks that eating breakfast is a waste of time.

14. (A) Rain is in the forecast.
    (B) Hail is expected at the end of the summer.
    (C) The dry spell will last for a while.
    (D) The heat wave is almost over.

15. (A) To buy a new book is cheaper than to borrow it.
    (B) To buy the book is cheaper than to pay the fine.
    (C) It's costlier to buy the book than to pay the fine.
    (D) It's better not to lose library books.

16. (A) Taking the letter to the post office
    (B) Giving the post office the correct address
    (C) Inquiring at the post office
    (D) Calling the addressee about the letter

17. (A) Larry is a terrible person.
    (B) Larry is staying only for two days.
    (C) The woman will see her friend.
    (D) The woman may change her mind.

18. (A) He is seeing Carol now.
    (B) He is dating Sally.
    (C) He saw this show last week.
    (D) He can't keep track of dates.

19. (A) A politician
    (B) A typist
    (C) A baseball player
    (D) A reporter

20. (A) Hiring an instructor
    (B) Lending her the calculator
    (C) Checking a phone book
    (D) Reading the directions

Part B

<u>DIRECTIONS</u>: Choose the one phrase or sentence that is the best answer to the question you heard on the tape. Answer the questions on the basis of what is stated or implied by the speakers.

21. (A) At birth
    (B) During parenthood
    (C) Predominantly in childhood
    (D) Over several decades

22. (A) Neighbors
    (B) Parents
    (C) Teachers
    (D) Siblings

23. (A) To enjoy their meals
    (B) To satisfy their hunger
    (C) To win their parents' approval
    (D) To develop poor eating habits

24. (A) They may have difficulty eating.
    (B) They become healthy and fit.
    (C) They can't always reduce their weight.
    (D) They are forced to count calories.

25. (A) It creates reflections.
    (B) It affects behavior.
    (C) It results in deviations.
    (D) It leads to disappointment.

26. (A) As an excuse
    (B) As a habit
    (C) To establish contacts
    (D) To appear intimidating

27. (A) By exercising to become fit
    (B) By excusing themselves
    (C) By building relationships
    (D) By eating to feel better

28. (A) As commonly known
    (B) As possibly direct
    (C) As probably inverse
    (D) As positively evident

Exercise 3: Specific Content Questions

Part C

<u>DIRECTIONS</u>: Choose the one phrase or sentence that is the best answer to the question you heard on the tape. Answer the questions on the basis of what is stated or implied by the speakers.

1. (A) In a physics laboratory
   (B) In a classroom
   (C) In an observatory
   (D) In a theater

2. (A) A janitor
   (B) A tour guide
   (C) A salesman
   (D) An optician

3. (A) To examine foreign objects
   (B) To magnify distant objects
   (C) To reflect object images
   (D) To collect light waves

4. (A) By turning the objective from left to right or from right to left
   (B) By modifying the distance between the eyepiece and the objective
   (C) By magnifying the image in the eyepiece or the objective
   (D) By enlarging the size of the eyepiece or the lens

5. (A) Cameras
   (B) Telescopes
   (C) Curved mirrors
   (D) Opera glasses

6. (A) One
   (B) Two
   (C) Three
   (D) Four

7. (A) They are more powerful.
   (B) They have more lenses.
   (C) They can be used in photography.
   (D) They can be placed within reach.

8. (A) To serve as an eyepiece
   (B) To angle light intensity
   (C) To disperse light rays
   (D) To reflect the observed image

Exercise 4: Emphasis, Stress, and Tone

Part A

<u>DIRECTIONS</u>: Choose the one sentence that is the best answer to the question you heard on the tape.

1. (A) Someone else should answer the door.
   (B) His job is to answer the phone.
   (C) He needs to turn the door handle.
   (D) He needs to give an answer.

2. (A) Dick has been hedging about the trees.
   (B) Dick planted the hedge and three trees.
   (C) Dick didn't get a shave and a trim.
   (D) Dick has done a lot of the yard work.

3. (A) Dennis paid for his parking sticker.
   (B) Dennis didn't pay for parking.
   (C) Dennis paid only his fine.
   (D) Dennis remembered to pay the man's fine.

4. (A) She is looking forward to seeing the desert.
   (B) She can't do without sweets after her meal.
   (C) She is happy about winning a trip to the desert.
   (D) She won't bother with making the dessert.

5. (A) He could fill in for her at chorus practice.
   (B) He feels they should look at the seashore.
   (C) She wouldn't like doing all the work.
   (D) He feels bad about doing his share of the work.

6. (A) She is proud.
   (B) She is sad.
   (C) She is concerned.
   (D) She is surprised.

7. (A) The restaurant service is slow.
   (B) The place has been closed.
   (C) He doesn't want to have dinner.
   (D) He'd prefer to go to the airport.

8. (A) He has known Emily for some time.
   (B) He doesn't know whether Emily is awake.
   (C) Emily must have left her light on.
   (D) Emily's room is different from his.

9. (A) She is too tired to watch the show.
   (B) The episode has been shown earlier.
   (C) She has no time to watch the episode.
   (D) The script for the show has to be written.

10. (A) His luck has been bad lately.
    (B) He forgot to check the time.
    (C) The break is almost over.
    (D) The car has broken down again.

Exercise 5: Sound Discrimination

Part A

<u>Directions</u>: Choose the one phrase or sentence that is the best answer to the question you heard on the tape.

1. (A) The butter is in the cup.
   (B) Corn tastes better with butter.
   (C) Service here should be better.
   (D) The corn that they served is bitter.

2. (A) The bill is sure to pass.
   (B) The bill needs to be sorted out.
   (C) Bill resorted to traveling.
   (D) Bill had the most popular idea.

3. (A) She will pay for the next drink.
   (B) She will pay for this round.
   (C) The man is in charge of packing.
   (D) The man has had too much to drink.

4. (A) He was wounded while climbing a tree.
   (B) He sat near the clock till morning.
   (C) He needn't be alarmed before tomorrow.
   (D) He needs to get up early tomorrow.

5. (A) He left without his cloths and pail.
   (B) He didn't take his belongings with him.
   (C) He filled the bin with clothes.
   (D) He could care less about closets.

6. (A) Test-takers receive a free gift when they leave.
   (B) Those who take the test get a pencil.
   (C) Buyers receive pencils with their purchases.
   (D) The purchase of pencils is limited.

7. (A) Moving the discs
   (B) Clearing off the desk
   (C) Shelving the task
   (D) Putting away the vials

8. (A) Arnold has been lucky with funding.
   (B) Arnold has run out of money.
   (C) Arnold is competing in the job search.
   (D) Arnold is fond of this research.

9. (A) She will talk to Rob about the rumor.
   (B) She won't mind taking just one piece.
   (C) She will confront Rob about his jokes.
   (D) She won't let Rob have peace.

10. (A) He's been looking for 50 minutes.
    (B) His sight has been declining.
    (C) He needs to get a taxi.
    (D) He's late for his flight.

Exercise 6: Comparisons

Part A

DIRECTIONS: Choose the one phrase or sentence that is the best answer to the question you heard on the tape.

1. (A) George writes as well as Phil does.
   (B) Sam and George write better than Phil.
   (C) Phil's German is not as good as Sam's.
   (D) Phil's essays are worse than George's.

2. (A) Her typing is as accurate as Martin's.
   (B) Martin's typing is slower than hers.
   (C) She types more accurately than Martin.
   (D) She types as slowly as Martin does.

3. (A) The road can be widened if the side-walks are too.
   (B) The sidewalks are narrower than the widened road.
   (C) The widening of the road will make for narrower sidewalks.
   (D) The sidewalks will be made wider than the road.

4. (A) Alex is heavier than Dan.
   (B) Alex is not as heavy as Dan.
   (C) Dan is shorter than Alex.
   (D) Dan is taller than Alex.

5. (A) In December, days are longer than nights.
   (B) In December, nights are longer than in March.
   (C) In March, days are shorter than in December.
   (D) In March, nights are longer than days.

6. (A) The red fabric is not as costly.
   (B) The red dress looks awful.
   (C) The blue dress is more elegant.
   (D) The blue dress is less expensive.

7. (A) Four
   (B) Thirteen
   (C) Sixteen
   (D) Twenty-eight

8. (A) Less than two hours
   (B) Two-and-a-half hours
   (C) Three hours
   (D) Three-and-a-half hours

9. (A) 12 percent
   (B) 16 percent
   (C) 24 percent
   (D) 30 percent

10. (A) The suit coat
    (B) The suit pants
    (C) The man's height
    (D) The man's weight

Part B

11. (A) Moving to a new suburb
    (B) Finding a larger place to live
    (C) Getting a new office
    (D) Increasing the commuting distance

12. (A) In the city
    (B) In the suburbs
    (C) Far from the woman's office
    (D) Near a highway

13. (A) Her commute
    (B) The roadway
    (C) The rent
    (D) The kitchen

14. (A) To the office
    (B) To a storage facility
    (C) To look at an apartment
    (D) To work at the office

Supplement to Listening Practice

Idioms in Daily Conversations

Idioms and conversational expressions are very frequently tested in the Listening Comprehension section of the TOEFL. Idioms and conversational expressions present two types of difficulties: there are many of them, and their meanings cannot be guessed from the meanings of the words that they consist of.

The words in idioms cannot be replaced with other words that have similar meanings. You can think of idioms as "frozen" phrases, the parts of which cannot be moved or changed. For example, *to be under the weather* means *not to feel well*. You cannot replace the words in this expression without changing its meaning. The meanings of idioms have to be learned or memorized, just as you have to memorize the meaning of words.

Conversational expressions are a little different from idioms. These expressions are not "frozen," and they represent the way people usually speak. For example, all of the following expressions can be used as greetings:

Hello.	*How are you?*
How are you today?	*How is everything going?*
How is everything with you?	*How have you been?*

Although there are differences among these expressions, their meanings and purposes are the same. In idioms, only one form and only one combination of words has a particular meaning.

Two- or three-word verbs are similar to idioms because the meaning of the whole cannot be guessed from the meanings of the parts, for example, *look up to = admire, look after (somebody) = to take care of (somebody), look (someone) up = visit,* and *look for = search.*

Because there are no rules that you can use to guess the meanings of idioms and two- and three-word verbs, these parts of the English language have to be learned individually.

The following common idioms and two- or three-word verbs are provided for you.

List of Idioms and Two- or Three-Word Verbs Frequently Used on the TOEFL

about time   indicates that something should have happened earlier. *After working for this company for 5 years, he felt that it was about time he received a promotion.*

about to   ready to, at the point of. *Now that she is about to enter college, she has moved out of her parents' place.*

ahead of time   early, in advance. *Preparing for business presentations ahead of time is essential for the success of any venture.*

all along   from the beginning, always, all the time. *Television networks have claimed all along that they do not attempt to influence their viewers.*

all at once   suddenly, surprisingly, unexpectedly. *All at once, with the collapse of the stock market, many people found themselves financially ruined.*

all day long   the entire day. *Educators frequently frown on the idea of studying the same material all day long.*

all in all   everything taken into account, everything considered. *All in all, environmental concerns have gained considerable attention in the media.*

all the time   (1) continually, regularly. *Ideally, adults should receive a consistent amount of sleep all the time.* (2) during a certain period of time. *This semester, students have been dropping and adding classes all the time.*

as for   referring to, concerning, regarding. *As for updating the physics curriculum, the current budget allows us few resources to spare.*

as usual   as occurs most of the time, typically. *As usual, the technical writers have missed the deadline for completion of the project.*

at first   at the beginning. *At first, adjusting to new schools may appear almost impossible to foreign students.*

at last   finally, after a long time. *The Admissions Office had been requesting Frank's transcript for six months and, at last, it arrived.*

at (the) least   no less than, minimum. *Although the entire managerial staff does not need to attend the conference, at least the production supervisors should be there.*

at (the) most   maximum, not more than. *A letter sent by first-class mail should take at most three days to travel from the east coast to the west coast.*

be broke   have no money. *Jane cannot afford to buy a new car; she is broke after her vacation.*

be out of   have none left. *I am sorry, sir, we are out of typewriter ribbons.*

be short of   not have enough. *The factory outlet where Mark shops is short of sports footwear.*

be/get used to   be/get accustomed to, accept (something) habitually. *Although maritime climates are famous for their abundance of rain, newcomers get used to it rather quickly.*

bring up   (1) mention, raise an issue or question, introduce for discussion. *Betsy thought that bringing up the constant shortage of office supplies would not be appropriate at the teachers' seminar.* (2) raise a child, care for during childhood. *Mr. and Mrs. Nickels brought up Tim as if he were their own son.*

by far   greatly, clearly, by a large margin. *The automobile inventory of midsize sedans exceeds by far the consumer demand for this type of car.*

by the way   mention in passing, incidentally. *Mr. Johnson, could you call my dentist and cancel my appointment for this afternoon. By the way, there is no need to reschedule.*

call off   decide not to do something, cancel. *The sightseeing tour was called off because a thunderstorm was forecast for the area.*

call on   (1) visit. *Maybe we should call on Mr. Smith to see his rose garden.* (2) ask or choose to participate or to contribute. *The university vice-president was called on to design a long-term plan for the expansion of laboratory facilities on campus.*

catch a cold   to become ill with a cold. *People who find themselves near to someone with a cold may be likely to catch a cold.*

change (one's) mind   alter/change an earlier decision/opinion. *Michael thinks that changing his mind about even minor issues signifies failure.*

check in/into   register at a hotel. *We can go out for dinner as soon as we check in.*

check into   investigate. *Because your invoice is long overdue, I suggest that you check into this matter with your bank.*

check out   (1) take a book out of the library. *I'm sorry, sir, this book is checked out.* (2) investigate. *If the advertised offer is as good as it appears, it is certainly worth checking out.* (3) leave a hotel. *What time do we have to check out?*

cheer up   make (someone) feel happier. *Jack tried to cheer Ann up but she was really upset about failing her math midterm.*

clean up   make clean and organized. *We can't leave until we clean up this mess we made.*

come across   meet by chance, accidentally. *Can you believe it? I came across this color TV at a garage sale, and it was only $10.*

come back   (1) return. *Dr. Bradford may not be able to come back to the office before his surgery this afternoon.* (2) remember, recall. *Even events that people consider long forgotten can come back to them in the right circumstances.* (3) return to popularity. *Have you noticed that platform shoes are coming back for the fall?*

come to/come down to   (1) grow to, gradually achieve enough familiarity to do something. *While some linguists disdain statistics as a mere manipulation of numbers, others may come to appreciate it as a powerful means to prove one's point.* (2) amount to. *The more we learn about human behavior, the more it comes down to heredity being a predominant factor.*

cut down on   reduce, decrease, lessen. *Cutting down on high calorie foods may lead to a substantial weight loss over an extended period of time.*

do over   do again. *His essay was so poorly written that he had to do it over.*

do with   (1) profit/benefit from, use to advantage. *I am cold and hungry; I could do with a cup of hot soup.* (2) be familiar with, associate with, work with. *How should I know where the computer manual is? I don't have anything to do with it.*

do without   manage without having. *The structure of American cities is such that urban dwellers cannot do without private transportation.*

drop by/in   visit informally, for a short period of time. *Whenever you are in town, please feel free to drop by any time.*

drop off   leave (something/someone) at a certain place. *If you are going downtown, can you drop me off at City Hall?*

drop out   stop going to school/a class/a club. *In general, the rate at which U.S. high school students drop out has reached 43 percent in the past decade.*

every other   every second one. *Liz is expected to undergo physical therapy sessions every other week.*

feel up to   be able to, be capable of. *Having spent the entire day editing my paper, I don't feel up to discussing it right now.*

figure out   (1) understand, achieve understanding by reasoning. *Historians dedicate themselves to figuring out the sequence of events that led to a particular outcome.* (2) calculate, solve. *The income tax laws have become so complicated that it takes an accountant to figure out all the intricacies.*

fill out   write/complete a form/a questionnaire. *Please read the instructions before you begin filling out the application form.*

find fault with   criticize, be dissatisfied with. *It is almost always easier to find fault with something than to improve it.*

find out   (1) learn, discover. *Physicists and astronomers have been attempting to find out how earth was created.* (2) inquire, ask. *I've tried to find out why Vicky has been so depressed lately, but she refuses to talk about it.*

for the time being   temporarily, for the present period of time. *For the time being, because of a series of budget cuts, the library has to postpone the acquisition of new journals.*

from now on   starting now and continuing into the future, from this moment forward. *In addition to quitting smoking, the patient must carry out a daily exercise program from now on.*

get along (with/without)   (1) be friendly with, agree on many things. *Many employers believe that getting along with one's co-workers is as important as being able to do one's job.* (2) make progress; advance. *How is Mary getting along with her Spanish lessons?* (3) manage; maintain. *Getting along without a word processor would seem impossible to professional writers.*

get/fall/be behind   (1) fail to be at an expected level. *If Nick continues to miss his chemistry classes, he will fall behind.* (2) support, help, assist. *Environmentalists are behind the new legislation for the protection of endangered species.*

get off   (1) leave a means of transportation (bus, train, plane, **but not car**). *I am going to the concert hall on Main Street; where should I get off?* (2) take off, remove. *Skiing boots can be difficult to put on and get off.*

get on   board a means of transportation (bus, train, plane, **but not car**). *After getting on the bus, Janet discovered that she did not have any money for the fare.*

get over   recover, overcome. *Some types of flu may take up to 2 weeks to get over.*

get out of   (1) leave a car. *Watch out for the oncoming traffic while getting out of a car on the left side.* (2) exit. *I was tired this morning and had a hard time getting out of bed.* (2) avoid unpleasant activity or work. *Greg succeeded in getting out of trimming the hedges after all!*

get rid of   eliminate, throw away, discard. *If I were you, I would get rid of that washing machine and buy a new one.*

get through   finish. *Look at all this paperwork we have to get through before the deadline.*

give up   stop. *How can you give up smoking when you continually borrow cigarettes from everyone in the office?*

go ahead   begin, start doing something. *After the artifacts are gathered, the archaeological team can go ahead with the dating analysis.*

go away   leave, depart. *I wish the mosquitoes would go away; they are ruining the picnic.*

go on   (1) happen. *I don't know exactly what went on during the meeting.* (2) continue. *The rehearsal for the outdoor scene should go on despite the rain.*

go over   check; review. *How could you turn in the report without going over it?*

go up   (1) rise, increase. *In most situations, prices go up as quickly as the inflation rate rises.* (2) ascent, mount. *Go up the stairs, turn right, and go through a set of glass doors.* (3) be constructed. *The new art center will go up on High Street before the end of the year.*

grow up   become an adult. *It is unusual to find someone who did not have to face social difficulties and peer pressure while growing up.*

had better/I'd (we'd) better   ought to, would be smart to. *It's getting cold; we had (or we'd) better close the window.*

hand in   submit, turn in. *Students must hand in their assignments before the deadline in order to receive full credit.*

hang up   end a telephone conversation. *After she hung up, Martha realized that she had forgotten to invite Wendy to her party.*

have a good time   enjoy oneself. *Bob and Carrie had such a good time in Los Angeles that they decided to go there again next summer.*

have (someone) do (something)   make (someone) do (something); cause (someone) to do (something). *Peter had his children help him paint the house.*

have in mind   plan, intend. *What exactly did you have in mind for dinner?*

have over   invite. *Let's have Mark over this Saturday; we haven't seen him in three weeks.*

hear from   (1) receive a letter or a phone call from. *Mary hasn't heard from Sue since Sue moved to Wisconsin.* (2) receive information from someone about someone else. *Frank heard from Diane that Professor Green is planning to retire.*

How come?   why? [an expression of surprise or questioning] *How come you decided to take that job in Washington? I thought you liked your current job.*

in a while   later, at some time in the future. *Mr. Collins will be able to see you in a while.*

in fact   in reality, really, specifically. *This exercise is particularly challenging; in fact, I think it is the most difficult in the book.*

instead of   in place of, rather than. *Wouldn't you rather have tea instead of beer?*

in time   (1) sufficiently early, early enough. *The letter must be typed in time for the 3 P.M. collection.* (2) eventually (not immediately). *All new undertakings are difficult; however, in time, most people adjust.*

it's no wonder/no wonder   predictably, expectably, naturally, it's not surprising. *It's no wonder John missed his flight; he left home just 20 minutes before the departure time.*

keep up with   (1) maintain one's familiarity with. *In many research fields, scientists are required to keep up with recent findings.* (2) go/move/progress as fast as (someone/something). *You are walking so fast that I cannot keep up with you.*

leave out   (1) omit. *Did you leave out your date of birth on the application form?* (2) leave available, set out. *If you come to the office after closing, I will leave your paper out for you.*

let (somebody) know   inform, tell. *It is crucial that the director let the crew know about the new project deadline.*

let (me/us) see   allow (me/us) time to think, find out, determine (something). *Well, I'm not sure which road we should take. Let me see here.*

look after   watch over, give care to. *Thank you for looking after my apartment while I was away.*

look for   search for, seek. *You've been looking for your file for 3 hours now!*

look forward to   anticipate with pleasure. *I'm sure Mrs. Lovely is looking forward to the trip to Hawaii.*

look into   investigate, examine. *Because this matter has not yet been clarified, I am requesting that you look into it.*

look like   resemble. *Not only does Margaret look like her father, she also acts like him.*

look out   beware, be careful. *Look out! This car is moving very fast.*

look up   (1) research, search in a book. *Students who cannot remember the specific weight of oxygen should look it up in the reference materials.* (2) improve. *Because of the economic stability of the past few months, business is looking up.* (3) visit. *When you are in town next month, look us up in our new house.*

look up to   respect. *Mary looks up to her older sister, and that's how it should be.*

make a difference   (1) change the existing situation, cause a change. *The hiring of the new city manager will make a difference in how things are run around here.* (2) be of importance. *It makes no difference to me which restaurant we go to.*

make a living   earn enough to have a satisfactory standard of living. *I find it rather amazing that Stephen can make a living by selling Christmas trees.*

make a point of   give importance to, insist on. *After Bob was late again this morning, his boss made a point of commenting on it.*

make fun of   laugh at. *Why are you making fun of her? Anyone can make a mistake.*

make out   (1) understand. *I can't make out his line of reasoning.* (2) distinguish, identify. *It was so dark when we finally arrived at the house that we couldn't make out the number over the door.* (3) complete, fill in. *Make out the check for me to give to Mr. Becker.* (4) achieve, succeed. *How did you make out in the card game last night?*

make sense   be reasonable, be intelligible. *You are not making any sense. Slow down and explain the situation to me again.*

make sure   be certain. *Rick made sure he had brought his passport to the registration hall.*

make up   (1) compose, invent. *For this assignment, you have to make up a story about an unfortunate experience.* (2) do past work. *Students can make up the test that was given on Friday at 10 A.M.* (3) renew good relations. *Most friends make up after they've had a fight.*

may/might as well   do with equal or better result/effect, be slightly preferable. *If Joe has so much work to do, he might as well stay home and study.*

more or less   to some extent. *In the past five years, we have more or less achieved all our sales goals.*

never mind   forget it, don't worry about it. *Can you help me to look for my glasses? Never mind, I found them.*

no matter   regardless of. *No matter what the weather, the game won't be called off.*

not at all   not in the least. *Do you mind dropping the paper off at the printing office? Not at all.*

no wonder   see **it's no wonder.**

of course   to be expected, naturally. *Of course, Peggy was late for the show; she's always late.*

once and for all   finally, permanently, conclusively. *If the changes in scheduling are implemented as planned, our timing problems will be solved once and for all.*

once in a while   occasionally, every so often, from time to time. *We don't get out of the house much, but once in a while we go to the movies.*

on purpose   intentionally, for a certain reason. *She came to the meeting late on purpose so she would miss the introductory speech.*

on the other hand   from the opposite point of view. *Snow covered roads are very pretty; on the other hand, driving conditions can be treacherous.*

on the whole   in general, all things considered. *Although the main character in the play was not very well developed, on the whole, I enjoyed the performance.*

on time   on schedule, exactly at the fixed time, punctually. *Unlike Linda, who is always late, Matthew comes to work on time.*

pick out   (1) choose, select. *She should have picked out just one blouse instead of buying all three.* (2) recognize. *They couldn't pick out their son among all the graduates.*

pick up   (1) lift. *The suitcase was so heavy that Grandma couldn't even pick it up.* (2) obtain, gather, acquire. *Claire stopped at the grocery store to pick up some milk for dinner.* (3) catch, arrest. *The criminal was picked up at the gas station on the corner.*

point out   (1) mention, explain. *I hate to point out that the report has not been completed yet.* (2) show. *Kathy pointed Jim out to Becky at the party yesterday.*

put away   return something to the usual place. *Don't forget to put away the dictionary when you are finished with it.*

put off   (1) postpone, delay. *Dr. Black announced that she would put off her retirement till the end of the year.* (2) discourage. *Bret's grade in chemistry was so low that I think he was really put off by it.* (3) somewhat repelled. *Many people were put off by the candidates' lack of candor.*

put on   (1) get dressed in. *On days like this, you need to put on your hat to stay warm.* (2) add. *Nicole looks as if she has put on a lot of weight.*

put up with   tolerate. *I am not going to put up with this disarray in the kitchen.*

quite a few   a number or a lot of. *We invited about 50 people to the reception, but quite a few of them did not show up.*

read up on   study by reading about. *Professor Douglas indicated that graduate students should read up on the current economic prognosis.*

right away   immediately. *Your waitress will bring you your appetizers right away.*

run into   (1) meet by chance, accidentally. *Imagine running into Sue in a drugstore!* (2) collide with, crash into. *This morning, Ruth ran into the mailbox while backing out of the driveway.* (3) encounter. *While trying to get the car out of the ditch, she ran into a problem with her tires.*

run out of   exhaust the supply of, come to the end of. *Sorry, sir, we have run out of paperback copies of this book.*

see to   give attention to. *I'm in charge here, and I'll see to it that the work gets done right.*

show up   appear. *They waited for Greg for about 45 minutes but he never showed up.*

so far   until now. *So far, we have discussed only basic and Pascal in our computer class.*

sooner or later   inevitably, eventually, ultimately. *Ryan has to start being more careful when he drives because sooner or later he'll hit someone.*

step by step   gradually. *A person can learn to do almost anything taking it step by step.*

stop by   visit. *We stopped by Rick's house, but he wasn't home.*

take advantage of   (1) profit/benefit from, make use of. *All those who need to familiarize themselves with various word processing packages can take advantage of the seminar offered at the Adult*

Education Center. (2) gain at the expense of another, use unfairly. *Criminals may take advantage of the elderly who live alone and rob them of their life's savings.*

take after   resemble. *My daughter takes after my husband more than after me.*

take a trip   go for a journey. *When did you take a trip to the Bahamas?*

take it easy   relax, don't worry. *During spring break, most students take it easy: they have fun with their friends and travel a bit.*

take off   (1) remove (clothing). *Bob took off his coat because he was getting warm.* (2) leave the ground and rise (of aircraft). *Flight attendants will serve drinks after the plane takes off.* (3) be absent from work. *I need to take a few days off to catch up on my domestic chores.* (4) deduct, reduce the price/cost. *You forgot to take the value of the coupon off my bill.*

take over   take control. *Yesterday, when the basement flooded, Linda took over the entire cleaning operation.*

take out   (1) remove, extract. *What do you use to take out oil stains from a wool fabric?* (2) prepared food bought in a restaurant but eaten at home. *We decided to get take out instead of cooking this evening.*

take part in   participate. *Many volunteers took part in the clean-up efforts in Florida.*

take place   occur, happen. *When does the English test take place?*

take up   (1) begin, undertake. *Can you believe that Harold took up dancing at his age?* (2) occupy space or time. *These old phone books should be thrown out because they take up too much room on the shelves.*

talk (something) over   discuss. *After I talk it over with my wife, I'll let you know whether this price is acceptable.*

tear down   demolish, reduce to nothing. *The old theater building was torn down in 1968.*

tell (one) from (another); tell apart   distinguish between. *The Steiner brothers look so much alike that I cannot tell Mark from Bruce. Identical twins can be difficult to tell apart.*

that is   say something more exactly, express better. *Peter left; that is, he has gone, and he is not coming back.*

think of   (1) have an opinion about (something). *What do you think of the new president?* (2) consider. *Karen has been thinking of opening her own business.* (3) give attention to. *The school year is almost over, and you need to think of preparing for your final exams.*

think (something) over   consider/think carefully before deciding/doing (something). *Nancy told the recruiter that she would like to think his offer over for a day or two.*

time off   period of vacation, release from work, time away for oneself. *Nick hasn't had any time off this year; he must be ready for a vacation.*

throw away/out   discard, get rid of. *Paper should be recycled instead of being thrown away.*

turn down   (1) decrease volume/intensity. *Could you turn down your radio?* (2) reject [frequently used in the passive]. *Although Paul did his best during the interview, his application for admission was turned down.*

turn in   (1) hand in/submit an assignment. *The test has to be turned in before the bell.* (2) go to bed. *Although it's only 8 o'clock, I'm so tired that I'm going to turn in.*

turn off   (1) shut off, close, stop. *Don't forget to turn off the fan before you leave.* (2) repel, something that repels (noun or verb). *The smell of raw meat turns me off.*

turn on   let flow, open, let come. *To turn on the hot water, you need to open the valve.*

turn out   (1) extinguish (a light). *The last person to leave has to turn out the lights.* (2) **turnout** attendance. *There was an impressive turnout at the lecture on global warming.*

turn up   (1) increase volume/intensity. *If you turn up the volume, you'll be able to hear better.* (2) appear. *The 20-dollar bill that we couldn't find two days ago has turned up in the washing machine.*

CHAPTER 5

Strategies for Structure and Written Expression

About the Structure and Written Expression Section of the Test

Section 2 of the TOEFL, Structure and Written Expression, contains 40 sentences with multiple-choice responses, 15 in Part A (Structure) and 25 in Part B (Written Expression). This section of the test must be completed in 25 minutes, so you have approximately 35–37 seconds to answer each question.

In Part A, you need to find the word or phrase that correctly completes the sentence. In Part B, you need to identify which one of the underlined words or phrases is incorrect in the sentence. One of the most important differences between Part A and Part B is that in Part A you must choose what is correct, and in Part B you must choose what is wrong.

In Part A, you are given sentences in which a missing phrase or word has been replaced by a dashed line: - - - - - - - - - . Below the sentence, you will find four choices of words or phrases, labeled (A), (B), (C), and (D). Only one of these four choices will complete the sentence correctly, although most of the words or phrases in the selection are correct in and of themselves.

Example of sentence completion in Part A:

California - - - - - - - - about 8,000 lakes.

(A) has
(B) has had
(C) is
(D) is having

In this example, the answer is (A) because the sentence states a fact that is true now. (B) is not appropriate because *has had* indicates a fact that was true over a period of time in the past. (C) results in the statement "California *is* about 8,000 lakes," but California *is not* lakes—it *is* a state. (D) is not appropriate because the present progressive tense means *currently* or *right now*; California does not just currently have 8,000 lakes; it has always had them.

In Part B, you will find sentences in which four phrases or words are underlined. Under each of the underlined phrases or words, you will see (A), (B), (C), and (D). One of these underlined phrases or words makes the sentence incorrect in written American English.

Example of error identification in Part B:

Candles have been use since the prehistoric era.
   A   B   C   D

In this example, the answer is (B). There is no problem with (A) because *candle* is a countable noun and can take the plural marker *-s*; (B) contains an error because the verb following *have* + *been* must take *-ed* or the past participle form. (C) "Since" is used correctly with the present perfect tense in this sentence. (D) is not the answer because *era* is a countable noun and therefore can be used in the singular.

What the Structure and Written Expression Section Is Designed to Test

The topics of the sentences in the Structure and Written Expression section are usually academic, and many of them express basic numerical, biographical, geographical, cultural, scientific, or historical facts. Most of these sentences are factually accurate. However, special knowledge of the subject matter is not required in order to answer them correctly.

The TOEFL tests a wide variety of phrase-level structures but few whole-sentence structures. When you prepare for the test, you need to concentrate on noun, verb, adjective, prepositional and adverbial phrases, and subordinate clauses in order to make the most efficient use of your time. Research on the tests administered from 1980 through 2003 shows that some structures appear more frequently than others.

In the tests administered since 1986, the structures most frequently tested on the TOEFL have been:

(1) the form and function of nouns, verbs, adjectives, and adverbs;
(2) parallel structure;
(3) subordinate clauses, adjective, adverb, noun clauses; and
(4) subject and verb presence and agreement.

Other frequently tested areas include:

(5) the active and the passive voice;
(6) gerunds and infinitives;
(7) prepositions, repeated meaning, verb tenses, and complete clauses.

Each of these is explained below, and examples are provided.

Examples of structures in the frequency table

Below you will find examples of structures listed above. The answer and a brief explanation are provided for each example. A more detailed explanation of structures and grammar rules will follow in "Tips for Guessing the Answer," page 59.

STRUCTURE 1: Form and Function

a. Nouns and Noun Phrases

> In 1848, Elizabeth Stanton organized the first - - - - - - - - rights convention in the United States.
>
> (A) woman
> (B) women
> (C) women's
> (D) woman's

The answer is (C). The plural possessive noun *women's* indicates *rights that belong to women*.

> Noise <u>pollution</u> can be <u>controlled</u> in <u>a number</u> of <u>way</u>.
>   A   B   C   D

The answer is (D). The phrase *a number of* implies that a plural noun, *ways*, should follow.

b. Verbs and Verb Phrases

In the past 200 years, the earth's atmosphere - - - - - - - - enriched in carbon dioxide.

(A) becoming
(B) have become
(C) becomes
(D) has become

The answer is (D). The present perfect tense is usually used with the phrase *in the past +* *[time]* (e.g., *in the past 3 weeks, in the past 2 hours*).

In <u>some religions,</u> people <u>fasts</u> for <u>a period</u> of <u>mourning</u>.
      A   B   C   D

The answer is (B). Because *people* is a plural noun, the verb *fast* should reflect the plural subject.

c. Adjectives and Adjective Phrases

The earth spins around - - - - - - - - that connects the geographic North and South Poles.

(A) the image and line
(B) imagined the line
(C) that line imagined
(D) the imaginary line

The answer is (D). In this sentence, the preposition *around* is followed by the noun phrase *the imaginary line.*

<u>Sweetly smelling</u> <u>perfumes</u> are <u>added</u> to soap to make <u>it appealing</u>.
     A   B   C   D

The answer is (A). The adjective *smelling* requires an adjective, *sweet*, to describe it, not an adverb. (For more information and examples, see page 81.)

d. Pronouns

Young rabbits learn to feed - - - - - - - - when they are one day old.

(A) so
(B) and
(C) much
(D) themselves

The answer is (D). The plural form of the reflexive pronoun *themselves* refers to the noun *rabbits*.

<u>Instead</u> of <u>going</u> to a <u>beauty salon,</u> Mary cut <u>hers own</u> hair.
  A   B   C   D

The answer is (D). The possessive pronoun *her* (*not hers*) should be used when a noun (*hair*) follows.

e. Adverbs and Adverb Phrases

Art critics and historians alike claim that Van Gogh's art - - - - - - - - from that of his contemporaries.

(A) is a considerable difference
(B) is considerably different
(C) the difference is considerable
(D) was considerably and differently

The answer is (B). In the sentence, the preposition *from* is a part of the adjective-and-prepo-
sition structure *different from*.

Joseph Priestley <u>eventual</u> emigrated to the United States in 1794, where
                          A

<u>he lived</u> his <u>remaining</u> years in <u>relative</u> isolation.
     B   C   D

The answer is (A). An adverb is required to describe the verb *emigrated*, as in *eventually
emigrated*.

STRUCTURE 2:   Parallel Structure

Before any food is canned, it is thoroughly - - - - - - - - or sliced.

(A) clean cut
(B) cleaned and cut
(C) clean and cut
(D) cleaned or cut

The answer is (B). Only (B) and (D) are possible in this sentence because these choices
contain passive verbs, *cleaned and cut* and *cleaned or cut*, parallel to *sliced*. A structure containing two conjunctions, … *or* … *or*, as in (D) is not used in most parallel structures.

Many Americans believe that <u>food additive</u> and <u>other chemicals</u> used
                                       A   B

<u>in the production</u> and <u>processing</u> of foods harm the body.
        C   D

The answer is (A). *Food additive*, a singular expression, is not parallel to the plural form of
other chemicals.

STRUCTURE 3:   Subordinate Clauses

Proper packaging protects food - - - - - - - - in the freezer.

(A) while it is stored
(B) stored while it
(C) while storing
(D) is stored while

The answer is (A) because it is the only choice among the four that is a complete adverb
clause.

Many couples share <u>the cost</u> of a <u>date</u> and <u>decide</u> together what <u>will they</u> do.
                          A   B   C   D

The answer is (D). In a noun clause, the word order should be *what they will do*.

STRUCTURE 4: Subject/Verb Presence and Agreement; Repeated Subject

None of the nutrients in soil - - - - - - - - found in sand.

(A) are usually
(B) that is usually
(C) is usually
(D) typically

The answer is (C). *None* is the singular subject of this sentence, and the verb should also be the singular *is*.

Many old elephants <u>they die</u> after <u>they</u> lose <u>their teeth</u> and <u>can no longer</u>
                A   B   C   D

chew food.

The answer is (A). Having both *Many old elephants* and *they* causes the sentence to have a repeated subject.

STRUCTURE 5: Active/Passive Voice

Unless some rare plants - - - - - - - - , they may die out completely.

(A) protect them
(B) are protected
(C) protected
(D) are protecting

The answer is (B) because a plural passive verb is necessary after *plants*.

Calculus <u>was invented</u> to <u>deal with</u> problems that could not <u>be solving</u> using
          A   B   C

<u>algebra or</u> geometry.
   D

The answer is (C). The passive form of the verb is necessary here. The correct clause would be *that could not be solved using algebra or geometry*.

STRUCTURE 6: Gerunds/Infinitives

Most countries spend a large portion of their budgets - - - - - - - - for their citizens.

(A) education provided
(B) provide education
(C) to education provides
(D) providing education

The answer is (D). The sentence can be correctly completed by the gerund phrase *providing education*. None of the other three choices would form a grammatical sentence.

J. Davis devoted his <u>last years</u> <u>to write</u> at <u>his home</u> in Biloxi, Mississippi, near
                    A   B   C

<u>the Gulf</u> of Mexico.
  D

The answer is (B). The verb *devote* takes a noun or a gerund; in this sentence, the phrase *to writing* makes the structure correct.

STRUCTURE 7: Prepositions/Prepositional Phrases

Several nations may use the same colors - - - - - - - - .

(A) their flags with
(B) by their flags
(C) in their flags
(D) flags in their

The answer is (C). In this sentence, the correct prepositional phrase is *in their flags*, as *colors* are used *in flags*.

Often the bottom of a pan or skillet becomes black when it is placed among a fire.
           A   B   C   D

The answer is (D). The preposition *among* is used with more than two objects, as in *among the students. In a fire* would be correct.

STRUCTURE 8: Repeated Meaning (tested only in Part B of the Structure and Written Expression section)

Isadora Duncan danced in her bare feet and wore loose-fitting clothing garments
                    A   B   C
that allowed her freedom of movement.
     D

The answer is (C). *Clothing* and *garments* have similar meanings.

Light rays that enter the eye must come to a point focus for a clear vision to form.
  A   B   C   D

The answer is (C). *Come to a point* and *focus* have similar meanings.

STRUCTURE 9: Articles/Article Form

- - - - - - - - who determines similarities in human group behavior lives with a group of people.

(A) Anthropologists
(B) Anthropologist
(C) An anthropologist
(D) The anthropologists

The answer is (C). Because in English most countable singular nouns are used with articles or pronouns, (B) would not be correct. (A) and (D) are plural, but a singular subject is necessary.

A adult elephant has so little hair that it appears almost hairless.
  A   B   C   D

The answer is (A). The correct form of the indefinite article before a word that begins with a vowel (*a, e, i, o,* or *u*) is *an*.

STRUCTURE 10:   Verb Tenses/Inversion

Electric trains travel faster than other types of trains, and they - - - - - - - - smoke or exhaust.

(A) did not produce
(B) do not produce
(C) had not produced
(D) are not produced

The answer is (B) because the simple present tense *travel* is used in the first part of this compound sentence.

Not <u>only new</u> ideas change <u>the development</u> of modern science but
         A   B
<u>they also make</u> new inventions <u>a part of daily</u> life.
         C   D

The answer is (A). When a sentence begins with a negative such as *not*, the helping verb (or sometimes the main verb) should be used before the subject, as in *Not only do new ideas change the development of modern science….*

STRUCTURE 11:   Adverb Placement

A guest - - - - - - - - respond to a written invitation by telephone or by mail within five days of receiving it.

(A) that should always
(B) should always
(C) always
(D) all ways should

The answer is (B). When a verb phrase consists of a modal and a main verb, the adverb is placed between them.

Dictatorships <u>generally lack</u> the approval of <u>the people</u> and are <u>never almost</u>
                    A   B   C
hereditary when established <u>through violence</u>.
                                    D

The answer is (C). *Almost* usually precedes the adverb it describes: *almost never.*

STRUCTURE 12:   Main Clause Structure; Complete and Partial Clauses

Experts - - - - - - - - feel that they are related to the deep wishes and fears of the dreamer.

(A) study dreams
(B) who dream study
(C) whose dream study
(D) who study dreams

In (A), the word *study* can be either a noun or a verb. It cannot be a noun because the word *Experts* in front of it and the word *dreams* after it are both plural. If *study* is a verb, then the subject *Experts* has two verbs *study* and *dream* without a conjunction. (A) is not a good choice. (B) is also not a good choice because the phrase *dream study* includes a verb *study*, followed by another verb *feel*. In (C), *dream* is a noun because *whose* precedes nouns, and in this case, there is no conjunction between *study* and *feel*.

The answer is (D). The word order in a clause follows the subject-verb-object pattern: *who* (subject) *study* (verb) *dreams* (object).

> Because children <u>grow rapidly</u>, <u>need</u> food not only <u>to replace</u> worn-out tissue
>   A   B   C
> <u>but also to provide</u> energy.
>   D

In (A), the adverb *rapidly* follows the verb *grow*; (A) is correct. In (B), if *need* is a verb, it has no subject. If *need* is a noun, it has no verb. (B) is a possible answer. (C), *to replace*, is correct if *need* is a verb. The choice (D) also seems correct because *to replace* may be parallel to *to provide*. The answer is (B). The subject *they* is missing from the main clause: *they need food....*

Strategies for Guessing the Answer

Remember that in Part A, Completion, most of the phrases in the multiple-choice selections are correct in and of themselves and become inappropriate only in the context of the sentence. Therefore, you should not examine them in detail and try to find errors in the four possible answers independently of the context of the sentence. Three of the four selections either would not complete the sentence grammatically, or have meanings that would not make sense when combined with the rest of the sentence.

The sentences in both Part A and Part B seldom contain more than two clauses, that is, they consist of a simple sentence, a compound sentence consisting of two simple sentences, or a complex sentence with one main clause and at least one subordinate clause. The capitalization and punctuation (commas, semicolons, colons, periods, and question marks) are always correct. You should note commas and question marks because they can help you recognize parallel structures, beginnings and ends of clauses, and whether the sentence is a statement or question. The sentences in the Structure and Written Expression section never have spelling mistakes.

Sometimes, you will not be able to guess the answer. If you really have no idea what the answer may be, be sure to mark one of the choices anyway; there is no penalty for inappropriate answers on the test. The rest of this chapter will be devoted to strategies for narrowing down your choice of the correct answer out of the four possibilities.

The more inappropriate answers you can eliminate from your selection, the higher the probability of your choosing the appropriate answer. If you are choosing one answer out of four, the probability of your selecting the correct response is 25 percent. After you have eliminated one of the answers, the probability that you will choose the appropriate response increases to 33 percent. Eliminating two of the four possible answers raises the probability to 50 percent. As you can see, the ability to eliminate as many unlikely answers as possible provides you with the advantage of a more accurate, less random, guess. The following section, "Tips for Guessing the Answer," and the examples presented here can help you to make better guesses, but you must still prepare for the test thoroughly. The tips will help you analyze most but not all sentences on the test.

In addition to helping you guess the answers on the TOEFL, the grammar information contained in the Study Tips will make you more aware of English sentence structure. If you are planning to enter a university in the United States, you will have to complete many homework assignments and papers. The grammar regularities presented in the Tips will help you produce correct sentences in both writing and speech. They will also aid you in your reading comprehension in English. Chapter 6 provides specific rules for each of the frequently tested structures.

Tips for Guessing the Answer

STUDY TIP

Some answer choices in both Parts A and B of the Structure and Written Expression section contain extra words while others are missing words.

The sentence

Tip 1. A basic sentence consists of at least a subject and a verb. Special sentences, such as commands (for example, "Sit down"), have an understood subject (you), but a sentence cannot be correct without a verb.

Every subject must have a verb, and every verb except a command must have a subject. A double comparative, the *more/-er...*, the *more/-er...* , is the only other exception you need to keep in mind.

> The deeper the lake, the bigger the fish.
> The determinist theory contends that the more logical the reasoning process, the fewer the chances for a fallacious decision.

STUDY TIP

Even if you do not understand the meaning of a sentence, you should try to identify the subject and the verb because both must be present for most sentences to be grammatical.

The subject, noun phrase, and noun clause

Tip 2. The subject can be:

a. A noun or noun phrase:

> Students usually read a great deal.
> Rain and snow wash out aerosols, making the air fresher after the precipitation.
> Many people came to see the new zoo.
> A geological engineer guides the search for mineral deposits and estimates their value.

b. A pronoun: *I, we, you, he, she, it, they*

> He became known for his sketches of nature.
> At her country home, she painted views of the cathedral or of a haystack under changing atmospheric conditions.

c. A "dummy" subject (empty of meaning): *it* or *there*

> It is seldom possible to win large sums of money.
> It has not been established with certainty whether global warming is taking place.

In structures with *there*, the subject follows the verb, which must be singular or plural to agree with the subject.

<u>There</u> is a lot of precipitation in the tropics.
<u>There</u> are three or more groups of motives that arouse humans.

In the first sentence, the subject is *a lot*. In the second sentence, the subject is *groups*. Therefore, the verb is singular in the first sentence and plural in the second.

d. A gerund, that is, a noun ending with *-ing* that is formed from a verb:

<u>Skiing</u> is one of the most popular sports in Canada.
<u>Dredging</u> is cost efficient only where mineral-bearing sand and gravel layers are exceptionally thick.

e. An infinitive, that is, a verb form preceded by *to*:

<u>To see</u> is to believe.
<u>To regulate</u> the nation's money supply has become the responsibility of the Federal Reserve System.

f. A clause that begins with a clause word such as *that, who, what, when, where, how, which, if, and whether*:

<u>That he was late</u> upset his girlfriend.
<u>That Samuel Morse was scientifically inexperienced</u> baffled his collaborator, Leonard Gale, who taught chemistry at the University of New York.
<u>What he said</u> is not true.
<u>What distinguishes moose from other members of the deer family</u> is their big shoulders and broad hooves.

STUDY TIP

Once you identify the subject, you can decide what kind of verb must follow and what kind cannot, depending on the subject's form and number (singular/plural).

Tip 3. *This* and *that* precede singular nouns; *these* and *those*, plural nouns. Nouns that are preceded by one of these words do not take an article.

<u>This</u> organization freed able-bodied men for combat and scouting duties.
Because ballpoint pens depend on gravity to pull the ink to the ball, <u>these</u> instruments do not work well when held sideways.

Tip 4. Possessive pronouns (sometimes called possessive adjectives), such as *my, our, your, his, her, its,* and *their*, can also help you distinguish a noun from a verb because they precede only nouns or noun phrases.

<u>Their</u> English teacher is from Australia.
John H. Loud patented a ballpoint pen in 1888, but <u>his</u> invention received little notice until World War II.

Prepositions and the prepositional phrase

Tip 5. Prepositions, such as *about, at, across, among, around, by, behind, down, during, except, in, on, of, out, through, together, toward, with, without,* and *upon,* almost always come before nouns, noun phrases, or noun clauses. Rarely, a preposition may appear at the end of an adjective or a noun clause.

> About 14,000 soldiers returned <u>to</u> Britain.
> Pencils consist <u>of</u> a writing core set <u>within</u> a case <u>of</u> wood, metal, or plastic.

Tip 6. Prepositional phrases, that is, prepositions with nouns, are never part of the subject phrase. The grammatical subjects and verbs are underlined in the following sentences. Note that the prepositional phrases do not affect subject-verb agreement in any way.

> <u>Mr. Smith</u>, with his wife, <u>is</u> coming for dinner.
> <u>Mr. Smith and his wife</u> <u>are</u> coming for dinner.
> <u>The average amount</u> of vegetables consumed in the United States <u>is</u> derived from the weight of retail sales.
> <u>The drawing and extrusion</u> of metal <u>are</u> the fundamental processes in die-making.

Phrase conjunctions and markers; parallel structures

Tip 7. The word *and* ties together pieces of a compound subject and makes it plural:

> <u>Mary, John, and Bill</u> <u>are</u> late.

And also ties together pieces of a compound verb:

> Mary <u>reads and writes</u> at her desk.

And makes all phrases parallel, that is, repetitive in their grammatical patterns.

> Mary went <u>to the library</u> <u>and</u> <u>to the bank</u>.
> Dorothea Dix led the drive <u>to build</u> state hospitals <u>and</u> <u>to improve</u> prison conditions in the mid-1800s.
> <u>Fleas, mosquitoes, and other parasitic insects</u> transmit the pathogens responsible for the spread of <u>plague, malaria, and typhus</u>.

Tip 8. Articles indicate nouns and can have only three forms: *the, a,* and *an.*

> <u>the</u> book, <u>a</u> bird, <u>an</u> umbrella

Abstract nouns, which represent ideas (*science, knowledge, education*), uncountable nouns (*milk, bread, coffee*), and, rarely, nouns that represent a class of similar nouns may have no article.

> <u>Life</u> is an object of study for poets and biologists.
> The purpose of professional conventions, conferences, and seminars is to exchange and expand <u>knowledge</u>.

STUDY TIP

Articles are very important because they can help you distinguish a noun from a verb—*a drive* is a noun, but *drive* is a verb. Most singular nouns in English must have an article or a possessive pronoun. If you see an article, a possessive pronoun, or a preposition, you can be sure that you are working with a noun phrase. Remember: prepositional phrases are not part of a subject.

Tip 9. The ending -s serves a variety of functions for both nouns and verbs. For nouns, -s indicates the plural form and usually marks the last noun of a plural noun phrase: *school days, lamp shades, noodle dishes.*

> cornfield flower<u>s</u>
> five-credit-hour course<u>s</u>
> ten-year-old boy<u>s</u>

The structures *cornfields flowers* and *five-credit-hours courses* are **INCORRECT**.

For verbs, -s indicates the singular present form and tells you whether a third person subject is singular or plural.

> The girl read<u>s</u>. The girl<u>s</u> read.

A large percentage of sentences on the TOEFL are constructed using third person singular or plural.

STUDY TIP

In the third person singular present, either the subject (*he, she,* or *it*) or the verb must end in -*s*, but both the subject and the verb cannot have -*s*. If a noun describes another noun (*work schedule*), the plural -*s* can be used only on the last noun.

(See Chapter 7 for more information about -*s* for nouns.)

The verb and the verb phrase

Tip 10. A verb phrase consists of at least one main verb. Sometimes, in addition, you will find auxiliary verbs such as *be, do* and *have*, or modal verbs such as *will, would, need to, must, have to, can, may, to be able to, should, might, could,* and *ought to.* All auxiliary and modal verbs come before the main verb.

> The experiment <u>will be completed</u> in three days.
> Tourists <u>must protect</u> their belongings from thieves.
> Solar radiation, along with cosmic rays, <u>can change</u> the chemical composition
>   of the atmosphere in the thermosphere.

Tip 11. Two-word verbs such as *go on, give up, find out, bring up, make up, turn on, turn out,* and many others represent one meaning unit. To avoid confusing two-word verbs and prepositions, you need to memorize the common two-word verbs listed in almost all grammar texts.

> When <u>looking for</u> a lost contact lens on a carpeted surface, using bright and
>   directed flashlight beam can expedite the process. [look for = search]
> From very early childhood, Americans are conditioned to <u>look up to</u> authority
>   figures. [look up to = respect, admire]
> Stock brokers <u>look over</u> charts of share, gold, and foreign currency prices up
>   to two dozen times a day. [look over = examine, inspect]

Tip 12. Certain verbs are usually not followed by direct objects. Other verbs usually are. Linking verbs can be followed by a variety of structures. In formal English, the following frequently used verbs are rarely followed by a direct object: *explode, jump, rest, sleep, arrive, walk, talk,* and *come.*

The verbs *benefit, break, bring, carry, cause, compose, cover, dismiss, encounter, explain, find, give, grow, help, launch, learn, locate, make, mark, pass, please, precede, reach, receive, see, situate, store, strike,* and *use* are almost always followed by a direct object (without a preposition).

> Several software packages marketed for commercial purposes can <u>compose</u> short business <u>letters</u> and <u>locate</u> grammatical <u>errors</u> in writing.
> Good language learners <u>find</u> their own <u>way</u> and develop sophisticated strategies when they <u>are learning</u> a second <u>language</u>.

If you encounter one of these verbs, in most cases you must have a direct object following it. Forms of these verbs are often used in the passive voice; passive verbs do not take direct objects.

> If a customer <u>is not pleased</u> with the purchase, practically all businesses will either exchange the merchandise or refund the amount of purchase.
> When corn <u>is grown</u> for fodder, it <u>is stored</u> in special silos.

In many sentences, you will also find objects, which follow the verb with or without a preposition. To find out if the verb must take a direct object, you can ask a *what* or *whom* question:

> The student broke <u>the measuring cup</u>.
> <u>What</u> did the student break? [the measuring cup]
> Research benefits <u>science</u>.
> <u>What</u> does research benefit? [science]

English nouns have the same form whether they are functioning as subjects or as objects.

> Indirect objects can take the prepositions *to* and *for*.
> I bought a sandwich <u>for</u> you. I gave the book <u>to</u> Jim.

In sentences such as "I bought you a sandwich" use *what* or *whom* questions to figure out if the direct object is necessary.

The verbs *be, become,* and other linking verbs can be followed by nouns, adjectives, verbs with *-ing, -ed* (or in the past participle form), prepositional phrases, or sometimes adverbs without *-ly*:

> John is <u>a student</u>. Mary is <u>tall</u>.
> Mr. Johnson was <u>working</u>. Mr. Smith was <u>tired</u>.
> Mr. Robinson was <u>in the park</u>. Mr. Nixon is <u>out</u>.

Tip 13. Active verbs with *-ing* must be preceded by a form of *be* (*be + verb + -ing*):

> Mary <u>is laughing</u>.
> While F. Scott Fitzgerald <u>was working</u> on his acclaimed novel, *The Great Gatsby*, his health continued to decline.
> In 1943, millions of people <u>were receiving</u> government checks from the armed forces, the Social Security Board, and other agencies.

The verbs *happen, occur, belong* and *consist* are always active.

A passive verb always consists of at least *be + verb + ed* (e.g., *be isolated*), *be + past participle* (e.g., *be sold*), or *get + verb + ed/past participle* (e.g., *get married*):

> Most fruit <u>is cleaned</u> before it <u>is packaged</u> and <u>sold</u>.
> Paleontologists, archaeologists, and geologists dedicate a great deal of research to events that <u>occurred</u> before history <u>was recorded</u>.

The verb *become* can sometimes be used instead of *be* in such structures (e.g., *become tired*).

Tip 14. A group of verbs that are mostly used in the passive voice (although they can also sometimes be used in the active voice) are usually followed by specific prepositions in passive verb + preposition combinations:

> *accustomed to, acquainted with, bored with, committed to, composed of, covered with, dedicated to, devoted to, disappointed with/in, dressed in, finished (done) with, interested in, located in, made of, married to, opposed to, related to, scared of, satisfied with, used to, worried about, upset about/with.*

If a verb can be used in a combination with two different prepositions, the meaning of the phrase changes, e.g., *upset about* usually refers to a thing or an event, and *upset with* usually refers to a person or a living creature, such as an animal.

> Mary is <u>accustomed to</u> rain, but John is <u>used to</u> dry weather.
> A sheet of metal made of an aluminum alloy is <u>covered with</u> plastic before being shipped.
> The board of directors was <u>disappointed with</u> the work of the chief accountant.
> But: The board of directors was <u>disappointed in</u> the manager of operations.

STUDY TIP

When working with the verb phrase, pay attention to auxiliaries and modals, two-word verbs, and verbs that require direct objects. If the verb phrase includes any form of *be*, make sure the main verb has *-ing* for active or *-ed*/past participle for passive voice.

Tip 15. The tense is expected to be the same in the main and in the subordinate clauses unless time markers, which allow one to switch tenses, are included.

> <u>Last year</u> John <u>lived</u> in California, but <u>this year</u> he <u>lives</u> in Hawaii. [Mention of the different years allows the tense change.]
> Although Susan <u>was</u> an excellent student in <u>high school</u>, her grades in <u>college</u> <u>are</u> not very good. [Mention of *high school* and *college* allows the tense switch.]

In English, future and past tenses, as well as present perfect and past perfect tenses, generally cannot be used in the same sentence. When the past tense is used in the main clause, the verb *would* instead of *will* is usually used in the subordinate clause.

> My brother <u>said</u> he <u>would</u> come to see us.

(The sentence "My brother said he will come to see us" is considered **INCORRECT** in standard written English, although this structure is often used in daily conversations.)

> The report <u>mentioned</u> that the city commissioner <u>would</u> oversee the bridge repair.

(The sentence "The report mentioned that the city commissioner will oversee the bridge repair" is also **INCORRECT**.)

Tip 16. Some verbs, usually called stative, do not take progressive tenses (present, past, or past perfect progressive) in formal English, although they occasionally do in spoken language. These verbs are: *appear, be, believe, belong, hate, have, hear, know, like, look like, love, mean, need, note, notice, owe, own, prefer, realize, recognize, remember, resemble, see, seem, smell* (as in *The coffee smells good*), *taste* (as in *The soup tastes great*), *understand, want, weight, wish*.

> For many years before the new nutrition guidelines were issued by the U.S. government, many dietitians <u>believed</u> that adults preferred meat to other types of foods. (It is incorrect to use *believe* and *prefer* in the progressive tense **were believing* and **were preferring*).

STUDY TIP

Make sure that the tense of the verbs in a sentence is consistent. Pay attention to the tense of the first verb and other time words and be sure that the parts of the sentence that follow reflect the correct time.

Clauses

Tip 17. Clauses can be main or subordinate. Main clauses are simple sentences that always contain at least one verb and almost always have a subject. (In imperative structures, such as *Stop!*, and double comparatives, such as *The more, the merrier,* the subject is omitted; see Tip 1 for more information.) Generally, a subordinate clause contains a clause word as well as the basic subject-verb structure. In addition to the clause words listed in Tip 2, the following words can also indicate clauses: *after, although, as, as soon as, because, before, even though, everywhere, if, since, so, so that, such, such that, that, though, unless, when, where, whereas, which, while,* and *who.*

> It has not been determined <u>where</u> life first began.
> <u>Because</u> liquids have no shape of their own, they take the shape of any container in <u>which</u> they are placed.
> Henry Arnold did not get a chance to go overseas during World War I, <u>since</u> he was assigned to Panama.

Tip 18. Clause words, except *that, who,* and *which,* are almost never directly followed by a verb.

> The building <u>where the Admissions Office is located</u> is one of the oldest on campus.
> <u>Although they were skilled in construction</u>, the Romans depended on the Greeks for their ideas for decoration.
> Gordon Gee, <u>who arrived yesterday</u>, is the university president.
> The Romanesque style of architecture <u>that became immediately popular for building churches, schools, and department stores</u> was introduced to the United States in the late 1800s.

Tip 19. In adjective clauses, the object pronouns *which* and *whom* can be omitted when followed by a noun. In noun clauses, the conjunction *that,* also when followed by a noun, may be omitted. Both adjective and noun clause examples are given below.

> The energy <u>(that/which)</u> the sun emits is referred to as solar radiation.
> Mr. Smith is the physicist <u>(whom)</u> the committee selected for nomination.
> Scientists have determined <u>(that)</u> polar regions are arid.

Tip 20. The pronouns *that, who, which,* or *whom* can be omitted if they are followed by the subject of the subordinate clause:

> Geologists <u>say (that) they</u> cannot always date fossils accurately.

That, who, and *whom* cannot be omitted when they are immediately followed by a verb:

> Prairie grasses <u>that are dormant during drought</u> become a fire hazard.
> To speed lawmaking, bills <u>that are introduced to the Senate</u> are referred to committees.

Tip 21. An adjective clause must follow the noun it describes.

> <u>Diamonds</u>, <u>which are pure carbon</u>, are mined from ancient crustal rocks.
> In law, the term *fixture* refers to personal property <u>that has been affixed to houses or land</u>.

The structure in the example below is **INCORRECT**:

> "The new meteorology textbook costs 50 dollars <u>that is published by the university</u>."

STUDY TIP

In clauses, check for words that introduce clauses, a subject and a verb. Check if the subject follows the clause word—watch out for *who* and *which* in the *clause* subject position.

Adjectives and adjective phrases

Tip 22. An adjective without a phrase always precedes the noun it describes.

> <u>Bright</u>, <u>yellow</u> ribbons are symbolic in <u>American</u> culture.
> A <u>prominent</u> characteristic of <u>living</u> things is adaptation to <u>harsh</u> or <u>new</u> environments.

The only exceptions are adjectives that follow the verbs *be, become, get,* and other linking verbs.

> The topic of viral diseases <u>became common</u> in medical literature after the invention of the microscope.

An adjective phrase always follows the noun it describes.

> Tobacco <u>raised in Kentucky</u> is considered the best in the United States.
> Daniel Boone, <u>hired to lead a group of farmers west in 1775</u>, chose a place to settle and built a fort <u>called Boonesborough</u>.

Tip 23. The words *every* and *each* (as well as nouns beginning with *every-, some-, any-, no-/body/one/thing*) require singular verbs.

> <u>Each</u> of the students in my class <u>works</u> on an individual project.
> <u>Everybody</u> <u>has</u> decided to attend the school picnic.
> When <u>something</u> <u>is extinct</u>, it no longer has living specimens or organisms.

Tip 24. The comparative forms *more* and *-er*, used when two nouns are compared, most often require the preposition *than* (except in the structure *the more/-er ... the more/-er. The thicker the book, the higher the price*). If a sentence has the word *than*, a comparative adjective should be used.

> Usually, freight trains are long<u>er</u> <u>than</u> passenger trains.
> Anthrax is <u>more</u> ancient <u>than</u> any other animal disease known to man.
> Of the two brothers, John is the faster.

The superlative forms, used when more than two nouns are compared, are *most* and *-est*.

> Basketball players are some of the <u>tallest</u> people in the world.
> Anthropology, the study of humans, is one of the <u>most observational</u> sciences.

Exceptions:

Adjective ➤	Comparative ➤	Superlative
good	better	best
little	less	least
bad	worse	worst

Equality is marked by *as ... as*.

> This book is <u>as</u> thick <u>as</u> that one.
> Social anthropology is <u>as</u> complex and ambiguous <u>as</u> physical anthropology.

Comparative or superlative adjectives cannot be used with *as ... as*. Occasionally, in the case of two comparisons, the second comparison need not contain the final *as*.

> John is younger than Mary, and he is not <u>as</u> tall.

This sentence has the same meaning as:

> John is younger than Mary, and he is not <u>as</u> tall (as she is).

STUDY TIP

Check to see whether adjective clauses or phrases follow the nouns that they describe. An adjective without a phrase precedes the noun. Check for comparative signals: *more/-er, than,* and *as ... as*.

Adverbs

Tip 25. Adverbs, which often end in *-ly,* are also never a part of the subject of a sentence. So you can ignore them when matching the subject and the verb.

> During snow storms, travelers <u>frequently</u> have to spend the night in airport terminals.
> Bongo antelopes are <u>beautifully</u> colored in orange-red with thin white lines.

The comparative and superlative forms of adverbs take *more/most* and *as ... as*, similar to those of adjectives.

> ### STUDY TIP
>
> Adverbs can describe verbs (*go quickly*), adjectives (*especially pretty*), and other adverbs (*very quickly*). Check to see whether adverbs have the ending *-ly*.

Using the Guessing Tips

It is not always easy to understand the meaning of a sentence or the meanings of all the words used in the sentence. If you do not understand the meaning of a sentence, do not stop trying to guess the answer (keep in mind that you have about 35 seconds per question). The grammatical markers and other signal words can prompt you as to which selection is more likely to be the correct answer.

The following examples show you how to take advantage of sentence markers and the preceding "Tips for Guessing the Answer."

Examples for Part A

EXAMPLE 1:   Simple sentence
Begin by reading the sentence.

> The planning of television dramas - - - - - - - - in the programming departments of broadcasting stations.

You see that the first word is the article *the*, followed by *planning*. Because articles usually come before nouns (gerunds are nouns formed from verbs) or noun phrases, you know that *planning* is a noun (Tip 2). The next word after *planning* is the preposition *of*. Because the prepositional phrase *of television dramas* is not part of the subject (Tip 6), *the planning* is the subject. Notice that it is singular—no *-s*.

After the blank, you see both the preposition *in* and the article *the*. Clearly, *programming departments* is a noun phrase, followed by the prepositional phrase *of broadcasting stations*. So far, you have found only nouns and no verb. You already know that you need a verb (Tip 1) and that, since the subject is singular, the verb may end in *-s* in the present tense.

The next step is to look at the multiple choice selections:

    (A) which begin
    (B) begins
    (C) are beginning
    (D) which begins

(A) is not a good choice because the verb *begin* has no *-s* (Tip 9). (B) is a possible answer, so you should keep it in mind while you are looking at the other selections. In (C), *are* is plural, so (C) is not a likely choice.

If you insert (D) in the sentence, you obtain: *The planning of television dramas which begins in the programming departments of broadcasting stations.* Here the word *begins* is the verb for the pronoun *which*, and the subject *the planning* still has no verb (Tip 1).

The answer is (B).

EXAMPLE 2: Complex sentence with one subordinate clause

> Before electric - - - - - - - common, Europeans used candles as a source of artificial light.

Again, begin by reading the sentence. The first word you see is *before*, which can be a preposition or a clause word (Tip 18). Then comes an adjective, *electric. Europeans used candles as a source of artificial light* is a complete sentence, *common* is an adjective, and there is no noun after it (Tip 22). This means that you need another subject and another verb to complete the *before* clause (Tip 17). The four selections include forms of the verb *become*, which can be followed by an adjective without a noun.

(A) lighting it became
(B) the lighting became
(C) becomes the lighting
(D) lighting became

Each of these choices contains a word, *lighting*, that looks like a noun, and each contains a verb. (A) contains a noun and a pronoun but only one verb. This would give the clause two subjects but only one verb. (A) is not a good choice. (B) is not good because an article should come before a noun phrase and not in the middle of it. In (C), the verb *becomes* is in the present tense, but the verb in the main clause, *used*, is in the past (Tip 15); also, the verb usually follows a noun—but *electric* is an adjective.

The answer is (D) because the subject and the verb are in the correct order, and the verb is in the past tense, just as is the verb in the main clause, *Europeans used candles as a source of artificial light.*

EXAMPLE 3: Complex sentence with two subordinate clauses

> Man-made satellites in space carry instruments - - - - - - - - .

(A) that record where flooding is worst can
(B) where is the worst flooding that can be recorded
(C) where can they record the worst flooding
(D) that can record where flooding is worst

The sentence in this example has a subject and a verb. Three of the four choices (A, B, and D) have two possible clause words, *that* and *where* (Tip 1). The verb *can* cannot end a sentence except in a comparison: "She can run faster than I can" or when the main verb is omitted: *call me when you can (call me)* (Tip 10), so (A) is not the answer. Because there is no question mark at the end of the sentence, it is a statement, not a question. In a statement, the word *where* cannot be followed by a verb, so (B) and (C) can be ruled out (Tip 18).

By default, the answer is (D).

EXAMPLE 4: Complex sentence with a reduced clause

> Equipment failures or damage - - - - - - - - can interrupt local service of electric power.

(A) are caused by storms
(B) they are caused by storms
(C) which caused
(D) caused by storms

The sentence contains a subject, *equipment failures or damage*, and a verb, *can interrupt*. If you choose (A), you will have two verbs, *are caused* and *can interrupt*, not connected by *and*. You will also have only one subject, so (A) is not a good choice. In (B), *they are caused by storms* is a complete sentence; if (B) is inserted in the sentence, *equipment failures or damage* and *they* would make for two subjects. (B) is not a good choice, either. (C) is not appropriate because *caused* must be followed by an object (Tip 12) or by a *by* phrase if it is used in the passive voice, as in (D).

The answer is (D).

Examples for Part B

EXAMPLE 5: Simple sentence

> <u>Helicopters</u> are <u>small than</u> most <u>airplanes and</u> cannot fly <u>as far</u>.
>   A   B   C   D

There is no error in (A) because *helicopters* is a plural countable noun and is a possible subject. In (B), *than* signals the need for the comparative *-er, smaller* (Tip 24). In (C), the phrase <u>airplanes and</u> has no error because *airplanes* are compared to *helicopters* — both plural. In (D), *as far* is acceptable because it completes the comparison between *helicopters* and *airplanes* (*than* marks the first comparative structure).

The answer is (B).

EXAMPLE 6: Complex sentence with one subordinate clause

> <u>There is</u> no definite <u>record of</u> who created or <u>first use</u> traffic <u>control devices</u>.
>   A   B   C   D

(A) is not wrong (Tip 2). (B) is also appropriate (Tips 5 and 12). In (C), the word *use* can be either a noun or a verb. If it is a noun, it needs an article (Tip 8). If it is a verb, *use* is in the present tense but the verb *created* is in the past (Tip 15). In either case, the error is in (C).

EXAMPLE 7: Complex sentence with two or three subordinate clauses

> Fortunetellers <u>say they</u> possess a certain <u>power that</u> makes <u>them aware</u> of events
>   A   B   C
> before <u>them happen</u>.
>   D

(A) is correct because the verb *say* is plural to match the plural subject of the sentence, and *they* is the subject of *possess* (Tip 1); *that* can be omitted (Tip 20). (B) is also correct because *that* can be a clause word (Tips 2 and 17); (C) contains no errors (Tip 12). The answer is (D) because the clause should be *before they happen* with the subject pronoun *they* instead of *them* (Tip 2).

EXAMPLE 8: Complex sentence with a reduced clause

> Nearly <u>all crops</u> <u>grown in</u> the United States <u>are planted</u> by machines <u>call</u> planters.
>   A   B   C   D

(A) has no error because in English *crop* is a countable noun and can be made plural; neither does (B) because the adjective phrase *grown in the United States* follows the noun *all crops* (Tip 22). (C) is plural, as it should be because *crops* is the subject. The answer is (D): the passive form, *called*, is necessary in this adjective phrase. It has been reduced from "… machines that are called planters."

STUDY TIP

Chapter 6 provides structure-specific tips and rules that you need to know, as well as exercises to provide practice for the Structure and Written Expression section of the TOEFL.

Practice for Structure and Written Expression

Exercise 1: Nouns and Noun Phrases

Countable nouns can be singular or plural. Most nouns belong in this group: *students, schools, books, pens, tests* and many others.

Uncountable nouns are always singular: *information, knowledge, equipment, furniture, news, evidence, education, intelligence, space, energy, pollution,* all fields of study, natural phenomena such as *weather, fog, rain,* and *electricity,* fluids such as *blood, water, coffee, oil,* and *tea,* solids such as *ice, silver, gold,* and *bread,* gases such as *oxygen, smoke,* and *steam,* particles such as *rice, chalk, wheat, dust,* and *dirt,* and some others.

Some nouns can be either countable or uncountable, depending on the meaning and context. For example, *hair* is usually uncountable, but can used in the plural to refer to strands of hair:

> Two human <u>hairs</u> found at the scene of the crime led the detectives to the eventual arrest of the murderer.

Occasionally, the noun *water* can be used in the plural form, *waters;* in this case, its meaning changes to denote the ocean or sea water near a specific land or country, or bodies of water in an earth's region.

> British territorial <u>waters</u> are regulated by stringent laws.
> The <u>waters</u> of the Black Sea conceal numerous archaeological treasures.

Some nouns that are usually uncountable and that refer to *drinks* can be plural when the reference is to a common quantity of the drink.

> A typical diner can sell as many as 200 coffees a day. [meaning *cups of coffee*]
> Two beers in an hour can raise the blood alcohol level above 0.1 percent.
> [meaning *two cans* or *bottles of beer*]

But nouns that can be either countable or uncountable are rare and are unlikely to appear in the TOEFL.

Nouns with *-ing* are called gerunds. They are formed from verbs and denote the process of the activity described by the verb.

> <u>Developing</u> new technology is time-consuming and expensive. [the process of practically applying new scientific discoveries or concepts]

Names of areas of study ending in *-ics,* such as *mathematics, physics, civics,* and *politics* are singular. A few nouns that indicate a set end in *-s* but are actually singular, for example, *species, series,* and *means.* The noun *statistics* can be both singular and plural: the singular refers to the field of study, and the plural to *data sets.*

> Many American high school students think that <u>mathematics</u> <u>is</u> difficult.
> <u>A series</u> of lectures <u>is</u> being presented at Lapidus Hall this week.

Some nouns have adjective forms: *nation, national*. If a noun has an adjective form, this form is used to describe another noun. The expression *nation flag*, for example, is **INCORRECT** because the noun *nation* has an adjective form, *national*. If, however, a noun does not have an adjective form, it can describe other nouns and function as an adjective, for example, *vegetable soup, a shoe store, a computer course*. Nouns that describe other nouns almost never take *-s*.

The possessive *-'s* can be used with nouns that refer to human beings, body organs, some animals, geographic locations, money, time, and collective nouns.

> the teacher's pen, the doctor's wife, the elephant's tusk, Germany's economic policy, one dollar's worth, a week's vacation, the team's uniforms, the jury's verdict

The possessive of a plural noun is indicated by *noun + s + '*: *the boys'* lunch. For irregular plural nouns, such as *men, women*, and *children*, the possessive is formed in the same way that it is for singular nouns: *the men's room, women's jobs*, and *the children's toys*.

Names of peoples, such as *the Chinese, the Japanese*, and *the French*, can be singular or plural nouns as indicated by the article; the singular form *a Chinese* or *a Japanese* refers to an individual person. Without an article, these words are adjectives referring to languages.

Part A

<u>Directions</u>: Choose the one word or phrase that best completes the sentence.

1. At the beginning of this book, the author discusses the effects - - - - - - - - on the environment.

   (A) of pollution
   (B) they are of the polluted
   (C) of the polluted
   (D) they pollute

2. Psychologists have observed that a large part of the - - - - - - - - activity is beyond one's awareness.

   (A) brain that
   (B) brainless
   (C) brain's
   (D) brain whose

3. Tax laws are passed by - - - - - - - - who usually want to be re-elected.

   (A) political it is
   (B) politicians
   (C) politics for
   (D) politician

4. Paul Samuelson was the first American to win the Nobel Prize in - - - - - - - - - .

   (A) economy
   (B) economic
   (C) economical
   (D) economics

5. Various societies define - - - - - - - - in many rather complex ways.

   (A) that is successful
   (B) what success is
   (C) that success is
   (D) what is success

6. - - - - - - - - warfare duties primarily to males was imperative when combat was hand-to-hand.

   (A) Assigning
   (B) Assigned
   (C) They who assigned
   (D) That they were assigning

7. One approach to the study of stress is to identify events that cause psychological - - - - - - - - .

   (A) disrupting
   (B) disrupts
   (C) disrupt
   (D) disruption

8. - - - - - - - budget depends on the state of its economy and the stability of its currency.

   (A) The country
   (B) The countries
   (C) Countries
   (D) The country's

9. When items appear to vanish gradually from short-term - - - - - - - - , the process of displacement is noted.

   (A) memory
   (B) memorial for
   (C) in the memory
   (D) memorize

10. Wendell Willkie gained prominence for - - - - - - - to President Roosevelt's social reforms.

   (A) he opposed
   (B) his opposition
   (C) opposing him
   (D) he was opposite

Part B

Directions: In each sentence, identify the one underlined word or phrase that would not be considered correct in standard written English.

1. The British labor <u>movement</u> developed as <u>a means</u> of <u>improve</u> working <u>conditions</u> through
                 A   B   C   D
   group efforts.

2. <u>Poverty</u> in the United States is <u>noticeably</u> different <u>from</u> that in other <u>country</u>.
     A   B   C   D

3. <u>Five-credits-hour</u> courses <u>are approved</u> for the <u>student's</u> work in the major field <u>of interest</u>.
     A   B   C   D

4. A small <u>antelope</u> similar to the chamois lives in <u>rocky places</u> from <u>southern African</u> to
          A   B   C
   <u>the Sahara</u>.
     D

5. Emily Dickinson, <u>whose poems</u> were published after <u>her dead</u>, wrote <u>about</u> love, <u>nature</u>, and
              A   B   C   D
   eternity.

6. <u>The article</u> provides general <u>informations</u> about animals and tells <u>why animals</u> are important to
     A   B   C
   <u>human beings</u>.
      D

7. William Harvey, the <u>English doctor</u> who <u>discovered</u> the <u>circulate</u> of the <u>blood</u>, was born in
                A   B   C   D
   1578.

8. Roman <u>numericals</u> are <u>written</u> from left to right using the <u>principle</u> of <u>addition</u>.
         A   B   C   D

9. Farmers in all parts of Asia own their own farms, but tenant farmers are also practiced.
    A   B   C   D

10. After King Askia's many military victories, he seized deserts towns and consolidated
                    A   B   C

 his government.
     D

Exercise 2: Verbs and Verb Phrases

The basic sentence word order is:

Subject	Verb	Object
Good reading	requires	practice.

The word order in negatives is:

Subject	Auxiliary	not	Main Verb (+ Object)
Mary	did	not	study.

The basic question word order is:

(Wh- word)	Auxiliary	Subject	Main Verb	Object
	Is	he	coming?	
What	did	they	ask	you?

A command does not need a subject and takes the simple form of the verb:

Verb	(Object)
Stop.	
Close	the door.

A negative command requires an auxiliary *do:*

Do	not	Main Verb	(Object)
Do	not	open	the window.

Make, have (except when it means *must*), *must, can, could, should, let, will, would, may,* and *might* are never followed by *to.*

> John had his brother help him with his paper.

The verbs *force, ought, have* (meaning *must*), and *need* are followed by *to; force* can be also followed by a direct object (e.g. *force a smile*).

> I need to go home to study.
> Cornwallis was forced to surrender.

Verbs following all forms of *be* must have either the *verb + ing* form for the active voice or the *verb + ed/past participle* form for the passive.

| Active: | The boy | has been crying | for an hour. |
| Passive: | The experiment | was completed | on time. |

Part A

<u>Directions</u>: Choose one word or phrase that best completes the sentence.

1. Before the 1900s, children - - - - - - - - the yards of their homes and in the streets.

   (A) playing alone in
   (B) played in
   (C) has played in
   (D) they are playing

2. Many critics of plea bargaining - - - - - - - allows large numbers of criminals to escape appropriate punishment.

   (A) believed it
   (B) believe it to
   (C) believing that it
   (D) believe it

3. To get an idea of a soil's porosity, - - - - a small amount of top soil in your hand.

   (A) to rub
   (B) rubbing
   (C) rubbed
   (D) rub

4. The risks of developing cancer can - - - - - - - - by not smoking and by drinking in moderation.

   (A) be significantly reduced
   (B) to be significantly reduced
   (C) significantly reduce
   (D) to reduce significantly

5. Even though many couples - - - - - - - - smaller families, the number of births could rise.

   (A) now having
   (B) now has
   (C) are now having
   (D) is now having

6. To make up for losses in revenue, bus companies - - - - - - - - service and maintenance.

   (A) cutting
   (B) tends to cut
   (C) tending to cut
   (D) tend to cut

7. City planners in St. Paul - - - - - - - - models for building compact towns and cities.

   (A) proposing
   (B) have proposed
   (C) proposition
   (D) proposal

8. Refrigeration - - - - - - - - food spoilage by keeping temperatures near or below freezing.

   (A) and the prevention of
   (B) prevents
   (C) preventing that
   (D) is prevented from

9. Every year both large and small businesses - - - - - - - - financial difficulties.

   (A) that develop
   (B) are developed
   (C) they are developing
   (D) develop

10. Why - - - - - - - - to sell products consumers want in order to earn profit?

    (A) companies have
    (B) do companies have
    (C) companies do have
    (D) companies did have

Part B

<u>Directions</u>: In each sentence, identify the one underlined word or phrase that would not be considered correct in standard written English.

1. <u>Thousands</u> of settlers <u>gone</u> west <u>after</u> the Civil War <u>ended</u> in 1865.
      A   B   C   D

2. <u>Studies</u> of the sun <u>may leads</u> to the discovery of how the core of the sun <u>heats</u> its <u>outer</u>
    A   B   C   D
atmosphere.

3. Until the 1400s, <u>most books</u> and texts were <u>producing</u> by scribes who <u>copied</u> them <u>by hand</u>.
                  A   B   C   D

4. When <u>an object</u> moves or <u>vibrates</u>, it makes the <u>surrounding</u> air <u>vibrates</u>.
        A   B   C   D

5. <u>Approximately</u> 30 percent <u>of all</u> parents in the world let <u>their</u> children <u>to attend</u> school.
       A   B   C   D

6. Norman Rockwell <u>illustrating</u> <u>covers</u> of magazines, <u>books for</u> children, and <u>advertisements</u>.
                      A   B   C   D

7. <u>Organic</u> material, in <u>various</u> stages of decay, <u>releasing</u> nutrients <u>into</u> the soil.
    A   B   C   D

8. The <u>female turtle</u> often <u>walks away</u> after <u>covering</u> her eggs and <u>not return</u>.
       A   B   C   D

9. People <u>can reduce</u> stress <u>by accepting</u> events <u>as they are</u>, rather than as they would <u>likes them</u>
           A   B   C   D
to be.

10. When a bee <u>stings</u> an animal, <u>the insect's</u> stinger <u>remaining</u> in <u>the wound</u>.
           A   B   C   D

Exercise 3: Adjectives and Adjective Phrases

The adjectives *few, a few,* and *many* can be used for countable nouns:

> <u>A few</u> students registered for the course. [some, several]
> <u>Few</u> students registered for the course. [a small *number*]

The adjectives *little, a little,* and *much* can be used for uncountable nouns:

> I like <u>a little milk</u> in my coffee. [*some, but not much*]
> This project received <u>little</u> support. [*almost none*]

Forms of *other:*   *another*   for singular nouns (<u>another book</u>)
                        other   for plural nouns (<u>other books</u>)

Others and *the others* are also pronouns. They replace plural nouns:
                  others   is an unspecified plural.
                  the others   is a specific plural.

Many students study at night, but <u>others</u> prefer daytime.
Five students in my class study in the library, but <u>the others</u> study in their homes.

Part A

<u>Directions</u>: Choose the one word or phrase that best completes the sentence.

1. Caffeine is - - - - - - - - , slightly bitter substance, added to many carbonated soft drinks.

   (A) odor
   (B) odorless
   (C) an odorless
   (D) more odorous

2. Spain has little good farmland and lacks many - - - - - - - - raw materials.

   (A) important industry
   (B) industrious and important
   (C) important industrial
   (D) important industries

3. Nuclear engines operate without air and consume - - - - - - - - fuel than do other engines.

   (A) much less
   (B) most
   (C) much
   (D) most of the

4. Raising and selling cut flowers and - - - - - - - - potted plants is a large industry.

   (A) decoration
   (B) decorates
   (C) decorate
   (D) decorative

5. Calcite is one of - - - - - - - - minerals in the earth, and is prevalent in mountainous regions.

   (A) the more commonly
   (B) the most common
   (C) as common as
   (D) common

6. The mass of the sun is about 750 times - - - - - - - - that of all the planets combined.

   (A) the greatest
   (B) as great as
   (C) greatly
   (D) greater

7. Charles Dickens was one of - - - - - - - - writers of all time.

   (A) the popularity
   (B) the most popularly
   (C) the most popular
   (D) mostly popular

8. The divorce rate is - - - - - - - - in the United States than in almost any country.

   (A) very high
   (B) higher
   (C) the highest
   (D) highly

9. Martha Thomas was an American educator who stood for equal - - - - - - - rights for women.

   (A) well-educated
   (B) educational
   (C) educating of
   (D) educationally

10. The fewer the number of threads per inch, the - - - - - - - - texture.

    (A) loose fabric is
    (B) looser the fabric
    (C) fabric has loose
    (D) loose fabric

Part B

Directions: In each sentence, identify the one underlined word or phrase that would not be considered correct in standard written English.

1. Each climate zone <u>has</u> its <u>specially</u> features, <u>which this</u> research describes <u>in detail</u>.
              A   B   C   D

2. Although parents exert the <u>strongest</u> influence on <u>a child's</u> development, <u>another</u> adults also
                            A   B   C

   have <u>an effect</u>.
          D

3. The <u>more precipitation</u> there is, the <u>high is</u> the groundwater <u>table</u> <u>in low-lying</u> areas.
             A   B   C   D

4. Harold Pinter's <u>plays</u> show <u>ordinary</u> people being <u>threatened</u> or attacked by <u>mystery</u> forces.
                 A   B   C   D

5. <u>A little</u> drivers realize <u>how</u> many <u>individual</u> parts are <u>necessary</u> to assemble a car.
     A   B   C   D

6. <u>Much species</u> of cacti live in <u>places</u> that have warm <u>temperatures</u> at least <u>part of</u> the year.
      A   B   C   D

7. <u>According</u> to experts, <u>few regions</u> have as <u>little</u> plant life <u>than</u> deserts do.
    A   B   C   D

8. <u>Reinforced</u> plastics are strong, <u>lightweighted</u> combinations of plastics and <u>glass</u> fibers, <u>cloth</u>, or
    A   B   C   D

   paper.

9. The <u>essence problem</u> of <u>ethics</u> concerns <u>knowledge</u> and power when they are combined and
          A   B   C

   manipulated.
     D

10. Plato <u>argued</u> that it <u>is bad</u> to commit <u>an injustice</u> than to <u>suffer one</u>.
        A   B   C   D

Exercise 4: Pronouns

The possessive form of pronouns should be used before nouns with *-ing*. The object form of pronouns should not be used.

> I enjoy <u>his singing</u>. [not *him singing*.]

Possessive pronouns have special forms that are required when a noun has been mentioned and is not mentioned again. These forms are: *mine, yours, his, hers, ours,* and *theirs*.

> I like my coat better than <u>hers</u>. [her coat]
> Their house is as big as <u>ours</u>. [our house]

Usually, a reflexive pronoun should be used when the pronoun refers to the subject:

> John spilled coffee all over himself.

The forms of reflexive pronouns are:

I	myself	he	himself
we	ourselves	she	herself
you (singular)	yourself	it	itself
you (plural)	yourselves	they	themselves

Part A

<u>Directions</u>: Choose the one word or phrase that best completes the sentence.

1. During the American Revolutionary War, about 14,000 British loyalists returned to Britain, - - - - - - - - in 1783.

   (A) most of whom
   (B) most of them
   (C) mostly, they
   (D) much

2. The sense of touch is essential in locating external objects if - - - - - - - - close to our bodies.

   (A) their are
   (B) they are
   (C) their
   (D) they

3. We thank the many editors - - - - - - - - assisted us in the preparation of this book.

   (A) they
   (B) whose
   (C) whom
   (D) who

4. A language laboratory has audio equipment placed in booths - - - - - - - - students listen to language tapes.

   (A) how
   (B) in that
   (C) where
   (D) who

5. Mothers - - - - - - - - read to their children during the day and before bedtime give their children a great advantage in school.

   (A) their having
   (B) who have gotten
   (C) whose
   (D) who

6. Mary Cassatt was an inventive printmaker, and - - - - - - - - were always at the service of the public.

   (A) her talents
   (B) she was talented
   (C) talent of hers
   (D) hers, talents

7. Linguistics studies the structure of language and regularities - - - - - - - - .

   (A) it's used in
   (B) in its usage
   (C) people use it
   (D) using its

8. The judges at the fair are delighted to inform you that - - - - - - - - are one of the selected finalists.

   (A) your
   (B) yours
   (C) you
   (D) yourself

9. An organism cannot grow without food, - - - - - - - - materials to build its cells.

   (A) who delivers
   (B) whose delivery
   (C) which delivers
   (D) it delivers

10. A sizable proportion of high school students claim - - - - - - - - hope is to be admitted to college.

    (A) that is their
    (B) that their
    (C) it is that their
    (D) is that their

Part B

<u>Directions</u>: In each sentence, identify the one underlined word or phrase that would not be considered correct in standard written English.

1. Caruso <u>was a</u> famous Italian tenor, and <u>thousands</u> of people came <u>to listen</u> to <u>him singing</u>.
        A   B   C   D

2. Playing <u>jokes on</u> April Fool's Day is common in many regions, although <u>none</u> knows <u>how</u> the
           A   B   C

   tradition <u>began</u>.
            D

3. During the 1960s, the <u>state of</u> Alaska improved <u>it's</u> transportation <u>facilities</u> and put together a
                   A   B   C

   <u>statewide</u> ferry fleet.
      D

4. An <u>interest</u> in <u>architecture</u> often involves <u>preserving old</u> buildings and <u>modifying it</u> for new
          A   B   C   D

   uses.

5. Plants with short <u>root systems</u> are best <u>suited</u> for areas <u>where do</u> not receive <u>much rainfall</u>.
                 A   B   C   D

6. Earthworms belong to the <u>family</u> of segmented worms <u>their</u> body is <u>divided</u> into <u>a series</u> of
                         A   B   C   D

   segments.

7. <u>You can</u> think of <u>a species</u> as a group of <u>living</u> organisms most of <u>who are</u> very much alike.
     A   B   C   D

8. Benedict Arnold led <u>its</u> division into Canada <u>where he</u> participated in an <u>unsuccessful</u> <u>attack</u>
                       A   B   C   D

   on Quebec.

9. By the time babies are seven <u>months</u> old, <u>their</u> able to <u>sit up</u> without <u>support</u>.
                               A   B   C   D

10. <u>Currents</u> in <u>the South</u> Pacific are <u>slower</u> than <u>that</u> in the North Pacific.
      A   B   C   D

Exercise 5: Function and Placement of Adverbs

Adverbs describe verbs, adjectives, and other adverbs.

> Ann <u>immediately ran</u> after the bus.
> My brother is <u>almost always</u> happy and cheerful.
> Professor Thom speaks <u>very quickly</u>.

Most adverbs are formed from adjectives by adding -ly. Here are some exceptions: *already, always, everywhere* (and all other *-where* words), *here, never, next, now, nowadays, often, quite, rather, seldom, so, sometimes, then, there, today, yesterday,* and *yet.*

> The adverb form of *good* is *well*.

Costly, early, elderly, friendly, likely/unlikely, lively, manly, lovely, sickly, silly, shapely, womanly, and *ugly,* although ending in *-ly,* are adjectives.

The words *deep, early, fast, hard, high, late, long,* and *low* are used as both adjectives and adverbs:

> He is a <u>fast/hard</u> worker. [adjective]
> He works <u>fast/hard.</u> [adverb]

The words *hard* and *hardly* can be adverbs. However, they have different meanings: *hard* means *with great effort*, and *hardly* means *almost not/almost none*.

> He works <u>hard.</u> [diligently]
> He <u>hardly</u> works. [almost not at all]

Adjectives following linking verbs, such as: *appear, be, become, feel, go, grow, remain, smell, seem, get, prove,* and *turn,* do not take *-ly*.

> John's father appears/looks/seems <u>young</u>.

When the action of sensing is described, an adverb with *-ly* is used.

> Mary <u>carefully smelled</u> the coffee.
> John <u>slowly tasted</u> the tea.

When no action is involved, the adjective form should be used.

> Susan's perfume <u>smells sweet</u>.
> The kettle <u>feels hot</u>.

Verbs in certain special structures (*open wide, stand still, hold tight, keep quiet*) are also described by words without *-ly*.

> Please <u>keep quiet</u> for a while.

Adverbs can also be used at the beginning of sentences.

> <u>Occasionally</u>, Bob takes his sister to the movies.
> <u>Usually</u>, public universities have a semester schedule.

The words *already, always, afterwards, away, ever, everywhere, here, just, never, next, not ever, now, often, seldom, sometimes, soon, somewhere, still, then, today, there, tomorrow, upright, yesterday,* and *yet,* and words ending with *-ward* and *-wise (forward, otherwise)* are adverbs.

The words *deep, even, early, far, fast, high, late, long, low,* and *near* can be both adjectives and adverbs. When these words are followed by nouns or noun phrases, they function as adjectives. Otherwise, they function as adverbs.

> John walked at a <u>fast pace.</u> [Fast is followed by the noun *pace;* therefore, *fast* is an adjective.]
> John <u>walked fast</u>. [*Fast* is not followed by a noun, and it describes the verb *walked;* therefore, it is an adverb.]

The words *above, around, behind, below, down, up, in, inside, outside,* and *out* can be both prepositions and adverbs. When these words are followed by a noun or a noun phrase, they function as prepositions. Otherwise, these words function as adverbs.

> The car turned <u>around the corner.</u> [*Around* is followed by the noun phrase *the corner; around* is a preposition.]
> The car <u>turned around</u>. [*Around* is not followed by a noun or a noun phrase; therefore, *around* is an adverb.]

In addition to being placed at the beginning of a sentence (e.g., *"Yesterday* we went *to the movies"*), adverbs can be placed:

1. Between the subject and a simple form of a verb.

   John <u>never</u> comes on time.

2. After *be* in the simple present or past tense.

   John is <u>usually</u> late.

3. Before the main verb and after the auxiliary verbs.

   John has <u>occasionally</u> missed classes this semester.

4. After the main verb in the present perfect or past perfect tense.

   High winds have occurred <u>repeatedly</u> during the last six months.

Part A

<u>Directions</u>: Choose the one word or phrase that best completes the sentence.

1. By the end of the 1950s, portions of the Atlantic around New York had become - - - - - - - - .

   (A) extremely dirty
   (B) extreme dirtiness
   (C) more dirty
   (D) extremely dirtily

2. Because so much of the Sudan is dry land, irrigation - - - - - - - - for farming.

   (A) essentially
   (B) is essential
   (C) has essentially
   (D) has essential

3. Pilots who prepare for military careers train on the ground - - - - - - - - in the air.

   (A) as good as
   (B) as well as
   (C) well as
   (D) good as

4. None of the exercises provides students with practice in understanding - - - - - - - questions.

   (A) really difficult
   (B) real difficulty
   (C) reality, difficulty
   (D) really, difficulty

5. Saul Bellow has - - - - - - - - life in Chicago where he spent his childhood.

   (A) vivid portrayal
   (B) vividly portrayed
   (C) vividly portrays
   (D) vivid portrait

6. Knight Dunlap conducted his famous photography experiment - - - - - - - - sixty years ago.

   (A) nearing
   (B) nears
   (C) ear
   (D) nearly

7. The elderly person whose family moves to a new city may find it - - - - - - - - to make friends of similar age.

   (A) particularly hard
   (B) particular, hard
   (C) hardly particular
   (D) hard, particularly

8. Beethoven's nephew became his pupil, but this relationship turned out - - - - - - .

   (A) bad
   (B) badly
   (C) worst
   (D) more badly

9. Edgar Degas was - - - - - - - - visual information about faces, movement, and light.

   (A) constant accumulation
   (B) constantly accumulate
   (C) constantly accumulating
   (D) constant, accumulated

10. People who are - - - - - - - - cannot tell light from dark.

    (A) blind totally
    (B) a total blind
    (C) totally blind
    (D) totally blindly

Part B

Directions: In each sentence, identify the one underlined word or phrase that would not be considered correct in standard written English.

1. The <u>treatment of</u> cancer presents a <u>real</u> <u>urgent</u> task for researchers because many patients are
      A   B   C

   <u>affected</u>.
   D

2. When <u>there is</u> a recession, businesses are <u>serious</u> <u>concerned</u> about <u>taking risks</u>.
        A   B   C   D

3. It is <u>probably</u> that a <u>well-developed</u> memory is <u>crucial</u> in <u>learning</u> a foreign language.
       A   B   C   D

4. <u>Partial</u>, an <u>author's</u> inspiration comes from a <u>creative</u> idea that motivates him or her <u>to write</u>.
   A   B   C   D

5. <u>Approaching</u> a problem <u>creative</u> means <u>being able</u> to discern <u>its multiple</u> components.
    A   B   C   D

6. During the <u>finally</u> stage of <u>making</u> a dress, it is pressed and <u>carefully</u> packaged for <u>shipping</u>.
         A   B   C   D

7. Road racing is the <u>original</u>, and most popular, <u>form of</u> bicycle racing <u>wide</u> <u>accepted</u> in Canada.
               A   B   C   D

8. If one type of manufacturing <u>expands</u>, it is <u>like</u> that <u>another</u> type will shrink <u>considerably</u>.
                     A   B   C   D

9. Basil, an <u>annual</u> herb <u>usually grown</u> from seed, <u>is used</u> to make food <u>taste well</u>.
        A   B   C   D

10. The Saudi Arabian <u>economy</u> depends <u>large</u> on the petroleum <u>industry</u> and oil <u>production</u>.
                A   B   C   D

Exercise 6: Parallel Structure

The term *parallel structure* refers to "a string" of nouns, verbs, adjectives, phrases, or clauses that have similarities in structure and are often joined by one of the following conjunctions: *and, but, or,* or *nor.* If the string consists of more than two pieces, commas are used to separate them, and the conjunction comes before the last item.

> You may bring only pens, pencils, <u>and</u> erasers to the test.

All pieces of the string must be of the same type. For example, all should be adjectives or adjective phrases, or all should be verbs of the same tense and number, or all should be phrases.

> Little children enjoy <u>toys</u>, board <u>games</u>, and <u>books</u>.
> Before meat is cooked, it should be <u>washed</u>, <u>trimmed</u>, and <u>cut</u>.

Correlative conjunctions tie together **pairs** of structures: *both … and, either … or, neither … nor, whether … or, not only … but also,* and comparisons:

> Children enjoy <u>both</u> swimming <u>and</u> running.
> <u>Either</u> Mary with her sister <u>or</u> John with his brother is coming for dinner.

If the pieces of the string are the subject of a verb and the first element in the string is singular but the second one is plural, the verb must be plural. If the first item is plural but the second one is singular, the verb must be singular. In other words, the second part of the two parallel strings determine the number of the verb, whether it is singular or plural. An exception is *both ... and,* which always indicates a plural subject.

> Neither the teacher nor <u>the students are</u> in the classroom.
> Either the students or <u>the teacher is planning</u> to attend the conference.
> <u>Both the students and the teacher are planning</u> to attend the meeting.

Part A

<u>Directions</u>: Choose the one word or phrase that best completes the sentence.

1. Professional gardeners appreciate flowers for their - - - - - - - -, gorgeous colors, and pleasant fragrance.

    (A) attractively shaped
    (B) shape and attract
    (C) shaped attractively
    (D) attractive shapes

2. Customs influence - - - - - - - - and how they prepare, serve, and eat foods.

    (A) people eat that
    (B) people eat it
    (C) what people eat
    (D) what do people eat

3. Students of economics take courses in such related fields as history, political science, and - - - - - - - - .

    (A) statistical
    (B) statistics
    (C) statistic
    (D) statistician

4. To bake fish, - - - - - - - - butter and place it in a generously greased rectangular pan.

    (A) it brushes with
    (B) with its brushes
    (C) brushing it with
    (D) brush it with

5. Free electrons are not tightly bound to their atoms and - - - - - - - from one to another.

    (A) can move easy
    (B) can easily move
    (C) can move more easily
    (D) easy move

6. If you are seated when a newcomer enters the room, stand up to be greeted or - - - - - - - - .

    (A) introduces himself
    (B) introduce
    (C) introduction
    (D) introduced

7. Good manners should always govern the way people - - - - - - - - .

    (A) driving and parking
    (B) drive and park
    (C) to drive and to park
    (D) driven and parked

8. Classical ballet dancers perform their movements with an - - - - - - - - bearing.

    (A) openly and directly
    (B) openness and direction
    (C) open and direct
    (D) opening and directly

9. The brain centers of - - - - - - - - and hearing enable a person to understand written and spoken language.

    (A) vision
    (B) visual
    (C) the vision
    (D) a visual

10. The D'Aulaires were the - - - - - - - - team who wrote and illustrated children's books.

    (A) husband and wife
    (B) husband and a wife
    (C) husband and the wife's
    (D) husbands and wifes

Part B

<u>Directions</u>: In each sentence, identify the one underlined word or phrase that would not be considered correct in standard written English.

1. Americans share <u>a number</u> of values, <u>among them</u> achievement, <u>practical</u>, material comfort,
                  A   B   C

   and <u>democracy</u>.
        D

2. Some individuals see the issue of <u>smoking</u> as <u>a matter</u> of personal <u>freedom</u> or <u>choices</u>.
                                     A   B   C   D

3. Stores can <u>bring in</u> more customers when they <u>staying</u> open <u>longer</u> hours or <u>stock</u> more things.
            A   B   C   D

4. In long-term memory, the <u>stronger</u> the connection between <u>events</u>, the <u>likely</u> they are to
                        A   B   C

   <u>be retrieved</u>.
     D

5. Society uses <u>such human</u> emotions as <u>proud</u>, shame, <u>guilt</u>, and fear to maintain <u>itself</u>.
                  A   B   C   D

6. <u>A competitive</u> company <u>can increase</u> <u>its profit</u> by cutting its costs or <u>increase its</u> sales.
    A   B   C   D

7. Newspaper editor Arthur Brisbane emphasized <u>clearly</u> and <u>brief</u> stories and <u>the use</u> of bold
                                        A   B   C

   <u>headlines</u>.
     D

8. Eskimos <u>were</u> <u>the first</u> people to <u>live</u>, hunt, and <u>traveling</u> in the Siberian tundra.
          A   B   C   D

9. Decorations on <u>book</u> covers include <u>fabric</u> embossing, <u>colorfully</u> inking and metal <u>etching</u>.
                 A   B   C   D

10. Daniel Boone was <u>born</u> in Pennsylvania <u>but</u> lived <u>in several</u> states and <u>die in</u> Missouri.
                   A   B   C   D

Exercise 7: Subordinate Clauses

A *wh-* word in an adjective clause carries the following information about the noun to which it refers: person or thing (*who* for person and *which* for thing), and singular or plural (if the noun referred to is singular, the verb that follows the *wh-* word is also singular).

> The <u>boy who is</u> playing baseball is my brother.
> The <u>boys who are</u> playing baseball are my brothers.
> The <u>book, which was</u> published last year, is a best seller.
> The <u>books, which were</u> published last year, are best sellers.

The clause word *that* does not carry the person or thing information, but it does carry the same number (singular or plural) as the noun to which it refers. Therefore, the verb must agree with the number of the noun that the clause word "copies."

> The <u>information</u> that <u>was</u> given to me is very important. (singular)
> The <u>book</u> that <u>costs</u> twenty dollars is a textbook. (singular)

The <u>books</u> that <u>go</u> on sale today are marked down 20 percent. (plural)
The <u>vehicles</u> that <u>have been registered</u> with the sheriff's office are exempt from the new tax. (plural)

Adjective clauses with *wh-* words or *that* can be reduced to make adjective phrases of many kinds, such as some prepositional phrases, and active or passive adjective phrases. When an adjective clause is reduced to an adjective phrase, the first step is to delete the subject of the clause. If the verb is in progressive tense (present or past progressive), the helping verb *-be* also needs to be deleted.

The student who/that is reading in the library majors in chemistry.
The student - - - - - - - - reading in the library majors in chemistry.
The student - - - - - - - - - - - - - - in the library majors in chemistry.

If the verb in the clause is in the active voice, the adjective phrase remains active. If the verb is in the passive voice, the adjective phrase stays in the passive voice. The tense of the verb in the clause has little effect on the reduction.

The letter which/that was received in the office has/had a foreign stamp.
The letter - - - - - - - - - - received in the office has/had a foreign stamp.

If the verb in the clause is not in a progressive tense, another step is needed to reduce the adjective clause: for active adjectives, *-ing* has to be added to the simple form of the verb (without the present or the past tense). Passive verbs remain unchanged. For example:

<u>Active</u>
The technician, who works in the lab, can help you with the experiment.
The technician, - - - - - - - - work+ing in the lab, can help you with the experiment.

<u>Passive</u>
Abraham Lincoln, who was born in Illinois, became president.
Abraham Lincoln, - - - - - - born in Illinois, became president.

Unlike adjective clauses that describe nouns or noun phrases, adverb clauses usually describe the entire main clause.

When the soil has no drainage channels, the pooling of water occurs on the surface.

Adverb clauses can be reduced to participial phrases. The reduction takes several steps and is a little more complex than the reduction of adjective clauses. Participial phrases are frequently tested on the TOEFL. Examples of participial phrases are:

<u>After finishing our homework assignment</u>, we went for a walk.
<u>While looking for appropriate housing</u>, prospective renters need to consider the cost of utilities that varies widely.

Adverb clause reduction:
1. A very important condition for the reduction process is that the subject of the main clause and the subject of the adverbial clause must be the same. If the subjects of the main and adverbial clauses are not the same, the reduction cannot occur. For example:

After the rain stopped, we went for a walk.

The participial phrase *after stopping, we went for a walk* is **INCORRECT** because it means that *we stopped,* not that *the rain stopped.*

2. If the subject of the adverbial clause is replaced by a pronoun in the main clause, the subject of the clause has to be moved:

> After John and Mary finished their homework, they went for a walk.
> After - - - - - - - - - - finishing their homework, John and Mary went for a walk.

3. If the verb in the adverbial clause is active, -ing needs to be added to the simple form of the verb.

> After - - - - - - - - - - finish+ing their homework, John and Mary went for a walk.

4. If the verb in the adverbial clause is passive, -ing is added to the helping verb *be*.

> After the letter is received at the office, it will be filed.
> After - - - - - - - - being received at the office, the letter will be filed.

If -ing is already added to *be,* it does not need to be added again.

> While the new engine was being designed, it went through testing.
> While - - - - - - - - - - - - - being designed, the new engine went through testing.

5. When reducing adverbial clauses, *as* and *because* must be deleted. The words *before* and *since* cannot be deleted in clauses of time. The words *after, while,* and *when* have to remain if the adverbial clause follows the main clause; if the adverbial clause is in front of the main clause, they may be deleted.

6. If the time of the action in the adverbial clause (but not necessarily the verb tense) precedes the time of the action in the main clause, the helping verb becomes *having*. In clauses with the active verb, *having* is followed by V_3 (the past-participle form).

> After they stopped working, John and Mary went for a walk.
> Having stopped working, John and Mary went for a walk.

In clauses with passive verbs, *having* is added in front of the helping verb *been + main verb.*

> After the letter had been received at the office, it was filed.
> Having been received at the office, the letter was filed.

If the verb in the adverbial clause is negative, *not* is placed in front of the participle.

> When Mary did not know the answer, she skipped the test question.
> Not knowing the answer, Mary skipped the test question.

> Because John had not finished his assignment, he stayed home.
> Not having finished his assignment, John stayed home.

Part A

Directions: Choose the one word or phrase that best completes the sentence.

1. Dolphins and whales are mammals that - - - - - - - - lives in water.

(A) spend their entire
(B) their entire
(C) spend there entirely
(D) spending their entire

2. - - - - - - - - a wrong number, it is important to apologize before hanging up.

(A) You dial
(B) If dials
(C) If dialing, you
(D) If you dial

3. The study of etymology rests upon basic principles - - - - - - - - to all languages.

   (A) that applying
   (B) that they apply
   (C) that apply
   (D) applied that

4. Juries determine facts from what is said and from the manner - - - - - - - - .

   (A) which is said in
   (B) which said it in
   (C) in which it is said
   (D) which said it

5. No one knows when or why Monet abandoned his largest canvas, of which - - - - - - - - .

   (A) only the survival of fragments
   (B) only fragmented survivors
   (C) only fragments survive
   (D) survived only as fragments

6. Evening programs have been opened for people - - - - - - - - during the day.

   (A) whom work
   (B) who work
   (C) who works
   (D) which work

7. Congress, acting on the recommendations of special subcommittees, decides how much money - - - - - - - - on education.

   (A) the government which is spending
   (B) the government will spend
   (C) will the government spend
   (D) the spending of the government

8. Colonists who came to America created schools similar to those - - - - - - - - in Europe.

   (A) they had known
   (B) had they known
   (C) which had known
   (D) that had known

9. The thirteen colonies stretched from - - - - - - - - Maine to Georgia.

   (A) that is now
   (B) what is now
   (C) now that is what
   (D) is that what

10. That - - - - - - - - by gases was established only recently.

   (A) surrounding the earth
   (B) surrounded the earth
   (C) the earth is surrounded
   (D) the earth surrounded

Part B

Directions: In each sentence, identify the one underlined word or phrase that would not be considered correct in standard written English.

1. In 1847, Mormons settled in the Utah region they called Deseret what stands for hard work.
                         A   B   C   D

2. Veterinary medicine is the branch of medical science where deals with the diseases of animals.
              A   B   C   D

3. What the violin-maker glues the violin parts together, he uses no nails or screws.
   A   B   C   D

4. Economists predict how much will the prices change and, what trends the stock market
              A   B   C
   should exhibit.
   D

5. Normal unemployment exists in efficiently working economies even then jobs are plentiful.
                        A   B   C   D

6. A mellophone is a curved brass instrument that resemblance a horn and has a harmonic voice.
                    A   B   C   D

7. For a <u>when</u> it appeared <u>that</u> chimpanzees <u>could</u> learn <u>spoken</u> language.
     A   B   C   D

8. Emotions are <u>complicated</u> psychological phenomena <u>those</u> we cannot <u>sum up</u> in <u>everyday</u> terms.
               A   B   C   D

9. In countries <u>depend</u> on their <u>citizens'</u> obedience, <u>governments</u> encourage <u>compliance</u>.
            A   B   C   D

10. <u>Research</u> indicates <u>that genetic</u> inputs influence <u>who we</u> react <u>to alcohol</u>.
     A   B   C   D

Exercise 8: Subject/Verb Presence and Agreement; Repeated Subject

If the subject is plural, the verb form must reflect the plural subject. If the subject is singular, the verb must be singular. In English, a statement or clause can have only one subject, simple or compound. Every subject must have a verb.

None, all, some, half, most, a majority, the majority, percent, and *any* can be singular or plural. Generally, these words are followed by a noun phrase or a prepositional phrase. If the noun in the phrase is singular, these words take a singular verb. If the noun is plural, they take a plural verb.

> <u>Half</u> of <u>the students are</u> not in class today.
> <u>Some</u> of the <u>water</u> in the lake <u>is</u> contaminated.

Measurements of time, temperature, weight, volume, linear dimensions (e.g., <u>Five miles</u> is a long walk.), and money always take a singular verb, as do diseases.

> <u>Seventy degrees is</u> going to make for a pleasant afternoon.
> <u>Mumps afflicts</u> children but rarely adults.

The words *police* and *percent* have no -*s;* they may appear singular, but they take plural verbs. There is one exception: One percent takes a singular verb.

> Only 70 percent of the unemployed <u>collect</u> unemployment benefits.

The noun *number* is used with countable nouns, the nouns *quantity* and *amount* with uncountable nouns.

> the <u>number</u> of <u>students</u>, the <u>quantity</u> of <u>gasoline</u>, the <u>amount</u> of <u>money</u>

Part A

<u>Directions</u>: Choose the one word or phrase that best completes the sentence.

1. Nondurable goods - - - - - - - - for immediate use and are often less expensive than durable goods.

   (A) is intended
   (B) are intended
   (C) intent
   (D) intends

2. There - - - - - - - - photographs and graphs in this book that meet the needs of instructors in introductory courses.

   (A) is many
   (B) are many
   (C) many are
   (D) many more

3. Flower experts - - - - - - - - three main classes of cultivated roses.

(A) recognition
(B) they recognize
(C) recognize
(D) recognizes

4. Each of the displayed antique garments - - - - - - - - of praise and admiration.

(A) worthy
(B) worth
(C) are worthy
(D) is worthy

5. Almost all vegetarian diets contain fewer calories than diets that - - - - - - - - meat.

(A) it includes
(B) they include
(C) include
(D) including

6. When the Winter Palace caught on fire, all of its library - - - - - - - - .

(A) were destroyed
(B) destroyed
(C) was destroyed
(D) it destroyed

7. Syndicated news - - - - - - - - than news from independent agents.

(A) are cheaper and faster
(B) is cheaper and faster
(C) are cheap and fast
(D) is cheap and fast

8. None of the departments in the university - - - - - - - - advance the students' reading skills.

(A) it set out to
(B) setting out
(C) sets out to
(D) they set out to

9. Cold pressing - - - - - - - - less oil from a plant than do other processes.

(A) removes
(B) removing
(C) it removes
(D) they remove

10. While reporters listen to a communication, - - - - - - - - the points the speaker is making.

(A) evaluate
(B) the evaluation
(C) he evaluates
(D) they evaluate

Part B

Directions: In each sentence, identify the one underlined word or phrase that would not be considered correct in standard written English.

1. Not everyone wish to or can afford to purchase a home.
   A   B   C   D

2. Each of the musicians in the orchestra were rehearsing daily before the concert tour began.
                  A   B   C   D

3. The plant leaf has vascular tissues just as the stem and the root does.
              A   B   C   D

4. Side photographic light it does not show surface detail as well as front lighting.
        A   B   C   D

5. In round numbers, 70 percent of contracts is simple affairs and prompt transactions that are
                          A   B   C
   soon forgotten.
        D

6. Although Japan is crowded, the Japanese has a high standard of living.
   A   B   C   D

7. <u>All of</u> the <u>recipes in</u> this cookbook <u>has been</u> tested and <u>adjusted for</u> quantity.
     A   B   C   D

8. Left to <u>themselves</u>, rain forests <u>sustains</u> their <u>ecological</u> systems <u>indefinitely</u>.
           A   B   C   D

9. <u>Equipment</u> breakdowns in industry <u>accounts</u> for annual <u>losses</u> of billions of <u>dollars</u>.
     A   B   C   D

10. During the day the sun <u>warm</u> the air near the <u>earth's</u> surface, and the <u>heated</u> air <u>rises</u>.
                A   B   C   D

Exercise 9: Active/Passive Voice

In passive constructions, the grammatical subject does not "do" the action expressed by a verb.

> The store <u>is closed</u>. [Someone closed the store.]
> The first computing device <u>was designed</u> in 1891. [Someone designed the first computing device in 1891.]

An adjective clause can be reduced to an adjective or an adjective phrase. Active or passive adjectives (e.g., *amusing, amused*) come from active or passive verbs in adjective clauses.

> The boy <u>who sits</u> in the back of the classroom is from Taiwan. [*Sits* is an active verb.]
> The boy <u>sitting</u> in the back of the classroom is from Taiwan. [*Sitting* is an active adjective.]
> The book <u>that is required</u> for this course is expensive. [*Is required* is a passive verb.]
> The book <u>required</u> for this course is expensive. [*Required* is a passive adjective.]

Inanimate nouns (referring to things) can be subjects of **active** verbs.

> My pencil <u>broke</u>.
> If the cup <u>turns over</u>, the coffee <u>will spill</u>.
> Be careful! The door <u>is closing</u>.

Part A

<u>Directions</u>: Choose the one word or phrase that best completes the sentence.

1. The raw materials present in the sugar beet - - - - - - - - make sugar.

   (A) need
   (B) are needed to
   (C) while needing
   (D) needs it

2. Hair, fingernails, and toenails - - - - - - - - from the skin.

   (A) forming
   (B) formed
   (C) are formed
   (D) forms

3. The Icelandic language - - - - - - - - very little over the past 800 years.

   (A) is changed
   (B) has changed
   (C) changes are
   (D) changing so

4. The climate of India is greatly influenced by strong winds - - - - - - - - monsoons.

   (A) calling them
   (B) called for
   (C) are calling to
   (D) are called

5. Many cultures, religions, and languages - - - - - - - - among the peoples of South America.

   (A) found
   (B) finding for them
   (C) are found
   (D) founded them

6. The cost of medical insurance - - - - - - - steadily over the current decade.

   (A) has risen
   (B) being risen
   (C) being raised
   (D) rose

7. The first American immigrants - - - - - - - political practices that have influenced the history of the United States.

   (A) were institutional
   (B) were instituted by
   (C) instituted
   (D) instituting for

8. William Penn, a Quaker, - - - - - - - - the colony of Pennsylvania in 1681.

   (A) was founded
   (B) was found
   (C) founded
   (D) has found

9. Education in Chile - - - - - - - - since the government reform in the 1960s.

   (A) has many improvements
   (B) been improved
   (C) has an improvement
   (D) has improved

10. The oldest extant American valentine card has a - - - - - - - - verse in German.

    (A) handwriting
    (B) handwritten
    (C) wrote by hand
    (D) writing by hand

Part B

<u>Directions</u>: In each sentence, identify the one underlined word or phrase that would not be considered correct in standard written English.

1. Video <u>cameras</u> pick <u>up</u> the <u>light</u> that <u>reflecting</u> from an object.
          A   B   C   D

2. Ponds, lakes, <u>and streams</u> never <u>remain</u> <u>the same</u> and are always <u>transform</u>.
          A   B   C   D

3. The <u>seasons</u> are <u>reversing</u> in <u>the two</u> hemispheres, with global-scale air systems <u>moving</u> north
   A   B   C   D
   and south.

4. The value of <u>advertising</u> that is <u>intending</u> to influence and <u>persuade</u> is often <u>questioned</u>.
          A   B   C   D

5. After the steam <u>has left</u> the turbine, it is <u>condensing</u> and <u>recycled</u> through the power <u>plant</u>.
          A   B   C   D

6. The yeast dough <u>prepared</u> for baking bread may <u>be lack</u> sufficient <u>amounts of</u> sugar <u>to rise</u> in
          A   B   C   D
   the oven.

7. Military academies are <u>prepared</u> young men <u>and women</u> for <u>careers</u> as <u>officers</u> in the armed
          A   B   C   D
   forces.

8. The Pueblo Indians <u>entered</u> their houses <u>by ladders</u> that could be <u>removing</u> in case <u>of attack</u>.
                         A   B   C   D

9. Miners were <u>attracting</u> to the Rocky Mountains by <u>their</u> rich <u>deposits</u> of gold, silver, and
                    A   B   C

    <u>other</u> metals.
    D.

10. Edison <u>was always</u> <u>strongly</u> independent and <u>was followed</u> his <u>own</u> ideas.
                A   B   C   D

Exercise 10: Gerunds/Infinitives

Gerunds (nouns ending in *-ing* formed from verbs) can be used as subjects and as objects of verbs or prepositions. The verbs *appreciate, avoid, consider, delay, discuss, enjoy, finish, give up, go, mention, postpone, quit, spend [time on],* and *suggest* may be followed by a gerund.

> <u>Writing letters</u> can be boring. [subject]
> In the past ten years, many Americans <u>have given up smoking</u>. [after the verb *give up*]
> John paid the mechanic <u>for fixing</u> his car. [object of the preposition *for*]

Infinitives and infinitive phrases can be used as subjects, objects, and sentence introductions (transitions).

> <u>To travel</u> around the world is a dream of many Americans. [subject of the sentence]
> <u>To begin</u>, we will define the term "cost." [sentence introduction]
> John and Mary <u>decided to buy</u> a new car. [after the verb *decide*]

The verbs *agree, appear, ask, decide, hope, expect, need, offer, plan, pretend, promise, refuse, seem, want,* and *would like* may be followed by an infinitive.

Infinitives can be used after verbs that require a direct object, following the pattern *verb* [someone] *to + infinitive* [something]:

> Mary <u>advised John to see</u> a doctor.
> John <u>asked Mary to pay</u> the doctor's bill.

Some verbs that allow this pattern are *allow (someone), ask (someone), encourage (someone), need (someone), order (someone), permit (someone), remind (someone), require (someone), tell (someone), want (someone), warn (someone),* and *would like (someone).*

To express purpose, infinitives are also used when *in order to* is omitted:

> Cut the paper [in order to] <u>to cover</u> the shelf completely.

The verbs *begin, forget, hate, like, love, regret, remember, start,* and *try* can be followed by either gerunds or infinitives.

The expression *too + adjective (+ for + noun/pronoun)* has a negative meaning or the implication *insufficient, not to the necessary degree.* These constructions require an infinitive:

> John is <u>too young</u> to vote. [John cannot vote.]
> The cake is <u>too hot</u> (for John/him) to serve. [The cake is so hot that it cannot be served.]

The expression *adjective + enough (+ for + noun/pronoun)* also requires an infinitive and has the meaning *sufficient, to the necessary degree:*

> John is <u>old enough to drive</u> a car.
> The water in the pot is <u>hot enough (for Mary) to make</u> tea.

Part A

<u>Directions</u>: Choose the one word or phrase that best completes the sentence.

1. In automotive companies, employees are rewarded for - - - - - - - - with the firm for lengthy time periods.

   (A) to stay
   (B) staying
   (C) to staying
   (D) stay

2. Graduate students often spend their weekends - - - - - - - - data for their research.

   (A) together
   (B) to gather
   (C) gathering
   (D) to gathering

3. Early craftsmen did not have the technology that would have allowed them - - - - - - - - their wares.

   (A) to storing and transporting
   (B) to store and transport
   (C) storing and transporting
   (D) store and transport

4. Language permits us - - - - - - - - our heritage through literature and narratives.

   (A) preserve
   (B) preserving
   (C) to preserve
   (D) preservation

5. Fingerprints have been employed - - - - - - - - criminals, amnesia victims, and unknown dead.

   (A) to identifying
   (B) identifies
   (C) identifying
   (D) to identify

6. The blood near the skin allows excess body heat - - - - - - - - from the skin.

   (A) to be lost
   (B) being lost
   (C) to be losing
   (D) losing

7. Amateur sportsmen believe that there are too many government restrictions on - - - - - - - - deer.

   (A) to hunting
   (B) hunts
   (C) hunting
   (D) to hunt

8. Botanists hope - - - - - - - - new methods of intensive cultivation of crops in Africa.

   (A) formulate
   (B) formula
   (C) to formulate
   (D) formulating

9. In June 1990, lawmakers were on the verge of - - - - - - - - a new clean air bill.

   (A) pass
   (B) passing
   (C) passage
   (D) pass to

10. China has made impressive efforts - - - - - - - - population growth under control.

    (A) to bring its
    (B) bringing to its
    (C) to bringing their
    (D) bring there

Part B

<u>Directions</u>: In each sentence, identify the one underlined word or phrase that would not be considered correct in standard written English.

1. To <u>cleaning</u> the computer, <u>spray</u> cleaner on a <u>cloth</u> and wipe the screen <u>gently</u>.
      A   B   C   D

2. The <u>responsibilities</u> of each <u>job are</u> included <u>to giving</u> the reader <u>an overview</u> of the office.
         A   B   C   D

3. <u>Living</u> creatures need <u>to have</u> energy in order <u>to move</u> or <u>carrying out</u> life functions.
     A   B   C   D

4. Until the 1700s, <u>the average</u> European <u>had no</u> means for <u>sweeten</u> drinks <u>other than</u> with
                   A   B   C   D

   honey.

5. Root caps <u>protect</u> the tips of <u>roots</u> from <u>be injured</u> by rock <u>particles</u>.
            A   B   C   D

6. Many Americans <u>have the</u> opinion that <u>sending</u> weapons <u>to small</u> nations contributes <u>to fight</u>.
              A   B   C   D

7. If the loan <u>interest</u> rate <u>goes up</u>, fewer <u>businesses</u> will want <u>borrowing</u> from banks.
            A   B   C   D

8. <u>It is</u> possible for firms <u>to made</u> too <u>numerous</u> and diversified investments to <u>generate</u> profit.
    A   B   C   D

9. <u>Farmers</u> cut <u>terraces</u> into hillsides <u>to increase</u> the amount of land <u>for farm</u>.
     A   B   C   D

10. When an episode <u>of frigid</u> winter weather <u>sets in</u>, meteorologists say that <u>it is too</u> cold
                   A   B   C

    <u>to snowing</u>.
     D

Exercise 11: Prepositions and Prepositional Phrases

In addition to simple one-word prepositions, such as *in, on, at,* and *of,* there are also two- and three-word prepositions that, like one-word prepositions, indicate prepositional phrases. Prepositional phrases are not part of a subject. The two-word prepositions are *according to, ahead of, as for, aside from, along with, because of, except for, instead of, next to, out of, prior to, thanks to,* and *up to.* The three-word prepositions are *in accordance with, by means of, in back of, in case of, in charge of, in front of, in search of, in spite of,* and *on behalf of.*

Prepositions should not be confused with conjunctions and adverbs that can tie together parts of a sentence: *and, but, for, or, nor, yet, so, still, also, then, in fact,* and *rather.*

The preposition *between* is used for two nouns and *among* for three or more.

> The United States stretches <u>between</u> the Atlantic and the Pacific.
> <u>Among</u> the students in my class, only two are from Korea.

The adjective *different* takes the preposition *from;* the adverb *differently* takes the preposition *than:*

> This color is <u>different</u> from that one.
> John did the experiment <u>differently than</u> Mary.

Part A

<u>Directions</u>: Choose the one word or phrase that best completes the sentence.

1. The final step in the research process is to draw conclusions based - - - - - - - of results.

   (A) of the analysis
   (B) on the analysis
   (C) the analysis
   (D) in the analysis

2. A correlation refers to a regular relationship - - - - - - - two variables.

   (A) in
   (B) about
   (C) between
   (D) on

3. Language dialects in the inner city are different - - - - - - - those in the suburbs or the countryside.

   (A) than
   (B) of
   (C) from
   (D) in accordance to

4. The microwave oven is one of the safest appliances - - - - - - - .

   (A) home
   (B) about the home
   (C) in the home
   (D) a home

5. Internal migration can affect society as deeply as movement - - - - - - - a country.

   (A) up and over
   (B) between and among
   (C) in and out of
   (D) up to

Part B

<u>Directions</u>: In each sentence, identify the one underlined word or phrase that would not be considered correct in standard written English.

1. <u>Cyclical</u> unemployment <u>figures</u> include workers who <u>lose</u> their jobs <u>because a</u> recession.
      A   B   C   D

2. <u>Early</u> factories <u>relied on</u> steam engines <u>for</u> turning out power <u>to fabricating</u> goods.
     A   B   C   D

3. <u>Of all</u> the paved roads <u>in the nation</u>, 93 percent <u>are cover</u> <u>by asphalt</u>.
     A   B   C   D

4. Edwin Booth, the <u>brother of</u> John Booth, had acted <u>in over</u> a hundred of Shakespeare's
                       A   B

   tragedies <u>when at</u> 1865, he retired from acting <u>for a</u> while.
           C   D

5. Water is often <u>referred of</u> <u>by chemists</u> as a universal solvent because so many <u>materials are</u>
                 A   B   C

   soluble <u>in it</u>.
         D

Exercise 12: Repeated Meaning (tested only in Part B of the Structure and Written Expression Section)

Two words or phrases that express the same meaning or idea are considered redundant and are not acceptable on the TOEFL. This aspect largely tests your knowledge of vocabulary rather than of grammar.

Watch for the following words with similar meanings:

main/major/principal/central
significant/important/vital/essential/crucial
short/brief/concise
extremely/exceedingly/particularly/especially
strong/powerful/mighty
fast/rapid
accurate/precise
specific/detailed
examine/investigate/analyze
supply/provide
accelerate/speed up
decrease/decline
dampen/moisten
increase/rise
perish/die
join/connect/unite/bring together
delay/postpone
choose/select
consider/evaluate
understand/comprehend.

Part B

<u>Directions</u>: In each sentence, identify the one underlined word or phrase that would not be considered correct in standard written English.

1. The <u>characteristic</u> west <u>coast climate</u> of the subtropics has <u>humid, moderate</u> winters and
      A   B   C

   <u>dry, arid</u> summers.
    D

2. The Pullman strike of 1894 <u>occurred took</u> <u>place during the era</u> <u>of rapid</u> <u>industrialization</u>.
                              A   B   C   D

3. <u>Schools</u> are <u>important, vital</u> means <u>by which</u> modern education <u>is provided</u>.
   A   B   C   D

4. A <u>good diet</u> must include <u>tiny, minute</u> <u>quantities</u> of nutrients <u>known as</u> vitamins.
     A   B   C   D

5. Pollen cones <u>on a pine</u> tree <u>are</u> small, <u>fragrant, aromatic,</u> and <u>soft</u>.
             A   B   C   D

6. Barges <u>carry and</u> transport <u>coal and</u> metal <u>slabs along</u> <u>navigable waterways</u>.
       A   B   C   D

7. <u>Irrigation</u> is becoming <u>increasingly</u> important, <u>significant</u>, and costly in desert <u>countries</u>.
   A   B   C   D

8. This article <u>examines and analyzes</u> the <u>impact of</u> the <u>tax base</u> on real estate <u>prices and sales</u>.
                      A   B   C   D

9. The Amish <u>community</u> demands a <u>huge enormous</u> commitment <u>and sacrifice</u> from its
                  A   B   C

   <u>members</u>.
     D

10. In modern <u>societies</u>, families must <u>frequently often</u> move <u>from</u> one <u>city to another</u>.
                  A   B   C   D

Exercise 13: Verb Tense/Inversion

When working with tenses, pay close attention to time words. Unless time words allow for a tense switch, sentence tenses should be consistent.

The word *since* in time phrases or clauses marks an exact starting time.

> John has lived in Ohio <u>since 1989.</u>
> John has lived in Ohio <u>since his family moved there</u>.

The preposition *for* marks a quantity of time.

> John has lived in Ohio <u>for three years</u>.
> I worked in Japan <u>for seven months</u>.

The word *ago* marks a past time point and requires past tense usage.

> Mary came to New York <u>four years ago</u>.

The future tense is never used in clauses of time or condition.

> If he <u>comes</u> tomorrow, I will give him the information.

(The sentence "If he <u>will come</u> tomorrow, I will give him the information" is **INCORRECT**.)

> When she <u>arrives</u> tomorrow, she will receive her diploma.

(The sentence "When she <u>will arrive</u> tomorrow, she will receive her diploma" is **INCORRECT**.)

In some sentences, the verb *be* or the auxiliary verb precedes the subject:

1. When the sentence begins with a negative word or the words *barely, hardly, rarely, scarcely, seldom, never, nowhere, at no time,* etc.

> Nowhere <u>is Martin</u> so happy as he is in Paris.
> Not only <u>did Peter come</u> but he also brought his wife.
> Never <u>had Peter seen</u> such a beautiful girl.

2. When the clause begins with *only, few, little, so,* or *such* not followed by a noun or a noun phrase.

> Only then <u>did Mary</u> understand what the man was trying to tell her.
> Little <u>did they</u> know that their village was destroyed.

3. When the conditional tense is used without *if* or *unless*.

> <u>Should John</u> need this form, I will get it for him.
> <u>Had Bob</u> called, Betty would have met him at the station.

Part A

<u>Directions</u>: Choose the one word or phrase that best completes the sentence.

1. Never - - - - - - - - concerned about money even though he was not well-to-do.

   (A) the doctor was
   (B) was the doctor
   (C) the doctor were
   (D) the doctor is

2. Marilyn Monroe - - - - - - - - to playwright Arthur Miller from 1956 to 1961.

   (A) has been married
   (B) had been married
   (C) was married
   (D) married

3. When the two alpine glaciers - - - - - - - , they will comprise a compound glacier.

   (A) will unite
   (B) had united
   (C) unite
   (D) united

4. Not only - - - - - - - - closed but also the adjoining roadways are completely blocked.

   (A) the airport is
   (B) the airport did
   (C) is the airport
   (D) did the airport

5. Since the new campus - - - - - - - - , it has grown to twice its original size.

   (A) opened a year ago
   (B) a year ago it opened
   (C) opening for a year
   (D) opens for a year

Part B

<u>Directions</u>: In each sentence, identify the one underlined word or phrase that would not be considered correct in standard written English.

1. On the <u>average</u>, men and women <u>remain</u> single <u>longer</u> than they once <u>do</u>.
          A   B   C   D

2. So extensive <u>the lakes are</u> that they <u>are viewed as</u> the <u>largest</u> bodies <u>of fresh water</u> in the
                  A   B   C   D
   world.

3. <u>For nearly</u> a century, the name of the drink <u>symbolizes</u> quality <u>refreshment</u> and <u>good taste</u>.
    A   B   C   D

4. <u>About</u> twenty years ago, the <u>island's army</u> officers <u>have taken</u> control of <u>the media</u> and the
    A   B   C   D
   government.

5. Without rice, <u>approximately</u> half of the <u>world's</u> population <u>had had</u> little <u>to eat</u>.
               A   B   C   D

Exercise 14: Main Clause Structure; Partial and Complete Main Clauses

If a sentence has a subject, it must have a verb, except in the double-comparison structure *the more/-er ... the more/-er.*

If a sentence consists of a main clause and a subordinate clause, each should have a subject and a verb.

The clause word is placed at or very near the boundary between the main and the subordinate clause.

Every sentence can have only one subject phrase, including simple or compound subjects, and only one verb phrase, consisting of simple or compound verbs.

If the subject, the verb, or the object consists of several parallel pieces, these must be connected with a conjunction.

Part A

<u>Directions</u>: Choose the one word or phrase that best completes the sentence.

1. Mnemonic systems - - - - - - - - information so that it can be remembered.

   (A) organic
   (B) organized
   (C) organization
   (D) organize

2. As they grow older, many children - - - - - - - - attachments to living creatures, such as cats, dogs, and birds.

   (A) forming
   (B) a form
   (C) form
   (D) forms

3. Always - - - - - - - - diskettes to their envelopes as soon as you remove them from the disk drive.

   (A) they return
   (B) it is returned
   (C) a return
   (D) return

4. According to a survey, test scores - - - - - - - - prominently in university admission decisions.

   (A) may be a figure
   (B) may figure
   (C) have a figure
   (D) may have figures

5. - - - - - - - - are periodic vibrations in the loudness of a sound.

   (A) There are beats
   (B) That beats
   (C) Beats
   (D) It beats

Part B

<u>Directions</u>: In each sentence, identify the one underlined word or phrase that would not be considered correct in standard written English.

1. During the 1930s, <u>large</u> corporations <u>failure</u>, causing the shareholders <u>to lose</u> their holdings
               A   B   C

    and <u>savings</u>.
         D

2. One <u>problem how</u> to institute, <u>oversee</u>, and <u>enforce</u> affirmative <u>action programs</u>.
         A   B   C   D

3. What <u>interests</u> sociologists these <u>days the</u> meaning participants <u>give to</u> social <u>interactions</u>.
       A   B   C   D

4. <u>Everything</u> we think <u>we have</u> disposed <u>of still</u> here on <u>our planet</u> and in the ecosystem.
   A   B   C   D

5. Cartographers <u>employment</u> the three <u>basic elements</u> of scale, <u>projection</u>, and symbolism to
            A   B   C

    convey <u>geographic</u> relationships.
         D

CHAPTER 7

Strategies for Reading Comprehension

> **STUDY TIP**
>
> **In this book, all vocabulary items in the examples, exercises, and Practice Tests are words that have been used on the TOEFL.**

About the Reading Comprehension Section

The Reading Comprehension section contains four to six reading passages of approximately 200–450 words each. A reading passage is usually followed by seven to twelve questions. Most test-takers have problems completing the Reading Comprehension section of the TOEFL, so the faster you can work on the reading passages and comprehension questions, the better your score can be.

The topics of reading passages are usually academic, typical of those you will find in textbooks for introductory courses in a university. Most frequently, the passages come from texts on biology, chemistry, geography, physics, American history, biography, economics, social sciences, and the arts. No knowledge of the subject matter is required for you to be able to answer the questions correctly.

Some questions will ask you to restate a sentence (use other words with similar meanings) or to paraphrase a word or a phrase according to the meaning it has in a particular passage. On the computer version of the test, you may also be asked to insert another sentence into the text at the most appropriate place or identify where in the text the particular information is given. However, the main purpose of this section is to test whether you understand the ideas expressed in the passage and the ways in which these ideas relate to one another.

Since 1995, the most frequently tested reading comprehension areas have been:

1. factual or text-based,
   for example: "According to the author of the passage, ..."

2. vocabulary items that are often not related to context,
   for example: "The word 'xxx' is closest in meaning to ..."

3. inference,
   for example: "It can be inferred from the passage that ..." "The author of the passage implies that ..." "What can be inferred from the passage/first/second paragraph about ..." "Which of the following about ... can be inferred from the passage/first/second paragraph?"

4. sentence-level (syntactic) reference,
   for example: "The word 'it'/'they'/'this ...' in line 'x' refers to ..."

5. textual organization and focus,
   for example: "The author describes/presents 'xxx' according to …"

6. main idea/point/purpose of the passage; best title for the passage,
   for example: "What is the main idea/topic of the passage?"

7. restatement (saying something in different words or in a different way),
   for example: "What does the author say/indicate/point out about 'xxx'?"

8. the author's tone/viewpoint,
   for example: "The author of the passage would probably agree with which of the following statements?"

9. textual analogy (usually found in passage examples or comparisons),
   for example: " 'xxx' is like 'yyy'," " 'xxx' is similar to 'yyy'," and sentences that include the words "compare."

Each of these areas is explained below.

A solid knowledge of vocabulary is very important in order to obtain a good score on the Reading Comprehension part. In factual/text-based questions, you will be tested on your ability to understand the text. These questions usually begin with *What, Who, Which, Where, Why, How,* or *When.* Although you will be asked questions about the information in the text, the actual words in the passage will not be used. Instead, the questions will restate the information in the passage. Therefore, to answer such questions correctly, you need to understand both the questions and the text.

Examples of questions in the Reading Comprehension Section

Here is a reading passage:

Badgers belong to the weasel family. All of the six species of badgers are heavy-bodied animals with short tails, short legs, and large flat heads. Many have white marks and spots either on their bodies or on their faces, but only rarely on both. Their thick fur, tough skin, powerful jaw muscles, and the foul, repelling odor from their scent glands make them foes that are difficult to beat. Badgers are strong and audacious enough to take on several dogs at a time. Because badgers have strong front legs and large claws, which they employ for digging, they live under the ground and in burrows. Nocturnal animals, they hunt and feed at night. Species that live in the northern climate zone hibernate during the winter.

The American badger populates the grassy, brush-covered plains of the West from southern Canada to northern Mexico. An average-sized animal weighs 12 to 14 pounds and is 2 to 3 feet long. Badgers usually bear one to five young in May or June when the weather conditions are mild. The honey badger is found in Africa, the Middle East, and northern parts of India. Highly adaptable, it can live in deserts, rocky country, or woods.

AN EXAMPLE OF A FACTUAL/TEXT-BASED QUESTION:

1. According to the passage, what are badgers known to be?

   (A) Cowardly weasels
   (B) Tireless hunters
   (C) Ferocious fighters
   (D) Voracious eaters

(A) is not correct because even though the text states that badgers belong to the weasel family, they are described as *audacious* (recklessly bold), not cowardly. (B) is incorrect because the text only briefly mentions that badgers hunt at night, not how they hunt. (C) is possible because the text describes badgers as strong, audacious animals capable of "taking on several dogs at a time" (you need to know that *take on* means *fight*). (D) is wrong as the text does not mention what or how badgers eat. The correct answer is (C).

AN EXAMPLE OF A VOCABULARY QUESTION:

2. In line 4, the word "repelling" is closest in meaning to

(A) disabling
(B) disgusting
(C) compelling
(D) appealing

The answer is (B).

AN EXAMPLE OF AN INFERENCE QUESTION:

3. It can be inferred from the passage that badgers

(A) can be seen clearly
(B) can rarely be spotted
(C) should be exterminated
(D) are comparatively unusual

When you read the question, you see the word *inferred,* which comes from the word *inference*. Therefore, you know that the answer requires you to arrive at information not directly stated in the text.

The passage states that badgers "live under the ground" and that "they hunt and feed at night." Thus, you can guess that (A) is incorrect.

In (B), the trick is that the word *spot* has more than one meaning. Words with several meanings are frequently used in TOEFL multiple-choice selections. *Spot* can mean *a mark* or *a stain* when it is used as a noun; it can be also used as a verb, meaning to *notice* or *see briefly*. Because *spot* is used as a verb in (B), (B) can be a correct answer. In (C), the word *exterminated* means *killed*. (C) is wrong because nothing in the text indicates action to be taken against badgers. (D) states that badgers are "comparatively unusual." This answer is not correct because the text says that badgers can be found in various parts of the world, implying that badgers are rather common. (B) is the correct answer.

4. In line 6, the word "they" refers to

(A) claws
(B) dogs
(C) legs
(D) badgers

The word "they" in line 6 is the subject of the adjective clause and follows "which." If the clause described "legs" or "claws," "which" would be followed by a verb. In this case, "which" would be the subject of the clause. However, "which" is followed by "they," so "they" is probably the subject of the verb "employ" *(they employ legs and claws)*. The word "dogs" is in a preceding sentence, and it is not a good choice. The subject of the clause that begins with "Because" is "badgers." The word "they" is also a subject, and it probably refers to the subject of the first clause, "badgers." The correct choice is (D).

AN EXAMPLE OF A TEXT ORGANIZATION (TEXTUAL-FOCUS) QUESTION:

5. The author describes badgers according to their

    (A) habitats and geographical distribution
    (B) physical features and characteristics
    (C) distinctive habits and preferences
    (D) distinctions from other animals

(A) is incorrect since a larger portion of the text describes badgers themselves rather than places where they live. (B) is possible, so you should keep it in mind while looking at other possibilities. (C) is wrong because badgers' habits and preferences are mentioned only briefly, and the text is not organized on this basis. *Distinctions* in (D) means *differences;* the text compares badgers only to dogs and only in one respect: a badger is a better fighter than several dogs. Therefore, (D) probably implies broader comparisons than just this one point. The correct answer is (B).

AN EXAMPLE OF MAIN IDEA/POINT/PURPOSE, BEST TITLE QUESTION:

6. Which of the following is the best title for the passage?

    (A) Badgers in the Wild
    (B) The Types of Badgers
    (C) A Description of Badgers
    (D) A Remarkable Badger

Questions such as this one are very general and require you to look at the text as a whole rather than focusing on details. (A) is probably not correct because all badgers live in the wild. The types of badgers were mentioned only briefly, so (B) is not correct. (C) seems to be a good possibility. (D) presumes a description of one "remarkable badger" (notice the article *a*); however, the text describes badgers in general. (C) is the correct answer.

AN EXAMPLE OF A RESTATEMENT QUESTION:

7. The author uses the phrase *hibernate during the winter* to mean that badgers

    (A) change their metabolic rate in cold temperatures
    (B) suffer and perish from cold weather
    (C) sleep through cold weather
    (D) change their coats to protect them in winter

To answer this question correctly, you need to know the meaning of the word *hibernate,* which is *to sleep during the winter.* If you are familiar with this word, you know that the correct answer is (C).

AN EXAMPLE OF A QUESTION REFERRING TO THE AUTHOR'S TONE:

8. The author's tone in the passage can be best described as

    (A) resentful
    (B) neutral
    (C) admiring
    (D) affectionate

Questions about the author's tone are very difficult to answer correctly. When working with such a question, you need to know both the words in which an author's tone can be described and ways to figure out what the author's tone is. You also need to know a large vocabulary because in the TOEFL the author's tone can be understood from the words he or she uses.

In particular, adjectives and verbs can help you determine the author's tone. For example, the word *remarkable* indicates admiration, whereas *cowardly* shows that the author doesn't like the person or animal he or she is describing.

In the multiple-choice selection for Question 6, *resentful* means *somewhat angry,* *neutral* means *neither approving nor disapproving,* *admiring* means *expressing respect,* and *affectionate* means *loving.* While the passage states that badgers do not smell good and can be difficult to beat, the author's tone is not angry. Anger can be indicated by calls to action against the person or animal described and/or by words that clearly show the author's feelings (emotionally charged vocabulary), such as *horrible, disgusting, terrifying,* or *malicious.* Therefore, (A) is not correct. (B) is possible because the text is a description. In the passage, there are no particularly positive words describing badgers as wonderful or lovable animals; answers (C) and (D) are wrong. The correct answer is (B).

AN EXAMPLE OF A QUESTION ABOUT TEXTUAL ANALOGY OR SIMILARITY:

9. The author compares the badger to several dogs in order to

    (A) demonstrate badgers' fighting ability
    (B) establish a similarity between dogs and badgers
    (C) define the limits of badgers' strength
    (D) exemplify badgers' geographical distribution

(A) is possible, and you should not dismiss it while looking at other options. (B) is incorrect because the passage only briefly compares badgers and dogs. (C) is incorrect because the author does not say exactly what the limits of badgers' strength are; the reader is not even told how many or what kind of dogs a badger can fight at one time. (D) is also possible; however, physical prowess or strength does not mean just fighting skill. The dogs are mentioned only for a comparison of fighting ability, and (D) is too broad (general) to be correct. The correct answer is (A).

Strategies for Reading Comprehension

As with other sections of the TOEFL, if you really have no idea which choice to select, be sure to mark an answer anyway; there is no penalty for incorrect answers. The rest of this chapter is devoted to strategies for narrowing down your choice of the correct answer out of the four possibilities.

The more answers you can eliminate from your selection, the higher the probability of your choosing the appropriate answer. If you are choosing one answer out of four, the probability of selecting the correct response is 25 percent. After you have eliminated one answer, the probability of choosing the appropriate response increases to 33 percent. If you can eliminate two of the four possible answers, the probability becomes 50 percent. In other words, the ability to eliminate as many unlikely answers as possible provides you with the advantage of a more accurate, less random, choice. The strategies and examples presented here can help you to make better guesses on your test but cannot reduce the necessity for good preparation.

If you are planning to enter a university in the United States, you will have to complete many reading assignments and tests. Your ability to analyze and understand written materials with the help of the strategies presented in this chapter will enable you to become a better reader and thus a better writer of academic papers in English. Chapter 8 provides additional reading comprehension practice.

The order of reading the text and answering questions

Usually, students begin working on the Reading Comprehension Section by reading the passage first. Then they read the first question and return to the text to look for the answer. Next, they read the second question and again return to the passage. This strategy is time consuming and inefficient.

Because the order of the questions follows the order in which information is presented in the passage, you will have to read the entire passage to find answers to all the questions. However, if you first read the passage and then return to it while looking for each answer, you end up reading the passage twice. A better strategy is to go directly to the questions and then read as much of the passage as necessary to answer each question. In that way, you will read the entire passage but will do so only one time.

Frequently, the first question following the passage is as follows: Which of the following is the main idea/point/purpose/topic/best title of/for the passage? Questions of this type are very general and require you to be familiar with the entire text. Therefore, if such a question comes first, do not answer it until you have answered all the other questions based on the passage.

STUDY TIP

Do not read the passage before you read the questions. Start by reading the first question. If it deals with the main idea/point/purpose or best title, you should answer this question last. By the time you have answered the other questions, you will be able to answer general ones.

STUDY TIP

The order of questions for each passage follows the order in which information is presented in the passage. Therefore, once you find an answer in a certain portion of the text you do not need to go back and look for any other answers in that portion of the text.

Dealing with the words you do not understand

All reading passages in the TOEFL contain a number of words that most test-takers would not understand. When students see these words, they sometimes attempt to figure out their meanings or they think about these words so long that they lose precious time.

A great deal of research has been carried out to learn how people read their first and second language and how much information they need in order to understand text. The results of many studies show that readers need less information than the text provides to understand the meaning. In fact, experts have concluded that readers do not read every single word in a sentence or text but omit a large number of words because they can guess the meaning of the text without them. For example, when you are reading a newspaper article in your native language, you probably skip about half of the words in it whether you are aware of doing so or not.

Students often feel, however, that they should read every word in an English text and look up in a dictionary the words they do not know. There are two reasons why many second-language learners have this view. First of all, this is the way they may have been taught to read in English. Second, they may believe that, if they do not read every word, they may miss some important information and misunderstand the text. This may be true of beginning learners who are attempting to read material that exceeds their reading skills. Intermediate and advanced learners, however, do not need to read every word in a passage. For experienced learners, this strategy does not substantially improve their comprehension of a text. In fact, when readers concentrate on the meanings of individual words and use a dictionary to look up every unfamiliar word, they frequently lose track of the information in the passage and have to reread it. This approach is definitely not the best one to use when reading for the TOEFL.

Also, when students look up words during their preparation for the test, they become dependent on their dictionaries and do not develop the skills necessary to figure out the meanings of words in context. Furthermore, such students may not even attempt to guess the meaning of a sentence if they do not understand one or more words in it.

There are certain key words that you must understand in order to understand the text, but skipping some other words will not prevent you from understanding a sentence or a passage reasonably well. While you are answering the questions, try to guess the meanings of the words you do not know and then skip altogether any that you cannot guess. For example, consider the following sentence:

> The mayfly is a dainty insect with lacy wings and a slender, forked tail that trails
> behind it in flight.

In this sentence, there are several words you may not know: *dainty, lacy, slender, forked,* and *trails.* However, the number of words that you do understand is sufficient (enough) for you to understand what the sentence is about:

> The mayfly is a - - - - - - insect with - - - - - - wings and a - - - - - - , - - - - - - tail
> that - - - - - - behind it in flight.

This sentence is a description of an insect that can fly and has a tail.

The same technique can also help you figure out meanings of more complex sentences by looking at the meanings of word parts, for example:

> Coastal areas dilute and filter out large amounts of waterborne pollutants,
> protecting the quality of waters used for swimming and fishing and as wildlife
> habitats.

With this sentence, if you simply skip over the words or parts of words that you do not understand, you might have:

> Coast- - areas - - - - - - and - - - - - - out large amounts of water - - - - - -
> pollut- - -s, protecting the - - - - - - of waters used for swimming and fishing and
> as wildlife - - - - - - .

Even with several important words in this sentence omitted, it is still possible to figure out that "coasts (take) out large amounts of water pollution, protecting the waters used for swimming, fishing, and wildlife." This is the basic idea of the sentence. However, there are several key words that you must know to understand the sentence: *coast, pollution, protect,* and, possibly, *wildlife.*

To see how this strategy can be applied to larger passages, you can look at the following example. In this passage the words that you may not know have been omitted:

> When light passes through water or glass, its direction is changed. This - - - - - -
> is called refraction, and the - - - - - - of change in direction of the light is called the
> - - - - - - of refraction. Refraction is caused by differences in the speed of light
> - - - - - - in different - - - - - - . When - - - - - - of light strike the - - - - - - of a - - - - -
> - at right angles, the - - - - - - do not bend. If the angle of the - - - - - - is other than
> 90°, they do. When light passes from air into glass or water, its speed - - - - - - .
> The - - - - - of light - - - - - - away from the - - - - - - at an angle greater than that
> at which the light struck the - - - - - - .
>
> Refraction of light was - - - - - - in several discoveries. One of the - - - - - -
> examples is the find - - - - - - that white light into - - - - - - of color, - - - - - - from
> red to - - - - - - , in the same, - - - - - - . Isaac Newton, who - - - - - - with the
> - - - - - - of refraction, termed the - - - - - - of light the spectrum, and the
> separation of light dispersion. Newton proved that white light consists of colors of

the spectrum mixed together and that the color of an object consists of the
- - - - - - of the spectrum that it does not - - - - - - and that is - - - - - - into the eyes.
If a red object is held under a blue light, it appears black as there is no red light
to - - - - - . Black is the absence of color, just as white is the presence of all colors.

This passage may be followed by several questions:

1. According to the passage, refraction occurs when

    (A) the angle at which light hits the surface of a substance equals 90°
    (B) light travels through different materials at different speeds
    (C) light and various substances come together at different angles
    (D) light travels through a substance at an angle greater than that at which it hit the
        surface

(A) is incorrect because you understand from the passage that "When - - - - - - of light strike
the - - - - - - of a - - - - - - at right angles, the - - - - - - <u>do not bend.</u>" (B) is possible: the
passage states, "Refraction is caused by differences in the speed of light - - - - - - in different
- - - - - - ." (C) is wrong because the passage does not mention how light and various
substances meet or the angles between them. Answer (D) is also incorrect; the passage says,
"The - - - - - - of light - - - - - - <u>away</u> from the - - - - - - at an angle greater than that at which
the light struck the - - - - - - ", whereas (D) states that "light travels <u>through</u> a substance," not
away. The correct answer is (B).

2. It can be inferred from the passage that the discovery of refraction led to

    (A) improvements in human vision
    (B) a change in the composition of objects
    (C) additional developments in physics
    (D) expansion of the spectrum

Although the passage mentions the <u>eyes,</u> it does not refer to improvements in vision; answer
(A) is incorrect. (B) is wrong because the passage states "the color of an object consists of a
- - - - - - of the spectrum that it does not - - - - - - and that is - - - - - - into the eyes." From
this partial sentence, you can understand that the passage establishes a connection between
the color of an object and the way the eyes see it; the passage does not discuss changes in the
composition of objects. (C) is clearly possible: the passage mentions several physical terms as
well as Isaac Newton, a famous physicist. (D) is wrong: the information in the passage
indicates that "white light - - - - - - into - - - - - - of color, - - - - - - from red to - - - - - - ,
<u>in the same,</u> - - - - - - ." The next sentence in the passage states that "Isaac Newton, who with
the - - - - - - of refraction, termed the - - - - - - of light the <u>spectrum.</u>" You can conclude that
the spectrum is always *the same.* Therefore, the correct answer is (C).

3. It can be inferred from the passage that black and white

    (A) are basically the same color
    (B) are not separate colors in the spectrum
    (C) have no color of their own
    (D) have nothing in common in terms of light

The passage says that red appears black in a blue light, but red would obviously appear red
in white light, as it does every day. Black is not the same as white; (A) is clearly incorrect. The
passage further states, "Black is the absence of color, just as white is the presence of all colors," so (B) is possible. (C) is wrong because the passage states that white light is a mixture
of all colors; thus, it is impossible that white has no color. (D) is also incorrect because white
and black are compared in the sentence "Black is the absence of color, just as white is the
presence of all colors"; in other words, black and white are both colors that depend on other
colors. Thus, the correct answer is (B).

STUDY TIP

Inference questions require you to make conclusions based on the information in the text. Correct inference is directly related to the facts mentioned in the passage.

4. Which of the following is the best title for the passage?

   (A) Refraction: The Mystery of Light
   (B) The Effect of Light on Color
   (C) The Discovery of the Spectrum
   (D) Refraction and the Spectrum

(A), although possible, is unlikely. Refraction is not a mystery; in fact, Newton studied it three centuries ago. (B) reflects only part of the topic that the passage discusses; for example, it does not mention refraction. Furthermore, according to the passage, light consists of various colors, and it is hard to say whether light actually has an effect on color—color *is* light. (C), like (B), focuses only on the portions of the passage that deal with the spectrum, without mentioning refraction. By default, the correct answer is (D).

STUDY TIP

Main-idea/best-title/main-topic questions use three types of distractors (tricks) in the answer choices: for the information provided in the passage, (1) the response is too broad (general); (2) it is too narrow; (3) one noun, verb, or adjective in the response makes a response false. The best strategy for answering such questions is to examine the multiple-choice selection carefully without returning to the text. The correct answer is the one that is closely related only to the facts in the text, not to possible inferences from the information in the passage.

Below is the full text of the passage on refraction. Read it and decide whether you were able to figure out the meaning of the text and to answer the comprehension questions without understanding every word in the passage.

When light passes through water or glass, its direction is changed. This process is called refraction, and the extent of change in direction of the light is called the index of refraction. Refraction is caused by differences in the speed of light
Line traveling in different substances. When rays of light strike the surface of a
(5) substance at right angles, the rays do not bend. If the angle of the ray is other than 90°, they do. When light passes from air into glass or water, its speed diminishes. The beam of light bends away from the surface at an angle greater than that at which the light struck the surface.

Refraction of light was instrumental in several discoveries. One of the notable
(10) examples is the finding that white light spreads into bands of color, ranging from red to violet, in the same, constant sequence. Isaac Newton, who experimented with the phenomenon of refraction, termed the spread of light the *spectrum,* and the separation of light *dispersion.* Newton proved that white light consists of colors of the spectrum mixed together and that the color of an object consists of

(15) the portion of the spectrum that it does not absorb and that is reflected into the eyes. If a red object is held under a blue light, it appears black, as there is no red light to reflect. Black is the absence of color, just as white is the presence of all colors.

STUDY TIP

A solid vocabulary base is necessary to obtain a good score in the Vocabulary and Reading Comprehension section. However, you do not need to understand every word in a sentence or a passage in order to answer questions reasonably well. Try to guess the meanings of the words you do not know, and skip over them if you cannot guess.

There can be so many unfamiliar words in a passage that you will not be able to guess the meanings of some sentences or larger portions of passages. The important thing is that you should attempt to guess answers to questions based on the information that you can understand.

While working on Part B of Section 3, you can apply the grammar skills and "Tips for Guessing the Answer" that you learned in Chapter 5, "Strategies for Structure and Written Expression," and in Chapter 6, "Practice for Structure and Written Expression." You can look for grammar cues such as the plural *-s* on nouns, the singular *-s* on verbs, the tenses of verbs (*-s, -ed,* or irregular verbs), noun suffixes (*-ion, -ity, -ment, -ness*), adjective suffixes (*-al, ful, -able/-ible, -ive*), and the adverb suffix *-ly.* All these markers will help you analyze the sentence or the text that you are working on and to make a relatively accurate guess. Do not leave any answer blank, and keep in mind that most answers in the TOEFL fall on (B) and (C) options.

Dealing with Vocabulary Questions

When ETS made changes in the TOEFL a few years ago, the Vocabulary Section of the test was removed. Originally, the Vocabulary and Reading Comprehension Section consisted of 60 questions, and 30 of them were devoted to vocabulary. In the new format, the Reading Comprehension Section includes 50 questions. Although vocabulary testing does not represent half of them, a high number of the questions test familiarity with vocabulary. A good vocabulary is essential to get a good score on the test.

Vocabulary items are found in the body of the passage. Below, you will find a passage used as an example:

> The increasing pace of life and the distance between people in modern society was first observed and researched by Charles Norton Cooley. Cooley, a sociologist who taught at the University of Michigan, was raised in a small town,
> *Line* and his investigations drew on his personal experiences to study American social
> *(5)* change. His major contribution to sociology lies in his studies of the industrialization and urbanization of the American population, combined with rising individualism and interpersonal competition. Cooley's conviction was that small, traditional, and cooperative social groups were tremendously important to the quality of people's lives. In his view, without small primary groups,
> *(10)* humans cannot develop a sense of belonging and maintain attitudes based on compassion and fairness.

In vocabulary questions, you will see a word or a phrase in quotation marks ("xxx"). Below the question, there will be four multiple choice selections. Your task is to choose the one item that is closest in meaning to the word in quotes. If the tested word is an adjective, the multiple choice selection will also have four adjectives. Similarly, if the word is a noun, a verb, or an adverb, the multiple choice selection will consist of words that belong to the same part of speech. For example:

1.   In line 2, the word "observed" is closest in meaning to

   (A) obtained
   (B) obscured
   (C) noticed
   (D) created

The answer is (C). The word "observed" is a part of a passive verb, and the multiple choice options are also parts of passive verbs.

Another example of vocabulary questions can be:

2.   In line 7, the word "conviction" is closest in meaning to

   (A) belief
   (B) conversion
   (C) contemplation
   (D) pride

The answer is (A). Because the word "conviction" is a noun, all words in the multiple choice selection are nouns.

Strategies for Vocabulary Questions

It is not always easy to guess the meaning of the word or phrase in quotes by simply reading the sentence in which it is included. The sentences and passages are written in such a way that most of the words or phrases in the multiple choice selection appear to be possible answers, but only one is correct. Because you should try to save as much time as possible while working on the Reading Comprehension Section, you need to follow two steps. First, read only the word in quotes in the question and the choices given to see which item approximates the meaning of the word. In the example (2) above, if you know the meaning of the word "conviction," you can readily see that the correct answer is (A). In this case, the rest of the sentence is irrelevant.

Sometimes, however, a word can have two or more meanings, only one of which would be correct in a particular context. In this situation, you need to read the entire sentence. Consider the following example:

3.   In line 4, the word "drew" is closest in meaning to

   (A) pulled
   (B) drifted
   (C) relied
   (D) dropped

In this question, two of the multiple choice selections, *pulled* and *relied,* could be possible, depending on the context. If you read the whole sentence, you can make the correct selection. From the sentence, it is clear that Cooley, a sociologist who was raised in a small town, "relied" on his personal experience to study American social change. The choice (A) would not fit well with the sentence because the meaning of the word "drew" as "pulled" can be used when physical objects are referred to. Therefore, the answer is (C).

Phrases can also have various meanings in different contexts. In such a situation, you will again need to read the entire sentence to decide which of the four meanings is correct:

4. In line 10, the phrase "based on" is closest in meaning to

(A) circumvented by
(B) stationed on
(C) deprived of
(D) grounded in

Choices (B) and (D) could both be possible meanings of the phrase "based on." After reading the sentence, you can see that (D) is a better choice because "stationed on" applies mostly to contexts dealing with the military or job-related topics. The correct answer is (D).

> **STUDY TIP**
>
> **To save as much time as possible when working with vocabulary questions, you should begin by reading only the word in quotes and then the multiple choice selections.**

> **STUDY TIP**
>
> **If, in your opinion, more than one of the choices could have a meaning close to the word in quotes, then read the entire sentence to figure out which answer is the closest to the meaning of the word.**

If you do not know the answer, guess, keeping in mind that most correct answers turn out to be choices (B) or (C).

Knowing what words not to study may be almost as important as knowing which ones to study. Not all words in the English language are included on the TOEFL.

> **STUDY TIP**
>
> **The test vocabulary does not include slang, or outdated, foreign, specialized, unusual, highly technical, or rare words. The tested vocabulary never includes names of plants, animals, fish, birds, minerals, chemical elements, or any other types of words that require definition. The tested vocabulary includes only words that have synonyms.**

In vocabulary questions, the distractors used in the test questions often include words that begin with the first letter or two letters. For example:

5. In line 10, the word "maintain" is closest in meaning to

(A) mandate
(B) magnify
(C) uphold
(D) predict

The same first letter or two does not indicate which of the four choices is a correct answer. You should concentrate on the meaning of the word or phrase in quotes and then select the most similar choice. The correct answer is (C).

Increasing your vocabulary

A good way to increase your vocabulary is to read. The more you read, the larger your vocabulary becomes. It is usually better to read books than newspaper or magazine articles because in a book some of the vocabulary items occur several times. The repetition of words in different contexts helps you to remember them. In addition, because a word can have several meanings, you can learn all of them by encountering the word in various sentences. Frequently, students believe that by choosing academic books they will learn more new words. While this can be true for some, it does not work for everyone. The problem is that an academic text may be too difficult. In this case, the student will probably not finish the book.

On the other hand, if students choose books that they enjoy, they are more likely to finish them. It really does not matter what type of books students read, as long as they continue reading.

When choosing a book to read, you need to keep in mind one important factor. For most adults, an average of approximately 12 new words per page represents the level of frustration (the limit of difficulty) that they can successfully overcome. If the average number of new words on a page is greater than 12, an adult reader probably will not finish the book because it is too hard.

If the difficulty of the text is appropriate for your reading level, it is better to use the dictionary only occasionally. If you look up every word you don't understand, you may become tired, bored, and frustrated. In addition, most adults remember meanings of words better if they have to figure them out from the context than if they look them up.

In fact, using dictionaries can be a little tricky. English-English dictionaries provide accurate explanations of word meanings and usage and there are many learner's dictionaries available. However, they may be difficult for some students to use. On the other hand, translating dictionaries may not be very accurate and can prove to be misleading. As many language learners already know, every language has words and ideas that are very difficult to translate into another language. In this case, translating dictionaries can be particularly deceptive. As a general rule, then, you should try to guess the meaning of a word from the sentence or the story in which it occurs. If you see a word two or three times but still cannot figure out its meaning, then look it up in a dictionary.

Another practical way to increase your vocabulary is to learn prefixes, stems (roots), and suffixes that result in new meanings or new grammatical categories of words. Sometimes, a prefix can completely change the meaning of a word; for example, the word *satisfactory* means *reasonably good,* but the word *unsatisfactory* means *not good*. Chapter 8 provides a list of prefixes and stems commonly used on the TOEFL and exercises to show how these word-units can be used.

An important thing to remember is that most words tested in Part A of the Vocabulary and Reading Comprehension section are adjectives and verbs, although nouns and adverbs are also tested. By learning adjectives, you can also increase your adverb vocabulary because most adverbs are formed by adding the suffix *-ly* to adjectives.

Practice for Reading Comprehension

Word Formation with Prefixes, Stems, and Suffixes

To increase your vocabulary, you can learn the prefixes, stems, and suffixes that are components of many English words. Learning them can help you guess the meanings of words that you do not understand in sentences and passages.

Prefixes

Prefixes come at the beginnings of words. They have meanings of their own and can change the meaning of a word. Below is a list of prefixes commonly occurring in words on the TOEFL.

ab-	out of; **absorb**—to take (something) out of something
ante-	before; **antecedent**—someone or something that existed in the past
anti-	against; **antigovernment**—against the government
bi-	two; **bidirectional**—in two or both directions
circum-	around; **circumvent**—to avoid, to work around something
co-, col-,	together, with; **cooperate**—to work together
com-, con-	**committee**—a group working together; **congregate**—to come together
dis-	not, take away; **dissatisfied**—not satisfied
em-, en-	in, into, inside; **enclose**—to surround, to include
ex-	out, from; **external**—outside, outer
for-, fore-	ahead, to the front; **forward**—ahead
il-, im-,	not; **illogical**—not logical; **impossible**—not possible
im-, in-	in, into; **import**—to bring into a country; **inhale**—to breathe in
in-, ir-	not; **inconvenient**—not convenient; **irresponsible**—not responsible
inter-	between, among; **interstate**—between or among states
micro-	very small; **microcomputer**—a small computer
mis-	wrong(ly); **misbehave**—to behave wrongly
over-	above, more; **overcrowded**—to be crowded above capacity
post-	after; **postwar**—after the war
pre-	before; **precede**—to come before
pro-	before, in front of, in favor of; **proclaim**—to present a claim before others; **progovernment**—for the government
re-	again, back; **revive**—to bring back to life; **reread**—to read again
sub-	below, under; **subsurface**—under the surface
syn-	same; **synchronic**—occurring at the same time
trans-	across; **transport**—to carry across
un-	not; **unclear**—not clear

Roots

Roots are basic components of words from which many words can be formed by adding prefixes, suffixes, or other roots. Because the stems below are commonly found in academic texts, they are also frequently used on the TOEFL.

alter	other, different; **alternative**—another choice
anthro	human; **anthropology**—the study of humankind
aqua	water; **aquarium**—water container/tank
astro	star; **astronomer**—a person who studies stars
auto	self; **automobile**—moving by itself (vehicle)
bio	life; **biography**—a description of someone's life
chron	time; **synchronic**—occurring at the same time
cycle	circle; **bicycle**—two circles (wheels)
demo	people; **demographics**—a description (science) of people (population)
dic, dict	to speak, to say; **dictate**—to say words (out loud)
equi	equal; **equilibrium**—balance (having equal weight on both or all sides)
extra	over, in addition; **extraordinary**—out of the ordinary
geo	earth; **geography**—a description (science) of the earth
graph	to write; **phonograph**—a device that records (writes) sounds
homo	same; **homogeneous**—of the same kind
hydr(o)	water; **hydrology**—a science of water
hyper	extra, over; **hyperactive**—overactive
judic	law; **judicial**—associated with the law
liber	free; **liberate**—to set free
log(y)	study of, description of; **sociology**—the study/description of society
manu	hand; **manufacture**—produce by hand
medi	middle; **Mediterranean Sea**—the sea that is in the middle of the earth; **medieval**—pertaining to the Middle Ages
meter	to measure; **geometry**—a science of measuring the earth
mit/s	to send; **transmit**—to send over
mobil	movable; **mobility**—motion, movement
mono	one; **monosyllabic**—consisting of one syllable
mort	death; **mortal**—(someone/thing that) can die
phon	voice, sound; **phonology**—a study (science) of voice or sounds
photo	light; **photosensitive**—sensitive to light
poly	many, several; **polysyllabic**—(consisting of) many syllables
port	to carry; **transport**—to carry over/to
prim	first; **prime minister**—the first (most important) minister
scope	to view; **microscope**—an instrument for viewing very small things
scrib, scrip	to write; **tapescript**—something written on tape
simu(l)	same time; **simultaneous**—occurring at the same time
spec(t)	to look; **spectacular**—worthy of being looked at, watched
tele	over (at a) distance; **telephone**—sound over distance
tempo	time; **temporary**—for a limited time
terra	land, earth; **terrain**—surface of the land
tract	to pull; **tractor**—a machine that pulls
uni	one; **uniform**—consistent (as one) in shape or appearance
ver	true, genuine; **verify**—to check for truthfulness, to prove to be true
vit(a)	life; **vital**—very important for life
vid, vis	to see; **visible**—can be seen

Suffixes

Suffixes can change a noun to a verb, verb to a noun, noun or verb to adjective, adjective to adverb, and so on. In comparison to prefixes, suffixes are limited in meaning and seldom change the basic meaning of a word. In the list below, the word in parentheses after each suffix indicates the part of speech resulting when that suffix is added to a word; for example, *love* (verb) + *able* (adjective) = *lovable* (adjective).

-able, -ible	(adjective) able; **lovable**—can be loved
-al, -ical, -ial	(adjective) belonging to, pertaining to, having to do with; **magical**—having to do with magic
-ance, -ence	(noun) state of being; **presence**—the state of being here; **absence**—the state of not being here
-ant, -ent	(noun) someone or something who does something; **student**—someone who studies
-er	(noun) someone who does something; **worker**—someone who works
-fic	(adjective) making, doing; **specific**—making special
-ful	(adjective) full of; **playful, joyful**
-fy	(verb) to add, to make; **simplify**—to make simple
-hood	(noun) state, condition; **brotherhood**—the state of being brothers
-ic	(adjective) belonging to; **public**—belonging to the people; (noun) **medic**—one who belongs to or is associated with medicine
-ion (-tion, -sion)	(noun) act, state; **motion**—the act of moving; **decision**—the act of deciding
-ious, -ous	(adjective) full of, having the quality of; **ambiguous**—having ambiguity
-ist	(noun) someone who is something or routinely does something; **violinist**—someone who plays a violin
-ism	(noun) belief, values of, practice of; **capitalism**—values based on capital
-ity, -ty	(noun) state; **clarity**—the state of being clear
-less	(adjective) without; **penniless**—without a penny
-ly	(adverb); **honestly, warmly**
-ment	(noun) result of an action/state; **development**—the result of developing
-ness	(noun from adjectives) state, condition; **kindness**—the state of being kind
-ship	(noun) state, condition; **relationship**—the state of being related to someone or something
-ure	(noun) act, process, state; **adventure, temperature**
-y	(adjective) characterized by, like; **lucky, happy**

Vocabulary Practice

When you come across words that you do not know, first decide whether the words include any prefixes, roots of words, or suffixes. If they do, try to apply your knowledge of components to arrive at the meaning of a word. Although you may not always be able to detect the exact meaning, being able to guess even an approximate meaning will help you make a more accurate guess from the multiple choice selection.

The vocabulary exercises below provide you with practice on various types of words.

Exercise 1

Directions: Select the one word or phrase that <u>best keeps the meaning</u> of the original sentence if it is substituted for the underlined word or phrase.

1. Quantum physics made great <u>headway</u> and found many applications after the end of World War II.

   The word "headway" as used in the sentence above is most similar in meaning to which of the following:

   (A) munitions
   (B) progress
   (C) weapon designs
   (D) defense projects

2. Synthetic plastics have become <u>an inexpensive</u> substitute for such materials as wood, metal, and fiber.

   The word "inexpensive" as used in the sentence above is most similar in meaning to which of the following:

   (A) a practical
   (B) a primitive
   (C) a cheap
   (D) a ubiquitous

3. With the aid of skin between their fore and rear paws, flying squirrels can <u>leap</u> from tree to tree.

   The word "leap" as used in the sentence above is most similar in meaning to which of the following:

   (A) signal
   (B) gather food
   (C) jump
   (D) seek shelter

4. <u>Oral</u> cultures, such as those of Polynesian peoples, have rich narrative histories and highly contrived tonal devices associated with recitals and chants.

   The word "oral" as used in the sentence above is most similar in meaning to which of the following:

   (A) Ancient
   (B) Spoken
   (C) Limited
   (D) Convoluted

5. Computer hardware and software have been <u>enormously</u> beneficial in the editing of newspapers, magazines, and journals.

   The word "enormously" as used in the sentence above is most similar in meaning to which of the following:

   (A) fundamentally
   (B) tremendously
   (C) pedantically
   (D) quintessentially

6. Copyright law stipulates conditions for <u>a collaboration</u> of authors to reduce the possibility of legal contests.

   The word "collaboration" as used in the sentence above is most similar in meaning to which of the following:

   (A) an ownership
   (B) a competition
   (C) fiscal obligations
   (D) a joint effort

7. Trees have to be <u>pruned</u> seasonally or annually to ensure that they continue to bear fruit.

   The word "pruned" as used in the sentence above is most similar in meaning to which of the following:

   (A) fertilized
   (B) trimmed
   (C) weeded
   (D) harvested

8. Mosquitoes and other parasitic insects can be so <u>bothersome</u> to deer that entire herds have been known to throw themselves off cliffs to be rid of the incessant attacks.

   The word "bothersome" as used in the sentence above is most similar in meaning to which of the following:

   (A) excessive
   (B) irritating
   (C) degrading
   (D) detrimental

9. Carbon monoxide expelled by exhaust systems may profoundly change the <u>climate</u> on the planet.

The word "climate" as used in the sentence above is most similar in meaning to which of the following:

(A) industrial production
(B) geological formations
(C) air composition
(D) weather conditions

10. Experts often forecast <u>an upswing</u> in an economy after a protracted slowdown.

The word "upswing" as used in the sentence above is most similar in meaning to which of the following:

(A) a decline
(B) inflation
(C) an improvement
(D) a reform

11. A complex mathematical problem can have several solution <u>paths</u> that are not necessarily comparably elegant.

The word "paths" as used in the sentence above is most similar in meaning to which of the following:

(A) equations
(B) apparati
(C) interludes
(D) algorithms

12. Before refrigeration, canning was one of the few methods of <u>preserving</u> vegetables with limited shelf-lives.

The word "preserving" as used in the sentence above is most similar in meaning to which of the following:

(A) storing
(B) ingesting
(C) increasing
(D) gleaning

13. Slang can be defined as a set of lexical, grammatical, and phonological regularities used in <u>informal</u> speech.

The word "informal" as used in the sentence above is most similar in meaning to which of the following:

(A) situational
(B) casual
(C) informative
(D) uneducated

14. The tempered glass from which almost all windshields are made <u>shatters</u> under considerable pressure.

The word "shatters" as used in the sentence above is most similar in meaning to which of the following:

(A) scratches and gouges
(B) resists impact
(C) breaks into shards
(D) rejects foreign objects

15. In rural Midwestern towns, the decisions that affect most residents are made at general <u>assemblies</u> in schools and churches.

The word "assemblies" as used in the sentence above is most similar in meaning to which of the following:

(A) concerts
(B) gatherings
(C) prayer services
(D) public libraries

16. Several chapters of Joan Steer's book describe <u>illegal</u> gambling activities in California in the 1970s.

The word "illegal" as used in the sentence above is most similar in meaning to which of the following:

(A) prosperous
(B) unlawful
(C) unusual
(D) embarrassing

17. When an infectious disease becomes highly contagious, it can <u>sweep</u> through a community in a very short time.

The word "sweep" as used in the sentence above is most similar in meaning to which of the following:

(A) spread
(B) stride
(C) creep
(D) maneuver

18. <u>Dissemination</u> of information is frequently carried out via satellite through local or national TV networks.

The word "dissemination" as used in the sentence above is most similar in meaning to which of the following:

(A) Compilation
(B) Condensing
(C) Sanctification
(D) Dispersal

19. Atoms that move <u>perpendicularly</u> to one another and collide do not regain their original velocities.

The word "perpendicularly" as used in the sentence above is most similar in meaning to which of the following:

(A) in a closed space
(B) at right angles
(C) in a vertical line
(D) at loose ends

20. Reclaiming clay-laden soil that has absorbed the <u>tainted</u> runoff from agricultural fields can be hampered by the soil's capacity to retain water.

The word "tainted" as used in the sentence above is most similar in meaning to which of the following:

(A) cleaned
(B) contaminated
(C) confined
(D) blocked

21. The debate as to whether Shakespeare was the author of the plays and sonnets published under his name has continued <u>posthumously</u> for several centuries.

The word "posthumously" as used in the sentence above is most similar in meaning to which of the following:

(A) with many interruptions
(B) after his death
(C) in light of new discoveries
(D) with an element of humor

22. Economic and ecological outcomes of political turmoil in strategically important regions of the world are impossible to <u>surmise</u>.

The word "surmise" as used in the sentence above is most similar in meaning to which of the following:

(A) guess
(B) survive
(C) coordinate
(D) prevent

23. Limestone grinding machines found at gravel excavations have two or three large flat plates that move <u>sideways</u>.

The word "sideways" as used in the sentence above is most similar in meaning to which of the following:

(A) noisily
(B) intermittently
(C) powerfully
(D) laterally

24. In the United States, elementary education is <u>compulsory</u> nationwide, with state governments having no say in the issue.

The word "compulsory" as used in the sentence above is most similar in meaning to which of the following:

(A) desirable
(B) mandatory
(C) perfunctory
(D) rational

25. The mountain resort industry advertises its sites as relaxing, picturesque, and <u>secluded</u>.

The word "secluded" as used in the sentence above is most similar in meaning to which of the following:

(A) affordable
(B) vogue
(C) healthy
(D) remote

26. The chemical element technetium was artificially created to serve as a <u>powerful</u> source of radiation.

The word "powerful" as used in the sentence above is most similar in meaning to which of the following:

(A) alternative
(B) obscure
(C) potent
(D) poisonous

27. A magician is an entertainer who performs a series of <u>deceptive</u> tricks based on the principles of physics, optics, and psychology.

The word "deceptive" as used in the sentence above is most similar in meaning to which of the following:

(A) skillful
(B) misleading
(C) incomprehensible
(D) unrivaled

28. The philosophical propositions of the Magna Carta made <u>an unequivocal</u> step toward the development of constitutional government in England.

The words "an unequivocal" as used in the sentence above are most similar in meaning to which of the following:

(A) a forbearing
(B) a formidable
(C) a definite
(D) a devastating

29. Belva Lockwood, who was trained as a teacher, gained recognition for her <u>selfless</u> dedication to women's suffrage.

The word "selfless" as used in the sentence above is most similar in meaning to which of the following:

(A) self-motivated
(B) unselfish
(C) self-centered
(D) unsettled

30. Expressionist drama <u>arose from</u> playwrights' interest in the revolutionary movement, which criticized social evils.

The words "arose from" as used in the sentence above are most similar in meaning to which of the following:

(A) deviated from
(B) extended to
(C) shed light on
(D) grew out of

Exercise 2

<u>Directions</u>: Select the one word or phrase that <u>best keeps the meaning</u> of the original sentence if it is substituted for the underlined word or phrase.

1. The Extension Program first established in 1873 at Cambridge University has successfully <u>withstood</u> changing popular trends.

The word "withstood" as used in the sentence above is most similar in meaning to which of the following:

(A) endured
(B) sponsored
(C) stood with
(D) stabilized in

2. A suppressed memory of <u>a traumatic</u> incident may be recovered under hypnosis.

The words "a traumatic" as used in the sentence above are most similar in meaning to which of the following:

(A) an enlightening
(B) an invigorating
(C) a subliminal
(D) a shocking

3. Surficial deposits of phosphorus produce a vague <u>illumination</u> that attracts animals after dark.

The word "illumination" as used in the sentence above is most similar in meaning to which of the following:

(A) light
(B) heat
(C) odor
(D) vibration

4. Private business negotiations and their outcomes, if commenced without a witness, are <u>extrajudicial</u>.

The word "extrajudicial" as used in the sentence above is most similar in meaning to which of the following:

(A) judgmental
(B) outside legal power
(C) extraprovincial
(D) outside regular measure

5. Olives are grown for their oil, which is used in cooking <u>predominantly</u> in ethnic and traditional cuisine.

The word "predominantly" as used in the sentence above is most similar in meaning to which of the following:

(A) pretentiously
(B) flagrantly
(C) preponderantly
(D) frequently

6. Margaret and Rachel McMillan were the <u>forerunners</u> of what is known today as early childhood education.

The word "forerunners" as used in the sentence above is most similar in meaning to which of the following:

(A) organizers
(B) benefactors
(C) precursors
(D) instructors

7. Although federal regulations pertain to all local legislative bodies, state legislatures exercise a significant degree of <u>autonomy</u>.

The word "autonomy" as used in the sentence above is most similar in meaning to which of the following:

(A) independence
(B) equitability
(C) jurisprudence
(D) reciprocity

8. <u>Pathways</u> in the mountains often follow the crests of ridges that are relatively treeless.

The word "pathways" as used in the sentence above is most similar in meaning to which of the following:

(A) Highways
(B) Caves
(C) Trails
(D) Cliffs

9. Tests with laboratory animals have <u>pinpointed</u> the danger of brain damage that monosodium glutamate may cause to infants.

The word "pinpointed" as used in the sentence above is most similar in meaning to which of the following:

(A) identified
(B) extrapolated
(C) projected
(D) hypothesized

10. The <u>emergence</u> of supersonic travel opened new horizons for the military, tourism, and commerce.

The word "emergence" as used in the sentence above is most similar in meaning to which of the following:

(A) profitability
(B) urgency
(C) appearance
(D) simplicity

11. In the 1920s, <u>amateur</u> theater performances benefited orphanages, poor families, and other charitable causes.

The word "amateur" as used in the sentence above is most similar in meaning to which of the following:

(A) nonprofessional
(B) pompous
(C) gregarious
(D) melodramatic

12. The invention of the microscope accelerated the advancement of microbiology at <u>an extraordinary</u> pace.

The words "an extraordinary" as used in the sentence above are most similar in meaning to which of the following:

(A) a remarkable
(B) an excruciating
(C) an elusive
(D) a rousing

13. Even the devoted fans of soap operas and serialized TV programming <u>deplore</u> the trivial plots of many episodes.

The word "deplore" as used in the sentence above is most similar in meaning to which of the following:

(A) divulge
(B) disdain
(C) lament
(D) ignore

14. Antique documents displayed in museum and library collections can be examined <u>strictly</u> by permission obtained in advance.

The word "strictly" as used in the sentence above is most similar in meaning to which of the following:

(A) frugally
(B) exclusively
(C) freely
(D) daily

15. Mayan <u>culture</u> and its artifacts illustrate the many mysteries surrounding the progression of the human race.

The word "culture" as used in the sentence above is most similar in meaning to which of the following:

(A) monument
(B) civilization
(C) edifice
(D) excavation

16. Soldering involves heating lead or lead alloys to <u>bind</u> metal objects by means of molecular diffusion.

The word "bind" as used in the sentence above is most similar in meaning to which of the following:

(A) melt
(B) meld
(C) solidify
(D) varnish

17. The <u>preeminence</u> of visual media as a source of pleasure has undermined the importance of reading for entertainment.

The word "preeminence" as used in the sentence above is most similar in meaning to which of the following:

(A) dominance
(B) frivolity
(C) pretentiousness
(D) idealization

18. The <u>widespread</u> use of pesticides and herbicides has led to contamination of groundwater basins in the Ohio River valley.

The word "widespread" as used in the sentence above is most similar in meaning to which of the following:

(A) extensive
(B) experimental
(C) occasional
(D) overwhelming

19. In order to enlist in the U.S. Air Force, a potential recruit must have a high school diploma.

The words "enlist in" as used in the sentence above are most similar in meaning to which of the following:

(A) rise in
(B) serve in
(C) conform to
(D) comply with

20. Hans Lippershey, a Dutch optician, built his telescope to scan the nighttime skies and chart the heavenly bodies.

The word "scan" as used in the sentence above is most similar in meaning to which of the following:

(A) visualize
(B) reflect
(C) magnify
(D) survey

21. Desert tribes avoid clinging attire in order to allow the body to expel perspiration without obstruction.

The word "clinging" as used in the sentence above is most similar in meaning to which of the following:

(A) embellished
(B) flowing
(C) dark-colored
(D) close-fitting

22. Giant kelp, one of the largest members of the seaweed family, propagates by sending out segments of its stems.

The word "segments" as used in the sentence above is most similar in meaning to which of the following:

(A) branches
(B) spores
(C) petals
(D) portions

23. In regions where industry is not a major source of employment, residents barter for sustenance and services.

The word "barter" as used in the sentence above is most similar in meaning to which of the following:

(A) bicker
(B) battle
(C) trade
(D) pay

24. Beer drinkers assert that they find the acrid taste and natural carbonation of this beverage refreshing.

The word "acrid" as used in the sentence above is most similar in meaning to which of the following:

(A) bitter
(B) flavorful
(C) pronounced
(D) compelling

25. Mollusks can cement their shells to virtually any solid underwater object and can eventually hinder the water flow.

The word "cement" as used in the sentence above is most similar in meaning to which of the following:

(A) float
(B) bond
(C) acclimate
(D) adapt

26. Perennially frozen ground on the north slope of Alaska is conducive to the emergence of ice mounds called pingos.

The word "perennially" as used in the sentence above is most similar in meaning to which of the following:

(A) Expectedly
(B) Sporadically
(C) Perpetually
(D) World-renowned

27. The Teamsters Union became the <u>foremost</u> labor organization in the United States during the 1950s and 1960s.

The word "foremost" as used in the sentence above is most similar in meaning to which of the following:

(A) most notorious
(B) most accessible
(C) leading
(D) forbidden

28. In the 1920s, the <u>changeover from</u> piecemeal to mechanized assembly quickened the rate of output in automobile factories.

The words "changeover from" as used in the sentence above are most similar in meaning to which of the following:

(A) conversion from
(B) contribution from
(C) supply of
(D) delivery of

29. Restoring <u>dilapidated</u> buildings can necessitate greater effort and expenditure than constructing new ones.

The word "dilapidated" as used in the sentence above is most similar in meaning to which of the following:

(A) ornate
(B) run-down
(C) old-fashioned
(D) obscure

30. A protective oil-based or silicon coating <u>deters</u> metal corrosion and the effects of road salt on steel, copper, and aluminum.

The word "deters" as used in the sentence above is most similar in meaning to which of the following:

(A) perpetuates
(B) masks
(C) inhibits
(D) integrates

Reading Comprehension Practice

Exercise 3

<u>Directions</u>: Answer all the questions following the passage on the basis of what is <u>stated</u> or <u>implied</u> in the passage. For each question, select the one best answer, (A), (B), (C), or (D).

No educational medium better serves as a means of spatial communication than the atlas. Atlases deal with such invaluable information as population distribution and density. One of the best, *Pennycooke's World Atlas,* has been widely accepted as a standard owing to the quality
Line of its maps and photographs, which not only show various settlements but also portray them in
(5) a variety of scales. In fact, the very first map in the atlas is a cleverly designed population cartogram that projects the size of each country if geographical size were proportional to population. Following the proportional layout, a sequence of smaller maps shows the world's population density, each country's birth and death rates, population increase or decrease, industrialization, urbanization, gross national product in terms of per capita income, the
(10) quality of medical care, literacy, and language. To give readers a perspective on how their own country fits in with the global view, additional projections depict the world's patterns in nutrition, calorie and protein consumption, health care, number of physicians per unit of population, and life expectancy by region. Population density maps on a subcontinental scale, as well as political maps, convey the diverse demographic phenomena of the world in a broad
(15) array of scales.

1. What is the main topic of this passage?

   (A) The educational benefits of atlases
   (B) Physical maps in an atlas
   (C) The ideal in the making of atlases
   (D) Partial maps and their uses

2. According to the passage, the first map in *Pennycooke's World Atlas* shows

   (A) national boundaries relative to population
   (B) geographic proportions of each country
   (C) the hypothetical sizes of countries
   (D) the population policy in each country

3. In line 2, the word "invaluable" is closest in meaning to

   (A) incremental
   (B) invalid
   (C) priceless
   (D) shapeless

4. In line 3, the phrase "owing to" is closest in meaning to

   (A) due to
   (B) in order to
   (C) instead of
   (D) in spite of

5. In line 5, the word "cleverly" is closest in meaning to

   (A) cleanly
   (B) collaboratively
   (C) intelligently
   (D) immaculately

6. Which of the following is NOT mentioned in the passage?

   (A) Calorie consumption
   (B) Currency exchange rates
   (C) A level of education
   (D) Population decline

7. It can be inferred from the passage that maps can be used to

   (A) pinpoint ethnic strife in each country
   (B) identify a shortage of qualified labor
   (C) give readers a new perspective on their own country
   (D) show readers photographs in a new form

8. In line 7, the word "layout" refers to

   (A) the geographic size
   (B) the cartogram
   (C) population
   (D) each country

9. In line 10, the word "perspective" is closest in meaning to

   (A) outlay
   (B) outlook
   (C) permission
   (D) permutation

10. In line 11, the word "depict" is closest in meaning to

    (A) amplify
    (B) implement
    (C) show
    (D) shrink

11. The author of the passage implies that

    (A) atlases provide a bird's-eye view of countries
    (B) maps use a variety of scales in each projection
    (C) maps of countries differ in size
    (D) atlases can be versatile instruments

12. In line 14, the word "convey" is closest in meaning to

    (A) convict
    (B) conjure up
    (C) demonstrate
    (D) devise

Exercise 4

Directions: Answer all the questions following the passage on the basis of what is <u>stated</u> or <u>implied</u> in the passage. For each question, select the one best answer, (A), (B), (C), or (D).

The returning boomerang is constructed in such a way that it sails on a circular trajectory and returns to the thrower. A trained hunter can throw a boomerang so that it will sweep up to a height of 50 feet, complete a circle 50 feet in diameter, and then spin along several smaller,
Line iterative circles before it lands near the thrower. Experts can make boomerangs ricochet off the
(5) ground, circle, and come back. Hunters use them to drive birds into nets by making the boomerang spin above the flock sufficiently high to fool the birds into reacting to it as if it were a predator. Ordinarily, a returning boomerang is 12 to 30 inches long, 1 to 3 inches wide, and less than half an inch thick. Its notorious pointed ends are not honed enough to allow the boomerang to serve as a weapon or to be even remotely threatening.
(10)   By contrast, the nonreturning boomerang is substantially heavier and can be used as a weapon. This type of boomerang is made to be 3 to 5 inches in diameter and 2 to 3 feet long, and may weigh up to 2 pounds. The power with which the boomerang hits its target is sufficient to kill or maim either an animal or a foe. All boomerangs are hurled in the same manner. The thrower grasps one end, pointing both ends outward. Having positioned the
(15) boomerang above and behind the shoulder, the thrower propels it forward with a snapping wrist motion to give it a twirl. The quality of the initial twirl conveys the propulsion to the weapon and provides its distinctive momentum.

1. In line 1, the word "sails" is closest in meaning to

   (A) flies
   (B) falls
   (C) surges
   (D) shirks

2. The author of the passage implies that throwing boomerangs

   (A) creates a circular air channel near the ground
   (B) can be useful in devising sailing trajectories
   (C) entails skill and requires practiced coordination
   (D) makes them pause in midair before they rise to a certain height

3. In line 4, the word "iterative" is closest in meaning to

   (A) robust
   (B) repeated
   (C) restrained
   (D) resolute

4. According to the passage, the boomerang can be used to

   (A) train birds
   (B) position a flock
   (C) flank birds
   (D) stupefy a flock

5. In line 7, the word "Ordinarily" is closest in meaning to

   (A) Orderly
   (B) Usually
   (C) Awkwardly
   (D) Obviously

6. In line 8, the word "honed" is closest in meaning to

   (A) heated
   (B) hooked
   (C) sharpened
   (D) shaded

7. In line 9, the word "remotely" is closest in meaning to

   (A) reluctantly
   (B) reportedly
   (C) vacantly
   (D) vaguely

8. It can be inferred from the passage that whether or not a boomerang can serve as a weapon depends primarily on

(A) its perimeter
(B) its weight
(C) the propulsion of its ends
(D) the power of the thrower

9. In line 10, the phrase "By contrast" is closest in meaning to

(A) On the other hand
(B) Therefore
(C) Thus
(D) Consequently

10. The author of the passage implies that boomerangs

(A) can disarm an enemy
(B) can locate a target
(C) are alike in shape
(D) are monumental in flight

11. In line 13, the word "hurled" is closest in meaning to

(A) threaded
(B) thrown
(C) thrashed
(D) thrust

12. In line 16, the word "twirl" is closest in meaning to

(A) reaction
(B) reflection
(C) rotation
(D) repulsion

Exercise 5

Directions: Answer all the questions following the passage on the basis of what is stated or implied in the passage. For each question, select the one best answer, (A), (B), (C), or (D).

Almon Strowger, an American engineer, constructed the first automatic telephone switching system, which had a horizontal, bladelike contact arm, in 1891. The first commercial switchboard based on his invention opened in La Porte, Indiana, a year later and
Line was an instant success with business users. To access the system, the caller pressed buttons to
(5) reach the desired number and turned the handle to activate the telephone ringer. During the same year, Strowger's step-by-step call advancement technology was implemented in the long-distance service between New York and Chicago when it proved to have the capacity of carrying signals through cable-joint extensions.

The first actual dial telephones, patented by Lee De Forest in 1907, were installed in
(10) Milwaukee in 1896. In 1912, their sound transmittal apparatus adapted an electronic tube to function as an amplifier. Transatlantic radio-telephone service linked New York and London in 1927. However, the long distance coaxial cable, which was hailed as unprecedented, came on the scene in 1936 connecting New York and Philadelphia. The Bell Laboratories research facility came up with the transistor to replace the cumbersome vacuum tube, thus diminishing the
(15) size of the electronic switch system to about 10 percent of that of the original. Crossbar switching, installed in terminals in 1938, operated on the principle of an electromagnetic force, which rotated horizontal and vertical bars within a rectangular frame and brought contacts together in a split second. A technological breakthrough in the form of underseas cables between the United States and Hawaii was implemented almost twenty years later.
(20) An extension was connected to Japan in 1964.

1. Which of the following would be the best title for the passage?

   (A) The Patent History of the Telephone
   (B) A Link between Research and Technology
   (C) The Telephone: A Technological Fantasy
   (D) The Developing Sophistication of the Telephone

2. In line 4, the word "instant" is closest in meaning to

   (A) impervious
   (B) impelling
   (C) immeasurable
   (D) immediate

3. In line 6, the word "implemented" is closest in meaning to

   (A) usurped
   (B) used
   (C) broken
   (D) breached

4. It can be inferred from the passage that initially telephones

   (A) utilized human operators
   (B) did not have a bell
   (C) were limited to businesses
   (D) revitalized business in La Porte, Indiana

5. Why did Strowger's switchboard find application in long-distance lines?

   (A) It could carry connections through cable extensions.
   (B) It could handle a large volume of simultaneous calls.
   (C) It required the caller to activate switches.
   (D) It was prevalent in commercial enterprises.

6. How did Lee De Forest improve the existing telephone?

   (A) He integrated the mouthpiece and the receiver.
   (B) He modified a pipe to transmit sound.
   (C) He created a device to boost the reception quality.
   (D) He made implementation of the dial system possible.

7. In line 12, the word "hailed" is closest in meaning to

   (A) praised
   (B) proposed
   (C) prepared
   (D) preserved

8. In line 14, the word "cumbersome" is closest in meaning to

   (A) culpable
   (B) curious
   (C) unwieldy
   (D) unyielding

9. In line 15, the phrase "of that" refers to

   (A) of the system
   (B) of the percent
   (C) of the tube
   (D) of the size

10. The author of the passage implies that telephone networks expanded because of

    (A) a series of breakthroughs
    (B) the work of a few inventors
    (C) multiple technical blunders
    (D) staunch public and private support

Exercise 6

<u>Directions</u>: Answer all the questions following the passage on the basis of what is <u>stated</u> or <u>implied</u> in the passage. For each question, select the one best answer, (A), (B), (C), or (D).

Psychology recognizes two types of research, experimental and differential. The former is concerned mainly with the overall processes governing human activities, and the latter sets out to establish individual differences in performance. More recent studies have demonstrated the
Line need for a third type of psychological study, namely, that which has to do with human
(5) development. Rather than considering this aspect of human performance as a part of the first two types, scientists have noted that developmental research indeed belongs in a separate category in and of itself. Piaget's work would indisputably fall in the area of developmental theories that have had great impact on both experimental and differential research. When examining Piaget's studies, it is necessary to keep in mind that, while his theories have been
(10) highly influential, his methodology has been strongly criticized. The primary shortfall of his work had to do with a lack of definition and standardization in his data and experiment design.

1. According to the passage, what is the central goal of experimental research?

   (A) To arrive at a general classification of individuals
   (B) To analyze individual differences in human activity
   (C) To establish the psychological processes governing humans
   (D) To administer experiments on humans and processes

2. In line 4, the word "namely" is closest in meaning to

   (A) specially
   (B) specifically
   (C) hence
   (D) nearly

3. It can be inferred from the passage that the author is a proponent of

   (A) reversing current trends in research
   (B) furthering a third branch of investigation
   (C) abolishing experimental and differential studies
   (D) assessing a need for human development

4. In line 7, the word "category" is closest in meaning to

   (A) case
   (B) cause
   (C) calling
   (D) class

5. In line 7, the word "indisputably" is closest in meaning to

   (A) indirectly
   (B) indiscreetly
   (C) undoubtedly
   (D) unduly

6. According to the passage, developmental psychology belongs in

   (A) the domain of Piaget's work
   (B) a category of dispute studies
   (C) its own unique area of study
   (D) other domains of research

7. It can be inferred from the passage that studies of human performance and of individual variations

   (A) should not be perceived as fundamental
   (B) should be taken with a grain of salt
   (C) cannot enumerate all facets of human brain
   (D) cannot account for all aspects of human psychology

8. In line 9, the phrase "to keep in mind" is closest in meaning to

   (A) remember
   (B) restate
   (C) remark
   (D) resolve

9. What is considered to be the greatest drawback of Piaget's research?

(A) His methodology was not based on an influential theory.
(B) His methodology was unsystematic, and his data were haphazard.
(C) His developmental theories and findings were not recognized.
(D) His studies did not undergo thorough examination.

10. According to the author's implications, which branch of psychology appears to be particularly controversial?

(A) Experimental
(B) Theoretical
(C) Differential
(D) Developmental

11. Which of the following is *not* mentioned in the passage as a type of psychology research?

(A) Differential
(B) Experimental
(C) Developmental
(D) Influential

Exercise 7

Directions: Answer all the questions following the passage on the basis of what is <u>stated</u> or <u>implied</u> in the passage. For each question, select the one best answer, (A), (B), (C), or (D).

Sir Anthony Van Dyck, one of the world's greatest masters of portraiture, was born in Antwerp and was the seventh of twelve children. His affluent father apprenticed him to a painter when he was just a little over ten. Having become a member of the Antwerp Guild of
Line painters before he was nineteen, he worked in the studio of Peter Paul Rubens for several years.
(5) In Italy, Van Dyck studied the great Venetian masters and painted flattering portraits of gorgeous ladies and haughty nobles in gilded velvet robes with lace and pearls. While he was sought after by the aristocracy for his acclaimed loose brushwork, his engravings and etchings also evinced his outstanding talent. Upon his return to Antwerp in 1628, he was influenced by Rubens's interpretation of the artistic form and produced numerous religious paintings while
(10) holding an appointment as the court painter. During his tenure, he proved that his use of color, his sensitive elegance, and his remarkable insight were unexcelled.

His fame preceded him to England, where he was invited by King Charles I. After years of faithful service, he was knighted in recognition of his achievements in painting countless portraits of the king, the queen, the royal children, and the titled nobility of England.
(15) However, Van Dyck's greatest piece is one of his religious works, a true masterpiece displayed in the Antwerp gallery. This group scene exhibits his artful polish in painting the folds of fabric, the delicacy of human skin, landscape, and other externals, and puts him above other accomplished contemporary masters. Although Charles paid Van Dyck a salary and granted him a pension, the painter's extravagant life-style and penchant for luxuries led him into debt,
(20) and he died without means.

1. It can be inferred from the passage that Van Dyck was raised

(A) in a large and wealthy family
(B) in a stable and loving household
(C) by his father alone
(D) without good work habits

2. What did Van Dyck do in his early youth?

(A) He was a brush cleaner.
(B) He was hired as a painter.
(C) He studied painting.
(D) He sold paintings.

3. The author of the passage implies that Van Dyck

   (A) had produced great paintings before he turned nineteen
   (B) had a great artistic talent even when he was young
   (C) joined other painters when he had little to occupy him
   (D) worked very hard in his youth to make a living

4. It can be inferred from the passage that after Van Dyck left Rubens

   (A) he accrued considerable wealth
   (B) he became a militant aristocrat
   (C) he refined his artistic tastes and skills
   (D) he incorporated southern styles in his art

5. The author of the passage implies that Van Dyck's fame had largely to do with his

   (A) artful portraits
   (B) wealthy family
   (C) elegance in clothing
   (D) religious beliefs

6. In line 7, the word "acclaimed" is closest in meaning to

   (A) reclaimed
   (B) recognized
   (C) recommended
   (D) rectified

7. According to the passage, when Van Dyck returned to Antwerp, he

   (A) had to schedule appointments at the court
   (B) found employment with a religious institution
   (C) proved that he was the best painter of his time
   (D) modeled elegant clothing for his religious paintings

8. How did Charles I honor Van Dyck?

   (A) Van Dyck painted members of the royal court.
   (B) Van Dyck received a noble title.
   (C) Van Dyck was allowed to travel widely.
   (D) Van Dyck displayed his work in the royal palace.

9. What does Van Dyck's masterpiece attest to?

   (A) His remarkable religious fervor.
   (B) His refined sense for texture.
   (C) His keen eye for polished surfaces.
   (D) His exorbitant tastes and habits.

10. In line 16, the phrase "this group scene" refers to

    (A) the Antwerp gallery
    (B) the masterpiece
    (C) Van Dyck's religious works
    (D) the titled nobility of England

11. What are the reasons given for Van Dyck's financial decline?

    (A) His employer's lack of generosity.
    (B) His ill health and lack of revenue.
    (C) His lavish spending.
    (D) His miserly attitudes.

12. The author's tone in the passage can be described as

    (A) critical
    (B) wistful
    (C) admiring
    (D) indifferent

Exercise 8

Directions: Answer all the questions following the passage on the basis of what is <u>stated</u> or <u>implied</u> in the passage. For each question, select the one best answer, (A), (B), (C), or (D).

Linen is yarn, thread, or fabric made from the stem fibers of flax, one of the oldest cultivated plants. Because the plant is grown in temperate climates, its production is limited. Archaeological evidence shows that flax was used for making ropes and fishing nets in
Line Switzerland over 10,000 years ago. Ancient Egyptians used flax more than any other fiber for
(5) making linen, which was employed in the manufacture of a diverse array of other materials. When the use of linen spread from the Mediterranean to Europe, linen became second only to wool as the most prevalent material for fabric, primarily because the spindle was no longer the sole device used for winding thread. It was during that time that the spinning wheel replaced the spindle and distaff for twisting and winding the flax fibers. By the end of the seventeenth
(10) century, a spinning wheel for linen was a fixture in almost every European and North American household.

Linen is relatively scarce now because the process of weaving flax fabric is comparatively work- and time-consuming. Upon harvesting, flax must be hackled to separate the linen fibers from the tow. Then the fibers are soaked and dried. Bundling the gleaned fiber precedes
(15) raking and thinning. The latter are essential steps since unraveling the fibrous mass of stems can facilitate winding. After the threads have been spun, they are laid on a loom and woven into the finished product, known as linen. As is the case with some other natural fibers, such as silk and wool, the price of linen fabric is rather high, and it is not as easy to care for as fabrics made of synthetic rayon, acetate, and viscose.

1. According to the passage, what precludes worldwide cultivation of linen?

   (A) Archaeologists do not put much stock in flax longevity.
   (B) Linen production has been restricted to increase prices.
   (C) Flax can be farmed only in certain geographical areas.
   (D) Flax plants are no longer grown where they used to be.

2. What promoted the proliferation of linen?

   (A) A shortage of materials in Europe
   (B) The replacement of wool by linen in textiles
   (C) Technological advancements in fiber processing
   (D) The dissipation of need for various materials

3. In line 8, the word "sole" is closest in meaning to

   (A) solar
   (B) soluble
   (C) only
   (D) likely

4. In line 10, the phrase "a fixture" is closest in meaning to

   (A) an attachment
   (B) a piece of furniture
   (C) common
   (D) complete

5. According to the passage, which of the following is the crucial phase in fiber preparation?

   (A) Harvesting and tying it
   (B) Towing and pulling it
   (C) Combing it to make it fine
   (D) Spinning it rapidly

6. In line 16, the word "facilitate" is closest in meaning to

   (A) fabricate
   (B) furnish
   (C) ease
   (D) elude

7. It can be inferred from the passage that the high cost of linen can be attributed to

(A) its relative popularity
(B) its laborious fabrication
(C) the labor-intensive care
(D) looming and weaving

8. The author of the passage implies that currently, linen is NOT as prevalent as

(A) wool
(B) silk
(C) synthetic fibers
(D) woven textiles

Exercise 9

Directions: Answer all the questions following the passage on the basis of what is <u>stated</u> or <u>implied</u> in the passage. For each question, select the one best answer, (A), (B), (C), or (D).

    Evaporation and recondensation of water entail an important step in purification called distillation. During evaporation, water molecules rise from the surface of a solution, but the salts and other minerals that had been dissolved in it crystallize and precipitate from the
Line solution, forming sediment. As water is heated, its molecules acquire sufficient energy to
(5) break the weak pull between them and rise in the form of vapor. As the vapor temperature falls, the attractive force between molecules grows to hold the molecules together, resulting in condensation. When water vapor recondenses, it consists only of water. Pure water used in chemical laboratories is obtained by this process. Water from the ocean and other sources is perpetually evaporated, purified, and eventually recondensed in the atmosphere.
(10)   Water can be purified by distillation or other methods. The hydrological cycle of the earth consists of water vapor entering the atmosphere through evaporation and coming back via condensation and precipitation. Since oceans occupy approximately 70 percent of the planet's surface, the largest amount of water in the cycle is derived from the evaporation of water from the ocean surfaces. A secondary source of water vapor lies in rivers, lakes, and soil. Plant
(15) transpiration occurs in areas with heavily vegetated land and adds to the vapor in the cycle.

1. Why does sedimentation develop?

(A) Salts and minerals solidify and accumulate.
(B) Distillation makes water rise.
(C) Solid water condenses at low temperatures.
(D) Recondensation dissolves salts and minerals.

2. What is the primary physical mechanism of evaporation?

(A) The reduction in the attraction of molecules
(B) The rise of water vapor into the air
(C) Molecular decomposition of water into atoms
(D) Vapor condensation to hold molecules together

3. In line 8, the phrase "this process" refers to

(A) evaporation
(B) precipitation
(C) condensation
(D) purification

4. In line 9, the word "perpetually" is closest in meaning to

(A) persistently
(B) perceptually
(C) always
(D) slowly

5. In line 11, the word "via" is closest in meaning to

(A) by means of
(B) without
(C) because of
(D) upward from

6. It can be inferred from the passage that regions near the ocean experience

   (A) high winds
   (B) high humidity
   (C) low precipitation
   (D) cold snaps

7. It can be inferred from the passage that evaporation

   (A) occurs only from the surfaces of oceans
   (B) takes place from all bodies of water
   (C) is only 70 percent effective
   (D) cannot take place from the soil

8. The author of the passage implies that

   (A) plants benefit from water vapor and precipitation
   (B) plants participate in the hydrological exchange
   (C) vegetables grow well near the ocean coastline
   (D) water is the main constituent of the earth's atmosphere

9. Which of the following is *not* mentioned in the passage as a source of vapor?

   (A) precipitation
   (B) oceans
   (C) water in plants
   (D) rivers and lakes

10. Which of the following would be the best title for the passage?

    (A) Purification of Water in Large Quantities
    (B) The Physical Consistency of Water Vapor
    (C) Evaporation of Molecules for Purification
    (D) Distillation in the Hydrological Cycle

Exercise 10

<u>Directions</u>: Answer all the questions following the passage on the basis of what is <u>stated</u> or <u>implied</u> in the passage. For each question, select the one best answer, (A), (B), (C), or (D).

Piracy began before the days of the Roman Empire when captured sailors and passengers were sold as slaves. Around the sixteenth and the seventeenth centuries, piracy became legitimized when famous English buccaneers were licensed by the government to attack
Line Spanish fleets and merchant ships while Spain and England were not at war. The hiring of
(5) pirates caught on because the governments had difficulty protecting their ships and citizens from foreign pirates. In 1668, Sir Henry Morgan, one of the best known captains of a conglomeration of pirate ships, practically declared a war on Jamaica. His lootings of Porto Bello, the Cuban coast, Maracaibo, and Panama earned him his title and the post of lieutenant governor of Jamaica. Numerous legends associated with his marine and coastal conquests have
(10) remained as part of the folklore both in England and in the Caribbean.

One of the most brutal pirates was Edward Teach, nicknamed "Blackbeard" for his long, thick beard, which he tied back over his ears with a ribbon. After the war between England and Spain ended and his services were no longer needed, he turned to piracy and terrorized the Virginia and Carolina coasts. In 1713, Teach lost a marine battle between his ships and the
(15) Virginian fleet and was never heard from again.

Piracy vanished gradually with the onset of steam-powered seaboats that were too fast and too well equipped for a pirate frigate to overtake. The last strongholds of piracy were Pacific islands and coastal havens where boats with long galleys rowed by slaves engaged in plundering villages and capturing prisoners. British and Dutch navy patrols finally did away
(20) with these enclaves in 1863. However, till this day, piracy can be a profitable endeavor in remote parts of the world.

1. This passage is probably taken from a longer text on

    (A) plots and episodes in historical tragedies
    (B) marine treasures and excavations
    (C) the maritime history of England
    (D) illustrious characters in the coastal battles

2. It can be inferred from the passage that the English government

    (A) penalized pirates for crimes
    (B) employed pirates to its advantage
    (C) protected pirates as citizens
    (D) set out to control roving pirates

3. According to the passage, who was Captain Morgan?

    (A) A mythological figure
    (B) A famous statesman
    (C) The governor of Jamaica
    (D) A notorious buccaneer

4. In line 7, the word "conglomeration" is closest in meaning to

    (A) flight
    (B) fleet
    (C) combination
    (D) connection

5. It can be inferred from the passage that Morgan's feats became a part of

    (A) the English language
    (B) the English heritage
    (C) maritime attractions
    (D) marine treasures

6. In line 11, the word "brutal" is closest in meaning to

    (A) brave
    (B) brusque
    (C) cruel
    (D) fashionable

7. According to the passage, Edward Teach

    (A) competed with Morgan for fame and fortune
    (B) claimed portions of Virginia and Carolina
    (C) sought solace in the New World
    (D) had been employed in the war

8. In line 16, the word "vanished" is closest in meaning to

    (A) disappeared
    (B) dispersed
    (C) vanquished
    (D) valorized

9. In line 17, the word "overtake" is closest in meaning to

    (A) override
    (B) overthrow
    (C) catch up with
    (D) pull away from

10. The author of the passage implies that piracy

    (A) provided plots for novels
    (B) is universally condemned
    (C) has not been fully eradicated
    (D) has been completely absolved

11. In line 19, the phrase "did away with" is closest in meaning to

    (A) refurbished
    (B) retreated
    (C) removed
    (D) rebuffed

12. In line 20, the word "endeavor" is closest in meaning to

    (A) activity
    (B) acumen
    (C) adversity
    (D) aggression

Exercise 11

<u>Directions</u>: Answer all the questions following the passage on the basis of what is <u>stated</u> or <u>implied</u> in the passage. For each question, select the one best answer, (A), (B), (C), or (D).

Anteaters are so named because they eat white termites. Few people realize that anteaters have no teeth. Their jawbones protrude and are almost entirely covered with skin, making their oral cavities very small. An anteater's tongue, covered with adhesive saliva to hold
Line termites on touch, can be extended a long way beyond its mouth. Then the animal draws it
(5) back and swallows. Although some termites build sizable mud nests, the anteater's powerful front paws have lengthy claws that can tear open the termites' nests, either on the ground or in trees.

The claws on anteaters' front legs are so long that the animals walk on the outer edges of their feet rather than on the soles. The longest claw folds back into a skin pouch in the sole of
(10) the foot. The solitary Tamandua anteater utilizes its prehensile tail as an arm to grasp a tree branch and lift itself as high as the tree crown. This physical characteristic enables the Tamandua anteater to live and hunt in trees. The silky anteater can also live in trees and sleeps curled up on a branch, to which it anchors itself by its tail and hind feet. Although the animals rarely attack, when disturbed they rear up on their hind legs and draw their forefeet alongside
(15) their head to strike an enemy with their claws or to squeeze it in their forearms. With only one offspring at a time, these mammals are extremely protective of their young, which ride on their mothers' backs. Little is known about anteaters' habitats and social organization.

1. According to the passage, anteaters

(A) cannot chew
(B) cannot lick
(C) cannot open their mouths
(D) have no nasal passages

2. What do anteaters do to grasp termites?

(A) They inhale and create pressure on their tongues.
(B) They use the sticky substance on their tongues.
(C) They expand their mouth openings.
(D) They apply force in their lateral grip.

3. What explains the anteaters' distinguishing walk?

(A) The length of their legs
(B) The size of their bones
(C) The length of their nails
(D) The sides of their feet

4. In line 10, the word "solitary" is closest in meaning to

(A) withdrawn
(B) soulful
(C) withheld
(D) somber

5. In line 11, the word "crown" is closest in meaning to

(A) hallow
(B) limb
(C) trunk
(D) top

6. Why is an anteater's tail compared to an arm?

(A) To symbolize the humanity of anteaters
(B) To elaborate on anteaters' sensibility
(C) To illustrate how it accords anteaters mobility
(D) To indicate that anteaters are advanced animals

7. In line 13, the word "anchors" is closest in meaning to

(A) glues
(B) drives
(C) attaches
(D) binds

8. It can be inferred from the passage that anteaters

(A) are rarely dormant
(B) are usually harmless
(C) can be exceptionally intelligent
(D) can be extraordinarily persistent

9. In line 16, the word "offspring" is closest in meaning to

(A) offing
(B) young
(C) offering
(D) yearning

10. Which of the following is the main topic of the passage?

(A) Anteaters' serene character
(B) A general description of anteaters
(C) Anteaters' peculiar feeding preferences
(D) Specific leaps and dives of anteaters

Exercise 12

Directions: Answer all the questions following the passage on the basis of what is <u>stated</u> or <u>implied</u> in the passage. For each question, select the one best answer, (A), (B), (C), or (D).

The New Scotland Yard, the most famous police unit in the world, is the headquarters of the Metropolitan Police in London. The police force in London was established in 1829 under an act of the British government. The police station and the office, whose task was to deal with
Line the public, was located at the back of the Westminster area, where mostly government
(5) buildings were located. The police station faced a vacant plot of land, called Great Scotland Yard. According to one legend, the land was set aside to build a residence for the kings of Scotland, who frequently visited the city. However, such a house was never constructed. Another story says that the plot was owned by an Englishman, named Adam Scot, but little proof of this version exists.
(10)   After the police force of London was founded, the building housed the police headquarters from September 29, 1829. The entire police division consisted of two commissioners, eight superintendents, 20 inspectors, 88 sergeants, and 895 constables. Together they represented a formidable force, and the 50-room building functioned as an administrative center that dealt with public inquiries, correspondence, and recruitment. By 1887, the staffing of the police
(15) force had grown to about 13,000, and it became evident that the accommodations had to be expanded. A new building on the Thames Embankment was erected in 1907 and another in 1940.
With the advent of new technology, paramount in police detective work, chemical, electronic, and forensic laboratories experienced a severe shortage of space. The diversification
(20) of police duties led to inevitable growth in the number of the enlisted men and women. As an outcome, Scotland Yard leased a 20-story office complex on Victoria Street at Broadway. The ever-expanding headquarters were named New Scotland Yard. It is curious to note that the vast amount of office space for the Metropolitan Police Force does not have a police station, but includes a citizens' information room.

1. What does the passage mainly discuss?

   (A) The work of the London police and the Scotland Yard
   (B) The internal organization of the Scotland Yard
   (C) The area of London where Scotland Yard is located
   (D) The name and location of the London police headquarters

2. According to the passage, the building where the first police office was located

   (A) got its name from the land lot on which it was built
   (B) was named after the owner to whom the land belonged
   (C) got its name from a facing parcel of land
   (D) got its name for several historical reasons

3. In line 6, the phrase "set aside" is closest in meaning to

   (A) reserved
   (B) seized
   (C) restored
   (D) sequestered

4. In line 13, the word "formidable" is closest in meaning to

   (A) formed
   (B) formulated
   (C) impressive
   (D) impudent

5. It can be inferred from the passage that the Scotland Yard building in the late 1800s

   (A) did not have room to accommodate the force
   (B) did not include an office for the public
   (C) housed the entire police administration
   (D) included police investigations

6. The author of the passage implies that in the past several decades

   (A) the police have begun to employ female personnel as police officers
   (B) the type of tasks the police perform has grown dramatically
   (C) police tasks have been relegated to office personnel
   (D) performing police duties has required training in science

7. The word "inevitable" in line 20 is closest in meaning to

   (A) unmistakable
   (B) undesirable
   (C) unavoidable
   (D) undisputed

8. How many buildings does Scotland Yard currently occupy?

   (A) One
   (B) Two
   (C) Three
   (D) Four

CHAPTER 9

Test of Written English

About the Test of Written English

The Test of Written English (TWE), administered in December, August, October, February, and May, was added to the TOEFL in 1986 and to all computer TOEFL tests in 2001. Until that time, the Structure and Written Expression section had the goal of testing writing skills. However, faculty and advisors in many academic institutions in the United States claimed that the ability to write cannot be tested adequately by multiple-choice questions.

The purpose of the TWE is to test for skills necessary in tasks associated with college writing: assignments, term papers, and responses to essay exam questions. Therefore, the TWE topics usually deal with academic subjects. As with other sections of the test, no specific knowledge of the subject matter is required to complete the tasks successfully. Controversial topics, such as religion, abortion, sex, divorce, death, violence, race, ethnic groups, and culture are not used for the TWE.

Unlike the scores for other sections of the test, TWE scores range upward from 1 through 6. The "passing" score for the TWE is determined by the institution to which you have applied for admission. Most colleges and universities in the United States and Canada require a TWE score of 4. Educational Testing Service administrators believe that, if your overall TOEFL score is between 530 and 550 (197 and 213, respectively, on computer tests), you will probably score 4 on the TWE, and if your overall score is slightly below or above 500 (173), you can expect your TWE score to be 3. In reality, however, this is not always the case, and often students who obtain an overall TOEFL score between 537 and 557 (203 and 220, respectively) score 3 on the TWE.

Your TWE score is included in your TOEFL score, and it can have a significant impact on whether you are admitted to the college or university of your choice. For example, if your grades are not particularly high and the general quality of your academic record is borderline, a low TWE score may result in the rejection of your application. Similarly, if a certain department in a university has received many applications, the applicants whose TWE scores are particularly low will be denied admission.

Scoring the TWE is a rather complicated process. Essays from all TWE administrations in all countries are collected by ETS and are scored at one time. The people who score the essays are usually teachers of ESL writing and composition from many universities in the United States. Each essay is read by at least two readers. If the two readers' scores differ by more than 1 point, the essay goes to a third reader who makes the final decision. If the original readers' scores differ by only 1 point, the reported score is averaged. Thus, students can receive scores such as 1.5, 2.5, 3.5, 4.5, and 5.5.

What Is Tested

In response to the TWE topic, you will need to write a developed essay, usually of 200–300 words, in 30 minutes. On the computer test, you have the option to write your essay by hand on paper or to type it into the computer. On both the computer test and the paper version of the test, you are given only one topic; you have no choice of topics. The information on the TWE answer sheet provided for you during the test will tell you that you must write on the given topic and that essays written on any other topic will not be scored.

Essays are evaluated according to the following criteria:

1. The essay is clearly organized.
2. The topic of the essay is addressed.
3. The ideas are well supported.
4. There is a clear relationship between all the parts and the whole essay.
5. Language structures and vocabulary are correct and appropriate.
6. The essay contains a variety of sentences and vocabulary items.

The organization of a successful TWE essay must follow the rhetorical patterns accepted in the English-speaking academic environment. What one reader may perceive to be a reasonably clear organization, however, may appear somewhat confusing to another. There are no objective criteria for evaluating writing, and the TWE is no exception.

Although the list of criteria by which TWE essays are evaluated focuses primarily on rhetorical issues, it would be a serious mistake to think that grammatical structure and vocabulary are not important. It would be practically impossible for an essay that displayed faulty grammar and limited vocabulary to receive a high score. According to the guidelines issued by ETS, only minor and occasional errors can be acceptable in essays scored 6.

TWE essays are evaluated on the basis of the criteria in Table 9–1. The points mentioned in this table also serve as the scoring guide.

STUDY TIP

An essay that contains numerous grammatical errors will not receive a high score on the TWE, even if the essay is well organized.

TABLE 9–1. THE TWE SCORING GUIDE

Score	Essay Evaluation Criteria
6	The essay demonstrates very strong rhetorical, grammatical, and vocabulary skills.
5	The essay demonstrates good rhetorical, grammatical, and vocabulary skills but has some errors.
4	The essay demonstrates generally satisfactory rhetorical, grammatical, and vocabulary skills but contains some consistent errors.
3	The essay demonstrates some rhetorical, grammatical, and vocabulary skills, all of which require improvement.
2	The essay demonstrates only basic rhetorical and grammatical skills; vocabulary is limited.
1	The ideas in the essay are difficult to understand.

What not to do in writing the essay

1. Do not think of an essay written on the TWE as an essay in your native language to be translated into English.
2. Do not try to support more than two or three main points. Do not simply list reasons why something is a good or bad idea.
3. State exactly what your main points are. Do not make the reader guess what your opinion is.
4. Do not defend your position or point of view by citing authority, proverbs, or facts that are considered common knowledge in your country. They may not be understood or recognized by the TWE readers, who were raised in a different culture.
5. Do not wait to state your opinion at the end of the essay after you have explained your reasons for having this opinion. Your position/opinion should be clearly stated early in the essay.
6. Do not describe the advantages and disadvantages of two points of view without stating your own view. Choose a clearly stated positive or negative position and defend it.
7. On the other hand, do not ignore all points of view that are different from your own. You should mention opposing opinions and argue against them.
8. Don't forget that the purpose of the TWE essay is not to persuade or inform the reader. Rather, you need to show the reader that you can write a good essay.
9. Don't include more than one stated and discussed idea in a paragraph. The information in the individual paragraphs should approach the idea from various aspects.
10. Don't generalize or make global statements. If you are discussing your own or someone else's experience, your opinion can be based only on this experience. Other people have had experiences different from yours.

Types of Topics and Essays

There are two basic types of topics: argumentation/position and technological inventions.

Argumentation/position

In an argumentation/position essay, you need to present two sides of an argument, choose one side, support it, and explain your reasons for making that particular choice. This type of topic has been found in most TWE administrations since 1990.

The topic in Example 1 requires an argumentation/position essay.

EXAMPLE 1:

> Some people believe that love comes after marriage, and that love before marriage is not necessary for the marriage to be a happy one. Others say that love before marriage is essential for the couple to be happy. Compare these two approaches to marriage and explain which you think might be more appropriate in your country.

Another form that argumentation/position topics can take is very similar to the topic in Example 1, but it presents only one side of the issue. In this case, it is up to the test-taker to supply the opposing point of view.

EXAMPLE 2:

> In the future, because of its low cost, nuclear energy should replace nonrenewable fossil fuels. Do you agree or disagree with this statement? Give reasons to support your opinion.

In this example, the opposing opinion can be "Nuclear fuels are not safe," or "Nuclear energy can be appropriate for countries with large populations but not for those with small populations."

EXAMPLE 3:

> Learning should be enjoyable, and the classroom environment should provide for an element of fun. Do you agree or disagree with this statement? State reasons to support your point of view.

In response to this topic, a counterargument may be "Learning is not equivalent to entertainment, and the classroom atmosphere should encourage students to concentrate on the subject matter."

Although topics such as those in Examples 2 and 3 require you to agree or disagree with a statement, you need to provide argumentation to defend the statement or to object to it.

Technological invention

Essays written in response to inventions/technology topics resemble those written on argumentation/position topics in that you need to state your view, support it, and describe your reasons for choosing a specific technological innovation.

EXAMPLE 4:

> Inventions such as the sewing needle and the refrigerator have had important effects on our lives. Choose another invention that you believe to be important. Give specific reasons for your choice.

Topics such as these usually mention two inventions: one a tool or an instrument (pen/pencil, nail, wheel, clock), and the other a complex machine/mechanism or a device of technological significance (printing press, computer, automobile, radio, TV). Two inventions are mentioned to indicate to test-takers that they are to choose from a wide array of inventions.

STUDY TIP

If you see a topic such as Example 4, do not write about the inventions that are mentioned.

It really does not matter what type of instrument or technological device you write about in your essay as long as you provide specific and detailed reasons to explain why you chose it.

STUDY TIP

Choose a simple tool or instrument. The more complex the machine or technology, the harder it is to describe its applications.

In the argumentation/position essays written in response to topics in Examples 1 to 3, and the technological invention, written in response to the topic in Example 4, the main idea is defined in the topic, but you have to decide how to approach the topic. Then you need to determine the amount and the type of information necessary to explain and support your opinion, and you must supply this information. Which position you choose to argue for (or defend) has no impact on your score. The list of practice topics at the end of this chapter provides many other examples for practice.

Writing Style and Information

TWE essays must be written in formal, academic English appropriate in university settings. The use of varied grammatical forms and of compound and complex sentences is preferable to relying on short, simple sentences. Similarly, advanced (academic) vocabulary and idioms may also contribute to your TWE score.

A well-written essay in English has to contain varied but related information that the writer presents to the reader. An essay cannot merely repeat the same idea in different ways. Academic writing has to follow an organizational pattern. A good essay usually contains a brief introduction with a clearly stated main idea and/or statement of the author's purpose (also called a thesis statement), several arguments (points) that support the thesis, and a clear, brief conclusion.

> ### STUDY TIP
>
> **The essay should be as long as you can make it in 30 minutes. An essay of fewer than 100 words will not get a good score. The preferred length for an essay is 200 to 300 words.**

Improving Your Writing and Vocabulary

One of the best ways to improve your writing skills is to read widely in English. By reading, you learn new sentence structures, increase your vocabulary, and see how text and ideas can be organized and presented.

A good way to start preparing for the TWE is to write summaries of articles you read in English-language newspapers, magazines, and reading texts. Your summaries need not be long: one to three paragraphs are sufficient in the beginning. The key point in writing summaries is not to copy portions of an article or phrases from sentences but to write down the main ideas of the text in the way that you remember them.

When you read books, you need to pay attention to sentence structure, paragraph and story development (plot), and vocabulary. After you finish reading, write a short (one- to four-page) essay about the book, and explain your specific reasons for liking or disliking it.

You can practice writing letters to real or imaginary friends. A good idea is to find a partner with whom you can prepare for the TWE. You can correct one another's mistakes and make suggestions for improving your essays.

Writing an Argumentation/Position Essay

In Example 5, you will find a TWE topic that requires an argumentation/position essay. Three essays, marked A, B, and C follow the topic. Essay A is likely to receive a score of 6. Essay B would probably receive a score of 4, the score that is usually required by U.S. and Canadian colleges and universities. On the other hand, Essay C is presented as an example of how not to write on the test—it would receive a score of 1. Be sure to read carefully the detailed analysis that follows each essay and explains its strong and weak points as judged by the criteria on page 144. All sample essays in this chapter are analyzed according to these criteria.

EXAMPLE 5:

Some people believe that it is better to have children when couples are young and are physically equipped to raise them, while others believe that parenting requires maturity and the solid financial foundation that often comes later in life. Discuss these two positions, and state which one you agree with and why.

The following argumentation/position essay would receive a score of 6.

Essay A

In my country, people traditionally get married and have children in their twenties. There is no doubt that 25-year-old parents have more energy than those who are 45. However, energy doesn't necessarily mean better parenting skills. In my view, parents should have children when they are mature and can afford to raise them without poverty.

Being able to play baseball with the children does not show parent's insight, patience, or maturity. Today, when life choices are becoming more and more difficult, raising children to be responsible, intelligent, and thinking adults is not as easy as teaching them baseball. We often think that youth means adaptability and flexibility. The truth of the matter is that flexibility comes with years of experience in dealing with people and situations.

Raising a child can be expensive. For example, in my country, young families cannot afford to buy a house or send their children to private schools, which have a higher quality of education than government schools. In most cases, few young people in their twenties make enough money to afford either, not to mention both. In general, couples who have children early cannot give them the best of what comfortable living has to offer: a nice house and good education.

Being a parent is probably the most difficult, work-consuming, but rewarding task a person can undertake. It requires a good deal more than the physical strength of youth. Parents in their forties have the advantages of maturity and economic security.

Essay analysis

1. **Is the essay clearly organized?** The essay is well organized. The first paragraph summarizes the argument and presents the two points of view on the topic. In addition, the fourth sentence of the first paragraph indicates the author's position on the issue (the thesis sentence), and the reader can easily figure out that the author will defend the view that older parents have more advantages in raising children than younger parents do.

The second paragraph discusses, for both younger and older parents, the physical aspects of raising children; the third paragraph deals with the financial aspects of having a family. The author's points of view in both paragraphs are supported by examples and discussion. In the second paragraph, the author compares the benefits of playing baseball and of helping children deal with people and situations. In the third, the author presents the specific example (marked by the phrase *For example*) of being able to afford a house or to send children to a good school.

The fourth and final paragraph clearly summarizes and restates the author's thesis. This paragraph serves as a conclusion for the essay.

2. **Is the topic of the essay addressed?** The author follows the topic closely and addresses the two points of physical capabilities and a solid financial base that are mentioned in the topic.

3. **Are the ideas well supported?** The ideas in the essay are supported in paragraphs 2 and 3 by specific (smaller and less broad) points that, together with many other aspects of the topic, give strength to the author's position.

Even though the author's point is illustrated by the clear contrast of playing baseball and parenting, the second paragraph is a little more abstract than it should be. There are too many general, abstract nouns, such as *insight, maturity, patience, adaptability,* and *flexibility.*

The third paragraph is stronger in that the author presents a point, "Raising a child can be expensive," and then gives specific examples (a nice house *and* good education) that illustrate expensive benefits that older parents are more likely to be able to provide their children.

4. **Are the parts of the essay clearly related to one another?** Throughout, the author continues to defend the main idea that older parents can do a better job of raising children than younger parents.

5. **Are language structures and vocabulary correct and appropriate?** The vocabulary in the essay is varied and appropriate. The author uses such words and phrases as *physical stamina, parenting skills, responsible, work-consuming, rewarding, adaptability, flexibility,* and others that show a good command of English and fluency (the ability to express one's ideas with ease). The author also uses expressions and idioms, such as *thinking adults, the truth of the matter, in most cases,* and *not to mention both.* These expressions, combined with complex and correctly used vocabulary give the reader the sense that the author can write papers on academic topics without having to look up many words in the dictionary.

> ### STUDY TIP
>
> **Do not repeat the same nouns, verbs, and adjectives unless they are necessary to explain your ideas. Try to use as many different words as you can. Use only words the meanings of which you understand well. Do not use complex words simply to sound "academic." Chances are that you will not be able to use these words correctly and will lose points for inappropriate vocabulary.**

6. **Does the text contain a variety of sentences and vocabulary items?** The essay contains a mixture of simple and complex sentences: "In my country, people traditionally get married and have children in their twenties" [simple], "There is no doubt that 25-year-old parents have more energy than those who are 45" [complex; notice the two subordinate clauses, *that 25-year-old parents have more energy than those* and *who are 45*].

Essay B would probably receive a score of 4 on the TWE. This score is required by most colleges and universities in the United States and Canada.

Essay B

In my country, many people believe that people who are thirty or forty are too old to have children. They think that twenty is the best age because both mother and father are healthy and strong and can give their kids best care. In my opinion, take care of children requires a lot of wisdom, time, and money, which come when people are thirty or forty.

My parents were 24 when I was born, and they had little money. When I was young child, I saw my father only on the weekend because he worked all the time. My mother stayed at home and took care of the house and the children but she was also so busy that she never had time to spend with us. She almost never played with us because she had a million things to do: she cooked for us, cleaned house, washed dishs and cloths, she even made our cloths for us. When they were twenty, neither of my parents understood that giving attention and love to children was more important than making money or cleaning house. In my opinion they lacked the experience and maturity to understand what was important for raise children.

Now that my parents are over 40 they have the money they needed when they were young. Now they don't have to run and hurry, and they have free time. But their children are grown and don't live with the parents. I think its sad that now when they have time and money, they can't have children to spend it with. I think now that they are more mature, they also regret that they didn't give us more attention when we were little.

Young people who are trying to get a good life from the point of view of time and finances and understanding of what their children really need should wait and have children until they have the time and the money to raise children with.

Essay analysis

1. **Is the essay clearly organized?** The essay is well organized: the first paragraph clearly presents the two sides of the issue and also specifies the author's opinion. As in Essay A, the reader can immediately understand that the essay will support the view that having children at an older age is better than when parents are young.

The second paragraph discusses the author's personal experience of being raised by two young parents and mentions the financial and the emotional difficulties of raising children when young people lack resources and maturity. The third paragraph deals with financial and emotional stability of older parents and contrasts it with that of younger parents. The fourth paragraph restates the argument that young parents may not be ready to raise children.

STUDY TIP

In general, this essay approaches the topic as a personal narrative (story), and in American universities, such an approach is not always considered appropriate. However, if the essay's main idea and the supporting information are clear and detailed, personal narrative can be acceptable.

2. **Is the topic of the essay addressed?** For the most part, the topic of the essay is addressed. The essay discusses the issues of maturity and solid financial foundation in sufficient detail; the point regarding physical capabilities is only mentioned without elaboration.

3. **Are the ideas well supported?** The two ideas of maturity and solid financial foundation are well supported by detailed information that ties them together to make the essay whole. The supporting information is clearly related to the author's main idea:

a. Financial foundation is important when raising children because it can provide parents an opportunity to spend time with their children and give them attention.

b. Experience and maturity that allow parents to make good judgments and choices come with age.

4. **Are the parts of the essay clearly related to one another?** The author provides several points to support the main idea that young parents cannot always do a good job raising children and that older parents are often in a better position.

5. **Are language structures and vocabulary correct and appropriate?** The vocabulary in the essay is relatively simple, but it is used appropriately. Some of the words and phrases that the author uses, such as *requires a lot of, giving attention and love, lack,* and *regret* show that he or she is comfortable with English and can express his or her ideas with ease. The phrases that are not necessarily idiomatic, such as *run and hurry* and *spend it with,* create interesting images that can help the reader "see" the picture the author is describing.

The essay contains some grammatical errors.

Correcting sentence structure and vocabulary errors in Essay B

Where necessary for clarity or the development of an idea, additional words and phrases have been supplied.

SENTENCE 2.   They think that twenty is the best age because the mother and the father are healthy and strong and can give their children the best care. (The word *kids* is not appropriate in academic texts.)

SENTENCE 3.   In my opinion, taking care of children requires a lot of life experience, time, and money, which come when people are thirty or forty.

SENTENCE 5.   When I was a young child, I saw my father only on weekends because he worked all the time.

SENTENCE 7.   She almost never played with us because she had a million things to do: she cooked for us, cleaned the house, washed dishes, and did the laundry; she even made some of our clothes.

SENTENCE 8.   When they were in their twenties, neither of my parents understood that giving us attention and love was more important than making money or cleaning the house.

SENTENCE 13.   I think it is sad that now when they have time and money, they do not have [little] children to give the time to and spend the money on.

SENTENCE 15.   Young people who are still trying to become established and who do not have a great deal of time, money, and understanding of what their children really need should [delay] having children until they have the necessary resources and maturity.

Although the grammatical errors in the essay are relatively small, they may cause a loss of a point on the TWE. When you are writing a TWE essay, it is important to pay careful attention to the mistakes that students often consider unimportant: missing articles, plural -*s,* and the form of nouns, verbs, adjectives, and adverbs.

6. **Does the text contain a variety of sentences and vocabulary items?** The essay uses simple, compound, and complex sentences: "But their children are grown and don't live with the parents" [simple], "In my country, many people believe that people who are thirty or forty are too old to have children" [complex; *who are thirty or forty* is an adjective clause].

Essay C would receive a score of 1 on the TWE.

Essay C

Old age of parent had been a problem among some families. Being a parent in the middle age have causing many problem. Some parents might afraid they can't get along their children because their children growing up. However, in my opinion, I think parent has to negitate aspect at all; instead old parent more mature and love children. A lot of young parent not enough maturity. On the contrary, old parent already have financial background and they stay at their home with their kids.

My country parent always have a lot of life experience which can teach their kids. They must know how teaching their kids compare to those young parent. They care their childrens more than those young parents because strong education background. Old parent kid might proud of his parent because of they has knowledges which from their life experience.

Come to my conclusion, old parent will not just bring pleasures and problems to parents, instead though the maturity they might care of their kids and love them as young. As a result, kid should happy if they are grown up in old parent family.

Essay analysis

1. **Is the essay clearly organized?** Clear organization is very important on the TWE. The organization of this essay, however, is difficult to understand. The introduction simply states that parents' *old age* creates *a problem among some families,* but it does not state exactly what this problem is. The essay does not discuss both positions mentioned in the topic and does not present a balanced point of view: the advantages of having children at a young age are not mentioned. Similarly, no drawbacks to parenting in later years are identified.

> ### STUDY TIP
>
> **You must discuss the topic as it is given to you. If the topic mentions some aspects of the argument for both sides, you should discuss these aspects in your essay. Stay on the topic.**

The author's main idea is stated in the first paragraph: "I think parent has to negitate aspect at all; instead old parent more mature and love children." After reading this sentence, the reader can expect the essay to discuss maturity and parents' love for children. However, the sentence at the end of the same paragraph mentions "financial background" and "stay[ing] … home with their kids."

It is difficult to see what particular pattern of organization the author followed. For example, an essay can begin with the least important ideas and move to the most important ones; it can begin with the most important ideas and move to the least important ones; it can compare the two points of view mentioned in the topic. However, Essay C does not seem to be organized at all; the paragraphs do not contain different ideas and do not have clearly stated topic sentences.

> ### STUDY TIP
>
> **In general, each paragraph should contain only one idea, which is discussed in some detail. Furthermore, each paragraph should contain a topic sentence, that is, a clear statement of the main idea in the paragraph. The main ideas of all the paragraphs should mention the various aspects of the topic as it is given and together should address the main points of the essay.**

The second paragraph of Essay C mentions three ideas: (1) teaching kids from experience, (2) caring for the children, and (3) pride that the child of older parents may feel. While teaching kids from experience is a good point, the sentence "They care their childrens more than those young parents because strong education background" is difficult to understand. The faulty construction of the sentence and the omission of words make it confusing.

However, even if the sentence structure is corrected, the reader may still have difficulty understanding the author's point. The corrected sentence is "Older parents can give their children better care than young parents because they have had a good education." The author does not explain what *better* care means, why older parents can give their children better care than younger parents, or what the connection between better care and a good education is. It is quite possible that the author knows the answers to these questions. However, an author's goal is to explain his or her point of view to the reader so that the reader can easily understand the author's reasons for making a particular statement.

The author's third point, that the child of older parents might be proud of his or her parents, approaches the issue from a completely different viewpoint (the child's). This statement is also not explained sufficiently. Merely stating that older parents have learned a great deal from their life experiences does not specify why their child can be proud of them.

The author mentions *financial background* in the last sentence of the first paragraph. However, this point is not discussed or explained in the essay. Thus, the essay does not address one of the topic aspects and so does not discuss the entire topic.

> ### STUDY TIP
>
> **The essay's thesis (main idea) needs to be clearly stated in the first paragraph, following a brief (one- or two-sentence) introduction. The thesis must be supported throughout the rest of the essay: you need to provide several different points, all of which describe the reasons for your opinion. Also, these points must be organized according to certain patterns: from the most important to the least important; from the least important to the most important; or, if you are comparing two points of view, by discussing the various aspects of both views in a parallel way.**

2. **Is the topic of the essay addressed?** In Essay C, the topic is largely addressed. However, the author did not develop the topic aspect that deals with the solid financial foundation.

3. **Are the ideas well supported?** Although the essay makes several general points (for example, that some parents might be afraid that they would not be able to get along with their children, that older parents are more mature and love their children, and that many young parents do not have enough maturity), very little support is provided for these statements. In other words, it is not clear on what specific information the author bases these opinions.

The ideas in an essay can be supported in a variety of ways. One of the best supports can come from examples that the author "invents," that is, provides from information available to him or her from experience, reading, or even imagination. No matter where the information comes from, it has to be clearly organized so as to support the author's main idea. If such information is not provided, the ideas in the essay can appear too general and unsupported.

For example, the author's ideas could be supported by developing each of the following points into a paragraph:

a. Young people in the process of maturing may be too busy becoming established in their careers to deal adequately with raising children.

b. Young people may be still adjusting to taking care of one another and providing for themselves and their household and thus be unable to take care of children.

c. Young people may have a number of family and social obligations they need to meet before they can focus on their children's needs.

STUDY TIP

The essay must provide specific and detailed examples and reasons to support the main points. If you cannot think of any, describe your own, your friends', or your parents' experiences, information you read in a newspaper article, or a tradition or custom that exists in your country as an example and "proof" for your opinion.

---

4. **Are the parts of the essay clearly related to one another?** Because Essay C does not follow a clear pattern of organization, the paragraphs do not contain different ideas related to the topic; the second paragraph seems to repeat the ideas mentioned in the first paragraph. Therefore, it is hard to judge whether parts of the essay are related to one another.

STUDY TIP

The ideas in the essay must be closely related to the topic. If the reader does not need to know something in order to understand your idea, do not include it.

---

5. **Are the language structures and vocabulary correct and appropriate?** Essay C contains many errors in both sentence structure and vocabulary. The grammar errors can be corrected as shown below. However, even if the sentence structure and grammar in the essay are corrected, the organizational and vocabulary flaws that remain are so numerous that the essay still would not receive a high score.

Correcting sentence structure and vocabulary errors in Essay C

Where necessary for clarity or the development of an idea, additional words and phrases have been supplied.

SENTENCE **1.**   When parents are older, various problems can arise.

SENTENCE **2.**   Becoming a parent in middle age can cause many problems.

SENTENCE **3.**   Some parents may worry that they can't get along with their children while the children are growing up.

SENTENCE **4.**   However, in my opinion, parents have to negitate [it is impossible to figure out which word the author intended to use here] aspect at all [this phrase is also impossible to understand]. Older parents are often more mature and love their children more than younger parents do.

SENTENCE **5.**   Younger parents may lack maturity.

SENTENCE **6.**   Compared to young parents, older parents may have an established financial base and can afford to stay home with their children.

SENTENCE **7.**   In my country, older parents are expected to have a great deal of life experience to which they can refer when raising their children.

SENTENCE **8.**   They are better prepared to teach their children.

SENTENCE **9.**   They can take better care of their children than can young parents because of their good education. [In this sentence, it is difficult to understand the connection between child care and education.]

SENTENCE **10.**   The children of older parents can be proud of their parents because such parents have knowledge derived from their life experiences.

SENTENCE **11.**   In conclusion, having children at an older age can bring parents both joy and problems. Because of their maturity, older parents can care for their children and love them just as much as younger parents. [The connection between the two ideas in this sentence is not clear.]

SENTENCE **12.**   Children of older parents can have a happy time while growing up.

STUDY TIP

Use only grammatical structures and words you know well. The TWE is not the place to experiment with new sentence types and vocabulary. If your sentences are all of the same type but are correct, your score may well be higher than if your sentences are varied but incorrect.

---

6. **Does the text contain a variety of sentences and vocabulary items?** Essay C contains many simple sentences and, as has been mentioned, the vocabulary is limited. Some of the words and expressions (*negitate, aspects at all*) are difficult to understand.

Writing an Essay on an Invention/Technology Topic

Example 6 is followed by three essays, D, E, and F, again with an analysis of each.

EXAMPLE 6:

Inventions such as photography and television have greatly changed the way we transmit information. Choose another invention that you believe to be important. Give specific reasons for your choice.

Essay D would receive a score of 6 on the TWE.

Essay D

Few technological innovations have had the impact on communication that the telephone has had. Socially, one is arranging dates, making restaurant or theater reservations, and keeping in touch over long distance by phone. Business matters are discussed and deals made between several people at various locations around the world through conference calls. Emergency help can be obtained around the clock just by pressing a few buttons on a telephone. It would be impossible to thoroughly discuss the role of the telephone in the modern world, therefore a look at how it is used in two areas of sales may indicate how important the telephone has become.

Nobody wants to receive unwanted phone calls from salespeople, or worse yet, tape-recorded sales talks, but telemarketing is much more than that. By providing a toll-free number, companies make it easy and inexpensive for potential customers to reach experienced and knowledgeable sales staff who can answer questions and even close a sale without inconveniencing the customer or taking much of his or her time. The product can be sent right away and arrive in a day or two.

Even after a sale, it is important to keep the customer satisfied. Another major use of the telephone in sales is product support. Customers can receive individual instruction on complex pieces of equipment or sophisticated software that can help them with special problems they may be having. Without the telephone, such service would be terribly expensive or even impossible because of time constraints.

By increasing customer convenience and making help immediately available, the telephone gives companies an opportunity to expand sales and keep customers satisfied.

Essay analysis

1. **Is the essay clearly organized?** The first paragraph introduces the topic and indicates that two areas will be addressed. The second paragraph talks about the first area; the third paragraph, the second area. The final paragraph is a general conclusion.

2. **Is the topic of the essay addressed?** Yes. Notice that the author does not try to mention every area that the telephone has affected. Trying to cover too broad a thesis would make it impossible to discuss supporting points adequately, and the essay would seem less unified.

3. **Are the ideas well supported?** Details are provided to explain each point. Each main point receives a paragraph of explanation. Particularly effective is the comment in paragraph 3: "Without the telephone, such service would be terribly expensive or even impossible because of time constraints." This reinforces the idea that the telephone is important in product support.

4. **Are the parts of the essay clearly related to one another?** All parts of the essay develop the main idea—the effect of the telephone on two areas of sales. The first sentence of the third paragraph links the two ideas and explains how they are related to each other.

5. **Are the language structures and vocabulary correct and appropriate?** The sentences in the essay are correct and varied; the vocabulary usage is appropriate.

Correcting sentence structure and vocabulary errors in Essay D

There were a few minor errors in the essay, but none of the errors made it difficult to understand the author's points.

SENTENCE 2. Socially, one arranges dates, makes restaurant or theater reservations, and keeps in touch over long distance by phone. [The wording has been changed to create parallel structures in sentences 2 and 3.]

SENTENCE 3. Business matters can be discussed and deals made between several people at various locations around the world through conference calls.

SENTENCE 5. It would be impossible to thoroughly discuss the role of the telephone in the modern world, but a look at how it is used in two areas of sales may indicate how important the telephone has become.

SENTENCE 6. Nobody enjoys receiving unwanted phone calls from salespeople … [*wants* was changed to *enjoys* to avoid repetitious vocabulary.]

6. **Does the text contain a variety of sentences and vocabulary items?** The essay contains several types of sentences and uses varied words and phrases.

Essay E would receive a score of 4 on the TWE.

Essay E

Today, in most industries and areas of study, doing one's job without a computer would not be possible. Although computers became our daily necessity only in the past ten years, it has greatly affected how we do most basic things. Computers are used for checking books out of a library, getting information from bank, controlling air traffic, and industrial production. However, the two most remarkable changes the computer brought are in diagnosing and treating diseases.

Diagnosing a disease is difficult because even a simple stomach ache can be a result of several causes. The doctor can input patient's medical data and results of tests into a computer that will analysis the data and produce several possible causes for the patient's condition.

After the diagnosis, the next step is to decide which treatment is the best for patients. The doctor can input patient information, such as age, medical history, and genetic condition, and have the computer find the best treatment. The computer can even warn the doctor about a problem that may develop during the treatment if a patient experiences diseases in addition to the one that is treated.

For example, last year, when my father had cancer, both he and all of us believed that he would die because in my country we have no computer diagnosis and modern equipment for treatment. When he came to American hospital, we were impressed because computer analyze his symptom and suggested treatment for his type of cancer in only two weeks. The treatment turned out the best possible for my father, and now he is completely cured.

Computers in medicine can save many lives and find treatment for serious diseases. I think even ten years ago, my father's cancer would not be diagnosed and cured. Personally, I am happy that we have them.

Essay analysis

1. **Is the essay clearly organized?** The first paragraph clearly states the topic, computers, and its two aspects to be discussed: diagnosing and treating diseases. The second and the third paragraph focus on the diagnosis of disease and its treatment. Because diagnosis logically precedes treatment, the author talks about diagnosis before treatment. The fourth paragraph presents an example that is related to both the diagnosis of a disease and the treatment and brings the two aspects of the topic together. The fifth paragraph is a brief conclusion.

2. **Is the topic of the essay addressed?** The author continues with the discussion of the role of computers in medicine. The amount of detail mentioned in the essay is balanced, that is, the author provides information sufficient for the reader to understand his or her points with-

out giving too much detail. The "proof" for points is mentioned and given the necessary supporting information (one to three sentences).

STUDY TIP

When supporting your main points, tell the reader what is necessary to make your ideas easy to understand. Do not give too much detail so that the reader can easily relate bits of information to one another; avoid giving too little so that he or she can understand your points clearly.

---

3. **Are the ideas well supported?** In the body of the essay (paragraphs 2, 3, and 4) the impact of the computer on medical diagnosis and treatment is supported. The author's point that diagnosis is not easy and benefits from computer analysis is supported by the observation that even simple problems can have several causes. The author lists specific information that the computer can use in diagnosis and the information that the computer can give a doctor. The author also includes an example of computer-assisted diagnosis and treatment that was successful.

4. **Are the parts of the essay clearly related to one another?** All parts of the essay describe the use of the computer in diagnosis and treatment of diseases. The first sentence in the third paragraph provides a transition between the discussion of diagnosis and the discussion of treatment. The first sentence in the fourth paragraph indicates that an example to support the previous statements is being offered.

5. **Are language structures and vocabulary correct and appropriate?** Most of the vocabulary is used correctly. The essay contains some grammatical errors that do not interfere with the understanding of the author's ideas. These errors are corrected below.

Correcting sentence structure and vocabulary errors in Essay E

Where necessary for clarity or the development of an idea, additional words and phrases have been supplied.

SENTENCE 2. Although computers have become a daily necessity only in the past ten years, they have greatly affected how people do many basic things.

SENTENCE 3. Computers are used for checking books out of a library, getting information from [a] bank, controlling air traffic, and [operating] industrial production [lines].

SENTENCE 5. Diagnosing a disease [can be] difficult because even a simple stomachache can result from several causes.

SENTENCE 6. The doctor can input the patient's medical data and results of tests into a computer that will analyze the data and indicate several possible causes for the patient's condition.

SENTENCE 7. After the diagnosis [is made], the next step is to decide which treatment is the best for [the] patient.

SENTENCE 8. The doctor can input patient information, such as age, medical history, and genetic conditions, and have the computer find the best [course of] treatment for the patient.

SENTENCE 9. The computer can even warn the doctor about problems that may [arise] during the treatment if a patient [suffers from other] diseases.

SENTENCE 10. For example, last year, when my father was diagnosed with cancer, both he and all of us believed that he would die because in my country, we have no computer diagnosis or modern equipment for treatment.

SENTENCE 11. When he came to [an] American hospital, we were impressed because his symptoms were analyzed by a computer in only two weeks. In addition to the diagnosis, the computer suggested the treatment for his type of cancer.

SENTENCE 12. The treatment turned out [to be] the best possible for my father, and now he is completely cured.

SENTENCE 14. I think even ten years ago, [it would not have been possible] to diagnose and cure my father's cancer.

SENTENCE 15. Personally, I am happy that computers are used to help both patients and doctors in treating [deadly] diseases.

6. **Does the text contain a variety of sentences and vocabulary items?** The vocabulary is appropriate and used correctly without many repetitions. There is a good balance of simple (for example, "Today, in most industries and areas of study, doing one's job without a computer would not be possible") and complex (for example, "Diagnosing a disease is difficult because even a simple stomach ache can be a result of several causes") sentences.

Essay F written on this topic would score 1 on the TWE.

Essay F

Radio change how we transmit information. Radio used for play music everyday. People uses radio listening songs. They enjoy radio in every place. Radio is very important in our daily lifes. Radio can play music and makes our life happy. You can listen news by radio. They give us new information and tell us what is happen everywhere in the world. You can't live your life without radio.

I have radio. I listening all the time. If I want listen music I turn black botton and music come out. Sometime, I come to my home and I'm boring. Then, I listen radio and feel happy because I like listening radio. I can move radio from one to another and it give me different music. When somethings happen in the world we listen to radio to tell if there exist a problem or something. Radio tell us what will be the weather tomorrow. If you know the weather tomorrow you can wearing cloths and be warm when is cold.

Last year, there was hurican in my country. We listen to radio all the time to tell us what should we do and what was the best way. We need radio because radio save us.

Essay analysis

1. **Is the essay clearly organized?** The essay mentions some benefits of having a radio instead of telling why the invention of the radio was important or how the radio has affected some aspects of society. The essay has no clear thesis statement and does not follow a recognizable pattern of organization. The paragraphs do not have just one main idea each. The second paragraph, for example, talks about entertainment, news reports, and weather forecasts.

2. **Is the topic of the essay addressed?** Although the essay is centered around radio, it does not discuss how the invention of radio has changed the ways of transmitting information. Rather, it describes why the author enjoys having a radio. Therefore, the topic of the essay is only partially addressed.

3. **Are the ideas well supported?** The ideas in the text are repetitious and do not provide sufficient detail. The author states several times that he or she enjoys radio because it plays music and reports news. The conclusion that radio can *save us* is too broad for the ideas presented earlier in the text.

4. **Are the parts of the essay clearly related to one another?** The parts of the essay are so similar that they provide little new information. The author does not examine various aspects of radio as an information-transmitting device.

5. **Are the language structures and vocabulary correct and appropriate?** As with Essay C, even if the many structure and vocabulary errors in Essay F were corrected, the essay would still receive a score of 1 or 2. Notice that several words are misspelled. Although spelling is not directly figured into the evaluation of the essay, misspelled words that make it difficult for the reader to understand your point may lower your score.

Correcting sentence structure and vocabulary errors in Essay F

Where necessary for clarity or the development of an idea, additional words and phrases have been supplied.

SENTENCE 1. Radio has changed how we transmit information.

SENTENCE 2. Radio can be used to play music every day.

SENTENCE 3. People use the radio when they listen to songs.

SENTENCE 4. They can listen to the radio almost anywhere in their cars, homes, stores, and restaurants.

SENTENCE 5. Radio can be very important in our daily lives.

SENTENCE 6. If people are sad, listening to music on the radio can cheer them up.

SENTENCE 7. In addition, radio newscasts can keep us informed about important events.

SENTENCE 8. By listening to the radio, we can learn new facts and be informed about events that happen anywhere in the world.

SENTENCE 9. It is impossible to imagine life without the radio.

SENTENCE 10. I have a radio.

SENTENCE 11. I listen to it all the time.

SENTENCE 12. If I want to listen to music, I turn the black button, and music comes out.

SENTENCE 13. Sometimes, when I come home and feel bored, radio can entertain me and make me happy. [Sentences 13 and 14 can be combined.]

SENTENCE 15. I can change stations to listen to different types of music.

SENTENCE 16. When something happens in the world, we can listen to the radio to learn about it.

SENTENCE 17. In addition, weather forecasts can help us be prepared for the next day.

SENTENCE 18. If we know what the weather is expected to be, we can dress appropriately.

SENTENCE 19. Last year, there was a hurricane in my country.

SENTENCE 20. At that time, we listened to the radio to receive instructions and be prepared for an emergency.

SENTENCE 21. The information broadcast during an emergency can save lives.

6. **Does the text contain a variety of sentences and vocabulary items?** The sentences in the essay lack variety, and the vocabulary is simple and repetitious.

Organizational and other errors frequently found in student essays

1. The essay does not have a clearly stated thesis.
2. The organization of the essay is not clear.
3. The essay does not support the thesis with specific, detailed, and relevant information.
4. The vocabulary is misused, and/or grammatical structures are flawed.
5. The essay is off the topic.

Proofreading the essay

> **STUDY TIP**
>
> **Budget your time to allow yourself 5 minutes for proofreading and editing at the end of the 30-minute period.**

When people begin to proofread their writing, they often become "caught up" in the flow of the text and start reading for meaning, instead of paying careful attention to grammatical forms, sentence structure, and correct vocabulary usage. This can be one of the reasons why students frequently cannot find any mistakes in their compositions.

> **STUDY TIP**
>
> **When you proofread, read the essay twice. First, read it through to make sure that you included all necessary points and that the text is easy to follow and understand. Then read the essay again. This time, begin with the last sentence, and focus on the grammatical structure of nouns, verbs, and clauses. Then move to the second to last sentence and then to the third sentence from the end, and so on until you reach the beginning of your essay.**

Use the following checklist to proofread your essay for grammatical accuracy (also see pages 59–68 of Chapter 5).

1. Find the verb(s) in each sentence or clause.
2. Check the verb forms; focus on verb endings. Use the correct forms of irregular verbs.
3. Move to the left of the verb and find the subject. Do not confuse the subject with noun(s) in prepositional or adjective phrases.

> **STUDY TIP**
>
> **Make sure that every singular countable noun has an article, a possessive pronoun (my, our, your, his/her, their), or a demonstrative pronoun (this, that, these, those).**

4. Check whether the singular/plural subject agrees with the singular/plural verb.

> **STUDY TIP**
>
> **Using the plural form for countable nouns in general statements is often better than the singular. Check for subject/verb agreement.**

5. Move to the right of the verb; if the verb requires an object, make sure that the object is present.

6. Check verb tenses. Tenses in the entire essay must be consistent unless time words are used to allow for tense switches.

STUDY TIP

In general, present tenses can be appropriate in many argumentation/position essays. Examples from personal experience, however, may be presented in the past tenses.

---

7. Is the essay long enough?
8. Does the essay include a brief and clear conclusion? Does the conclusion use vocabulary different from that in the thesis?

Practice Topics for the Test of Written English

Argumentation/position essays

TOPIC 1:   It is often argued that, because education resources are limited, college training should be accessible primarily to the talented. On the other hand, many people believe that the opportunity to receive a college education should be open to all those who have completed high school. Explain some of the arguments for each side, and tell which point of view you agree with and why you hold this opinion.

TOPIC 2:   Some people equate advancements in technology with progress, while others feel that the development of technology moves us farther away from traditional values. What is your position on this issue? Discuss the strengths and weaknesses of both positions, and use specific examples when you explain and support your point of view.

TOPIC 3:   Many people want to occupy positions of power and leadership in their places of employment, as such a position may give them independence and control. Others say that a position of power and leadership may also require them to accept more responsibilities and invest a greater amount of time in their jobs. Discuss the advantages and disadvantages of positions of power in employment, state which point of view you agree with, and give your reasons.

TOPIC 4:   In the past forty years, through improved health care, human life has been prolonged to an extent never believed possible. Some people say that merely prolonging life increases the size of the aging population and, therefore, the burden on the family and society. Other people object, arguing that prolonging life is one of the goals of medical science that should be accomplished at almost any cost. What do you think about the problems and benefits of prolonged life? Give reasons.

TOPIC 5:   Many people claim that having a large circle of friends and acquaintances provides them with a support network in both happy and hard times. By contrast, others claim that maintaining many social relationships takes a lot of time and energy that can be better spent in other ways. Compare these two views, state which one you agree with, and explain the reasons for your opinion.

TOPIC 6: Some people feel that those who occupy positions of power and authority in society should be expected to demonstrate honest and ethical behavior. Others believe that people in such positions are human beings with desires and values similar to our own. What is your position on this issue? Discuss the strengths and weaknesses of both positions, and use specific examples when you explain and support your point of view.

TOPIC 7: Some people value honesty very highly and believe that it is essential to be honest at all times. Others believe that there are situations when a lie is acceptable or even necessary. Explain some of the arguments for each side, and tell which belief you advocate. Give reasons.

TOPIC 8: Many educators believe that parents should help to form their children's opinions. Others feel that children should be allowed to develop their own opinions. Compare these two views, state which one you agree with, and explain the reasons for your opinion.

TOPIC 9: Today, in almost all universities in the United States, teachers are required to conduct a great deal of research in addition to teaching. While some feel that teachers need to carry out research in order to update their professional knowledge, others think that conducting research takes time away from teaching and does not allow teachers to concentrate fully on the needs of their students. What is your position on the issue of whether teachers should be required to conduct research? Discuss the strengths and weaknesses of both positions, and use specific examples to explain and defend your point of view.

TOPIC 10: Some educators believe that college education has the purpose of preparing young people for future careers, while others hold the view that the goal of college training is to provide students with access to knowledge. Discuss the advantages and disadvantages of these two approaches to college education and state which point of view you agree with and why you hold his opinion.

TOPIC 11: Many parents feel that their children should enter the best university possible because a degree from such a university can provide good employment opportunities. Others hold the view that a degree from a famous university is too expensive and does not guarantee successful employment or a bright future. Compare and contrast these points of view. Which do you prefer? Explain your reasons.

TOPIC 12: Many people feel that to be considered successful they need to have wealth and material possessions. Others consider that money is not necessary for success and believe that success can be measured in other ways. What do you believe? Give specific examples and explain the reasons for your opinion.

TOPIC 13: Some people choose their friends among those who have characteristics very similar to their own. Others prefer to have friends who are significantly different in their personal characteristics. Discuss how you choose your friends. What characteristics does a person need to have in order for you to consider him or her your friend? State your opinion and provide examples.

TOPIC 14: All students should be required to study art and music in high school. Do you agree or disagree with this statement? Give specific reasons to support your opinion.

TOPIC 15: Some people believe that participation in international sports events should be a source of national pride. Others feel that athletic events should be seen as contests among individuals, not nations. What is your position of this issue? Give reasons for your opinion.

TOPIC 16: Some people believe that television has undermined relationships between people and among family members. Do you agree with this opinion? Give reasons and examples to support your point of view.

Invention/technology essays

TOPIC 17: Inventions such as eyeglasses and the telephone have had a great deal of influence on our daily lives. Choose another innovation that you think is important. Give specific reasons for your opinion.

TOPIC 18: Technology has greatly affected the way we live and work today. In your view, how will technological innovations affect our lives in the future? Choose one example that you believe is important. Give specific reasons for your choice.

TOPIC 19: The bicycle and the refrigerator are two inventions that have greatly affected the quality of our lives. Choose another invention that you think is important. Give specific reasons for your opinion.

TOPIC 20: The invention of the light bulb and of the sewing machine have had a significant impact on our daily lives. Name another invention that you think has affected our lives. Explain the reasons for your choice.

Practice TOEFL 1

Section 1
Listening Comprehension

In this section, you will demonstrate your skills in understanding spoken English. There are three parts in the Listening Comprehension section, with different tasks in each.

Part A

DIRECTIONS: In Part A you will hear short conversations between two speakers. At the end of each conversation, a third speaker will ask a question about what the first two speakers said. Each conversation and each question will be spoken only one time. Therefore, you must listen carefully to understand what each speaker says. After you hear a conversation and the question, read the four choices and select the one that is the best answer to the question the speaker asked. Then, on your answer sheet, find the number of the question and blacken the space that corresponds to the letter for the answer you have chosen. Blacken the space completely so that the letter inside the space does not show.

Listen to the following example.

On the recording, you hear:

Sample Answer

(Man)	Does the car need to be filled?
(Woman)	Mary stopped at the gas station on her way home.
(Narrator)	What does the woman mean?

In your test book, you will read:

(A) Mary bought some food.
(B) Mary had car trouble.
(C) Mary went shopping.
(D) Mary bought some gas.

From the conversation you learn that Mary stopped at the gas station on her way home. The best answer to the question "Does the car need to be filled?" is (D), "Mary bought some gas." Therefore, the correct answer is (D).

Now let us begin Part A with question number 1.

GO ON TO THE NEXT PAGE. ➡

1. (A) Mike shouldn't skip classes and borrow notes.
   (B) Mike always borrows notes from his classmates.
   (C) Mike is least likely to skip classes.
   (D) Mike needs to get the material taught in class.

2. (A) The office is closed for the day.
   (B) The officer will return in the morning.
   (C) There is an opening at 9 tomorrow morning.
   (D) The office is open until 9 o'clock.

3. (A) She is sorry that she ordered that salad.
   (B) She didn't get the salad she ordered.
   (C) She is sorry, but this salad is not hers.
   (D) This salad does not taste very good.

4. (A) Did Mr. Calvert say something about his back?
   (B) Did Mr. Calvert say when he is planning to return?
   (C) Mr. Calvert forgot it's time for him to come back.
   (D) Mr. Calvert said he isn't going to come back.

5. (A) The library sells books and postcards.
   (B) Postcards are available to library users.
   (C) You need to have a card to have your books sent.
   (D) The library will let you know when the book arrives.

6. (A) He does not know how to cook.
   (B) He had dinner at a restaurant.
   (C) He doesn't like to stand while cooking.
   (D) He went shopping and then had dinner.

7. (A) Students are permitted to use bikes.
   (B) Students with bikes are counted regularly.
   (C) Permits for bikes are available.
   (D) Bikes can be purchased next door.

8. (A) They haven't told him when to turn in the paper.
   (B) They told him when the assignment is due, but he forgot.
   (C) He wishes they would tell him where to pay the dues.
   (D) He wanted to tell them when to turn in the assignment.

9. (A) The garbage can be stored in the garage.
   (B) The driver is parking in the garage.
   (C) The driver crashed into the garage.
   (D) The garbage can was near the garage.

10. (A) Joan didn't hear the first half of the speech.
    (B) Joan heard nothing from half of the speakers.
    (C) Half of the people in the room did not hear the speaker.
    (D) The speaker did not speak loudly enough.

11. (A) On campus, your phone can be hooked up only once.
    (B) Campus calls can't be made from your phone.
    (C) You cannot call off campus until your phone is connected.
    (D) You can't call collect unless you live on campus.

12. (A) The drug store sells toothpaste.
    (B) Drugstores used to sell toothpaste.
    (C) The drugstore does not have toothpaste.
    (D) Toothpaste and drugs are sold everywhere.

13. (A) The truck on your right has no ticket.
    (B) If you buy a ticket, you can pass the driving test.
    (C) Passing on the right is against the law.
    (D) Trucks get tickets for passing, but cars don't.

GO ON TO THE NEXT PAGE. ➡

14. (A) He didn't travel to college.
    (B) He didn't attend college.
    (C) He didn't go to school.
    (D) He didn't want to go far.

15. (A) Students don't read their instructor's forms.
    (B) If students can't read, they can't fill out forms.
    (C) Most students ignore the directions on paperwork.
    (D) Most forms for students don't have instructions.

16. (A) The movie theater is around the corner.
    (B) The movie theater is to your left.
    (C) The movie theater is a mile away.
    (D) The next turn is by the movie theater.

17. (A) Julie's courses are full and closed.
    (B) Julie is carrying a bag full of books.
    (C) Julie can't carry all these courses.
    (D) Julie is enrolled as a full-time student.

18. (A) Everyone who went on the trip fell.
    (B) The trip was not well attended.
    (C) The trip was hard to make in one day.
    (D) Many students tripped and fell.

19. (A) Neither team won.
    (B) Men swim better than women.
    (C) Did the men's team win?
    (D) Is Tim the head of the team?

20. (A) She had a good chance to see the report.
    (B) Chances are she was looking at a reporter.
    (C) Has this report been changed yet?
    (D) Has she had time to read the report?

21. (A) The weather is unpredictable.
    (B) Rain is predicted for today.
    (C) She heard the weather report.
    (D) This year, it's been raining often.

22. (A) At a police station
    (B) At a doctor's office
    (C) In a car repair shop
    (D) In an insurance agency

23. (A) A house-cleaning business
    (B) A plumbing company
    (C) A lawn service
    (D) An electrical supply store

24. (A) Finish her classes
    (B) Look for a job
    (C) Write a paper
    (D) Take a break

25. (A) Over to the next street
    (B) For dinner at a shop
    (C) To a cafe
    (D) For a walk

26. (A) The move in hot weather was costly.
    (B) The woman must have moved too soon.
    (C) A new heater must have been expensive.
    (D) The water heater never worked well.

27. (A) They don't need new computers at this time.
    (B) They don't have much time to work with new computers.
    (C) The computers should have been replaced much earlier.
    (D) The timing for replacing computers is about right.

GO ON TO THE NEXT PAGE. ➡

28. (A) She can come on another day, but not tomorrow.
    (B) She can see the man in three days.
    (C) She is thirsty and needs some water.
    (D) She doesn't know how to help the man.

29. (A) The man needs change for a vending machine.
    (B) The man will break expensive equipment.
    (C) The man shouldn't spend his money at the bar.
    (D) The man shouldn't give her candy.

30. (A) On the street
    (B) In the car
    (C) In a warehouse
    (D) At a grocery store

GO ON TO THE NEXT PAGE. ➡

Part B

DIRECTIONS: In this part of the test, you will hear longer conversations. After each conversation, you will hear several questions. The conversations and questions will not be repeated.

After you hear a question, read the four possible answers in your test book and select the best answer. Then, on your answer sheet, find the number of the question and fill in the space that corresponds to the letter of the answer you have chosen. Remember, you are not allowed to take notes or write in your test book.

Listen to the following example:

You will hear:

You will read:

Sample Answer

  (A) He has changed jobs.
  (B) He has two children.
  (C) He has two jobs.
  (D) He is looking for a job.

From the conversation you learn that Tom has taken an additional job. The best answer to the question "Why is Tom tired?" is (C), "He has two jobs." Therefore the correct answer is (C).

31. (A) Children's shoes
  (B) Business trips
  (C) Different types of glue
  (D) Various types of goods

32. (A) She had to leave early in the morning.
  (B) She needed to call her friend.
  (C) Her purse had ripped.
  (D) Her office didn't supply the hardware.

33. (A) Come to her house
  (B) Glue her purse
  (C) Suggest an adhesive
  (D) Go to a store to buy glue

34. (A) To show that he is a good father
  (B) To display his knowledge
  (C) As an indication of problems with cement
  (D) As an example of using epoxy

35. (A) He doesn't like to be bothered.
  (B) He wants to help the woman.
  (C) He wants the woman to like him.
  (D) He isn't interested in women's purses.

36. (A) New York
  (B) Seattle
  (C) Vancouver
  (D) Portland

37. (A) She gets the *New York Times*.
  (B) She reads about it in the *Seattle Post*.
  (C) She listens to the news on the radio.
  (D) She watches TV and goes to the movies.

38. (A) He reads the newspaper and listens to the radio.
  (B) He travels to Portland to attend conventions.
  (C) Usually, he pays attention to regional news.
  (D) He talks to tourists who come to visit the city.

GO ON TO THE NEXT PAGE. ➡

Part C

DIRECTIONS: In Part C you will hear short lectures and extended conversations. At the end of each, you will be asked several questions. Each lecture or conversation and each question will be spoken only one time. For this reason, you must listen carefully to understand what each speaker says. After you hear a question, read the four choices and select the one that best answers the question the speaker asked. Then, on your answer sheet, find the number of the question and blacken the space that contains the letter for the answer you have chosen.

Answer all questions according to what is stated or implied in the lecture or conversation.

Listen to this sample talk.
You will hear:

Now listen to the following example.
You will hear:

Sample Answer

Ⓐ ● Ⓒ Ⓓ

You will read:

(A) By cars and carriages
(B) By bicycles, trains, and carriages
(C) On foot and by boat
(D) On board ships and trains

The best answer to the question "According to the speaker, how did people travel before the invention of the automobile?" is (B), "By bicycles, trains, and carriages." Therefore, the correct answer is (B).

Now listen to another sample question.
(Narrator)   Approximately how many people are employed in the
                automobile service industry?

Sample Answer

Ⓐ Ⓑ ● Ⓓ

You will read:

(A) One million
(B) Ten million
(C) Twelve million
(D) Ninety million

The best answer to the question "Approximately how many people are employed in the automobile service industry?" is (C), "Twelve million." Therefore, the correct answer is (C).

You are not allowed to make notes during the test.

39. (A) How mail is processed in airports
    (B) How quickly goods can be delivered
    (C) How big and small airports work
    (D) How cargo is handled for shipment

40. (A) Mail and baggage
    (B) Mail and freight
    (C) Passengers and luggage
    (D) Baggage and freight

41. (A) It is routed to separate cargo terminals.
    (B) It is separated from mail by machine.
    (C) It is loaded when passengers board the planes.
    (D) It is shipped to smaller airports.

GO ON TO THE NEXT PAGE. ➡

42. (A) Together with passengers
    (B) Together with baggage
    (C) According to special schedules
    (D) Exclusively to its destination

43. (A) In postal offices
    (B) In airports
    (C) On aircraft
    (D) In commercial outlets

44. (A) Manufactured goods
    (B) Passengers and baggage
    (C) Livestock and crops
    (D) Cars and automobile mechanics

45. (A) Thousands
    (B) A few
    (C) Thirty
    (D) Sixty

46. (A) Green, yellow, and red
    (B) Green, white, or cream
    (C) Yellow, white, or red
    (D) White, cream, and yellow

47. (A) As soft or firm
    (B) As sweet or sour
    (C) As fresh or sour
    (D) As large or small

48. (A) They are eaten.
    (B) They are pressed for juice.
    (C) They are made into sauce.
    (D) They are processed as jam.

49. (A) Cold weather
    (B) Prolonged watering
    (C) Systematic consumption
    (D) Extensive roots

50. (A) Africa
    (B) South America
    (C) Australia
    (D) Eurasia

➤STOP◄

This is the end of Section 1.

Read the directions for Section 2.
Do not read or work on any other section of the test.
Look at the time now before you begin work on Section 2.
Use exactly 25 minutes to work on Section 2.

Section 2
Structure and
Written Expression

2

Time: 25 minutes

This section is designed to test your ability to recognize language structures that are appropriate in standard written English. The questions in this section belong to two types, each of which has special directions.

<u>DIRECTIONS</u>: Questions 1–15 are partial sentences. Below each sentence you will see four words or phrases, marked (A), (B), (C), and (D). Select the one word or phrase that best completes the sentence. Then, on your answer sheet, find the number of the question and fill in the space that contains the letter for the answer you have chosen. Fill in the space completely.

EXAMPLE I

Sample Answer

● Ⓑ Ⓒ Ⓓ

Drying flowers is the best way - - - - - them.

(A) to preserve
(B) by preserving
(C) preserve
(D) preserved

The sentence should state, "Drying flowers is the best way to preserve them." Therefore, the correct answer is (A).

EXAMPLE II

Sample Answer

Ⓐ Ⓑ ● Ⓓ

Many American universities - - - - - as small, private colleges.

(A) begun
(B) beginning
(C) began
(D) for the beginning

The sentence should state, "Many American universities began as small, private colleges." Therefore, the correct answer is (C).

After you read the directions, begin work on the questions.

1. Fort Niagara was built by the French in 1726 on land - - - - - the Seneca Indians.

(A) they buy from
(B) bought from
(C) buying from
(D) was bought from

2. Soil texture depends on the proportions of clay and sand particles, - - - - - soil porosity.

(A) both alter
(B) which alter
(C) where altered
(D) although altered

GO ON TO THE NEXT PAGE. ➡

3. The writers of the realist movement embraced the notion that art should depict life - - - - -.

(A) accurately and objectively
(B) accuracy and objectivity
(C) accurate and objective
(D) accurate objectivity

4. A ratio is a comparison of - - - - - whole or a part to another part.

(A) part to the
(B) a part to
(C) a part to the
(D) the part to the

5. The bones of the elderly are more prone to fractures and splintering - - - - - of young people.

(A) than that
(B) than those
(C) those than
(D) that than

6. English and Scottish settlers - - - - - Belfast as a trading post in 1613.

(A) they established
(B) established themselves
(C) established
(D) establishing

7. The formulation of economic policies necessitates meticulous consideration - - - - - large segments of the population.

(A) because they affect
(B) they are affected because
(C) affect them because
(D) because affecting them

8. Only - - - - - feathered creatures inhabit the Arctic region year round.

(A) fewer
(B) fewer than
(C) as few as
(D) a few

9. Before Richard Bennett accepted the appointment as the prime minister of Canada in 1930, he - - - - - as a lawyer.

(A) had achieved a successful
(B) had been achieved successfully
(C) has achieved success
(D) had achieved success

10. Gardeners transplant bushes and flowers by moving them from one place to - - - - -.

(A) other
(B) others
(C) another
(D) each other

11. Museums of natural history are ordinarily - - - - - by special interest groups created for that purpose.

(A) owned and operated
(B) they own and operate
(C) owning and operating
(D) the owner operates

12. A surge in the level of stress - - - - - the recurrence of nightmares.

(A) apparent increase
(B) apparently increase
(C) apparently increases
(D) apparent increases

13. Each bowler - - - - - in each frame, unless a strike is bowled.

(A) rolling the ball twice
(B) the ball is rolled twice
(C) rolls the ball twice
(D) the ball rolls twice

GO ON TO THE NEXT PAGE. ➡

14. William Hearst had five sons, - - - - - eventually became executives in the Hearst newspaper conglomerate.

    (A) all of them
    (B) of them all
    (C) all of whom
    (D) who of all

15. An axiomatic assumption in physics holds that all matter has kinetic energy - - - - - motion and mass.

    (A) because its
    (B) because of its
    (C) because it is
    (D) because of it

GO ON TO THE NEXT PAGE. ➡

② ② ② ② ② ② ② ②

<u>DIRECTIONS</u>: In questions 16–40 every sentence has four words or phrases that are underlined. The four underlined portions of each sentence are marked (A), (B), (C), and (D). Identify the one word or phrase that makes the sentence incorrect. Then, on your answer sheet, find the number of the question and fill in the space that contains the letter for the answer you have chosen. Fill in the space completely.

EXAMPLE I   **Sample Answer**

● Ⓑ Ⓒ Ⓓ

Christopher Columbus <u>has sailed</u> from Europe in 1492 and <u>discovered a</u> <u>new land</u> he
                          A   B   C

<u>thought to</u> be India.
    D

The sentence should state, "Christopher Columbus sailed from Europe in 1492 and discovered a new land he thought to be India." Therefore, you should choose answer (A).

EXAMPLE II   **Sample Answer**

Ⓐ ● Ⓒ Ⓓ

<u>As the roles</u> of people in society change, <u>so does</u> the <u>rules of</u> conduct in certain <u>situations.</u>
    A   B   C   D

The sentence should state, "As the roles of people in society change, so do the rules of conduct in certain situations." Therefore, you should choose answer (B).

After you read the directions, begin work on the questions.

16. <u>In summer</u>, warm southern <u>air carries</u> <u>moist</u> north to the eastern and <u>central</u> United States.
        A   B   C   D

17. Billie Holiday became <u>recognized</u> as the most <u>innovative</u> jazz singer of her <u>day</u> and was
                              A   B   C

<u>admiration</u> for her vocal range.
    D

18. To raise livestock <u>successfully</u>, farmers must <u>selecting</u> cattle for <u>breeding</u> and <u>apply</u> a dietary
                          A   B   C   D

regimen.

19. In the 1960s, <u>urban renewal</u> projects <u>cleared land</u> for <u>commerce</u> and <u>offices building.</u>
                      A   B   C   D

20. In 1868, Sioux leaders signed a <u>treaty</u> <u>preventing</u> whites from <u>traveling</u> through the Sioux
                                        A   B   C

<u>territorial</u>.
    D

GO ON TO THE NEXT PAGE. ➡

2 2 2 2 2 2 2 2

21. A number multiplied by zero is zero, and a number multiplied by one is the same as number.
    A   B   C   D

22. Muscles aids in attaching portions of the skeleton to one another and ultimately shape the torso.
    A   B   C   D

23. Thomas More, who fell into disfavor with the king, was a great English author, statesman, and
                      A   B   C

    scholars.
    D

24. The first microprocessors were fabricated in 1971 for installation in handhold calculators.
    A   B   C   D

25. If autistic children form an attachment, it predominantly was to inanimate objects.
                A   B   C   D

26. Technology is define as the tools, skills, and methods that are necessary to produce goods.
                  A   B   C   D

27. Fruit flies do not have to leap to take off because of they become airborne solely by
                    A   B   C

    wing movement.
    D

28. Historians postulate that Eskimos migrated from Alaska to Greenland in two greater
                          A   B   C   D

    movements.

29. Electric wires carry current for lighting and outlets designing for household appliances.
    A   B   C   D

30. Troops housing in Fort Bliss, Texas, train to operate aircraft equipment and artillery.
            A   B   C   D

31. Charles Kettering patented the first success spark-based starter for automotive vehicles in 1911.
                      A   B   C   D

32. During the 1700s, public concerts proliferated when composers wrote music for their
                                      A   B   C

    audiences' enjoying.
              D

33. The philosophers and artists of ancient Greece and Rome emphasized the study of human as
        A   B   C

    fundamental to their doctrine.
    D

34. Computer graphics software has infinite applications in a widely array of fields.
              A   B   C   D

35. The planet Mercury rotates slow than any other planet except Venus.
                      A   B   C   D

GO ON TO THE NEXT PAGE. ➡

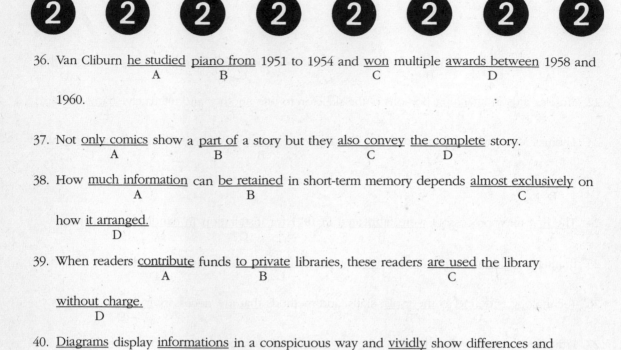

36. Van Cliburn <u>he studied</u> <u>piano from</u> 1951 to 1954 and <u>won</u> multiple <u>awards between</u> 1958 and
            A   B   C   D

    1960.

37. Not <u>only comics</u> show a <u>part of</u> a story but they <u>also convey</u> <u>the complete</u> story.
        A   B   C   D

38. How <u>much information</u> can <u>be retained</u> in short-term memory depends <u>almost exclusively</u> on
         A   B   C

    how <u>it arranged.</u>
         D

39. When readers <u>contribute</u> funds <u>to private</u> libraries, these readers <u>are used</u> the library
                   A   B   C

    <u>without charge.</u>
         D

40. <u>Diagrams</u> display <u>informations</u> in a conspicuous way and <u>vividly</u> show differences and
    A   B   C

    <u>similarities.</u>
    D

➤STOP◄

This is the end of Section 2.

Read the directions for Section 3.
Do not read or work on any other section of the test.
Look at the time now before you begin work on Section 3.
Use exactly 55 minutes to work on Section 3.

Section 3
Reading Comprehension

Time: 55 minutes

<u>DIRECTIONS</u>: In this section you will read several passages. Each passage is followed by a series of questions. For questions 1–50, you need to select the best answer, (A), (B), (C), or (D), to each question. Then, on your answer sheet, find the number of the question and fill in the space that contains the letter of the answer you have selected. Fill in the space completely.

Answer all questions following a passage on the basis of what is stated or implied in the passage.

Read the following passage:

A tomahawk is a small ax used as a tool and a weapon by the North American Indian tribes. An average tomahawk was not very long and did not weigh a great deal. Originally, the head of the tomahawk was made of a shaped stone or an animal bone and was mounted on
Line a wooden handle. After the arrival of the European settlers, the Indians began to use toma-
(5) hawks with iron heads. Indian males and females of all ages used tomahawks to chop and cut wood, pound stakes into the ground to put up wigwams, and do many other chores. Indian warriors relied on tomahawks as weapons and even threw them at their enemies. Some types of tomahawks were used in religious ceremonies. Contemporary American idioms reflect this aspect of American heritage.

EXAMPLE I

Sample Answer

● Ⓑ Ⓒ Ⓓ

Early tomahawk heads were made of

(A) stone or bone
(B) wood or sticks
(C) European iron
(D) religious weapons

According to the passage, early tomahawk heads were made of stone or bone. Therefore, the correct answer is (A).

EXAMPLE II

Sample Answer

Ⓐ Ⓑ ● Ⓓ

How has the Indian use of tomahawks affected American daily life today?

(A) Tomahawks are still used as weapons.
(B) Tomahawks are used as tools for certain jobs.
(C) Contemporary language refers to tomahawks.
(D) Indian tribes cherish tomahawks as heirlooms.

The passage states, "Contemporary American idioms reflect this aspect of American heritage." The correct answer is (C).

After you read the directions, begin work on the questions.

GO ON TO THE NEXT PAGE. ➡

Questions 1–12

Charles Lindbergh was born in Detroit, Michigan, in 1902 but was raised on a farm in Minnesota, where his father was elected to the U.S. Congress in 1907. From then on, he spent his boyhood alternately in Washington, D.C., Detroit, and Little Falls, Minnesota.
Line Because Lindbergh exhibited exceptional mechanical talent, in 1921 he was admitted to
(5) the University of Wisconsin to study engineering. However, the young man was seeking more challenging endeavors, and two years later he became a stunt pilot who performed feats at county fairs and public assemblies. This unusual and dangerous undertaking paid off handsomely in the sense that it allowed him to gain a diverse and well-rounded experience in aeronautics. He particularly delighted in what he called "wing-walking" and para-
(10) chute jumping.

After a year of training as a military cadet, Lindbergh completed his program at the Brooks and Kelly airfields at the top of his class and earned the rank of captain. Robertson Aircraft Corporation of St. Louis, Missouri, offered him employment as a mail pilot to run the routes between St. Louis and Chicago, and Lindbergh retained his position with the
(15) company until 1927. During this period, he set out to win the Raymond B. Orteig prize of $25,000 to be awarded to the first pilot to fly nonstop from New York to Paris. This ambition would irreversibly change his life and accord him a prominent place in the history of aviation.

Embarking on the greatest adventure of his time, Lindbergh left Roosevelt Field at 7:52
(20) A.M. on May 20, 1927, and landed at Le Bourget Field at 5:24 P.M. the next day. Fearing that he would be unknown when he arrived, Lindbergh carried letters of introduction to dignitaries in Paris, but when his plane came to a stop, he was overwhelmed by tremendous welcoming crowds. He was decorated in France, Great Britain, and Belgium, and President Coolidge sent a specially designated cruiser, the Memphis, to bring him back. His accom-
(25) plishments in aeronautics brought him more medals and awards than had ever been received by any other person in private life.

1. Which of the following is the best title for the passage?

   (A) A Benchmark Adventure in Aeronautics
   (B) The Early Life of Charles Lindbergh
   (C) Groundbreaking Events in Aviation
   (D) Charles Lindbergh's Explorations

2. According to the passage, Lindbergh did not complete his degree because he

   (A) opted for the life of an exhibition pilot
   (B) pursued training in the military
   (C) was seeking a sedentary life-style
   (D) set out to win recognition

3. In line 7, the word "assemblies" is closest in meaning to

   (A) hearings
   (B) houses
   (C) gatherings
   (D) shows

4. In line 7 the word "undertaking" refers to

   (A) studying at the university
   (B) exhibiting mechanical talent
   (C) seeking challenging endeavors
   (D) performing feats

GO ON TO THE NEXT PAGE. ➡

5. In line 8, the word "handsomely" is closest in meaning to

(A) honorably
(B) handily
(C) well
(D) in time

6. It can be inferred from the passage that as a military cadet, Lindbergh

(A) was in top form
(B) earned a good salary
(C) was the best among students
(D) trained with the best students

7. The author of the passage implies that Lindbergh's job with Robertson Aircraft Corporation

(A) required regular intercity flights
(B) was not intended as long-term employment
(C) required him to perform dangerous flights
(D) necessitated his running long distances

8. In line 17, the word "irreversibly" is closest in meaning to

(A) forever
(B) formerly
(C) irresistibly
(D) only

9. According to the passage, how old was Lindbergh when he carried out his challenging flight?

(A) Twenty-one
(B) Twenty-three
(C) Twenty-four
(D) Twenty-five

10. The author of the passage implies that Lindbergh did not anticipate becoming a

(A) pilot
(B) celebrity
(C) mail carrier
(D) army captain

11. It can be inferred from the passage that in the early 1920s it was NOT common for young people to

(A) study engineering
(B) train as officers
(C) go on exhibition tours
(D) be elected to an office

12. A paragraph following the passage would most probably discuss

(A) the development of commercial and military aviation
(B) the reaction of the government to Lindbergh's flight
(C) the effect of instant celebrity on Lindbergh
(D) Lindbergh's aircraft and engine modifications

GO ON TO THE NEXT PAGE. ➡

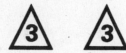

Questions 13–21

Lithography is a planographic process that performs a significant function in illustration and offset printing. It is based on the principle that water does not combine with grease-based substances, preventing them from smearing an outline on an unpolished surface. The
Line contour does not need to be engraved into the plate, as in the case of gravure printing, or
(5) raised above the surface, as in the letterpress process. These laborious operations ensure that only the design to be printed catches and retains the ink transferred to the paper.

In lithography, the artist draws on a leveled, grainy plate made of limestone, zinc, aluminum, or specially treated paper with a grease pencil, a crayon, or tusche, a greasy liquid. After sketching the contour on the plate, the artist coats both the drawn and the undrawn por-
(10) tions of the plate with an inking roller dipped in a solution of nitric acid and gum arabic. The gum arabic envelops the greased surfaces and prevents ink from penetrating into the greaseless areas. The artist dampens the surface with water, which is repelled by the greased areas. Then the surface is covered with thick, oily ink and pressed onto paper. The sheet picks up the ink from the design while the damp stone around the pattern keeps the ink
(15) from spreading.

In offset lithography, shiny sheets of zinc and aluminum are used instead of the heavy, hard-to-handle stone plates. The metal plates are scoured by emery dust and marble chips to give them a grained finish. The subjects to be printed are laid down photographically, and rotary presses automatically moisten, ink, and print hundreds of impressions per hour.

13. What does the passage mainly discuss?

(A) Commercial printing of mass-produced lithographs
(B) Steps in a technique for making impressions
(C) The equipment necessary for offset lithographs
(D) The evolution of lithograph printing to rotary presses

14. According to the passage, lithographic printing makes use of the fact that

(A) artists can draw on flat, greaseless surfaces
(B) oily substances do not mix with water
(C) gravure etching is work- and time-consuming
(D) limestone, zinc, and aluminum can be used as planes

15. In line 4, the word "contour" is closest in meaning to

(A) contrast
(B) content
(C) outline
(D) edge

16. In line 7, the word "leveled" is closest in meaning to

(A) elevated
(B) low
(C) flawed
(D) flattened

17. In line 11, the word "envelops" is closest in meaning to

(A) sends
(B) soils
(C) coats
(D) coils

18. It can be inferred from the passage that in making lithographic prints, the paper

(A) absorbs the ink from the printing plate
(B) spreads the ink on the greased areas
(C) shrinks away from the printing stone
(D) keeps the oil from sliding off

GO ON TO THE NEXT PAGE. ➡

19. Where in the passage does the author point out the advantages of lithography over other types of printing?

    (A) Lines 1–2
    (B) Lines 3–5
    (C) Lines 7–8
    (D) Lines 16–18

20. A paragraph following the passage would most probably discuss

    (A) photosynthesis in commercial lithographs
    (B) the offset printing of billboard advertisements
    (C) technological advancements in offset printing
    (D) types of unique lithographs printed in rare books

21. In line 19, the word "impressions" is closest in meaning to

    (A) originals
    (B) reproductions
    (C) photographs
    (D) plates

GO ON TO THE NEXT PAGE. ➡

Questions 22–32

Although a few protozoans are multicellular, the simplest are unicellular organisms, such as amoebas, bacteria, sarcodina, ciliates, flagellates, and sporozoans, which can be amorphous in shape and smaller than .001 inch. Cytoplasm fills the cell membrane that en-
Line closes it and functions as a barrier between cells. The membrane serves as the outer tissue,
(5)   and any compound that may destroy the cell has to penetrate it to reach the cytoplasm.

Some types of organisms are termed colonial because they represent loosely assembled groups of structurally similar and unifunctional cells. Colonial organisms maintain a symbiotic relationship within their particular environments.

Unlike colonial organisms, almost all species of animals and plants are multicellular and
(10) include various types of specialized or somatic cells, each with its own nucleus, genetic code, and RNA. The overall size of a multicellular body is contingent on the total number of cells that comprise it, not the size of individual cells. The simplest multicellular animals are hydras, sponges, and jellyfish, which have well-defined tissues, a cellular nucleus, and an element of cell functions. Sponges have a few specialized cells but largely resemble colonial or-
(15) ganisms that can readily form a new individual group. If the cells of a sponge are separated, they rejoin and continue as a newly formed colonial organism.

22. How many cells do the simplest
    organisms contain?

    (A) One
    (B) One hundred
    (C) Many
    (D) An unknown number

23. In line 4, the phrase "outer tissue" is
    closest in meaning to

    (A) outside force
    (B) outlying area
    (C) shell
    (D) cell

24. In line 5, the word "it" refers to

    (A) the cell
    (B) any compound
    (C) the membrane
    (D) the cytoplasm

25. It can be inferred from the passage that a
    cell serves as

    (A) a partition of organism functions
    (B) the smallest colonial group
    (C) the smallest genetic unit
    (D) a flagellate reproductive organ

26. In line 6, the word "loosely" is closest in
    meaning to

    (A) lively
    (B) naturally
    (C) freely
    (D) feebly

27. In line 8, the word "symbiotic" is closest
    in meaning to

    (A) mutually dependent
    (B) mutually exclusive
    (C) mutually hostile
    (D) mutually resistant

28. The author of the passage implies that
    large animals and plants have

    (A) larger cell sizes than amoebas and
        protozoans
    (B) larger quantities of protoplasm than
        smaller life-forms
    (C) stronger cellular membranes than
        flagellates
    (D) a greater number of cells than smaller
        life-forms

GO ON TO THE NEXT PAGE. ➡

29. In line 10, the word "each" refers to

   (A) animals
   (B) species
   (C) cells
   (D) plants

30. According to the passage, sponges and jellyfish are

   (A) the simplest one-cell organisms
   (B) the simplest multicellular animals
   (C) tissues and cellular nuclei
   (D) cellular and colonial organisms

31. The author mentions all of the following EXCEPT:

   (A) procreative mechanisms
   (B) colonial organisms
   (C) cell contents
   (D) specialized cells

32. This passage would most likely be found in a textbook on which of the following subjects?

   (A) Genetics
   (B) Anatomy
   (C) Biology
   (D) Biochemistry

GO ON TO THE NEXT PAGE. ➡

Questions 33–42

When parchment, which was extraordinarily costly, was replaced by papyrus, it became feasible to establish libraries. At the onset, they began as archives for record keeping and document storage. According to second-hand reports, the most renowned papyrus library
Line was the Alexandrian, founded by Alexander the Great around 330 B.C. in Alexandria, Egypt.
(5) His successors as rulers of Egypt, Ptolemy I and Ptolemy II, expanded the library into the greatest collection of scrolls in the ancient world. To acquire this collection, the rulers borrowed scrolls and manuscripts from libraries in Athens, Rome, and other localities and ordered them duplicated. At times, the library employed more than 100 scribes and illustrators. Some historians claim that the Alexandrian library purchased entire lesser libraries to
(10) contribute to and enhance the quality of its possessions.

The library owned a copy of every contemporary scroll known to the library's administrators and contained more than 400,000 items, all of which were classified and organized. The contents of the papyrus rolls were edited, and a bibliography of Greek literature was compiled and cross-referenced, reflecting the emergence and dissemination of a highly devel-
(15) oped Greek culture. Over time, a succession of leading scholars directed this library, which was acclaimed for the scholarly undertakings it supported as well as for the size of its collection. At one time, 72 scholars were engaged to translate religious testaments, historical annals, and mercantile accounts. Although the library flourished, it was accessible to only a minority of the population because in ancient times the vast majority of urban dwellers were
(20) illiterate. Because papyrus was extremely perishable, not a trace of the Alexandrian library remains today, and archaeologists have several hypotheses as to what became of it.

33. What does the passage mainly discuss?

(A) The use of papyrus in ancient scroll collections
(B) The origin and history of a library
(C) The cultural initiatives of Alexander the Great
(D) The expansion of libraries in ancient times

34. In line 2, the word "feasible" is closest in meaning to

(A) practicable
(B) easy
(C) prestigious
(D) ebullient

35. It can be inferred from the passage that reports of the Alexandrian library

(A) were highly exaggerated
(B) could not be verified
(C) were secondary in importance
(D) could not be made known

36. The author of the passage implies that the rulers of Egypt

(A) oversaw the expansion of the library directly
(B) devoted funds and other resources to the library collections
(C) sought to make the library self-contained
(D) marshaled worldwide support for the library collections

37. According to the passage, the main goal of the library in Alexandria was

(A) collecting scrolls loaned by other libraries
(B) gradually replacing papyrus with parchment
(C) translating scrolls in ancient Egypt and Greece
(D) accumulating translations and originals of texts

GO ON TO THE NEXT PAGE. ➡

38. In the second paragraph, the author implies that

(A) parchment was more durable than books
(B) libraries were necessary to conduct research
(C) the library collection cannot be examined
(D) the library was historically relevant

39. With which of the following statements about Greek literature is the author of the passage most likely to agree?

(A) It was nurtured in libraries in Athens and Rome.
(B) It was integral to Greek culture.
(C) It was compiled and cross-referenced in the library.
(D) It was beginning to emerge when the library was expanded.

40. In line 15, the word "succession" is closest in meaning to

(A) series
(B) success
(C) sundry
(D) substitution

41. It can be inferred from the passage that in ancient times

(A) books and scrolls were updated regularly
(B) libraries benefited upper social classes
(C) maintaining collections was fruitless
(D) the population should have been educated

42. In the last sentence, the phrase "not a trace" most probably means

(A) absolutely no one
(B) absolutely nothing
(C) not a penny
(D) not a soul

GO ON TO THE NEXT PAGE. ➡

Questions 43–50

According to data obtained from radioactive dating, the oldest rocks found on earth are approximately 500 million to 4 billion years old. Similar ages have been determined for meteorites and the rocks gathered from the moon's surface. Different methods of arriving at the
Line earth's age generate very similar results. Modern theories about the formation, develop-
(5) ment, and eventual burning out of stars suggest that the sun is about 5 billion years old. Experts contend that the earth and the sun were formed at almost the same time from a cloud of
dust and gas resulting from a cosmic explosion. The present rate of expansion of the galaxies
can be extrapolated to suggest that, if the universe began with a "big bang" about 15 billion
years ago, an age of 5 billion years for both the earth and the sun can be considered plausible.
(10)   Long before radioactive dating was implemented, mythology and oral narratives alluded
to a conjecture that the earth was nearly 6,000 years old. The methods of computation based
on the analysis of genealogical trees in scant archaeological findings provide evidence that
can be difficult to date accurately. Today, radioactive dating of particles and whole objects
has rejected this figure of the earth's age as unreliable.

43. What does the passage mainly discuss?

(A) Dating techniques in research
(B) Modern theories and radioactive dating
(C) Research and narratives about the earth's formation
(D) Establishing the earth's age

44. It can be inferred from the passage that radioactive dating is important for estimating the age of

(A) all known meteors
(B) all existing planets
(C) the earth
(D) the trees

45. In line 5, the word "eventual" is closest in meaning to

(A) ultimate
(B) eventful
(C) utter
(D) enduring

46. According to the passage, the moon is

(A) older than the earth and the sun
(B) newer than the earth and the sun
(C) approximately the same age as the earth and the sun
(D) approximately the same density as the earth and sun

47. The author of the passage implies that

(A) the earth and the sun are of similar origin
(B) the earth and the sun can be explosive
(C) meteorites and the moon have been analyzed
(D) the galaxies are expanding at a substantial rate

48. With which of the following statements would the author be most likely to agree?

(A) The moon and the sun are 15 billion years old.
(B) The moon can be viewed as a meteorite.
(C) The formation of galaxies is an on-going process.
(D) The earth can be dated as far back as 6,000 years.

GO ON TO THE NEXT PAGE. ➡

49. In line 9, the word "plausible" is closest in meaning to

(A) reasonable
(B) rational
(C) relative
(D) relational

50. What conclusion does the author of the passage make?

(A) Radioactive dating is refuted by researchers.
(B) Radioactive dating is more accurate than other methods.
(C) The earth is a part of a galaxy that includes many moons.
(D) The sun's radioactivity is scant and can be negligible.

Practice TOEFL 2

Section 1
Listening Comprehension

In this section, you will demonstrate your skills in understanding spoken English. There are three parts in the Listening Comprehension, with different tasks in each.

Part A

<u>DIRECTIONS</u>: In Part A you will hear short conversations between two speakers. At the end of each conversation, a third speaker will ask a question about what the first two speakers said. Each conversation and each question will be spoken only one time. Therefore, you must listen carefully to understand what each speaker says. After you hear a conversation and the question, read the four choices and select the <u>one</u> that is the best answer to the question the speaker asked. Then, on your answer sheet, find the number of the question and blacken the space that corresponds to the letter for the answer you have chosen. Blacken the space completely so that the letter inside the space does not show.

Listen to the following example.

On the recording, you hear:

Sample Answer
Ⓐ Ⓑ Ⓒ ●

(Man)	Does the car need to be filled?
(Woman)	Mary stopped at the gas station on her way home.
(Narrator)	What does the woman mean?

In your test book, you will read:

(A) Mary bought some food.
(B) Mary had car trouble.
(C) Mary went shopping.
(D) Mary bought some gas.

From the conversation you learn that Mary stopped at the gas station on her way home. The best answer to the question "Does the car need to be filled?" is (D), "Mary bought some gas." Therefore, the correct answer is (D).

Now let us begin Part A with question number 1.

GO ON TO THE NEXT PAGE. ➡

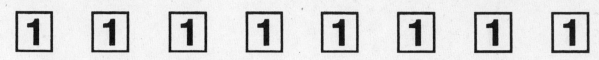

1. (A) Peter didn't pay Bill two times.
   (B) Peter didn't pay the phone company.
   (C) Peter is the second in line to pay.
   (D) Peter forgot to call Bill.

2. (A) The course is closed for registration.
   (B) The instructor decides who can enroll.
   (C) Registration for this course is permitted.
   (D) The instructor doesn't give students permission.

3. (A) We expected only fourteen people to come.
   (B) Forty people came to work in the shop.
   (C) More people came than had been expected.
   (D) We expanded the shop to include forty people.

4. (A) It's better to change this job.
   (B) Betty decided to take the job.
   (C) In my opinion, Betty should change her job.
   (D) I thought Betty was taking John with her.

5. (A) If she dropped Jack off.
   (B) If she took his jacket to be cleaned.
   (C) If she was leaving Jack.
   (D) If she had cleaned his jacket yet.

6. (A) The teachers didn't go to the meeting.
   (B) The meeting on Wednesday was crowded.
   (C) The teachers knew about the meeting.
   (D) Everyone forgot about the meeting.

7. (A) He was nice to give up his part.
   (B) He gave a party for the man.
   (C) He was kind to do his part.
   (D) He was kind to come to the party.

8. (A) Pharmacists shouldn't carry boxes to the station.
   (B) Paper goods are not usually sold in drug stores.
   (C) Mobile pharmacies are not stationed here.
   (D) The pharmacy needs to order paper goods.

9. (A) The exam seems to be easier than it first appeared.
   (B) He thinks the exam appears to cover the material.
   (C) He thinks they made the exam difficult on purpose.
   (D) The exam is more difficult than he thought.

10. (A) The number of the unemployed has been increasing.
    (B) Drama clubs have been helping the unemployed.
    (C) Unemployed actors can find work in drama.
    (D) Dramas about the unemployed are gaining popularity.

GO ON TO THE NEXT PAGE. ➡

11. (A) Linda's grades don't leave much room for improvement.
    (B) Linda deserves better grades in her courses.
    (C) Linda's grades aren't as high as they should be.
    (D) Linda's grades should be left alone.

12. (A) She had to add salt to her hamburger.
    (B) She had a hamburger at 1:30.
    (C) She needs something to drink.
    (D) Her hamburger was excellent.

13. (A) They dropped her sandwich.
    (B) She didn't have food on her mind.
    (C) They will bring her a sandwich.
    (D) She should be on her way home.

14. (A) Doug is too old to go on a boat.
    (B) Ducks can't be transported by boat.
    (C) Doug doesn't like to vote.
    (D) Doug is too young to vote.

15. (A) Harry is working to buy new shoes.
    (B) Harry's shoes are at school.
    (C) Harry is a student.
    (D) Harry walks to the seashore.

16. (A) There is no room on the third floor.
    (B) Room 7 is ready for the third meeting.
    (C) The room is on a different floor.
    (D) The floor in this room is dirty.

17. (A) After he broke a glass, he had to use a cup.
    (B) After the flat, he's been using a spare tire.
    (C) When he broke the glass, he cut himself.
    (D) He has been using different glasses.

18. (A) My brother had an idea for our father's gift.
    (B) My brother wants to buy our father a pool.
    (C) We wanted to bake a pie for my father.
    (D) We celebrated our father's birthday.

19. (A) Ann will be 21 next month.
    (B) No one now lives next to Ann.
    (C) Ann moved here three weeks ago.
    (D) Ann is going on a 21-day vacation.

20. (A) If he could sell her a product to remove grease.
    (B) If he knew he had a stain.
    (C) If he wanted to remove his shirt.
    (D) If she had a crease in her shirt.

GO ON TO THE NEXT PAGE. ➡

21. (A) She approves.
    (B) He is good at tennis.
    (C) He was nice to clean the house.
    (D) She wants to come, too.

22. (A) He is going out of town.
    (B) He is expecting guests.
    (C) He is changing companies.
    (D) He is moving to another town.

23. (A) At an amusement park.
    (B) In a restaurant.
    (C) On the sidewalk.
    (D) Near a parking meter.

24. (A) Buying vegetables.
    (B) Planting a garden.
    (C) Cooking a meal.
    (D) Loading a truck.

25. (A) Can you hear this noise?
    (B) Do you know this sound?
    (C) Where would you prefer?
    (D) Where is this sound coming from?

26. (A) At a craft show
    (B) At a bookstore
    (C) At a hardware store
    (D) At a video rental shop

27. (A) A gas station attendant
    (B) A university course grader
    (C) An income tax accountant
    (D) A technical team leader

28. (A) She is upset that she forgot to send the
        card.
    (B) She thinks the man should share
        responsibility.
    (C) She has been forgetting a lot of things
        lately.
    (D) She is asking whether the man sent his
        own card.

29. (A) Go for dinner
    (B) Order Italian food
    (C) Mail her report
    (D) Finish her report

30. (A) She believes her services should be
        noticed.
    (B) She is taking a two-week leave.
    (C) She was promoted to the position of a
        manager.
    (D) She is planning to take another job.

GO ON TO THE NEXT PAGE. ➡

Part B

DIRECTIONS: In this part of the test, you will hear longer conversations. After each conversation, you will hear several questions. The conversations and questions will not be repeated.

After you hear a question, read the four choices in your test book and select the best answer. Then, on your answer sheet, find the number of the question and fill in the space that corresponds to the letter of the answer you have chosen. Remember, you are not allowed to take notes or write in your test book.

Listen to the following example:

You will hear:

You will read:

Sample Answer

(A) He has changed jobs.
(B) He has two children.
(C) He has two jobs.
(D) He is looking for a job.

From the conversation you learn that Tom has taken an additional job. The best answer to the question "Why is Tom tired?" is (C), "He has two jobs." Therefore, the correct answer is (C).

31. (A) In a film studio
    (B) In a record company
    (C) At an art gallery
    (D) At a movie theater

32. (A) He thinks his children should watch educational programs.
    (B) His daughters are too old to watch cartoons.
    (C) He isn't a child any longer.
    (D) He doesn't want to watch cartoons.

33. (A) The drawings are made.
    (B) The story is created.
    (C) The shots are framed.
    (D) The artists are organized.

34. (A) To make cartoons a form of graphic art
    (B) To enhance the visual and auditory elements
    (C) To add action to animation
    (D) To speed up the feature plot

35. (A) At a county fair
    (B) In the woods
    (C) On a sidewalk
    (D) On a playground

36. (A) In the evening
    (B) In the morning
    (C) In the fall
    (D) In the spring

37. (A) They shed their leaves in the fall.
    (B) There are fewer daylight hours.
    (C) Young trees require a blanket.
    (D) Red and yellow are prettier than green.

38. (A) She doesn't care about his explanation.
    (B) She doesn't understand scientific facts.
    (C) She doesn't believe the man.
    (D) She doesn't like autumn.

GO ON TO THE NEXT PAGE. ➡

Part C

<u>DIRECTIONS</u>: In Part C you will hear short lectures and conversations. At the end of each, you will be asked several questions. Each lecture or conversation and each question will be spoken only one time. For this reason, you must listen carefully to understand what each speaker says. After you hear a question, read the four possible choices and select the one that best answers the question the speaker asked. Then, on your answer sheet, find the number of the question and blacken the space that corresponds to the letter for the answer you have chosen.

Answer all questions according to what is stated or implied in the lecture or conversation.

Listen to this sample talk.
You will hear:

Now listen to the following example.
You will hear:

Sample Answer

Ⓐ ● Ⓒ Ⓓ

You will read:

(A) By cars and carriages
(B) By bicycles, trains, and carriages
(C) On foot and by boat
(D) On board ships and trains

The best answer to the question "According to the speaker, how did people travel before the invention of the automobile?" is (B), "By bicycles, trains, and carriages." Therefore, the correct answer is (B).

Now listen to another sample question.

(Narrator)   Approximately how many people are employed in the automobile service industry?

Sample Answer

Ⓐ Ⓑ ● Ⓓ

You will read:

(A) One million
(B) Ten million
(C) Twelve million
(D) Ninety million

The best answer to the question "Approximately how many people are employed in the automobile service industry?" is (C), "Twelve million." Therefore, the correct answer is (C).

You are not allowed to make notes during the test.

39. (A) It changes climatic conditions.
   (B) It controls the indoor environment.
   (C) It circulates water particles in the air.
   (D) It reduces overhead expenditures.

40. (A) By cleaning off dirt and dust
   (B) By modifying the temperature
   (C) By removing and adding moisture
   (D) By bringing in and taking out air

GO ON TO THE NEXT PAGE. ➡

41. (A) To replace it with fresh air
    (B) To create a breeze
    (C) To retard heat conduction
    (D) To remove local moisture

42. (A) Hardly ever in cold regions
    (B) Exclusively in business settings
    (C) Basically as it does in summer
    (D) Mainly as needed for repairs

43. (A) They can dress comfortably.
    (B) They become tired.
    (C) They feel alert.
    (D) They stay healthy.

44. (A) Business and finance
    (B) Law and science
    (C) Sports
    (D) Chief editors

45. (A) Copy editing
    (B) Approaching people
    (C) Writing
    (D) Typing

46. (A) Many reports have been filed.
    (B) Many reporters have been laid off.
    (C) Many publications have closed.
    (D) Many are hiring new specialists.

47. (A) They will stay sluggish.
    (B) They may continue to decrease.
    (C) They are likely to expand.
    (D) They may be difficult to break into.

48. (A) It represents an essential supply of
        water.
    (B) Its sources can be renewed indefinitely.
    (C) It always provides a usable source of
        water.
    (D) Its development is important in the
        United States.

49. (A) Increased rain and agricultural irrigation
    (B) Increased use and contamination
    (C) Airborne bacteria and atmospheric
        oxygen
    (D) Surface runoff and turbulence

50. (A) Several years
    (B) Centuries
    (C) Dozens of years
    (D) Thousands of years

➤STOP◄

This is the end of Section 1.

Read the directions for Section 2.
Do not read or work on any other section of the test.
Look at the time now before you begin work on Section 2.
Use exactly 25 minutes to work on Section 2.

Section 2
Structure and
Written Expression

Time: 25 minutes

This section is designed to test your ability to recognize language structures that are appropriate in standard written English. There are two types of questions in this section, and each has special directions.

DIRECTIONS: Questions 1–15 are partial sentences. Below each sentence you will see four words or phrases, marked (A), (B), (C), and (D). Select the one word or phrase that best completes the sentence. Then, on your answer sheet, find the number of the question you have selected. Blacken the space so that the letter inside the circle does not show.

EXAMPLE I

Drying flowers is the best way - - - - - - them.

(A) to preserve
(B) by preserving
(C) preserve
(D) preserved

Sample Answer

● Ⓑ Ⓒ Ⓓ

The sentence should state, "Drying flowers is the best way to preserve them." Therefore, the correct answer is (A).

EXAMPLE II

Many American universities - - - - - - as small, private colleges.

(A) begun
(B) beginning
(C) began
(D) for the beginning

Sample Answer

Ⓐ Ⓑ ● Ⓓ

The sentence should state, "Many American universities began as small, private colleges." Therefore, the correct answer is (C).

After you read the directions, begin work on the questions.

1. The upper branches of the tallest trees produce more leaves - - - - - - other branches.

   (A) than do
   (B) than does
   (C) than they do
   (D) than it does

2. No one - - - - - - projections of demographic shifts are reliable and will prove to be valid in the future.

   (A) know how
   (B) knows whether
   (C) knows even
   (D) know who

GO ON TO THE NEXT PAGE. ➡

3. Senior executives often receive bonuses when their profit targets are reached or - - - - - - .

   (A) surpass
   (B) surpasses
   (C) surpassed
   (D) surpassing

4. Since the 1970s, riding bicycles - - - - - - in the United States.

   (A) becomes increasingly widespread
   (B) become increasingly widely spread
   (C) has become increasingly widespread
   (D) has increased and becomes spread widely

5. Horseradish has extended stems and a large root that is grated - - - - - - a spicy food sauce.

   (A) to making
   (B) to make
   (C) to be made
   (D) to the making

6. Vitamin A maintains the sharpness of human vision - - - - - - and promotes healthy bones.

   (A) at night
   (B) of the night
   (C) for the night
   (D) nighttime

7. - - - - - - , often used in children's poetry and rhymes, are a result of words used in ambiguous contexts.

   (A) Humorous and misunderstood
   (B) Misunderstand humorously
   (C) Humorous misunderstandings
   (D) Misunderstanding its humor

8. Modern scanning technology enables physicians to identify brain disorders earlier - - - - - - than in the past.

   (A) and more accurate
   (B) and more accurately
   (C) accurate and more
   (D) accurately and more

9. Educational toys and games give children an opportunity to enjoy themselves - - - - - - .

   (A) while their learning
   (B) while learning
   (C) are they learning
   (D) and they are learning

10. William Hazlitt's essays, written in - - - - - - style, appeared between 1821 and 1822.

   (A) vigorously and informally
   (B) vigorous and informally
   (C) vigor and informality
   (D) vigorous and informal

11. Wild hogs inhabited Europe and other parts of the world - - - - - - 6 million years ago.

   (A) as long
   (B) as long as
   (C) then it was
   (D) than it was

12. Electrically charged particles exert a magnetic force on one another even - - - - - - not in physical contact.

   (A) if there are
   (B) they are
   (C) if they are
   (D) are they

GO ON TO THE NEXT PAGE. ➡

13. F. Scott Fitzgerald's early literary success led to extravagant living and - - - - - - a large income.

   (A) a need for
   (B) to need for
   (C) needed for
   (D) for he needed

14. Water fire extinguishers must never be used for fires that involve - - - - - - .

   (A) electrically equipped
   (B) equipment, electrically
   (C) electricity equipped
   (D) electrical equipment

15. By the 1300s, the Spanish had learned that gunpowder could - - - - - - propel an object with incredible force.

   (A) use to
   (B) be used to
   (C) been used to
   (D) using it to

GO ON TO THE NEXT PAGE. ➡

② ② ② ② ② ② ② ②

<u>DIRECTIONS</u>: In questions 16–40 every sentence has four words or phrases that are underlined. The four underlined portions of each sentence are marked (A), (B), (C), and (D). Identify the one word or phrase that should be changed in order for the sentence to be correct. Then, on your answer sheet, find the number of the question and blacken the space that corresponds to the letter of the answer you have selected.

EXAMPLE I

Sample Answer

● Ⓑ Ⓒ Ⓓ

Christopher Columbus <u>has sailed</u> from Europe in 1492 and <u>discovered</u> <u>a new land</u> he <u>thought to</u>
               A   B   C   D

be India.

The sentence should state, "Christopher Columbus sailed from Europe in 1492 and discovered a new land he thought to be India." Therefore, you should choose answer (A).

EXAMPLE II

Sample Answer

Ⓐ ● Ⓒ Ⓓ

<u>As the roles</u> of people in society change, <u>so does</u> the <u>rules of</u> conduct in certain <u>situations</u>.
  A   B   C   D

The sentence should state, "As the roles of people in society change, so do the rules of conduct in certain situations." Therefore, you should choose answer (B).

After you read the directions, begin work on the questions.

16. During a recession, manufacturers may <u>be forced</u> to <u>decrease</u> the number of their workers
                                          A   B

    <u>to reduction</u> their <u>expenditures</u>.
        C   D

17. <u>Tides</u> constitute a <u>change in</u> the level of water in <u>the oceans</u> and are caused by the
  A   B   C

gravitational interaction between heavenly <u>body</u>.
                                         D

18. Most people <u>are surprising</u> to see <u>how rapidly</u> bacteria <u>can multiply</u> <u>under favorable</u> conditions.
              A   B   C   D

GO ON TO THE NEXT PAGE. ➡

2 2 2 2 2 2 2 2

19. Without <u>water</u>, food, shelter, and <u>clothing</u>, <u>person</u> could not survive a prolonged exposure to
          A   B   C

the <u>elements</u>.
          D

20. Ancestor <u>worship</u> reflects <u>a family's</u> reverence for the <u>advice</u> and guidance of its <u>died</u> members.
                          A   B   C   D

21. <u>A little</u> land animals live in the polar <u>regions</u> which <u>are covered</u> with snow <u>year round</u>.
          A   B   C   D

22. A dolphin, often <u>called</u> a "porpoise," is <u>considered</u> to be one of the <u>bright</u> among <u>animals</u>.
                                A   B   C   D

23. In Arizona, <u>regular</u> <u>annually</u> events include <u>horse</u> shows, art fairs, and folk <u>dances</u>.
                          A   B   C   D

24. <u>Artificial</u> intelligence is concerned with <u>designing</u> computer systems that perform such tasks as
          A   B

<u>reason</u> and <u>learning</u> new skills.
          C   D

25. Saccharin, <u>made</u> from toluene, is <u>about</u> 350 <u>times</u> as <u>sweeter</u> as sugar.
                          A   B   C   D

26. Work <u>affect</u> intellectual development and personal <u>characteristics</u>, and <u>personality</u> and life
                A   B   C

events <u>affect</u> work.
              D

27. <u>Because of</u> attitudes <u>shape</u> behavior, <u>psychologists</u> want to find out how opinions <u>are formed</u>.
          A   B   C   D

28. Although Connecticut occupies a <u>small</u> area, <u>its</u> weather can <u>vary</u> from one area to <u>others</u>.
                                                      A   B   C   D

29. The Great Depression <u>serves as</u> an example <u>of drama</u> fluctuations in <u>the balanced</u> <u>wage rate</u>.
                                          A   B   C   D

30. In some states, it <u>has</u> against <u>the law</u> <u>to ride</u> a motorcycle <u>without a</u> helmet.
                                A   B   C   D

31. The government <u>provides</u> financial support <u>for people</u> who <u>are unable</u> to support <u>themself</u>.
                                A   B   C   D

32. Robert Merton <u>studied</u> how <u>does</u> society <u>influences</u> the <u>development</u> of science.
                          A   B   C   D

33. The <u>available</u> of credit <u>influences</u> the rate of economic growth and the <u>increase</u> <u>in prices</u>.
                A   B   C   D

34. Pasteurization is the process <u>of heating</u> milk <u>to destroy</u> <u>disease-caused</u> organisms and <u>bacteria</u>.
                                            A   B   C   D

35. Paul Claudel, who <u>written</u> books about his <u>personal</u> <u>feelings</u>, was a <u>leading</u> French author of
                                A   B   C   D

the early 1900s.

GO ON TO THE NEXT PAGE. ➡

36. Astronomers do not have sufficient <u>information</u> <u>to determine</u> <u>what</u> the solar system
                                                A   B   C

<u>was created</u>.
    D

37. The soil and climate in the tropics are not <u>suit</u> to <u>produce</u> large <u>quantities</u> of <u>grain</u>.
                                                  A   B   C   D

38. Some <u>species of</u> bats <u>are dormant</u> <u>each days</u> and active <u>every night</u>.
          A   B   C   D

39. Paper was <u>so expensive</u> during the Middle Ages that <u>it has</u> to <u>be used</u> <u>sparingly</u>.
               A   B   C   D

40. Additives are <u>chemicals</u> that are <u>infused into</u> substances to <u>preventing</u> them from <u>spoiling</u>.
                   A   B   C   D

►STOP◄

This is the end of Section 2.

Read the directions for Section 3.
Do not read or work on any other section of the test.
Look at the time now before you begin work on Section 3.
Use exactly 55 minutes to work on Section 3.

Section 3
Reading Comprehension

Time: 55 minutes

<u>DIRECTIONS</u>: In this section you will read several passages. Each is followed by questions about it. For questions 1–50, you need to select the one best answer, (A), (B), (C), or (D), to each question. Then, on your answer sheet, find the number of the question and blacken the space that corresponds to the letter of the answer you have selected. Fill in the space completely.

Answer all questions following a passage on the basis of what is stated or implied in the passage.

Read the following passage:

> A tomahawk is a small ax used as a tool and a weapon by the North American Indian
> tribes. An average tomahawk was not very long and did not weigh a great deal. Originally,
> the head of the tomahawk was made of a shaped stone or an animal bone and was mounted on
Line a wooden handle. After the arrival of the European settlers, the Indians began to use toma-
(5) hawks with iron heads. Indian males and females of all ages used tomahawks to chop and cut
> wood, pound stakes into the ground to put up wigwams, and perform many other chores. Indian
> warriors relied on tomahawks as weapons and even threw them at their enemies. Some types
> of tomahawks were used in religious ceremonies. Contemporary American idioms reflect
> this aspect of American heritage.

EXAMPLE I   **Sample Answer**

Early tomahawk heads were made of   ● Ⓑ Ⓒ Ⓓ

(A) stone or bone
(B) wood or sticks
(C) European iron
(D) religious weapons

According to the passage, early tomahawk heads were made of stone or bone. Therefore, the correct answer is (A).

EXAMPLE II   **Sample Answer**

How has the Indian use of tomahawks affected American daily life today?   Ⓐ Ⓑ ● Ⓓ

(A) Tomahawks are still used as weapons.
(B) Tomahawks are used as tools for certain jobs.
(C) Contemporary language refers to tomahawks.
(D) Indian tribes cherish tomahawks as heirlooms.

The passage states, "Contemporary American idioms reflect this aspect of American heritage." The correct answer is (C).

After you read the directions, begin work on the questions.

GO ON TO THE NEXT PAGE. ➡

Questions 1–10

The Globe Theater, where most of Shakespeare's plays were staged and performed, was located in London. Cuthbert and Richard Burbage built the theater in 1599 with materials left over from the construction of London's first playhouse, the Theater. They constructed
Line the Globe on the south side of the Thames River in the little town of Southwark and counted
(5) on making the theater a draw for the locals. Little is known about the architectural design of the theater except what can be deduced from maps and the layout of the plays presented there. It appears that the Globe was either round or polygonal on the outside but most likely round on the inside. In keeping with the contemporary imitations of Roman government buildings, its roof was most probably shaped as a crude dome. It can be further deduced that
(10) the structure was decorated with pediments, arches, columns, and ornate staircases with carvings of shells, feathers, and cupids. The size of its audience is projected at as many as 3,000 spectators both in the amphitheater and in the balcony. The Globe burned down in 1613; it was rebuilt on the same foundation a year later, but its external walls were curved at an angle different from that of the original. The theater was built hastily, and evidently
(15) safety was not a top priority for either the engineer or the company. After several nearly fatal accidents, the Globe was torn down for good in 1644.

1. This passage most likely came from a longer work on

   (A) English deductive trivia
   (B) English monumental constructions
   (C) the history of the English theater
   (D) notable English disasters

2. According to the passage, the Globe Theater was built

   (A) from available contemporary materials
   (B) from materials remaining from another project
   (C) on a foundation designed to meet a temporary need
   (D) with ornaments intended to fool the spectators

3. In line 5, the phrase "a draw" is closest in meaning to

   (A) an option
   (B) an attraction
   (C) a drawing
   (D) a donation

4. It can be inferred from the passage that the Globe's exact architectural design

   (A) should be reconstituted
   (B) should be obliterated
   (C) cannot be determined
   (D) cannot be disregarded

5. In line 8, the word "imitations" is closest in meaning to

   (A) enumeration
   (B) elimination
   (C) elaborations
   (D) emulation

6. In line 11, the word "projected" is closest in meaning to

   (A) calculated
   (B) confirmed
   (C) embellished
   (D) entrenched

GO ON TO THE NEXT PAGE. ➡

7. The passage suggests that, for its time, the Globe Theater was

    (A) humble
    (B) harsh
    (C) austere
    (D) large

8. According to the passage, in how many buildings was the Globe Theater housed during its operation?

    (A) One
    (B) Two
    (C) Three
    (D) Four

9. The author implies that the last building housing the Globe was

    (A) dignified
    (B) unmistakable
    (C) hazardous
    (D) haunted

10. With which of the following statements is the author most likely to agree?

    (A) The architectural design of the theater was exemplary in the 1600s.
    (B) The builders did not invest a great deal of thought into the theater design.
    (C) The theater audience enjoyed plays, as well as the building design.
    (D) The theater location contributed to the opulence of its design and decorations.

GO ON TO THE NEXT PAGE. ➡

Questions 11–22

Vitamins, taken in tiny doses, are a major group of organic compounds that regulate the mechanisms by which the body converts food into energy. They should not be confused with minerals, which are inorganic in their makeup. Although in general the naming of vi-
Line tamins followed the alphabetical order of their identification, the nomenclature of individ-
(5) ual substances may appear to be somewhat random and disorganized. Among the 13 vitamins known today, five are produced in the body. Because the body produces sufficient
quantities of some but not all vitamins, they must be supplemented in the daily diet. Although each vitamin has its specific designation and cannot be replaced by another compound, a lack of one vitamin can interfere with the processing of another. When a lack of
(10) even one vitamin in a diet is continual, a vitamin deficiency may result.

The best way for an individual to ensure a necessary supply of vitamins is to maintain a
balanced diet that includes a variety of foods and provides adequate quantities of all the compounds. Some people take vitamin supplements, predominantly in the form of tablets. The
vitamins in such supplements are equivalent to those in food, but an adult who maintains a
(15) balanced diet does not need a daily supplement. The ingestion of supplements is recommended only to correct an existing deficiency due to unbalanced diet, to provide vitamins
known to be lacking in a restricted diet, or to act as a therapeutic measure in medical treatment. Specifically, caution must be exercised with fat-soluble substances, such as vitamins
A and D, because, taken in gigantic doses, they may present a serious health hazard over a pe-
(20) riod of time.

11. In line 1, the word "regulate" is closest in meaning to

(A) control
(B) refine
(C) refresh
(D) confine

12. According to the passage, vitamins are

(A) food particles
(B) essential nutrients
(C) miscellaneous substances
(D) major food groups

13. In line 4, the word "nomenclature" is closest in meaning to

(A) conservation
(B) classification
(C) concentration
(D) clarification

14. How many vitamins must be derived from nourishment?

(A) 5
(B) 7
(C) 8
(D) 13

15. The author implies that foods

(A) supply some but not all necessary vitamins
(B) should be fortified with all vitamins
(C) are equivalent in vitamin content
(D) supplement some but not all necessary vitamins

16. In line 7, the phrase "daily diet" is closest in meaning to

(A) weight loss or gain
(B) sufficient quantities
(C) nourishment intake
(D) vitamin tablets

17. A continual lack of one vitamin in a person's diet is

(A) contagious
(B) desirable
(C) preposterous
(D) dangerous

GO ON TO THE NEXT PAGE. ➡

18. With which of the following statements would the author be most likely to agree?

(A) A varied diet needs to be supplemented with vitamins.
(B) An inclusive diet can provide all necessary vitamins.
(C) Vitamins cannot be consistently obtained from food.
(D) Vitamins should come from capsules in purified form.

19. It can be inferred from the passage that vitamin supplements can be advisable

(A) in special medical cases
(B) in most restricted diets
(C) after correcting a dietary deficiency
(D) before beginning a therapeutic treatment

20. In line 17, the phrase "act as" is closest in meaning to

(A) play the role of
(B) pretend to be
(C) fight for
(D) attest to the fact that

21. The author of the passage implies that

(A) some vitamins are not fat-soluble
(B) vitamins can be taken in very small doses
(C) most vitamins are water-soluble
(D) all vitamins are found in measured doses

22. What does the passage mainly discuss?

(A) Adopting vitamins to control weight
(B) The individual's diet for optimum health
(C) Vitamin categorization and medical application
(D) The place of vitamins in nutrition

GO ON TO THE NEXT PAGE. ➡

Questions 23–33

When jazz began to lose its reputation as "low-down" music and to gain well-deserved ac-
claim among intellectuals, musicians began to feature many instruments previously considered inappropriate for jazz. Whereas before the 1950s, jazz musicians played only eight ba-
Line sic instruments in strict tempo, in this decade they started to improvise on the flute, electric
(5) organ, piccolo, accordion, cello, and even bagpipes, with the rhythm section composed for
strings or piano. Big bands no longer dominated jazz, and most changes emerged from small
combos, such as the Dave Brubeck Quartet and the Gerry Mulligan Quartet. The Gerry
Mulligan Quartet proved that a small, modern band could sound complete without a piano;
the rhythm section consisted only of a set of drums and a string bass.

(10)   Jazz continued to move in new directions during the 1960s. Saxophonist and composer
Ornette Coleman led a quartet playing "free" jazz that was atonal. Pianist Cecil Taylor also
conducted similar experiments with music, and John Coltrane included melodies from India in his compositions. In the 1970s musicians blended jazz and rock music into fusion jazz
which combined the melodies and the improvisations of jazz with the rhythmic qualities of
(15) rock 'n' roll, with three or five beats to the bar and in other meters. The form of jazz music
was greatly affected by electric instruments and electronic implements to intensify, distort,
or amplify their sounds. However, the younger musicians of the time felt compelled to include a steady, swinging rhythm which they saw as a permanent and essential element in
great jazz.

23. Which of the following would be the best title for the passage?

   (A) Popular Beats in Classical and Modern Jazz
   (B) Quintessential Moments in Jazz Music
   (C) The Achievements of Famous Jazz Musicians
   (D) The Rising Prestige and Diversity of Jazz

24. In line 2, the word "feature" is closest in meaning to

   (A) profess
   (B) prohibit
   (C) protest
   (D) promote

25. The paragraph preceding this passage would most likely describe

   (A) instruments used in jazz
   (B) instrumental pieces in jazz
   (C) jazz in the 1940s
   (D) the origins of jazz

26. The author of the passage implies that in the 1950s, jazz musicians

   (A) strictly adhered to its traditions and compositions
   (B) probably continued with its tempo and instrumentation
   (C) experimented with rhythm and instruments
   (D) increased the tempo to keep up with the changes

27. The author of the passage mentions all of the following EXCEPT

   (A) bagpipes
   (B) percussion
   (C) string bass
   (D) harpsichord

GO ON TO THE NEXT PAGE. ➡

28. It can be inferred from the passage that small jazz bands

    (A) were dominated by large orchestras
    (B) consisted of drums and a string bass
    (C) were innovative in their music
    (D) included modern sound systems

29. The author believes that the developments in jazz described in the passage

    (A) should be seen as precocious
    (B) should be considered influential
    (C) appear largely suggestive
    (D) may be perceived as discrete

30. The passage implies that representative jazz musicians

    (A) concentrated on melodious combinations of sounds
    (B) blended improvisations and sheet music together
    (C) created and modernized sophisticated devices
    (D) sought novel techniques in form and content

31. According to the passage, the changes in jazz music in the 1970s came from

    (A) another harmonious scale
    (B) another musical trend
    (C) ambitious aspirations
    (D) sound amplifications

32. In line 17, the word "compelled" is closest in meaning to

    (A) forced
    (B) challenged
    (C) obligated
    (D) censored

33. Which of the following best describes the organization of the passage?

    (A) Chronological innovations in jazz music
    (B) Definitions of diverse jazz styles
    (C) A classification of prominent jazz musicians
    (D) Descriptions and examples to illustrate jazz rhythms

GO ON TO THE NEXT PAGE. ➡

Questions 34–41

The killdeer is a commonly found shore bird that inhabits the area between southern Canada and South America. As with all plovers, its soft contour feathers with barbs and barbules impart a sleek appearance to its body while its down feathers insulate it from the winter cold
Line and the summer heat. The male's loud shrill, which seems to say kill-deer, warns other males
(5) away from his territory. Ornithologists do not consider the killdeer a true songbird because its throat muscles are not structured to make melodious notes.

Killdeers are distinguished by the two black bands that mark their chest and neck. Camouflaged by their protective grayish brown pigment, killdeers build nests that cradle the eggs and the young in shallow depressions in fields and open meadows. Because their
(10) nests lie directly on the ground, the young are able to run about as soon as they hatch. Killdeer are incubatory creatures and brood their own babies. When a predator approaches the nest or the bird's young, the mother tries to distract the intruder by dragging one of her wings as if it were injured. Farmers are particularly fond of killdeers because they feed on insects that damage crops. Because whole flocks of killdeers in the wild have vanished due to
(15) overhunting, game laws have been enacted to protect these plovers from poaching.

34. It can be inferred from the passage that killdeer usually live

(A) in the brush
(B) in mountains
(C) near oceans
(D) near cities

35. In line 3, the word "impart" is closest in meaning to

(A) give
(B) import
(C) link
(D) imprint

36. What is the reason given for the bird's name?

(A) It has distinctive bands.
(B) It has a peculiar song.
(C) It kills young deer.
(D) It eats deer fodder.

37. In line 6, the word "melodious" is closest in meaning to

(A) memorable
(B) musical
(C) mellow
(D) marvelous

38. It can be inferred from the passage that killdeers are

(A) inarticulate
(B) inconspicuous
(C) irreverent
(D) irresolute

39. How does the mother bird mislead its enemies?

(A) By pretending to be vulnerable
(B) By blending in with the background
(C) By building low-lying nests
(D) By scaring them away with her cry

40. According to the passage, farmers

(A) form foundations to protect killdeers
(B) appreciate the effects of killdeers
(C) camouflage killdeer nests and eggs
(D) provide killdeers with food and insects

41. Which of the following best describes the author's attitude toward the killdeer?

(A) Menacing
(B) Warm
(C) Detached
(D) Humorous

GO ON TO THE NEXT PAGE. ➡

Questions 42–50

In 1752, Benjamin Franklin made his textbook experiment with a brass key and a silk kite that he flew in a thunderstorm to prove that lightning and electricity are the same thing. In 1920, a kite-flying championship for families and individuals was held in London.
Line These two seemingly unrelated events underscore the fact that kites can be flown for both
(5) pleasure and scientific purposes. For example, in the 1800s weather bureaus flew kites to record temperature and humidity at certain altitudes. On one occasion, ten kites were strung together and flown at a height of four miles to lift men and carry cameras aloft.

The kite's ability to fly depends on its construction and the way that its line is attached. The familiar diamond-shaped kite flies when its covered face is aligned against the wind
(10) flow. The line attached to the nose of the kite pulls it into the wind, thus creating the necessary angle for the lift force. If the kite's construction and the angle of the air stream are correct, the kite will encounter greater pressure against its face and lower pressure against its back. The difference in the pressure creates a lift that causes the kite to rise until it hangs level from its bridle. Its angle against the wind should be sufficiently large or small to create
(15) maximum lift to overcome both drag and gravity. The towing point to which the line is attached is important because it sets the kite's angle relative to the air flow. Although the kite must be headed up and into the wind with a velocity of 8 to 20 miles per hour, it can maintain its position through a tail, a rudder, a keel, vents, or tassels.

42. What is the main topic of the passage?

(A) How kites can be utilized
(B) Why kites were spurned
(C) What parts kites consist of
(D) What makes kites stay aloft

43. In line 1, the word "textbook" is closest in meaning to

(A) textual
(B) tentative
(C) classic
(D) outrageous

44. In line 4, the word "seemingly" is closest in meaning to

(A) ostensibly
(B) oncoming
(C) optimistic
(D) opposite

45. In line 7, the word "aloft" is closest in meaning to

(A) in flight
(B) in the flood
(C) for the analysis
(D) for amusement

46. According to the passage, the kite flies when its nose is

(A) pointed away from the ground
(B) pointed into the wind flow
(C) balanced with the tail
(D) aligned parallel to the wind flow

47. What is the necessary condition for the kite to fly?

(A) The kite must be sufficiently strong to withstand great pressure.
(B) The kite must be diamond-shaped, and the wind of a certain velocity.
(C) The pressure against its back must be lower than the pressure against its face.
(D) The pressure of the air flow must be lower than the weight of the kite.

GO ON TO THE NEXT PAGE. ➡

48. According to the passage, the line of the kite is important because it

    (A) lifts the kite's cover and frame into the air space

    (B) contributes to the shape of the kite and extends it

    (C) determines the angle between the kite and the air flow

    (D) conveys the direction of the wind and the air flow

49. In line 17, the phrase "headed up" is closest in meaning to

    (A) diverted

    (B) deviated

    (C) directed

    (D) drafted

50. The paragraph following the passage most would likely discuss

    (A) fiberglass kites flown in competitions

    (B) the cords and wires needed for kite flying

    (C) bowed kites curved on their faces

    (D) elements of kite design and composition

Practice TOEFL 3

Section 1
Listening Comprehension

In this section, you will demonstrate your skills in understanding spoken English. There are three parts in the Listening Comprehension section, with different tasks in each.

Part A

DIRECTIONS: In Part A you will hear short conversations between two speakers. At the end of each conversation, a third speaker will ask a question about what the first two speakers said. Each conversation and each question will be spoken only one time. Therefore, you must listen carefully to understand what each speaker says. After you hear a conversation and the question, read the four selections and choose the one that is the best answer to the question the speaker asked. Then, on your answer sheet, find the number of the question and blacken the space that corresponds to the letter for the answer you have chosen. Blacken the space completely so that the letter inside the space does not show.

Listen to the following example.

On the recording, you hear:

Sample Answer

Ⓐ Ⓑ Ⓒ ●

(Man)	Does the car need to be filled?
(Woman)	Mary stopped at the gas station on her way home.
(Narrator)	What does the woman mean?

In your test book, you will read:

(A) Mary bought some food.
(B) Mary had car trouble.
(C) Mary went shopping.
(D) Mary bought some gas.

From the conversation you learn that Mary stopped at the gas station on her way home. The best answer to the question "Does the car need to be filled?" is (D), "Mary bought some gas." Therefore, the correct answer is (D).

Now let us begin Part A with question number 1.

1. (A) She didn't expect to fail.
   (B) She went sailing.
   (C) She had her hearing examined.
   (D) She passed her driving test.

2. (A) We have 40 minutes to spare.
   (B) We have to be there in 14 minutes.
   (C) We had a hard time parking the car.
   (D) The parking lot is around the corner.

GO ON TO THE NEXT PAGE. ➡

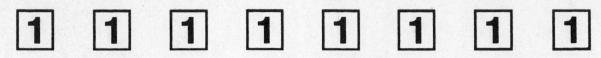

3. (A) I'm wearing his shoes.
   (B) He needs a new broker.
   (C) I broke my shoe strap.
   (D) The manager made investments.

4. (A) She can go right in.
   (B) She can arrive by herself.
   (C) He can't let her in my house.
   (D) He doesn't have a key for her.

5. (A) Seventy flavors are sold regularly.
   (B) Vanilla is the favorite flavor.
   (C) Ice cream was created in the past decade.
   (D) Vanilla accounts are 70 percent accurate.

6. (A) She should buy a new desk light.
   (B) She had to think of a new headline.
   (C) She is having trouble with her car.
   (D) She should talk to the new hires.

7. (A) Mark missed Joanna.
   (B) Joe and Ann love canoeing.
   (C) Joanna left after 10 o'clock.
   (D) Mark called his brother.

8. (A) Their revenue has increased.
   (B) Their salaries were reduced.
   (C) The income has been cut off.
   (D) The bay has been divided.

9. (A) Mrs. Bailey was cheated out of $38.
   (B) Mrs. Bailey charged the flowers on her credit card.
   (C) Mrs. Bailey charges a lot for her flower delivery.
   (D) Mrs. Bailey paid $50 for the flowers.

10. (A) The new hospital works better than the old one.
    (B) The hospital was built six years ago but still looks good.
    (C) They built a hospital here six years ago.
    (D) This proposal has a better chance than the previous one.

11. (A) The bell sounds like it's coming from the library.
    (B) The library has a sound strategy for patrons.
    (C) The library users should leave when the bell rings.
    (D) Parents shouldn't leave children in the library.

12. (A) We can go to the music hall separately.
    (B) We don't have to stand during the concert.
    (C) Let's have a meat dish after the concert.
    (D) We can have the meeting in the hall.

13. (A) She prepared the slides carefully.
    (B) She was sure she did well at the presentation.
    (C) She presented the slides to the sales personnel.
    (D) She checked the slides out of the sales office.

14. (A) Four people are coming.
    (B) Will you come for the break?
    (C) Would you like to visit us?
    (D) Eight friends are invited.

15. (A) Margaret already has a college degree.
    (B) Margaret is considering taking classes.
    (C) Margaret's children are away at college.
    (D) Margaret's children are outside.

16. (A) It's difficult to say what Ralph is thinking.
    (B) The boys are doing well, and Ralph is not worried.
    (C) Ralph only seems worried, but he is really not.
    (D) Ralph is always thinking about the boys.

GO ON TO THE NEXT PAGE. ➡

17. (A) A receptionist in a car repair shop.
    (B) An operator at a telephone company.
    (C) A veterinarian at an animal clinic.
    (D) A secretary in an insurance company.

18. (A) The grocery store has an odd schedule.
    (B) Arthur stores things at his place.
    (C) It's possible to go shopping at that hour.
    (D) Only strange people go to the store so late.

19. (A) He ran out of the station.
    (B) He didn't have enough gas.
    (C) He has been thinking a lot.
    (D) He pulled over to buy gas.

20. (A) Two-syllable words are common.
    (B) Stress can affect pronunciation.
    (C) Two-part words are very rare.
    (D) Most words have only one stress.

21. (A) In a kitchen
    (B) In a living room
    (C) In a bathroom
    (D) In a hallway

22. (A) At her father's
    (B) At her sister's
    (C) At her own home
    (D) At her children's

23. (A) At a post office
    (B) At a bank
    (C) At a pharmacy
    (D) At a deli

24. (A) She thinks her car will be ready before 5:00.
    (B) She is surprised that her car is not finished.
    (C) She doesn't believe her car will be ready at 3:30.
    (D) She wants the man to give her a ride to the shop.

25. (A) He is tired.
    (B) He ate too much.
    (C) He is out of breath.
    (D) He made soup.

26. (A) She couldn't be bothered.
    (B) She invited the Nixons.
    (C) She didn't mind.
    (D) She has a brother.

27. (A) Nick plays tennis all the time.
    (B) The woman went out with Nick.
    (C) The town has many nightclubs.
    (D) The woman finds Nick boring.

28. (A) Four hundred students will take it.
    (B) Two hundred students are in it.
    (C) It's restricted to the waiting list.
    (D) Its instructor has strict rules.

29. (A) At a laundromat
    (B) At a printmaker's
    (C) In an appliance store
    (D) In a tailor's shop

30. (A) A doctor
    (B) A flight attendant
    (C) A hospital nurse
    (D) A pilot

GO ON TO THE NEXT PAGE. ➡

Part B

DIRECTIONS: In this part of the test, you will hear longer conversations. After each conversation, you will hear several questions. The conversations and questions will not be repeated.

After you hear a question, read the four choices in your test book and choose the best answer. Then, on your answer sheet, find the number of the question and fill in the space that corresponds to the letter of the answer you have chosen. Remember, you are not allowed to take notes or write in your test book.

Listen to the following example:

You will hear:

You will read:

Sample Answer

Ⓐ Ⓑ ● Ⓓ

(A) He has changed jobs.
(B) He has two children.
(C) He has two jobs.
(D) He is looking for a job.

From the conversation you learn that Tom has taken an additional job. The best answer to the question "Why is Tom tired?" is (C), "He has two jobs." Therefore, the correct answer is (C).

31. (A) The life of sociable creatures
    (B) Special features of dolphins
    (C) The differences between fish and dolphins
    (D) Communication between groups of dolphins

32. (A) In a museum
    (B) On a seashore
    (C) In a laboratory
    (D) At a zoo

33. (A) For about 2 months
    (B) For almost 12 months
    (C) Approximately 2 years
    (D) Approximately 20 years

34. (A) By visual contact
    (B) By sounds
    (C) Through warning one another
    (D) With the help of scientists

35. (A) The contents and structure of dictionaries
    (B) The benefits and pitfalls of dictionary use
    (C) The acquisition of words in dictionaries
    (D) The various applications of dictionary entries

36. (A) Formal and technical
    (B) General and specialized
    (C) Small and unabridged
    (D) American and English

37. (A) Took a writing class
    (B) Used a technical dictionary
    (C) Studied many new words
    (D) Taught a reading class

38. (A) Learners need to abandon dictionaries when their vocabulary increases.
    (B) Teachers think that students shouldn't always depend on dictionaries.
    (C) One can't use a dictionary effectively without knowing word usage.
    (D) Although dictionaries contain many entries, some word definitions can be irrelevant.

GO ON TO THE NEXT PAGE. ➡

Part C

DIRECTIONS: In Part C you will hear short lectures and conversations. At the end of each, you will be asked several questions. Each lecture or conversation and each question will be spoken only one time. For this reason, you must listen carefully to understand what each speaker says. After you hear a question, read the four selections and choose the one that is the best answer to the sentence the speaker asked. Then, on your answer sheet, find the number of the question and blacken the space that corresponds to the letter for the answer you have chosen.

Answer all questions according to what is stated or implied in the lecture or conversation.

Listen to this sample talk.
You will hear:

Now listen to the following example.
You will hear:

Sample Answer

Ⓐ ● Ⓒ Ⓓ

You will read:

(A) By cars and carriages
(B) By bicycles, trains, and carriages
(C) On foot and by boat
(D) On board ships and trains

The best answer to the question "According to the speaker, how did people travel before the invention of the automobile?" is (B), "By bicycles, trains, and carriages." Therefore, the correct answer is (B).

Now listen to another sample question.

(Narrator)   Approximately how many people are employed in the automobile service industry?

Sample Answer

Ⓐ Ⓑ ● Ⓓ

You will read:

(A) One million
(B) Ten million
(C) Twelve million
(D) Ninety million

The best answer to the question "Approximately how many people are employed in the automobile service industry?" is (C), "Twelve million." Therefore, the correct answer is (C).

You are not allowed to take notes during the test.

39. (A) It's the northern.
    (B) It's the southern.
    (C) It's the deepest.
    (D) It's the smallest.

40. (A) It's heavily traveled all year round.
    (B) It's not navigable for large boats.
    (C) It has less traffic than the other Great Lakes.
    (D) Its shores are inaccessible for landing.

GO ON TO THE NEXT PAGE. ➡

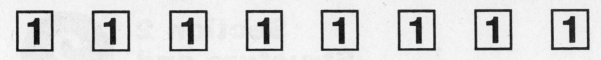

41. (A) 53 miles
    (B) 193 miles
    (C) 480 miles
    (D) 7,500 miles

42. (A) Its water is used for irrigation of trees.
    (B) It moderates the weather patterns in the region.
    (C) It cools the air in the surrounding areas.
    (D) It has a considerable capacity to store water.

43. (A) England
    (B) Scotland
    (C) Richmond
    (D) Boston

44. (A) They were well-to-do.
    (B) They didn't love young Poe.
    (C) They were English.
    (D) They abandoned him.

45. (A) 9
    (B) 11
    (C) 15
    (D) 18

46. (A) He was a competent student.
    (B) He preferred studying in the academy.
    (C) He did not do well in his academics.
    (D) He decided to travel to Scotland instead.

47. (A) John Allan could not afford Poe's education.
    (B) Poe became involved in gambling.
    (C) John Allan had to leave for England.
    (D) Poe decided to become a writer.

48. (A) It is nonpersonal.
    (B) It consists of presentations.
    (C) It cannot be bought.
    (D) It includes hamburgers and soft drinks.

49. (A) Product sponsors
    (B) Many people
    (C) TV viewers
    (D) Buyers of media time

50. (A) Advertising is paid for.
    (B) Advertising can be subject to skepticism.
    (C) Publicity reaches a greater audience.
    (D) Publicity usually benefits political leaders.

➤STOP◄

This is the end of Section 1.

Read the directions for Section 2.
Do not read or work on any other section of the test.
Look at the time now before you begin work on Section 2.
Use exactly 25 minutes to work on Section 2.

Section 2
Structure and
Written Expression

Time: 25 minutes

This section is designed to test your ability to recognize language structures that are appropriate in standard written English. The questions in this section belong to two types, each of which has special directions.

D̲i̲r̲e̲c̲t̲i̲o̲n̲s̲: Questions 1–15 are partial sentences. Below each sentence you will see four words or phrases, marked (A), (B), (C), and (D). Select the one word or phrase that best completes the sentence. Then, on your answer sheet, find the number of the question you have selected. Blacken the space so that the letter inside the circle does not show.

EXAMPLE I

Drying flowers is the best way - - - - - - them.

(A) to preserve
(B) by preserving
(C) preserve
(D) preserved

Sample Answer

● Ⓑ Ⓒ Ⓓ

The sentence should state, "Drying flowers is the best way to preserve them." Therefore, the correct answer is (A).

EXAMPLE II

Many American universities - - - - - - as small, private colleges.

(A) begun
(B) beginning
(C) began
(D) for the beginning

Sample Answer

Ⓐ Ⓑ ● Ⓓ

The sentence should state, "Many American universities began as small, private colleges." Therefore, the correct answer is (C).

After you read the directions, begin work on the questions.

1. The smoke from burning fuels causes pollution if - - - - - - into the atmosphere.

   (A) it releases
   (B) it is released
   (C) it will be released
   (D) it released

2. While preparing an issue, newspaper editors decide what - - - - - - in the editorials.

   (A) viewpoint to take
   (B) viewpoint takes
   (C) take a viewpoint
   (D) takes to a viewpoint

GO ON TO THE NEXT PAGE. ➡

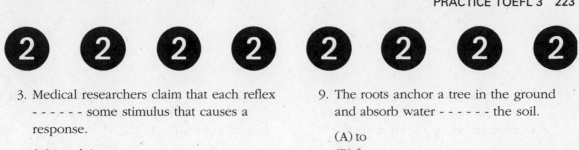

3. Medical researchers claim that each reflex - - - - - - some stimulus that causes a response.

   (A) involving
   (B) involvement
   (C) involves
   (D) involve

4. A law of physics stipulates that energy in any system cannot be created or - - - - - -.

   (A) destroy
   (B) to destroy
   (C) destroyed
   (D) destruction

5. Until the late 1800s, shopkeepers advertised - - - - - - on pictorial signs because their customers were illiterate.

   (A) they produced
   (B) their products
   (C) produced their
   (D) they are produced

6. Amnesia is the - - - - - - or total loss of memory concerning past experiences.

   (A) part
   (B) partially
   (C) partly
   (D) partial

7. A sharp sense of smell enables hunting dogs - - - - - - wild animals.

   (A) to tracking
   (B) to track
   (C) to be tracking
   (D) track them to

8. The popularity of early melodrama promoted the creation of realistic settings and - - - - - - effects.

   (A) elaborate special
   (B) elaborated specially
   (C) specially elaborating
   (D) specially to elaborate

9. The roots anchor a tree in the ground and absorb water - - - - - - the soil.

   (A) to
   (B) from
   (C) into
   (D) due to

10. Viruses are so tiny that - - - - - - only by means of an electron microscope.

    (A) they can see
    (B) they can be seen
    (C) can be seen
    (D) can see them

11. When Arturo Toscanini began his career, music was regarded as one - - - - - - expressing emotions.

    (A) means by
    (B) meant by it
    (C) means of
    (D) the meaning of

12. In diving competitions, women perform - - - - - - men do.

    (A) dive the same as
    (B) the same dives as
    (C) dive the same way as
    (D) the diving is the same

13. Syllables are the - - - - - - of a word according to pronunciation.

    (A) naturally divided
    (B) divided by nature
    (C) natural divisions
    (D) dividing them naturally

GO ON TO THE NEXT PAGE. ➡

14. Mesopotamian civilizations did not
- - - - - - history until meaning-symbol
correspondences had been devised.

   (A) beginning to record
   (B) record the beginning
   (C) began recording
   (D) begin to record

15. Before the 1700s, when children worked
together with adults, childhood - - - - - -
did not exist.

   (A) as we have known
   (B) as we know it
   (C) it is known
   (D) is known as

GO ON TO THE NEXT PAGE. ➡

② ② ② ② ② ② ② ②

DIRECTIONS: In questions 16–40 every sentence has four words or phrases that are underlined. The four underlined portions of each sentence are marked (A), (B), (C), and (D). Identify the one word or phrase that should be changed in order for the sentence to be correct. Then on your answer sheet, find the number of the question and blacken the space that corresponds to the letter of the answer you have selected.

EXAMPLE I

Sample Answer

● Ⓑ Ⓒ Ⓓ

Christopher Columbus <u>has sailed</u> from Europe in 1492 and <u>discovered a</u> <u>new land</u> <u>he thought to</u>
               A   B   C   D

be India.

The sentence should state, "Christopher Columbus sailed from Europe in 1492 and discovered a new land he thought to be India." Therefore, you should choose answer (A).

EXAMPLE II

Sample Answer

Ⓐ ● Ⓒ Ⓓ

<u>As the roles</u> of people in society change, <u>so does</u> the <u>rules of</u> conduct in certain <u>situations</u>.
  A   B   C   D

The sentence should state, "As the roles of people in society change, so do the rules of conduct in certain situations." Therefore, you should choose answer (B).

After you read the directions, begin work on the questions.

16. Carl Anderson <u>discovered</u> two atomic <u>particles</u> that he <u>identified</u> while <u>studied</u> cosmic rays.
                    A   B   C   D

17. No one <u>knows</u> exactly how many <u>species</u> of <u>animals</u> <u>lives</u> on earth.
        A   B   C   D

18. Assessment instruments in nursery schools <u>they feature</u> items and <u>other materials</u> different
                                              A   B

<u>from those</u> on elementary <u>school tests</u>.
  C   D

19. Michigan's rivers, inlets, <u>and lakes</u> attract tourists <u>who derive</u> pleasure <u>from canoeing</u> and
                              A   B   C

<u>water-ski</u>.
  D

20. Analysts <u>have translated</u> clay <u>tablets that</u> demonstrate <u>that the</u> Babylonians were <u>high skilled</u> in
            A   B   C   D

arithmetic.

GO ON TO THE NEXT PAGE. ➡

2 2 2 2 2 2 2 2

21. The visual <u>nerves of</u> the brain <u>interprets</u> <u>wavelengths</u> of <u>light as</u> perceptions of color.
  A　　　　　　　　B　　　　　　C　　　　　　D

22. <u>It is</u> possible to have wealth but <u>little</u> income and <u>having</u> income but <u>no wealth</u>.
  A　　　　　　　　　　　　　B　　　　　　C　　　　　　　D

23. When a criminal case goes to <u>trial</u>, the defendant may <u>election</u> to have it heard <u>either</u> by a jury
  　　　　　　　　　　　　A　　　　　　　　　　　B　　　　　　　　　C

  or by <u>a judge</u>.
  　　　D

24. John Keynes <u>used</u> his <u>knowledges</u> of economics to <u>help</u> his college and <u>himself</u>.
  　　　　　　A　　　　B　　　　　　　　C　　　　　　　　D

25. Government <u>offices store</u> and maintain <u>such documents</u> as certificates of birth, <u>married</u>, and
  　　　　　　　A　　　　　　　　　　　B　　　　　　　　　　　　　　C

  <u>death</u>.
  D

26. <u>After the</u> Constitution was <u>signed</u>, Delaware became <u>the first</u> state to <u>ratifying</u> it.
  A　　　　　　　　　　B　　　　　　　　　　　　　C　　　　　　　D

27. Migrant <u>workers live</u> in <u>substandard</u> <u>unsanitary</u>, and dilapidated housing and often <u>are lacking</u>
  　　　　　A　　　　　　　B　　　　　　C　　　　　　　　　　　　　　　　　　　D

  medical care.

28. The <u>mining</u> of minerals often <u>bring about</u> <u>the destruction</u> of landscapes and <u>wildlife</u> habitats.
  　　　A　　　　　　　　　　B　　　　　　C　　　　　　　　　　　　　D

29. Christopher Marlowe <u>established</u> his <u>theatrical</u> reputation with *Tamburlaine the Great,* <u>written</u>
  　　　　　　　　　　　A　　　　　　B　　　　　　　　　　　　　　　　　　　　C

  in high verse and <u>reflected</u> his unconventional thought.
  　　　　　　　　　D

30. William H. Bonney, <u>better known</u> as Billy the Kid, <u>shoot a man</u> to <u>death in a quarrel</u> and
  　　　　　　　　　A　　　　　　　　　　　　B　　　　　　C

  <u>had to flee</u> to New Mexico.
  　　D

31. Foxes stay in <u>closely knit</u> family groups <u>while the</u> <u>young ones</u> are <u>grow up</u>.
  　　　　　　A　　　　　　　　　　B　　　　C　　　　　　D

32. By 1938, the <u>sale</u> of <u>records album</u> <u>had reached</u> $26 <u>million</u> a year.
  　　　　　　A　　　　B　　　　　　C　　　　　D

33. Egyptian artisans <u>made</u> glass that was <u>colored</u> by the <u>present</u> of <u>impurities</u>.
  　　　　　　　A　　　　　　　　　B　　　　　　C　　　　D

34. A theory <u>called</u> plate tectonics <u>explain</u> the <u>formation</u> of the surface <u>features</u> of the earth.
  　　　　　A　　　　　　　　　B　　　　　　C　　　　　　　　　　D

GO ON TO THE NEXT PAGE. ➡

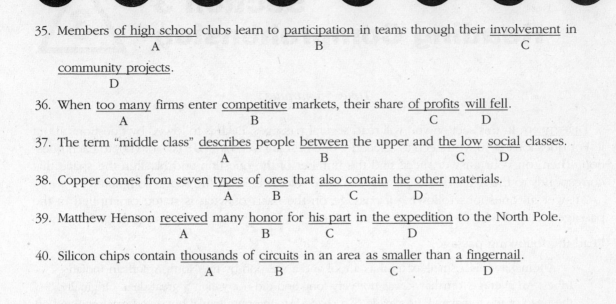

35. Members <u>of high school</u> clubs learn to <u>participation</u> in teams through their <u>involvement</u> in
           A   B   C

    <u>community projects</u>.
           D

36. When <u>too many</u> firms enter <u>competitive</u> markets, their share <u>of profits</u> <u>will fell</u>.
           A   B   C   D

37. The term "middle class" <u>describes</u> people <u>between</u> the upper and <u>the low</u> <u>social</u> classes.
                         A   B   C   D

38. Copper comes from seven <u>types</u> of <u>ores</u> that <u>also contain</u> <u>the other</u> materials.
                            A   B   C   D

39. Matthew Henson <u>received</u> many <u>honor</u> for <u>his part</u> in <u>the expedition</u> to the North Pole.
                       A   B   C   D

40. Silicon chips contain <u>thousands</u> of <u>circuits</u> in an area <u>as smaller</u> than <u>a fingernail</u>.
                         A   B   C   D

➤STOP◄

This is the end of Section 2.

Read the directions for Section 3.
Do not read or work on any other section of the test.
Look at the time now before you begin work on Section 3.
Use exactly 55 minutes to work on Section 3.

Section 3
Reading Comprehension

Time: 55 minutes

<u>DIRECTIONS</u>: In this section you will read several passages. Each is followed by questions about it. For questions 1–50, you need to select the one best answer, (A), (B), (C), or (D), to each question. Then, on your answer sheet, find the number of the question and blacken the space that corresponds to the letter of the answer you have selected. Fill in the space completely.

Answer all questions following a passage on the basis of what is stated or implied in the passage.

Read the following passage:

> A tomahawk is a small ax used as a tool and a weapon by the North American Indian tribes. An average tomahawk was not very long and did not weigh a great deal. Originally, the head of the tomahawk was made of a shaped stone or an animal bone and was mounted on
> *Line* a wooden handle. After the arrival of the European settlers, the Indians began to use toma-
> *(5)* hawks with iron heads. Indian males and females of all ages used tomahawks to chop and cut wood, pound stakes into the ground to put up wigwams, and do many other chores. Indian warriors relied on tomahawks as weapons and even threw them at their enemies. Some types of tomahawks were used in religious ceremonies. Contemporary American idioms reflect this aspect of American heritage.

EXAMPLE I

Early tomahawk heads were made of

(A) stone or bone
(B) wood or sticks
(C) European iron
(D) religious weapons

Sample Answer

● Ⓑ Ⓒ Ⓓ

According to the passage, early tomahawk heads were made of stone or bone. Therefore, the correct answer is (A).

EXAMPLE II

How has the Indian use of tomahawks affected American daily life today?

(A) Tomahawks are still used as weapons.
(B) Tomahawks are used as tools for certain jobs.
(C) Contemporary language refers to tomahawks.
(D) Indian tribes cherish tomahawks as heirlooms.

Sample Answer

Ⓐ Ⓑ ● Ⓓ

The passage states, "Contemporary American idioms reflect this aspect of American heritage." The correct answer is (C).

After you read the directions, begin work on the questions.

GO ON TO THE NEXT PAGE. ➡

Questions 1–12

Even with his diverse experience as an elected official at the state level, Andrew Johnson was the first president of the United States ever to be impeached, primarily because of his violent temper and unyielding stubbornness. His career started in 1828 with his election to
Line the city council of Greenville, Tennessee, and after two years as an alderman, he took office
(5) as mayor. His advancements followed in rapid succession when he was elected to the Tennessee state senate, then as the state governor, and later to the U.S. House of Representatives for five consecutive terms.

In 1864, Johnson ran for the office of vice-president on the Lincoln-Johnson ticket and was inaugurated in 1865. After Lincoln's assassination six weeks into his term, Johnson
(10) found himself president at a time when southern leaders were concerned about their forced alliance with the northern states and feared retaliation for their support of the secession. Instead, however, with the diplomatic skill he had learned from Lincoln, Johnson offered full pardon to almost all Confederates on the condition that they take an oath of allegiance. He further reorganized the former Confederate states and set up legislative elections.

(15) Congressional opposition to his peace-making policies resulted in gridlock between the House and Johnson, and the stalemate grew into an open conflict on the issue of the emancipation of slaves. While Johnson held the view that newly freed slaves lacked understanding and knowledge of civil liberties to vote intelligently, Congress overrode Johnson's veto of the Civil Rights Bill, which awarded them citizenship and ratified the Fourteenth Amend-
(20) ment. In the years that followed, Congress passed bills depriving the president of the power to pardon political criminals, stripping away his status of commander-in-chief, and taking away Johnson's right to dismiss civil and executive officers from their duties. Johnson vetoed each bill, and each veto was overridden. When Johnson dismissed the secretary of war, Edwin Stanton, Stanton refused to step down and was supported by the House of Repre-
(25) sentatives, which voted to impeach Johnson. At the trial, the Senate came one vote short of the two-thirds majority necessary to remove him from office. After Johnson's term expired, he returned to his home state, but in 1875 he was elected senator and went back to Washington to take his seat.

1. What does the passage mainly discuss?

   (A) Andrew Johnson's personal characteristics
   (B) Andrew Johnson's career as a politician
   (C) Congressional decisions in the late 1800s
   (D) Congressional decisions and procedures in the late 1800s

2. In line 4, the phrase "took office" is closest in meaning to

   (A) moved into an office
   (B) became an official
   (C) began a government job
   (D) rearranged the office

3. What can be inferred from the first paragraph about Andrew Johnson's work in Tennessee?

   (A) His personality precluded him from important positions.
   (B) His work became known to the governor.
   (C) He was elected to several important posts.
   (D) He was represented to the posts five times.

GO ON TO THE NEXT PAGE. ➡

4. In line 11, the word "alliance" is closest in meaning to

(A) union
(B) counsel
(C) allowance
(D) allotment

5. According to the passage, what led to Johnson's downfall?

(A) The state of the nation's economy
(B) His liberal position on slavery
(C) His personal characteristics
(D) His waffling and hesitation

6. The author of the passage implies that when Johnson became president he

(A) was a dedicated supporter of civil rights
(B) was a soft-spoken and careful diplomat
(C) had an extensive background in politics
(D) had already experienced political turmoil

7. According to the passage, at the beginning of Johnson's term as president southerners were

(A) expected to secede from the union
(B) apprehensive about their future
(C) singled out as scapegoats
(D) afraid of his violent temper

8. According to the passage, Congress's disapproval of Andrew Johnson's policies was

(A) short-lived and groundless
(B) detrimental to his presidency
(C) directed at his civic duties
(D) stopped as soon as it emerged

9. In line 21, the word "pardon" is closest in meaning to

(A) parade
(B) patronize
(C) exonerate
(D) extricate

10. The author of the passage implies that the Stanton affair proved the president's

(A) lack of stamina
(B) lack of electoral vote
(C) loss of willpower
(D) loss of authority

11. In line 23, the word "dismissed" is closest in meaning to

(A) distanced
(B) fired
(C) disdained
(D) flounced

12. According to the passage, the attempt to impeach Andrew Johnson

(A) succeeded as expected by the House
(B) failed by a minimal margin
(C) put an end to his political career
(D) overwhelmed his supporters in Tennessee

GO ON TO THE NEXT PAGE. ➡

Questions 13–24

Sex-trait stereotypes may be defined as a set of psychological attributes that characterize men more frequently than women. Thus, males are often described as ambitious, unemotional, and independent and, on the other hand, selfish, unrefined, and insensitive. Females
Line are described as emotional, irrational, high-strung, and tentative. In spite of the egalitarian
(5) movement, recent studies have demonstrated that sex-trait stereotypes remain common among young adults today. In fact, such stereotyping has proved to be the psychological justification for social beliefs concerning the appropriateness of various activities for men and women that further perpetuate the different sex roles traditionally ascribed to men and women.

(10)   The awareness of sex-trait stereotypes in the United States develops in a linear fashion between the ages of four and ten. Generally, knowledge of male stereotypical characteristics develops earlier, whereas knowledge of female characteristics increases more rapidly between the ages of four and seven. While the reasons for this learning are not fully understood, evidence suggests that at the preschool level children's literature and television pro-
(15) grams provide powerful models and reinforcement for stereotyped views.

Studies designed to compare sex-trait stereotypes cross-nationally show a high degree of correspondence in the characteristics ascribed to men and women. As findings have been obtained in other countries, two hypotheses have been advanced to explain the commonalities in sex trait stereotyping. One states that pancultural similarities play a role in the psy-
(20) chological characteristics attributed to men and women, and the second states that the general picture is one of cultural relativism.

13. Which of the following is the best title for the passage?

(A) A Relativist Perspective on Stereotyping
(B) The Pervasiveness of Sex-Trait Stereotypes
(C) A Unilateral Approach to Sex-Trait Stereotyping
(D) A Cross-examination of Stereotypical Behaviors

14. In line 2, the word "ambitious" is closest in meaning to

(A) enterprising
(B) ambiguous
(C) anxious
(D) honest

15. In line 4, the word "high-strung" is closest in meaning to

(A) high-class
(B) fair-minded
(C) nervous
(D) hideous

16. Which of the following statements is supported in the passage?

(A) The egalitarian movement has been a resounding success.
(B) The beliefs of young adults have shown little change.
(C) Young adults have participated in many common studies.
(D) The beliefs of young adults are more common among the old.

17. In line 8, the word "perpetuate" is closest in meaning to

(A) personalize
(B) perplex
(C) maintain
(D) mount

GO ON TO THE NEXT PAGE. ➡

18. It can be inferred from the passage that social beliefs precipitate

   (A) the on-going egalitarian change
   (B) the rationalization for stereotyping
   (C) nontraditional gender roles
   (D) concerns for the legitimacy of sex traits

19. It can be inferred from the second paragraph that young children learn about sex-trait stereotypes

   (A) by watching their parents
   (B) by being exposed to various media
   (C) after they start school
   (D) when their learning is reinforced

20. Where in the passage does the author refer to limitations of sex-trait research?

   (A) Lines 1–3
   (B) Lines 4–6
   (C) Lines 13–15
   (D) Lines 16–19

21. According to the passage, character-izations of men and women as having particular sets of attributes are

   (A) reflected in modern fashion
   (B) found in several countries
   (C) uniform across all groups
   (D) contingent on a socioeconomic class

22. In line 17, the word "correspondence" is closest in meaning to

   (A) letters
   (B) writing
   (C) agreement
   (D) discord

23. The author of the passage would most probably agree with which of the following statements?

   (A) Social attitudes toward women have been updated and made more balanced.
   (B) Social attitudes toward men are continually nullified and modernized.
   (C) The women's liberation movement has borne little fruit.
   (D) Social attitudes are not likely to change radically.

24. The passage is probably an excerpt from an article on

   (A) demographics
   (B) sociology
   (C) sociobiology
   (D) psychotherapy

GO ON TO THE NEXT PAGE. ➡

Questions 25–32

There are many reasons why food fads have continued to flourish. Garlic has long been touted as an essential ingredient of physical prowess and as a flu remedy, squash has been thought by some to cure digestive disorders, and red pepper has been alleged to promote en-
Line   durance. The natural human desire for a simple solution to a difficult problem sets the stage
(5)   for promoting miraculous potions, pills, and combinations of chemicals. The gullible individuals who eagerly embrace any second-hand information with scientific overtones provide the foundation for healthy business enterprises.

A person who has never crossed the threshold of a health food store may be astounded, bewildered, or overjoyed. Countless elixirs, herbs, powders, sweeteners, and other fascinating
(10)   extracts are only a fraction of the high-profit selection. The available literature includes pamphlets extolling the amazing return of youth one can anticipate while drinking a potion steeped with tropical weeds, as well as volumes assuring the reader of an almost eternal longevity.

The store is directly keyed to arouse visitors' concern over their health and to capitalize on
(15)   real and imagined problems by offering solutions that, incidentally, cost more than the customer may be able to afford. Health food store patrons are often cajoled into buying tonics that promise to make the functioning of healthy organs even better, regardless of whether an improvement is called for. Promotion of expensive products that consumers do not actually need takes considerable initiative and insight. On occasion, there may even be some
(20)   slight disregard for truth in an entrepreneur's zeal to cure customers of ills—for a price.

25. Which of the following is the main topic of the passage?

(A) Invigorating claims regarding health food
(B) Praising the health food store inventory
(C) Proving the wonders of health food products
(D) Marketing bogus miracles in health food stores

26. Which of the following best describes the author's tone?

(A) Approving
(B) Factual
(C) Sarcastic
(D) Hesitant

27. In line 2, the word "touted" is closest in meaning to

(A) talked about
(B) figured out
(C) identified
(D) known

28. Why does the author mention garlic and squash?

(A) To explain their prevalence in diets of some ethnic groups
(B) To promote their sales as healing agents for various ills
(C) To compare them to modern and beneficial health products
(D) To exemplify the persistence of misconceptions regarding food

29. Where in the passage does the author give reasons for the commercial success of the health food industry?

(A) Lines 1–2
(B) Lines 8–9
(C) Lines 10–13
(D) Lines 14–15

GO ON TO THE NEXT PAGE. ➡

30. In line 16, the word "cajoled" is closest in meaning to

(A) trained
(B) frightened
(C) drilled
(D) coaxed

31. It can be inferred from the passage that health food store operators are primarily concerned with

(A) persuading their customers of the high quality of their wares
(B) arriving at long-term solutions for health maintenance
(C) maximizing profits by taking advantage of consumer naïveté
(D) exposing the grave consequences of neglecting one's health

32. The author would most probably agree with which of the following statements?

(A) Health food articles are positively exotic and exorbitant.
(B) Promoting and selling health foods verges on cheating.
(C) Health food enterprises are dedicated to absolute honesty.
(D) Inducing patrons to buy health products is criminal at best.

GO ON TO THE NEXT PAGE. ➡

Questions 33–41

Because geologists have long indicated that fossil fuels will not last indefinitely, the U.S. government finally acknowledged that sooner or later other energy sources would be needed and, as a result, turned its attention to nuclear power. It was anticipated that nuclear power *Line* plants could supply electricity in such large amounts and so inexpensively that they would
(5) be integrated into an economy in which electricity would take over virtually all fuel-generating functions at nominal costs. Thus, the government subsidized the promotion of commercial nuclear power plants and authorized their construction by utility companies. In the 1960s and early 1970s, the public accepted the notion of electricity being generated by nuclear reactors, and the Nuclear Regulatory Commission proceeded with plans for numerous
(10) nuclear power plants in or near residential areas. By 1975, 54 plants were fully operational, supplying 11 percent of the nation's electricity, and another 167 plants were at various stages of planning and construction. Officials estimated that by 1990 hundreds of plants would be on line, and by the turn of the century as many as 1,000 plants would be in working order.
(15) Since 1975, this outlook and this estimation have changed drastically, and many utilities have canceled existing orders. In some cases, construction was terminated even after billions of dollars had already been invested. After being completed and licensed at a cost of almost $6 billion, the Shoreham Power Plant on Long Island was turned over to the state of New York to be dismantled without ever having generated electric power. The reason was
(20) that residents and state authorities deemed that there was no possibility of evacuating residents from the area should an accident occur.

Just 68 of those plants under way in 1975 have been completed, and another 3 are still under construction. Therefore, it appears that in the mid 1990s 124 nuclear power plants in the nation will be in operation, generating about 18 percent of the nation's electricity, a fig-
(25) ure that will undoubtedly decline as relatively outdated plants are shut down.

33. What was initially planned for the nation's fuel supply in the 1950s and in the early 1960s?

(A) Expansion and renovation of existing fuel-generating plants
(B) Creation of additional storage capacities for fossil fuels
(C) Conversion of the industry and the economy to nuclear power
(D) Development of an array of alternative fuel and power sources

34. How does the author describe the attitude of the population in regard to nuclear power as fuel in the early to mid 1970s?

(A) Apprehensive
(B) Ambivalent
(C) Receptive
(D) Resentful

35. In line 6, the word "nominal" is closest in meaning to

(A) so-called
(B) minimal
(C) exorbitant
(D) inflated

36. In line 8, the word "notion" is closest in meaning to

(A) nonsense
(B) notice
(C) idea
(D) consequence

GO ON TO THE NEXT PAGE. ➡

37. In line 15, the phrase "this outlook" refers to

(A) the number of operating nuclear plants
(B) the expectation for the increase in the number of nuclear plants
(C) the possibility of generating electricity at nuclear installations
(D) the forecast for the capacity of the nuclear plants

38. It can be inferred from the passage that government officials made a critical error in judgment by

(A) disregarding the low utility of nuclear power plants
(B) relying on inferior materials and faulty plant design
(C) overlooking the possibility of a meltdown, however remote
(D) locating installations in densely wooded areas

39. The author of the passage implies that the construction of new nuclear power plants

(A) is continuing on a smaller scale
(B) is being geared for greater safety
(C) has been completely halted for fear of disaster
(D) has been decelerated but not terminated

40. Which of the following best describes the organization of the passage?

(A) The exposition of the public opinion polls on nuclear power
(B) A narration of power-source deliberation in nuclear power plants
(C) Causal connections in the government's position on nuclear power
(D) Point and counterpoint in the nuclear power debate

41. The author of the passage implies that the issue of finding adequate sources of fuel and power for the future

(A) has long been ignored by short-sighted government authorities
(B) may be condoned by vacillating officials
(C) has lost its pertinence in light of new discoveries
(D) has not yet been satisfactorily resolved

GO ON TO THE NEXT PAGE. ➡

Questions 42–50

Collecting maps can be an enjoyable hobby for antiquarian booksellers, a captivating interest for cartographers, a lucrative vocation for astute dealers, and an inspirational part of the occupational functioning of map catalogers, archivists, and historians. Among recog-
Line nized collectibles, maps are relatively rarer than stamps, but they have had their avid enthu-
(5) siasts and admirers ever since copies were made by hand only for the affluent, the commanding officer, and the ship captain.

Whether the interest is business-related or amateur, the economic means abundant or slim, a collection needs a theme, be it associated with contemporary changes in cartographic representation or geographic knowledge, or a more accessible goal centered on a particular
(10) mapmaker, technique, or type of subject matter. Collectors should not overlook topical maps issued predominantly or exclusively after World War II, such as navigational charts, industrial compound road layouts, or aerial projections. Potential collectors ought not to disregard two superficially prosaic, yet important themes: maps of travel routes for family trips, and maps that, for aesthetic reasons, they personally find intriguing or simply attrac-
(15) tive. In the first case, like the box with old family photos, the collection will give the travelers the opportunity to reminisce and relive the journey.

In most cases, photocopies are worthy alternatives to originals. For example, historical society collections customarily include the high quality facsimiles needed to make a collection as comprehensive and practical as possible, supplementing the contributions made by
(20) well-to-do donors and benefactors. If not predisposed to wait patiently, and possibly ineffectually, for a lucky find, collectors may choose to sift through dealer stock, peruse through advertisements in local, regional, or national periodicals, and solicit the assistance of the U.S. Library of Congress and private agencies. Government and public agencies, companies, and trade associations can advise the collector about maps currently in circulation and
(25) pending sales of dated reproductions, editions, and prints.

42. What is the main idea of the passage?

(A) Why hobbyists always flaunt their map collections
(B) How maps can be collected by professionals and enthusiasts
(C) How to assure an interrupted flow of collectibles
(D) What cartographers advocate as a worthy undertaking

43. In line 2, the word "lucrative" is closest in meaning to

(A) instructive
(B) insensitive
(C) profitable
(D) profuse

44. According to the passage, map collecting as a hobby is

(A) not deserving of the time and resources
(B) not as conventional as collecting stamps
(C) as eccentric as collecting dolls
(D) conformist in the best sense of the word

45. It can be inferred from the passage that, at a time when maps were accessible to the upper socioeconomic classes, they appealed also to a fair number of

(A) professional copiers
(B) ardent devotees
(C) buried-treasure hunters
(D) obscure amateur dealers

GO ON TO THE NEXT PAGE. ➡

46. In line 7, the phrase "economic means" is closest in meaning to

    (A) economic maps
    (B) fiscal responsibility
    (C) available funds
    (D) capital investment

47. The author of the passage mentions all of the following as sources of procuring maps EXCEPT:

    (A) fellow collectors
    (B) map vendors
    (C) personal archives
    (D) publishers

48. In line 13, the author uses the phrase "superficially prosaic" to mean

    (A) described in informal prose
    (B) seemingly boring and unimaginative
    (C) useful for travelers who enjoy a change
    (D) potentially uncovered in a box of photos

49. In line 20, the word "predisposed" is closest in meaning to

    (A) pressured
    (B) provoked
    (C) condemned
    (D) inclined

50. A paragraph following the passage would most likely discuss

    (A) specific organizations to contact about map acquisition
    (B) specific mapping techniques used to enlarge the scale
    (C) trimming and framing valuable acquisitions
    (D) volunteering time and work to maintain obsolete maps

Practice TOEFL 4

Section 1
Listening Comprehension

In this section, you will demonstrate your skills in understanding spoken English. There are three parts in the Listening Comprehension Section, with different tasks in each.

Part A

DIRECTIONS: In Part A you will hear short conversations between two speakers. At the end of each conversation, a third speaker will ask a question about what the first two speakers said. Each conversation and each question will be spoken only one time. Therefore, you must listen carefully to understand what each speaker says. After you hear a conversation and the question, read the four selections and choose the one that is the best answer to the question the speaker asked. Then, on your answer sheet, find the number of the question and blacken the space that corresponds to the letter for the answer you have chosen. Blacken the space completely so that the letter inside the space does not show.

Listen to the following example.

On the recording, you hear:

Sample Answer
Ⓐ Ⓑ Ⓒ ●

(Man)	Does the car need to be filled?
(Woman)	Mary stopped at the gas station on her way home.
(Narrator)	What does the woman mean?

In your test book, you will read:

(A) Mary bought some food.
(B) Mary had car trouble.
(C) Mary went shopping.
(D) Mary bought some gas.

From the conversation you learn that Mary stopped at the gas station on her way home. The best answer to the question "Does the car need to be filled?" is (D), "Mary bought some gas." Therefore, the correct answer is (D).

Now let us begin Part A with question number 1.

GO ON TO THE NEXT PAGE. ➡

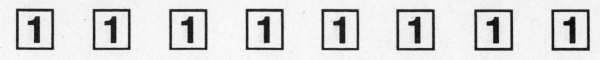

1. (A) Professor White holds advanced classes.
   (B) Professor White's students have graduated.
   (C) Students have great respect for Professor White.
   (D) Students are taking Professor White's seminar.

2. (A) You have to be careful in the desert.
   (B) You shouldn't eat so many sweets.
   (C) May I offer you some dessert?
   (D) Can you help me with the sweets?

3. (A) He never has any money.
   (B) He has no money on him.
   (C) He is out getting cash.
   (D) He has been out of work.

4. (A) The machine shouldn't be left running.
   (B) Turn on the copying machine when you leave.
   (C) The machine has to be turned around.
   (D) You made enough copies already.

5. (A) Tom passed up a Latin course.
   (B) Tom was expected to fail Latin.
   (C) He's surprised Tom is late.
   (D) Tom's Latin class is last.

6. (A) She buys exotic clothes.
   (B) She bought a $115 dress.
   (C) She spent $210.
   (D) She has a new house.

7. (A) The new engineering building is far from here.
   (B) The building is not what I thought it would be.
   (C) I don't know what I expected the engineer to do.
   (D) They are building a new house for the engineer.

8. (A) The man has put off going to a dentist.
   (B) The man likes getting his teeth cleaned.
   (C) She is not happy that the man went to a dentist.
   (D) Everyone should have their teeth cleaned regularly.

9. (A) The rent for the hall is high.
   (B) The wedding hall is for rent.
   (C) The hall is too small.
   (D) There are not enough guests.

10. (A) She can cash the check.
    (B) Only the manager can cash the check.
    (C) Traveller's checks cannot be cashed there.
    (D) A thousand dollars is a large sum of money.

11. (A) They worked together as a team.
    (B) The windows and carpets are beautiful.
    (C) They now have clean windows and rugs.
    (D) They are always cleaning their house.

12. (A) She got lost one more time.
    (B) She didn't know what to say.
    (C) She is learning many new words.
    (D) She had less than the price of the book.

13. (A) He is staying in this hotel.
    (B) He keeps going to bed late.
    (C) He lives by himself in this house.
    (D) He started early and finished late.

14. (A) Ronald won't travel this summer.
    (B) She doesn't know to what country Ronald is going.
    (C) She wants to travel with Ronald.
    (D) Ronald wants to travel out of the country.

GO ON TO THE NEXT PAGE. ➡

15. (A) They can't deliver her dress.
    (B) They don't know where she lives.
    (C) They didn't touch her dress.
    (D) They aren't familiar with the city.

16. (A) We'll be there on time.
    (B) We'll be late.
    (C) We'll take the next turn.
    (D) The turn is forty miles away.

17. (A) Only a third of the students are
        enrolled in the business school.
    (B) The third enrollment prediction for the
        business school was accurate.
    (C) The enrollment is three times higher
        than what was predicted.
    (D) The enrollment figures are about 66
        percent lower than expected.

18. (A) He likes to sing old songs.
    (B) The rumors about him are
        unbelievable.
    (C) To start singing at his age is unusual.
    (D) You shouldn't talk about him this way.

19. (A) He doesn't feel good, and he won't go
        to class.
    (B) He couldn't hear the lecture because
        students were talking.
    (C) Students don't pay attention to what he
        says.
    (D) In this class, the same thing happens
        every day.

20. (A) They passed the river.
    (B) They went for a walk.
    (C) They visited her sister.
    (D) They were looking at the sunset.

21. (A) Stand in line
    (B) Try to order tickets
    (C) Go to the game
    (D) Call their office

22. (A) She doesn't need another phone.
    (B) She is not as busy as it seems.
    (C) They can't afford another line.
    (D) They have to use the phone less.

23. (A) The man administers math placement
        tests.
    (B) The woman should take a math course.
    (C) The woman has to take the placement
        test.
    (D) The woman can transfer her math
        credit.

24. (A) A florist
    (B) A gardener
    (C) A barber
    (D) A custodian

25. (A) Listening to the radio
    (B) Watching a contest
    (C) Repairing a car battery
    (D) Attending a conference

26. (A) An insurance company
    (B) A car rental agency
    (C) A real estate agency
    (D) An apartment complex

27. (A) The man shouldn't attend the exam.
    (B) The instructor isn't proctoring the exam.
    (C) In this situation, the man should stay
        home.
    (D) She doesn't know what the man should
        do.

28. (A) She is a demanding person.
    (B) She is sympathetic to the man.
    (C) She doesn't fault the course.
    (D) She got out of the course.

29. (A) A bookstore
    (B) A publishing house
    (C) A craft show
    (D) An art exhibition

30. (A) He walked ten miles.
    (B) He came here first.
    (C) He won a ski competition.
    (D) He lives across the country.

GO ON TO THE NEXT PAGE. ➡

Part B

<u>DIRECTIONS</u>: In this part of the test, you will hear longer conversations. After each conversation, you will hear several questions. The conversations and questions will not be repeated.

After you hear a question, read the four possible answers in your test book and choose the best answer. Then, on your answer sheet, find the number of the question and fill in the space that corresponds to the letter of the answer you have chosen. Remember, you are not allowed to take notes or write in your test book.

Listen to the following example:

You will hear:

You will read:

Sample Answer

Ⓐ Ⓑ ● Ⓓ

(A) He has changed jobs.
(B) He has two children.
(C) He has two jobs.
(D) He is looking for a job.

From the conversation you learn that Tom has taken an additional job. The best answer to the question "Why is Tom tired?" is (C), "He has two jobs." Therefore, the correct answer is (C).

31. (A) In a movie theater
    (B) In a baseball stadium
    (C) At the man and woman's house
    (D) At a concession stand

32. (A) Corn on the cob
    (B) Four types of oil
    (C) A cooking pot
    (D) A small heater

33. (A) They are not good for you.
    (B) They are cheap.
    (C) They were invented by settlers.
    (D) They need moisture.

34. (A) It's necessary.
    (B) It adds calories.
    (C) It's good for you.
    (D) It tastes terrible.

35. (A) The liquid coats the corn.
    (B) Oil puffs up the corn.
    (C) It makes the kernel explode.
    (D) Moisture expands at the seams.

36. (A) You could eat the corn all day long.
    (B) The corn kernels would burn.
    (C) The kernels will expand from heating.
    (D) The corn would have more kernels.

37. (A) It's many times larger.
    (B) It's comparatively small.
    (C) It's hard to measure.
    (D) It grows steadily.

GO ON TO THE NEXT PAGE. ➡

Part C

DIRECTIONS: In Part C you will hear short lectures and conversations. At the end of each, you will be asked several questions. Each lecture or conversation and each question will be spoken only one time. For this reason, you must listen carefully to understand what each speaker says. After you hear a question, read the four selections and choose the one that is the best answer to the question the speaker asked. Then, on your answer sheet, find the number of the question and blacken the space that corresponds to the letter for the answer you have chosen.

Answer all questions according to what is stated or implied in the lecture or conversation.

Listen to this sample talk.

You will hear:

Now listen to the following example.

You will hear:

You will read:

Sample Answer

Ⓐ ● Ⓒ Ⓓ

(A) By cars and carriages
(B) By bicycles, trains, and carriages
(C) On foot and by boat
(D) On board ships and trains

The best answer to the question "According to the speaker, how did people travel before the invention of the automobile?" is (B), "By bicycles, trains, and carriages." Therefore, the correct answer is (B).

Now listen to another sample question.

(Narrator) Approximately how many people are employed in the automobile service industry?

Sample Answer

Ⓐ Ⓑ ● Ⓓ

You will read:

(A) One million
(B) Ten million
(C) Twelve million
(D) Ninety million

The best answer to the question "Approximately how many people are employed in the automobile service industry?" is (C), "Twelve million." Therefore, the correct answer is (C).

You are not allowed to take notes during the test.

38. (A) Course assignments
    (B) Course policies
    (C) Class participation
    (D) Writing projects

39. (A) By the time the paper is due
    (B) Over a three-day period
    (C) Before the end of the term
    (D) During the week assigned

GO ON TO THE NEXT PAGE. ➡

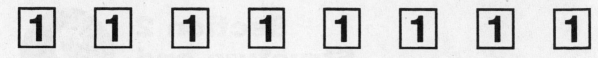

40. (A) Assign more homework
    (B) Take class attendance
    (C) Give a makeup test
    (D) Send in a notice

41. (A) By informing the speaker of the circumstances
    (B) By talking to their advisers about the class
    (C) By handing in assignments
    (D) By taking makeup tests they have missed

42. (A) Special circumstances may arise at any time.
    (B) No reasonable excuse will ever be accepted.
    (C) Assignment grades will be lowered otherwise.
    (D) Urgent matters must be taken care of in any event.

43. (A) The spread of disease
    (B) The flu epidemic
    (C) Flu symptoms
    (D) Disease variations

44. (A) The multiplying of viruses
    (B) Viruses transported by air
    (C) Drops of contaminated water
    (D) The regular breathing of air

45. (A) By adhering to droplets in the air
    (B) Only by tactile contact
    (C) Similarly to viral infections
    (D) Frequently through complications

46. (A) People who have overt flu symptoms
    (B) Humans who seek contact
    (C) Persons who are not self-aware
    (D) All those infected with a virus

47. (A) Product manufacturers
    (B) Opinion researchers
    (C) Restaurant owners
    (D) Commodity traders

48. (A) Time
    (B) Money
    (C) Fast-food restaurants
    (D) Household services

49. (A) Lawns
    (B) Fast-drying paints
    (C) Looks
    (D) Disposable goods

50. (A) To stay healthy
    (B) To improve their appearance
    (C) To become energetic
    (D) To satisfy personal creativity

➤STOP◄

This is the end of Section 1.

Read the directions for Section 2.
Do not read or work on any other section of the test.
Look at the time now before you begin work on Section 2.
Use exactly 25 minutes to work on Section 2.

Section 2
Structure and
Written Expression

2

Time: 25 minutes

This section is designed to test your ability to recognize language structures that are appropriate in standard written English. The questions in this section belong to two types, each of which has special directions.

<u>DIRECTIONS:</u> Questions 1–15 are partial sentences. Below each sentence you will see four words or phrases, marked (A), (B), (C), and (D). Select the one word or phrase that best completes the sentence. Then, on your answer sheet, find the number of the question you have selected. Blacken the space so that the letter inside the circle does not show.

EXAMPLE I

Drying flowers is the best way - - - - - - them.

(A) to preserve
(B) by preserving
(C) preserve
(D) preserved

Sample Answer

● Ⓑ Ⓒ Ⓓ

The sentence should state, "Drying flowers is the best way to preserve them." Therefore, the correct answer is (A).

EXAMPLE II

Many American universities - - - - - - as small, private colleges.

(A) begun
(B) beginning
(C) began
(D) for the beginning

Sample Answer

Ⓐ Ⓑ ● Ⓓ

The sentence should state, "Many American universities began as small, private colleges." Therefore, the correct answer is (C).

After you read the directions, begin work on the questions.

1. Tennessee has about 140 newspapers, - - - - - - 25 are issued daily.

   (A) about which
   (B) of which about
   (C) which are about
   (D) which is about

2. When consumers cannot have everything they want, they have to choose - - - - - - most.

   (A) they want what
   (B) what they want
   (C) they want it
   (D) that they want

GO ON TO THE NEXT PAGE. ➡

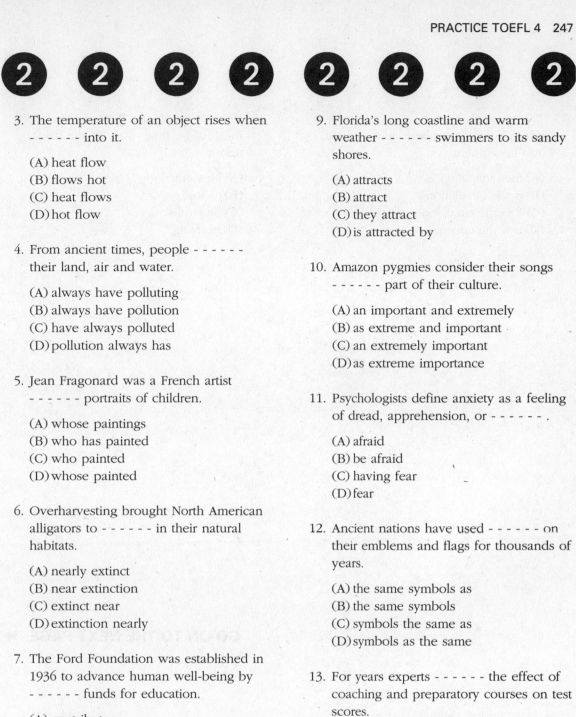

2   2   2   2   2   2   2   2

3. The temperature of an object rises when
   - - - - - - into it.

   (A) heat flow
   (B) flows hot
   (C) heat flows
   (D) hot flow

4. From ancient times, people - - - - - -
   their land, air and water.

   (A) always have polluting
   (B) always have pollution
   (C) have always polluted
   (D) pollution always has

5. Jean Fragonard was a French artist
   - - - - - - portraits of children.

   (A) whose paintings
   (B) who has painted
   (C) who painted
   (D) whose painted

6. Overharvesting brought North American
   alligators to - - - - - - in their natural
   habitats.

   (A) nearly extinct
   (B) near extinction
   (C) extinct near
   (D) extinction nearly

7. The Ford Foundation was established in
   1936 to advance human well-being by
   - - - - - - funds for education.

   (A) contribute
   (B) contribution
   (C) to contribute
   (D) contributing

8. Fireweed received its name because it
   - - - - - - after a forest fire.

   (A) quick growth
   (B) grows quickly
   (C) quickly grown
   (D) growing quickly

9. Florida's long coastline and warm
   weather - - - - - - swimmers to its sandy
   shores.

   (A) attracts
   (B) attract
   (C) they attract
   (D) is attracted by

10. Amazon pygmies consider their songs
    - - - - - - part of their culture.

    (A) an important and extremely
    (B) as extreme and important
    (C) an extremely important
    (D) as extreme importance

11. Psychologists define anxiety as a feeling
    of dread, apprehension, or - - - - - - .

    (A) afraid
    (B) be afraid
    (C) having fear
    (D) fear

12. Ancient nations have used - - - - - - on
    their emblems and flags for thousands of
    years.

    (A) the same symbols as
    (B) the same symbols
    (C) symbols the same as
    (D) symbols as the same

13. For years experts - - - - - - the effect of
    coaching and preparatory courses on test
    scores.

    (A) are examining
    (B) had been examined
    (C) have been examining
    (D) having been examined

GO ON TO THE NEXT PAGE. ➡

14. The nitrogen cycle - - - - - - of nitrogen through the atmosphere, hydrosphere, and lithosphere.

    (A) the circulation is
    (B) is the circulation
    (C) it is the circulation
    (D) is it the circulation

15. While working as a clerk, Edison spent much of his time - - - - - - the stock ticker.

    (A) he studied
    (B) to study
    (C) on study
    (D) studying

GO ON TO THE NEXT PAGE. ➡

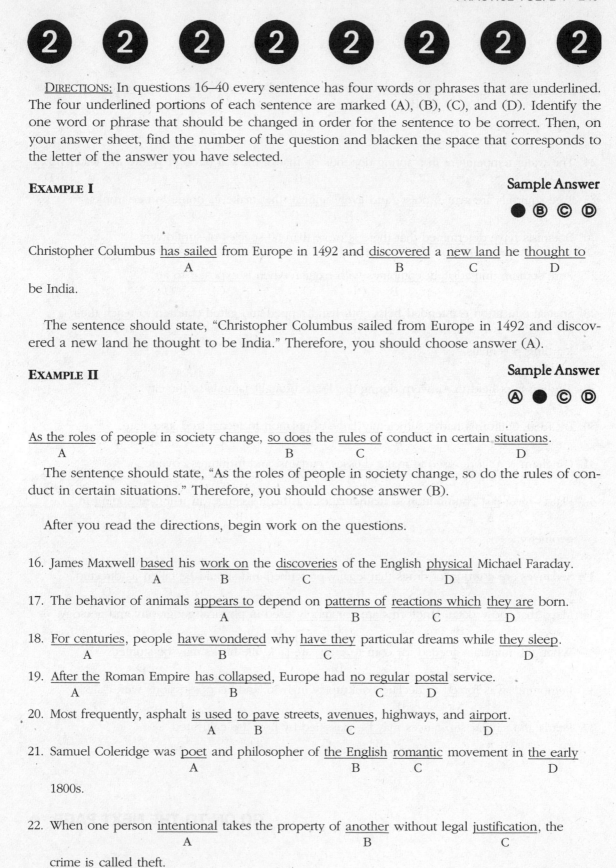

② ② ② ② ② ② ② ②

<u>DIRECTIONS:</u> In questions 16–40 every sentence has four words or phrases that are underlined. The four underlined portions of each sentence are marked (A), (B), (C), and (D). Identify the one word or phrase that should be changed in order for the sentence to be correct. Then, on your answer sheet, find the number of the question and blacken the space that corresponds to the letter of the answer you have selected.

EXAMPLE I

Sample Answer

● Ⓑ Ⓒ Ⓓ

Christopher Columbus <u>has sailed</u> from Europe in 1492 and <u>discovered</u> a <u>new land</u> he <u>thought to</u>
                                  A   B   C   D
be India.

The sentence should state, "Christopher Columbus sailed from Europe in 1492 and discovered a new land he thought to be India." Therefore, you should choose answer (A).

EXAMPLE II

Sample Answer

Ⓐ ● Ⓒ Ⓓ

<u>As the roles</u> of people in society change, <u>so does</u> the <u>rules of</u> conduct in certain <u>situations</u>.
      A   B   C   D

The sentence should state, "As the roles of people in society change, so do the rules of conduct in certain situations." Therefore, you should choose answer (B).

After you read the directions, begin work on the questions.

16. James Maxwell <u>based</u> his <u>work on</u> the <u>discoveries</u> of the English <u>physical</u> Michael Faraday.
                            A   B   C   D

17. The behavior of animals <u>appears to</u> depend on <u>patterns of</u> <u>reactions which</u> <u>they are</u> born.
                                          A   B   C   D

18. <u>For centuries</u>, people <u>have wondered</u> why <u>have they</u> particular dreams while <u>they sleep</u>.
         A   B   C   D

19. <u>After the</u> Roman Empire <u>has collapsed</u>, Europe had <u>no regular</u> <u>postal</u> service.
         A   B   C   D

20. Most frequently, asphalt <u>is used</u> <u>to pave</u> streets, <u>avenues</u>, highways, and <u>airport</u>.
                                          A   B   C   D

21. Samuel Coleridge was <u>poet</u> and philosopher of <u>the English</u> <u>romantic</u> movement in <u>the early</u>
                                      A   B   C   D
1800s.

22. When one person <u>intentional</u> takes the property of <u>another</u> without legal <u>justification</u>, the
                                A   B   C
crime is <u>called</u> theft.
                D

GO ON TO THE NEXT PAGE. ➡

2   2   2   2   2   2   2   2

23. <u>Computers</u> programs, <u>catalogues</u>, directories, and <u>collections</u> of data are <u>protected</u> by
    A   B   C   D

    copyright laws.

24. The water temperature in <u>a spring</u> depends <u>on that</u> of the soil through <u>where</u> the water <u>flows</u>.
                        A   B   C   D

25. Tree squirrels are active, <u>noisy</u>, and <u>lively</u> <u>animals that</u> make <u>its home</u> in tree trunks.
                     A   B   C   D

26. Botanists <u>have determined</u> that <u>there is</u> more than 60 <u>species</u> of <u>sunflowers</u>.
                A   B   C   D

27. Pure sodium <u>immediately</u> <u>combines</u> with oxygen when <u>is exposed</u> to <u>air</u>.
                A   B   C   D

28. Special education is intended <u>help</u> <u>both</u> handicapped and gifted children to <u>reach</u> their
                                 A B   C

    <u>learning</u> potentials.
     D

29. <u>Trading</u> fairs <u>held</u> in Antwerp during the 1300s <u>brought</u> <u>famous</u> to the city.
     A   B   C   D

30. By 1850, California had <u>a sufficiently</u> <u>large population</u> <u>to recognized</u> <u>as a state</u>.
                      A   B   C   D

31. Gingham is <u>a fabric</u> used to make <u>dresses</u>, <u>curtains</u>, and <u>furnitures</u> covers.
             A   B   C   D

32. Plato's most <u>last</u> contribution to mathematics was his <u>insistence</u> on <u>using</u> <u>reasoning</u> in
            A   B   C   D

    geometry.

33. Sedatives are <u>a group</u> of drugs <u>that legally</u> prescribed and should <u>be taken</u> <u>as directed</u>.
                A   B   C   D

34. Maps <u>that show</u> <u>detail</u> landforms <u>are commonly</u> <u>used</u> in physical geography and geology.
         A   B   C   D

35. When the minerals <u>needed for</u> corn <u>to grow</u> <u>are lack</u>, the husks may <u>be stunted</u>.
                     A   B   C   D

36. Rembrandt was <u>forced</u> to <u>declare</u> bankruptcy in 1656, and his <u>possessions</u> were <u>sale</u>.
               A   B   C   D

37. Pearls and <u>similar</u> substances <u>may be</u> <u>classified</u> by <u>how are</u> cultivated.
              A   B   C   D

GO ON TO THE NEXT PAGE. ➡

38. During <u>winter</u>, grizzly bears <u>live in</u> dens, caves or <u>the other</u> natural <u>shelters</u>.
            A   B   C   D

39. The neck of a <u>classical</u> guitar is <u>wider</u> than <u>those</u> of a steel-<u>string</u> guitar.
                  A   B   C   D

40. <u>Insufficient</u> oxygen causes lactic acid to <u>built up</u> in the <u>muscles</u> of long-<u>distance</u> runners.
    A   B   C   D

►STOP◄

This is the end of Section 2.

Read the directions for Section 3.
Do not read or work on any other section of the test.
Look at the time now before you begin work on Section 3.
Use exactly 55 minutes to work on Section 3.

Section 3
Reading Comprehension

Time: 55 minutes

This section is designed to measure your reading comprehension of standard written English. The questions in this section belong to two types, each of which has special directions.

<u>DIRECTIONS</u>: In this section you will read several passages. Each is followed by questions about it. For questions 1–50, you need to select the one best answer, (A), (B), (C), or (D), to each question. Then, on your answer sheet, find the number of the question and blacken the space that corresponds to the letter of the answer you have selected. Fill in the space completely.

Answer all questions following a passage on the basis of what is stated or implied in the passage.

Read the following passage:

> A tomahawk is a small ax used as a tool and a weapon by the North American Indian tribes. An average tomahawk was not very long and did not weigh a great deal. Originally, the head of the tomahawk was made of a shaped stone or an animal bone and was mounted on
> *Line* a wooden handle. After the arrival of the European settlers, the Indians began to use toma-
> *(5)* hawks with iron heads. Indian males and females of all ages used tomahawks to chop and cut wood, pound stakes into the ground to put up wigwams, and do many other chores. Indian warriors relied on tomahawks as weapons and even threw them at their enemies. Some types of tomahawks were used in religious ceremonies. Contemporary American idioms reflect this aspect of American heritage.

EXAMPLE I

Early tomahawk heads were made of

Sample Answer

● Ⓑ Ⓒ Ⓓ

(A) stone or bone
(B) wood or sticks
(C) European iron
(D) religious weapons

According to the passage, early tomahawk heads were made of stone or bone. Therefore, the correct answer is (A).

EXAMPLE II

How has the Indian use of tomahawks affected American daily life today?

Sample Answer

Ⓐ Ⓑ ● Ⓓ

(A) Tomahawks are still used as weapons.
(B) Tomahawks are used as tools for certain jobs.
(C) Contemporary language refers to tomahawks.
(D) Indian tribes cherish them as heirlooms.

The passage states, "Contemporary American idioms reflect this aspect of American heritage." The correct answer is (C).

After you read the directions, begin work on the questions.

GO ON TO THE NEXT PAGE. ➡

Questions 1–10

During the Middle Ages, societies were based on military relationships, as landowners formed their own foot armies into which they drafted their tenants and hired hands. The infantry that fought its way forward against the opposition engaged in heavy ground battles
Line that proved costly in the ratio of losses to wins. These soldiers carried darts, javelins, and
(5) slings to be used before closing ranks with the enemy, although their swords and halberds delivered crushing blows on contact. Such armed forces were active for limited periods of time and had a predominantly defensive function, displayed in hand-to-hand combat.

Because this sporadic and untrained organization was ineffective, the ruling classes began to hire mercenaries who were generously compensated for their tasks and subject to con-
(10) tractual terms of agreement. The greatest idiosyncrasy of a hired military force was that the troops sometimes deserted their employers if they could bank on a higher remuneration from the opposition. The Swiss pikemen became the best-known mercenaries of the late Middle Ages. In the 1300s, they practically invented a crude body armor of leather and quilted layered head gear with nose and skull plates, ornamented with crests. Their tower
(15) shields proved indispensable against a shower of arrows, and their helmets progressed from cone cups to visors hinged at the temples. As their notoriety increased, so did their wages, and eventually they were rounded into military companies that later grew into the basic units in almost all armies. During the same period, the first full-size army of professional soldiers emerged in the Ottoman Empire. What set these troops apart from other contempo-
(20) rary armies was that these soldiers remained on duty in peacetime.

Companies of mercenaries were employed on a permanent basis in 1445, when King Charles VII created a regular military organization, complete with a designated hierarchy. Gunpowder accelerated the emergence of military tactics and strategy that ultimately affected the conceptualization of war on a broad scale. Cannons further widened the gap be-
(25) tween the attacking and the defending lineups, and undermined the exclusivity of contact battles.

1. What is the main purpose of the passage?

   (A) To distinguish between laborers and mercenaries
   (B) To change the existing view of the military
   (C) To cite examples of armor in the Middle Ages
   (D) To trace the origins of military organization

2. In line 4, the word "ratio" is closest in meaning to

   (A) quota
   (B) reason
   (C) proportion
   (D) pace

3. Which of the following statements can be inferred from the first paragraph?

   (A) Temporary armies of farmers were not well trained.
   (B) Drafting farmers into armies was costly.
   (C) Heavy ground battles were won during combat.
   (D) Infantry was directed to the opposition for support.

4. In line 8, the word "sporadic" is closest in meaning to

   (A) spirited
   (B) splendid
   (C) irreverent
   (D) irregular

GO ON TO THE NEXT PAGE. ➡

5. Which of the following statements about the Swiss pikemen is supported by the passage?

   (A) Their weapons and skills were ahead of their time.
   (B) Their gear ensured their fame as well-dressed soldiers.
   (C) The demand for their cavalry made them the best-paid army.
   (D) Their weapons were issued to nonprofessionals as well.

6. Where in the passage does the author state the reasons for the emergence of professional armies?

   (A) Lines 1–4
   (B) Lines 8–10
   (C) Lines 12–14
   (D) Lines 15–18

7. The author of the passage implies that the soldiers in mercenary armies were

   (A) not loyal
   (B) not effective
   (C) well guarded
   (D) well rounded

8. In line 19, the phrase "these troops" refers to

   (A) the Swiss pikemen
   (B) military companies
   (C) almost all armies
   (D) Ottoman soldiers

9. According to the passage, the first army of professionals was mobilized

   (A) only in peacetime
   (B) only in wartime
   (C) in times of anticipated war
   (D) both during war and during peace

10. In line 25, the word "undermined" is closest in meaning to

   (A) underestimated
   (B) reduced
   (C) undersized
   (D) shred

GO ON TO THE NEXT PAGE. ➡

Questions 11–18

Observations of nature gained a foothold in art in the 1860s and 1870s when painters interested in science attempted to analyze the effects of light on color by means of physics. If the goal of impressionist painters was to copy the visual qualities of sunlight at different an-
Line gles, they needed to reproduce light as it appears to the spectator when reflected from the
(5) surfaces of structures. In painting, the effects of shade were conveyed by using small strokes to minimize breaks between hues. The so-called divided color method appeared to grasp a shimmering reflection of shadows when minimal portions of primary-color paints were applied directly to the canvas, instead of being blended on the palette.

Edouard Manet departed from the fairy-tale style of painting with its tacit symbolism
(10) and centered his compositions around the visual reality of ordinary objects. Mary Cassatt followed with her spontaneous and subtle portraits of children, and Edgar Degas depicted ballet dancers in their artful poses and the color schemes of their costumes in soft colors.

Postimpressionism built on the techniques developed by impressionists and supplemented it with keen insight into other dimensions of objects and scenes. Paul Gaugin chose
(15) to disregard the classical conventions of composition, the application of color, and the shaping of form and imitated primitivist art that upheld the beauty of native drawings in Tahiti. Henri Matisse created a unique style of poster graphics, deceptively simplistic in its rhythm and texture. In his view, paintings were intended to brighten and improve reality, not copy it. He noted that photography can accomplish this latter goal just as well, or even better.

11. This passage probably comes from a longer work on

(A) science and the fine arts
(B) great masters of impressionist painting
(C) light in the paintings of the 1800s
(D) new techniques in the art of the 1800s

12. The author of the passage implies that the goal of the impressionists was to

(A) reproduce light and shadow exactly as they appeared
(B) depict light as it appeared on different surfaces
(C) copy the pattern of sun rays at different angles
(D) reflect light and shadow from surfaces of structures

13. In line 7, the word "shimmering" is closest in meaning to

(A) gleaming
(B) strong
(C) trembling
(D) spotless

14. In line 8, the word "blended" is closest in meaning to

(A) replenished
(B) placed
(C) rendered
(D) mixed

15. What technique did painters employ to represent light as it appeared to the artist?

(A) They used as little paint as was necessary.
(B) They graded the shades of color in hues.
(C) Their paint colors were dark and muted.
(D) Their brush strokes were slow and cautious.

GO ON TO THE NEXT PAGE. ➡

16. It is implied in the passage that in the late 1800s artists painted

    (A) fantastic images and swirling action
    (B) luxurious ornaments and shapely figures
    (C) unusual textures and luscious colors
    (D) ordinary objects in varied intensities of light

17. It can be inferred from the passage that postimpressionism

    (A) developed into a trend parallel to impressionism
    (B) followed impressionism in the development of technique
    (C) flourished independently of impressionism
    (D) negated impressionist insight into objects and scenes

18. According to the passage, Matisse saw the purpose of his art as

    (A) depicting life realistically
    (B) enhancing life and reality
    (C) showing life through photography
    (D) imparting rhythm to drawings

GO ON TO THE NEXT PAGE. ➡

Questions 19–30

The symptoms of hay fever include watery and itchy eyes and a runny, congested nose. People suffering from hay fever may experience occasional wheezing and repeated bouts of sneezing and may even lose their sense of smell. Some victims of hay fever may also have
Line stopped-up ears. About 30 percent of those who suffer from hay fever may develop the symp-
(5) toms associated with periodic asthma or a sinus infection. The allergen-antibody theory does not fully explain allergic reactions because the membranes and glands in eyes and ears are controlled by the independent nervous system, which keeps these organs in balance. But the independent nervous system itself is part of the emotional-response center and may cause the feelings of anger, fear, resentment, and lack of self-confidence in reaction to al-
(10) lergy-causing substances.

The most common cause of hay fever is the pollen of ragweed, which blossoms during the summer and autumn. When airborne pollen particles, as well as mold, come into contact with the victim's membranes, they can cause allergic reactions that release histamine and re-sult in a virtual blockage of air passages. To prevent hay fever or to decrease the severity of its
(15) symptoms, contact with the ragweed pollen should be reduced. Although some communi-ties have attempted to eliminate the plants that cause the reactions, elimination programs have not been successful because airborne pollen can travel considerable distances. Antihis-tamine can help with short but severe attacks. Over extended periods of time, however, pa-tients are prescribed a series of injections of the substance to which they are sensitive in order
(20) to increase immunity and thus be relieved of the seasonal allergy.

19. It can be inferred from the passage that the phrase "hay fever" refers to

(A) fodder for cattle
(B) a seasonal discomfort
(C) viral bacteria
(D) a lung disease

20. According to the passage, the symptoms of the allergy are predominantly

(A) abdominal
(B) intestinal
(C) respiratory
(D) chronic

21. What can be inferred from the first paragraph?

(A) Hay fever may cause severe allergic reactions and even death.
(B) The cause of allergic reactions has not been determined.
(C) The nervous system balances allergic reactions.
(D) People should not have an emotional response to allergic reactions.

22. According to the passage, patients suffering from hay fever may also experience

(A) hunger pains
(B) mood swings
(C) nervous blockages
(D) sensory perceptions

23. In line 9, the word "resentment" is closest in meaning to

(A) reprieve
(B) reprisal
(C) acrimony
(D) grief

24. It can be inferred from the passage that a frequent source of allergy-causing irritants can be

(A) organic matter
(B) larynx infections
(C) human contact
(D) ear membranes

GO ON TO THE NEXT PAGE. ➡

25. According to the passage, the irritants are transported by

(A) wind
(B) food
(C) travelers
(D) air passages

26. In line 14, the word "blockage" is closest in meaning to

(A) obstruction
(B) bleeding
(C) enlargement
(D) dryness

27. According to the passage, to avoid incidents of hay fever, patients need to

(A) avoid interactions with other patients
(B) avoid exposure to pollen
(C) increase their self-confidence
(D) take doses of prescribed medicine

28. Which of the following is *not* mentioned in the passage as a cause of allergies?

(A) pollen
(B) mold
(C) flowers
(D) injections

29. It can be inferred from the passage that hay fever

(A) has no effective antibodies
(B) has no known cure
(C) is rooted in the human psyche
(D) can be likened to a breakdown

30. A paragraph following this passage would most probably discuss

(A) how the nervous system alerts patients
(B) how the immune system reacts to allergens
(C) what other diseases can be relieved by vaccines
(D) what flowers are harmless to hay fever patients

GO ON TO THE NEXT PAGE. ➡

Questions 31-40

Prehistoric horses were far removed from the horses that Christopher Columbus brought on his ships during his second voyage to the New World. Although fossil remains of "dawn horses" have been excavated in several sites in Wyoming and New Mexico, these animals,
Line which were biologically different from contemporary horses, had become extinct millennia
(5) before the onset of the Indian era. Although moviegoers visualize an Indian as a horse rider, Indians were not familiar with horses until the Spanish brought them to Mexico, New Mexico, Florida, and the West Indies in 1519. Those that escaped from the conquerors or were left behind became the ancestors of the wild horses that still roam the southwestern regions of the country. The Indian tribes scattered in the western plains began to breed horses about
(10) 1600.

The arrival of the horse produced a ripple effect throughout the Great Plains as the Indians living there were not nomadic and were engaged in rudimentary farming and grazeland hunting. Tracking stampeding herds of buffalo and elk on foot was not the best way to stock quantities of meat to adequately feed the entire tribe during the winter. However,
(15) mounted on horses, the hunting teams could cover ground within a substantial distance from their camps and transport their game back to be roasted, dried into jerky, or smoked for preservation. The hunters responsible for tribe provisions stayed on the move almost continuously, replacing their earth-and-sod lodges with tepees. Horses carried not only their riders but also their possessions and booty. The Blackfoot Indians of the Canadian plains
(20) turned almost exclusively hunters, and the Crow split off from the mainstream Indian farming in favor of hunting. In fact, some of the Apache splinter groups abandoned agricultural cultivation altogether.

The horse also drastically altered Indian warfare by allowing rapid maneuvering before, during, and after skirmishes. With the advent of the horse, the Apache, Arapahoe, and
(25) Cheyenne established themselves as a territorial monopoly in the Plains. Because Indians did not have the wheel and had dragged their belongings from one settlement to another, horses also enabled them to become more mobile and expedient during tribal migrations. In fact, the Cheyenne abolished the custom of discarding belongings and tepee skins simply because there were no means to transport them.

31. In line 3, the word "excavated" is closest in meaning to

(A) exasperated
(B) extinguished
(C) hunted down
(D) dug up

32. According to the passage, how many genetic species of horses are known today?

(A) One
(B) Two
(C) Three
(D) Four

33. In line 7, the word "those" refers to

(A) West Indies
(B) The Spanish
(C) horses
(D) Indians

34. According to the passage, American Indians

(A) tamed horses in the early 1500s
(B) farmed with horses in the 1500s
(C) were exposed to horses in the 1500s
(D) have ridden horses since prehistoric times

GO ON TO THE NEXT PAGE. ➡

35. The author of the passage probably believes that the popular image of American Indians before the arrival of Europeans

(A) is not theoretically viable
(B) cannot be realistically described
(C) cannot be discussed briefly
(D) is not historically accurate

36. According to the passage, after the arrival of Europeans, the Indian tribes inhabiting the Great Plains

(A) herded undomesticated buffalo
(B) played complicated hunting games
(C) had sedentary and tranquil life-styles
(D) improved their hunting techniques

37. In line 17, the word "provisions" is closest in meaning to

(A) supplies
(B) health
(C) weapons
(D) attire

38. According to the passage, American Indians invented various methods for

(A) dislocating their traps
(B) communicating over great distances
(C) conducting their hostile excursions
(D) keeping their possessions

39. It can be inferred from the passage that Indians did NOT

(A) accrue tribal wealth
(B) assign sustenance tasks
(C) pursue stampedes
(D) use covered wagons

40. It can be inferred from the passage that the arrival of horses in the Americas

(A) led to the dispersal of Indian tribes throughout the continent
(B) made Indian tribes relinquish their territorial monopolies
(C) altered the future course of the Indian way of life
(D) shattered the advancement of the Indian culture

GO ON TO THE NEXT PAGE. ➡

Questions 41–50

Lighthouses and lightships employ signal lights and foghorns to warn boaters of shoals and of oncoming foul weather. In recreational marinas, Coast Guard stations and yacht clubs inform boaters of weather and water conditions with storm flag signals displayed dur-
Line ing the daytime. Amateur boaters are required to acquaint themselves with the signals that
(5) can make them aware of oncoming storms and small craft advisories. Boaters who can recognize an approaching storm when no warnings are posted have the advantage of time when heading for shelter. Compasses and marine charts identify the locations of anchored whistles and floating buoys that have battery-powered lights, bells, or horns to sound or show warnings with the onset of high winds. On the marine charts, radio beacons and flashing buoys
(10) are assigned numbers that help navigators to identify their locations and to mark the edges of channels, underwater obstructions, reefs, and wrecks.

In each section of the coastline, lighthouses emit characteristic lights, published in light lists, so that mariners can zero in on their bearings by observing the beam pattern and consulting the list. "Making lights" signal approaching vessels to make land, and "leading
(15) lights" guide navigators into bays and harbors along navigable waterways.

The lighthouse tower, constructed on solid rock and pneumatic caissons, contains lighting mechanisms, engines, and spare parts, as well as the keeper's quarters. Saucerlike Fresnel lenses with pentagonal prisms project light at irregular, alternating intervals, while sealed-beam lenses rotate at varying speeds, similarly to the traditional long-range search
(20) light. The older, barrel-shaped lenses and kerosene-burning lamps, made up of prisms and glass panels attached to a metal frame, have been replaced by acetylene gas burners and incandescent lamps that can be operated either manually or automatically and that shut off at daybreak.

41. What is the best title for the passage?

   (A) The Function of Naval Signals and Buoys
   (B) Marine Installations for Boaters' Safety
   (C) Lighthouses and Maritime Signaling Devices
   (D) Lighthouses and Occulting Instrumentation

42. According to the passage, what is the purpose of lighthouses?

   (A) To measure weather and water conditions
   (B) To lead navigators to their destination
   (C) To flag down oncoming vessels
   (D) To display light-coded messages

43. According to the passage, buoys can be best described as

   (A) hanging constructions
   (B) electrical horns
   (C) floating devices
   (D) underwater anchors

44. Why do recreational mariners need to be familiar with the Coast Guard signaling system?

   (A) To learn navigation and rowing
   (B) To chart the course of storms
   (C) To learn about oncoming storms
   (D) To overtake rivals in boating races

45. In line 6, the phrase "the advantage of time" means most nearly

   (A) an early warning
   (B) a stable bearing
   (C) a timed landing
   (D) a timely arrival

GO ON TO THE NEXT PAGE. ➡

46. The author of the passage implies that flashing lights from lighthouses function as

    (A) a characteristic marine elevation
    (B) beams with a constant rotating speed
    (C) an indication of the lens thickness
    (D) an identification of its location

47. According to the passage, lighthouses can assist navigators in

    (A) identifying underwater obstructions
    (B) preparing their boats for advisories
    (C) finding their positions in the open sea
    (D) ignoring their charts of inland channels

48. In line 13, the phrase "zero in on" is closest in meaning to

    (A) cast about for
    (B) disguise
    (C) pinpoint
    (D) point out

49. In line 15, the word "navigable" is closest in meaning to

    (A) nauseating
    (B) passable
    (C) pernicious
    (D) calamitous

50. What can be inferred from the last paragraph?

    (A) Lighthouses do not contain a living space for maintenance personnel.
    (B) Lighthouse beams are projected intermittently during nighttime.
    (C) Technological expertise is expected of the lighthouse maintenance personnel.
    (D) Lighthouse technology is outdated and should have been replaced.

Practice TOEFL 5

Section 1
Listening Comprehension

In this section, you will demonstrate your skills in understanding spoken English. There are three parts in the Listening Comprehension section, with different tasks in each.

Part A

DIRECTIONS: In Part A you will hear short conversations between two speakers. At the end of each conversation, a third speaker will ask a question about what the first two speakers said. Each conversation and each question will be spoken only one time. Therefore, you must listen carefully to understand what each speaker says. After you hear a conversation and the question, read the four selections and choose the <u>one</u> that is the best answer to the question the speaker asked. Then, on your answer sheet, find the number of the question and blacken the space that corresponds to the letter for the answer you have chosen. Blacken the space completely so that the letter inside the space does not show.

Listen to the following example.

On the recording, you hear:

Sample Answer
Ⓐ Ⓑ Ⓒ ●

(Man)   Does the car need to be filled?
(Woman)   Mary stopped at the gas station on her way home.
(Narrator) What does the woman mean?

In your test book, you will read:

(A) Mary bought some food.
(B) Mary had car trouble.
(C) Mary went shopping.
(D) Mary bought some gas.

From the conversation you learn that Mary stopped at the gas station on her way home. The best answer to the question "Does the car need to be filled?" is (D), "Mary bought some gas." Therefore, the correct answer is (D).

Now let us begin Part A with question number 1.

1. (A) They gave me a lift.
   (B) He didn't stand close to the door.
   (C) He walked through the door on the left.
   (D) The door was left open.

2. (A) Rich students don't take math.
   (B) Rich didn't know much math.
   (C) Rich is taking a math course.
   (D) Rich should take math next year.

GO ON TO THE NEXT PAGE. ➡

3. (A) They wanted to know if they could buy the picture.
   (B) They were wandering around looking for a picture.
   (C) They stopped by the picture gallery to ask questions.
   (D) They thought that the picture was wonderful.

4. (A) He spent 15 minutes reading.
   (B) He talked for 50 minutes.
   (C) He found the magazine.
   (D) He enjoyed the article.

5. (A) He's looking for a new apartment.
   (B) He decided to buy a new car.
   (C) He doesn't have the figures.
   (D) His apartment is better than hers.

6. (A) The police stop most drivers.
   (B) The speed limit is unreasonable.
   (C) Drivers don't watch the traffic carefully.
   (D) Few people drive within the speed limit.

7. (A) Pink looks great on you.
   (B) Black is out of style.
   (C) The fashion changes every year.
   (D) I don't know the date of the fashion show.

8. (A) The banks are open at this hour.
   (B) The river is overflowing its banks.
   (C) Their bank is located nearby.
   (D) The banks close too early.

9. (A) The teacher taught about dreams.
   (B) The students are required to take the course.
   (C) The lecture on dreams was a great success.
   (D) Hardly anyone was listening to the teacher.

10. (A) They haven't had much luck with the weather.
    (B) The door was locked because of severe weather.
    (C) She's not sure if the door is locked.
    (D) She can't remember where the key to the door is.

11. (A) She gave away my half.
    (B) She is a half hour late.
    (C) She is very angry.
    (D) She is very hungry.

12. (A) It's easy to get along with Paul.
    (B) Paul was not feeling well.
    (C) She is sorry that Paul is ill.
    (D) Paul was uncomfortable.

13. (A) They showed us the back entrance.
    (B) When they return, the show will have started.
    (C) They don't know what time the show starts.
    (D) When they came back, there was no time left.

14. (A) She doesn't need any help.
    (B) She has two people helping her.
    (C) She's had enough.
    (D) The man is very kind.

15. (A) There is no light in number 8.
    (B) Smoking in the lounge is prohibited.
    (C) The management doesn't allow complaints.
    (D) The conversation in the lounge is too loud.

16. (A) Six copies were made last week.
    (B) The copier doesn't work well.
    (C) Eleven copies is plenty.
    (D) There are 11 jars of jam.

GO ON TO THE NEXT PAGE. ➡

17. (A) The club has stopped serving the Johnsons.
    (B) If the Johnsons want to, they can serve themselves.
    (C) The Johnsons think the service is bad.
    (D) The Johnsons are going to the club.

18. (A) The new paint makes the house look clean.
    (B) They worked for three days.
    (C) They ran out of paint on the second day.
    (D) They were in pain for two days.

19. (A) There are more students in the first class than in the second.
    (B) First class mail delivery is better than second.
    (C) First class postage is more expensive than second class.
    (D) The packaging comes in two prices, first and second.

20. (A) Mike didn't sleep well.
    (B) Mike slipped last night.
    (C) The car is parked for the night.
    (D) The neighbor has a white dog.

21. (A) In a taxi
    (B) In a hotel
    (C) Downstairs
    (D) Downtown

22. (A) The snow will stop soon.
    (B) The man is wrong about the situation.
    (C) The man is happy.
    (D) A call isn't necessary.

23. (A) Make up her mind
    (B) Take the man to work
    (C) Go to school
    (D) Do the right thing

24. (A) He doesn't like the company.
    (B) He has ordered some books.
    (C) He is a businessman.
    (D) He is selfish.

25. (A) A picture
    (B) A brochure
    (C) A letter
    (D) A flier

26. (A) Joe is not French.
    (B) Joe is going the wrong way.
    (C) Joe has passed his exam.
    (D) Joe will probably fail.

27. (A) Room 217
    (B) Room 17
    (C) The conference room
    (D) The meeting room

28. (A) They don't sell milk at the store.
    (B) They already have enough milk.
    (C) It's their breakfast.
    (D) It's too late to go out.

29. (A) The woman
    (B) A bakery
    (C) The woman's husband
    (D) The woman's mother

30. (A) The Stevensons have a lot of money.
    (B) The Stevensons will have to make many arrangements.
    (C) Will they go by boat or by plane?
    (D) The Stevensons don't appear to be rich.

GO ON TO THE NEXT PAGE. ➡

Part B

DIRECTIONS: In this part of the test, you will hear longer conversations. After each conversation, you will hear several questions. The conversations and questions will not be repeated.

After you hear a question, read the four possible answers in your test book and choose the best answer. Then, on your answer sheet, find the number of the question and fill in the space that corresponds to the letter of the answer you have chosen. Remember, you are not allowed to take notes or write in your test book.

Listen to the following example:

You will hear:

You will read:

Sample Answer

Ⓐ Ⓑ ● Ⓓ

(A) He has changed jobs.
(B) He has two children.
(C) He has two jobs.
(D) He is looking for a job.

From the conversation you learn that Tom has taken an additional job. The best answer to the question "Why is Tom tired?" is (C), "He has two jobs." Therefore, the correct answer is (C).

31. (A) Leaves
    (B) Cloth
    (C) Skins
    (D) Fibers

32. (A) Elegant
    (B) Functional
    (C) Pretentious
    (D) Sturdy

33. (A) 100 years
    (B) 300 years
    (C) 600 years
    (D) 1600 years

34. (A) Leather has become cheaper.
    (B) Computers have come down in price.
    (C) Shoes are made by machines.
    (D) The cost of labor has declined.

35. (A) In an airport
    (B) In a bus depot
    (C) At a wedding
    (D) On a school campus

36. (A) To Baltimore
    (B) To Philadelphia
    (C) To Chicago
    (D) To New York

37. (A) While visiting their children in college
    (B) While the man was attending a convention
    (C) When they went to college together
    (D) When the woman was in high school

38. (A) One
    (B) Two
    (C) Three
    (D) Four

GO ON TO THE NEXT PAGE. ➡

Part C

<u>DIRECTIONS</u>: In Part C you will hear short lectures and conversations. At the end of each, you will be asked several questions. Each lecture or conversation and each question will be spoken only one time. For this reason, you must listen carefully to understand what each speaker says. After you hear a question, read the four selections and choose the one that is the best answer to the question the speaker asked. Then, on your answer sheet, find the number of the question and blacken the space that corresponds to the letter for the answer you have chosen.

Answer all questions according to what is stated or implied in the lecture or conversation.

Listen to this sample talk.
You will hear:

Now listen to the following example.

You will hear:

You will read:

Sample Answer

Ⓐ ● Ⓒ Ⓓ

(A) By cars and carriages
(B) By bicycles, trains, and carriages
(C) On foot and by boat
(D) On board ships and trains

The best answer to the question "According to the speaker, how did people travel before the invention of the automobile?" is (B), "By bicycles, trains, and carriages." Therefore, the correct answer is (B).

Now listen to another sample question.

(Narrator)   Approximately how many people are employed in the automobile service industry?

Sample Answer

Ⓐ Ⓑ ● Ⓓ

You will read:

(A) One million
(B) Ten million
(C) Twelve million
(D) Ninety million

The best answer to the question "Approximately how many people are employed in the automobile service industry?" is (C), "Twelve million." Therefore, the correct answer is (C).

You are not allowed to make notes during the test.

39. (A) How thrilling police work can be
    (B) Why police work is enlightening
    (C) That police work has its mundane aspects
    (D) That serving on the police force is difficult

40. (A) As full of risk and adventure
    (B) As straightforward but demanding
    (C) As routine but necessary
    (D) As guaranteed employment

GO ON TO THE NEXT PAGE. ➡

41. (A) Directing traffic
    (B) Enforcing speed laws
    (C) Patrolling streets
    (D) Resolving disputes

42. (A) Changing tires for motorists
    (B) Verifying vehicle licenses
    (C) Walking the beat on city streets
    (D) Producing reports and correspondence

43. (A) It's physically exhausting.
    (B) It's ineffectual.
    (C) It can be boring.
    (D) It may be exhilarating.

44. (A) The first American government
    (B) Writing in the early colonial times
    (C) Population mobility in the colonial times
    (D) The establishment of first libraries

45. (A) To describe their new lives
    (B) To produce literary volumes
    (C) To conquer wilderness
    (D) To improve their writing skills

46. (A) To gain insight and understanding
    (B) To help shape them into novels
    (C) To make them a part of legal institutions
    (D) To develop American national character

47. (A) Jamestown colony
    (B) Virginia Company
    (C) English tailors
    (D) Religious organizations

48. (A) In Virginia
    (B) In Pennsylvania
    (C) In Boston Bay
    (D) In Middle Colonies

49. (A) Philadelphia
    (B) London
    (C) Jamestown
    (D) Salem

50. (A) Chronicles
    (B) Observations and essays
    (C) Government documents
    (D) Novels and poetry

►STOP◄

This is the end of Section 1.

Read the directions for Section 2.
Do not read or work on any other section of the test.
Look at the time now before you begin work on Section 2.
Use exactly 25 minutes to work on Section 2.

Section 2
Structure and
Written Expression

2

Time: 25 minutes

This section is designed to test your ability to recognize language structures that are appropriate in standard written English. The questions in this section belong to two types, each of which has special directions.

DIRECTIONS: Questions 1–15 are partial sentences. Below each sentence you will see four words or phrases, marked (A), (B), (C), and (D). Select the one word or phrase that best completes the sentence. Then, on your answer sheet, find the number of the question you have selected. Blacken the space so that the letter inside the oval does not show.

Example I

Drying flowers is the best way - - - - - - them.

(A) to preserve
(B) by preserving
(C) preserve
(D) preserved

Sample Answer

● Ⓑ Ⓒ Ⓓ

The sentence should state, "Drying flowers is the best way to preserve them." Therefore, the correct answer is (A).

Example II

Many American universities - - - - - - as small, private colleges.

(A) begun
(B) beginning
(C) began
(D) for the beginning

Sample Answer

Ⓐ Ⓑ ● Ⓓ

The sentence should state, "Many American universities began as small, private colleges." Therefore, the correct answer is (C).

After you read the directions, begin work on the questions.

1. The Boston Public Library, - - - - - - 1854, was the first library to be financed by donations and proceeds from raffles.

   (A) found it in
   (B) founded in
   (C) was founded in
   (D) it was found

2. Toolmakers not only - - - - - - elaborate tools but also test them for reliability and utility.

   (A) does it help to construct
   (B) help in the construction
   (C) help to construct
   (D) do help to construct

GO ON TO THE NEXT PAGE. ➡

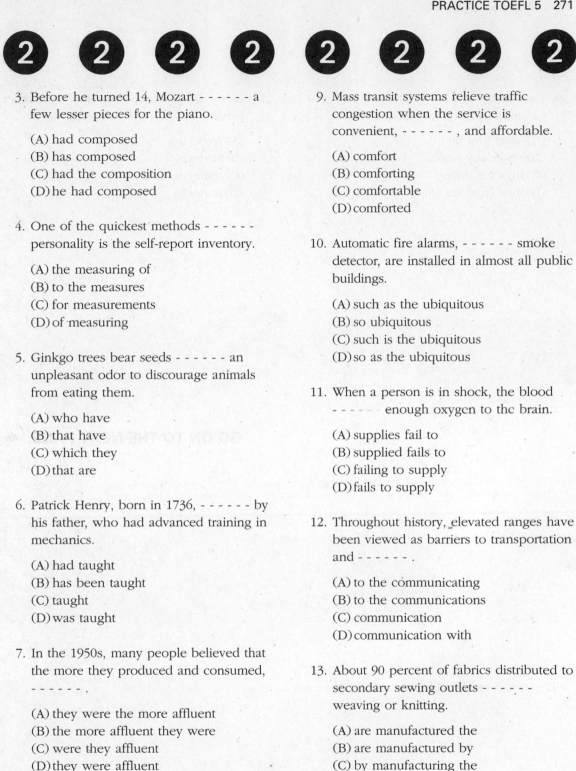

3. Before he turned 14, Mozart - - - - - - a few lesser pieces for the piano.

(A) had composed
(B) has composed
(C) had the composition
(D) he had composed

4. One of the quickest methods - - - - - - personality is the self-report inventory.

(A) the measuring of
(B) to the measures
(C) for measurements
(D) of measuring

5. Ginkgo trees bear seeds - - - - - - an unpleasant odor to discourage animals from eating them.

(A) who have
(B) that have
(C) which they
(D) that are

6. Patrick Henry, born in 1736, - - - - - - by his father, who had advanced training in mechanics.

(A) had taught
(B) has been taught
(C) taught
(D) was taught

7. In the 1950s, many people believed that the more they produced and consumed, - - - - - - .

(A) they were the more affluent
(B) the more affluent they were
(C) were they affluent
(D) they were affluent

8. A meteor burns brightly - - - - - - through the earth's atmosphere.

(A) as it descends
(B) as descending
(C) whether it descends
(D) when descends

9. Mass transit systems relieve traffic congestion when the service is convenient, - - - - - - , and affordable.

(A) comfort
(B) comforting
(C) comfortable
(D) comforted

10. Automatic fire alarms, - - - - - - smoke detector, are installed in almost all public buildings.

(A) such as the ubiquitous
(B) so ubiquitous
(C) such is the ubiquitous
(D) so as the ubiquitous

11. When a person is in shock, the blood - - - - - - enough oxygen to the brain.

(A) supplies fail to
(B) supplied fails to
(C) failing to supply
(D) fails to supply

12. Throughout history, elevated ranges have been viewed as barriers to transportation and - - - - - - .

(A) to the communicating
(B) to the communications
(C) communication
(D) communication with

13. About 90 percent of fabrics distributed to secondary sewing outlets - - - - - - weaving or knitting.

(A) are manufactured the
(B) are manufactured by
(C) by manufacturing the
(D) manufactured by

GO ON TO THE NEXT PAGE. ➡

14. Deer ticks - - - - - - vacationers hiking or camping in mixed deciduous forests.

    (A) never trouble
    (B) never any trouble
    (C) troubles never
    (D) trouble never

15. Either the goalkeeper or one of the other players - - - - - - the ball from the goal.

    (A) retrieving
    (B) retrieval
    (C) retrieves
    (D) retrieve

GO ON TO THE NEXT PAGE. ➡

2 **2** **2** **2** **2** **2** **2** **2**

<u>DIRECTIONS</u>: In questions 16–40 every sentence has four words or phrases that are underlined. The four underlined portions of each sentence are marked (A), (B), (C), and (D). Identify the one word or phrase that should be changed in order for the sentence to be correct. Then on your answer sheet, find the number of the question and blacken the space that corresponds to the letter of the answer you have selected.

Example I

Sample Answer

● Ⓑ Ⓒ Ⓓ

Christopher Columbus <u>has sailed</u> from Europe in 1492 and <u>discovered a</u> <u>new land</u> he <u>thought to</u>
               A   B   C   D
be India.

The sentence should state, "Christopher Columbus sailed from Europe in 1492 and discovered a new land he thought to be India." Therefore, you should choose answer (A).

Example II

Sample Answer

Ⓐ ● Ⓒ Ⓓ

<u>As the roles</u> of people in society change, <u>so does</u> the <u>rules of</u> conduct in certain <u>situations</u>.
 A   B   C   D

The sentence should state, "As the roles of people in society change, so do the rules of conduct in certain situations." Therefore, you should choose answer (B).

After you read the directions, begin work on the questions.

16. The Slater Mill, <u>built in</u> 1793, <u>it was</u> one of the first <u>successful</u> <u>mills in</u> the United States.
                 A   B   C   D

17. In kindergarten, <u>children</u> are generally <u>unrestricted in</u> expressing <u>their ideas</u> by <u>talk</u>.
              A   B   C   D

18. <u>Japanese</u> initially <u>used</u> <u>jeweled</u> objects to <u>decorate</u> swords and ceremonial items.
    A   B   C   D

19. The legal <u>age which</u> a person <u>is considered</u> to <u>be an</u> adult <u>is customarily</u> 18.
           A   B   C   D

20. Australian aborigines <u>adhere to</u> their tribal traditions and <u>few</u> <u>marriage</u> <u>outside</u> the tribe.
                   A   B   C   D

21. During a radio <u>broadcast</u>, a microphone <u>picks up</u> speech and <u>another</u> live <u>sounds</u>.
              A   B   C   D

22. Although both are the bread and butter of <u>recreational</u> vehicles, camping trailers are <u>smaller</u>
                                        A   B

and <u>compacter</u> than <u>travel</u> trailers.
    C   D

GO ON TO THE NEXT PAGE. ➡

2 2 2 2 2 2 2 2

23. The <u>leathery fruit</u> burr of the horse chestnut <u>splits openly</u> when <u>ripe and releases</u> a
         A   B   C

    <u>roundish brown</u> seed.
       D

24. Blacksnakes <u>ascend</u> trees to reach <u>bird's</u> <u>nests</u> and ingest the eggs and young <u>birds</u>.
                 A   B   C   D

25. Although rhubarb is <u>technically</u> a vegetable, <u>it usually</u> <u>prepared as</u> a <u>dessert</u>.
                      A   B   C   D

26. Colonial craftsmen <u>pieced</u> bed <u>covers</u> together from scraps of linen and wool <u>because</u> cloth
                       A   B   C

    was <u>scarcely</u>.
       D

27. In art, <u>relief is</u> sculpture <u>in which</u> the <u>figures</u> or designs <u>projects</u> from their background.
           A   B   C   D

28. Edith Roosevelt was a <u>devoted</u> mother <u>of five</u> children, <u>as well</u> a <u>gracious</u> hostess.
                       A   B   C   D

29. Vocational counseling <u>guides</u> students and helps them <u>to understand</u> how <u>occupations differ</u>
                       A   B   C

    and what job opportunities <u>are exist</u>.
                          D

30. Newtonian physics <u>holds true</u> if the velocities of the <u>objects</u> <u>being study</u> <u>are negligible</u>.
                   A   B   C   D

31. Roman doctrine <u>stipulated</u> every man <u>was</u> born with a <u>spiritual</u> who <u>guarded</u> him against
                 A   B   C   D

    travail.

32. <u>When</u> wine grapes <u>contain</u> the proper <u>amounts</u> of acid and sugar <u>required</u> to produce wine.
     A   B   C   D

33. Beef and dairy cattle <u>is major</u> sources of <u>income in</u> Louisiana, <u>which has</u> a <u>mild climate</u>.
                     A   B   C   D

34. After the new dollar bills are <u>printed</u> and <u>cut</u>, the <u>inspectors</u> scrutinize them for <u>imperfectives</u>.
                        A   B   C   D

35. Psychologists take <u>it for granted</u> that girls are <u>more</u> <u>empathetic</u> than <u>do boys</u>.
                    A   B   C   D

36. Henry Richardson was <u>the first</u> prominent architect <u>to incorporate</u> geometric <u>form in</u>
                     A   B   C

    <u>his concave</u> designs.
       D

GO ON TO THE NEXT PAGE. ➡

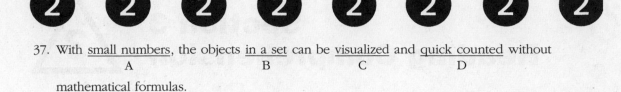

37. With <u>small numbers</u>, the objects <u>in a set</u> can be <u>visualized</u> and <u>quick counted</u> without
          A   B   C   D

mathematical formulas.

38. In <u>group dancing</u>, couples <u>step in</u> tandem, bow, <u>join hands</u>, and <u>change partner</u>.
          A   B   C   D

39. Additives are <u>chemicals</u> infused into <u>perishable</u> foods to prevent <u>it from</u> <u>spoiling</u>.
                          A   B   C   D

40. Football is a <u>fast-moving</u> <u>team sport</u> <u>playing</u> <u>mainly</u> in the United States and Canada.
               A   B   C   D

➤STOP◄

This is the end of Section 2.

Read the directions for Section 3.
Do not read or work on any other section of the test.
Look at the time now before you begin work on Section 3.
Use exactly 55 minutes to work on Section 3.

Section 3
Reading Comprehension

Time: 55 minutes

<u>DIRECTIONS:</u> In this section you will read several passages. Each is followed by questions about it. For questions 1–50, you need to select the one best answer, (A), (B), (C), or (D), to each question. Then, on your answer sheet, find the number of the question and blacken the space that corresponds to the letter of the answer you have selected. Fill in the space completely.

Answer all questions following a passage on the basis of what is stated or implied in the passage.

Read the following passage:

>   A tomahawk is a small ax used as a tool and a weapon by the North American Indian
>   tribes. An average tomahawk was not very long and did not weigh a great deal. Originally,
>   the head of the tomahawk was made of a shaped stone or an animal bone and was mounted on
> *Line* a wooden handle. After the arrival of the European settlers, the Indians began to use toma-
> *(5)* hawks with iron heads. Indian males and females of all ages used tomahawks to chop and cut
>   wood, pound stakes into the ground to put up wigwams, and do many other chores. Indian
>   warriors relied on tomahawks as weapons and even threw them at their enemies. Some types
>   of tomahawks were used in religious ceremonies. Contemporary American idioms reflect
>   this aspect of American heritage.

Example I

Early tomahawk heads were made of

(A) stone or bone
(B) wood or sticks
(C) European iron
(D) religious weapons

Sample Answer

● Ⓑ Ⓒ Ⓓ

According to the passage, early tomahawk heads were made of stone or bone. Therefore, the correct answer is (A).

Example II

How has the Indian use of tomahawks affected American daily life today?

(A) Tomahawks are still used as weapons.
(B) Tomahawks are used as tools for certain jobs.
(C) Contemporary language refers to tomahawks.
(D) Indian tribes cherish them as heirlooms.

Sample Answer

Ⓐ ● Ⓒ Ⓓ

The passage states, "Contemporary American idioms reflect this aspect of American heritage." The correct answer is (C).

After you read the directions, begin work on the questions.

GO ON TO THE NEXT PAGE. ➡

Questions 1–11

The Mayo Clinic in Rochester, Minnesota, where staff physicians practice a special integrated approach to patient care, is one of the largest medical facilities in the world. The clinic staff consists of a 12-member, committee-based board of governors and 900 physi-
Line cians and medical personnel whose records are updated by approximately 200 auxiliary per-
(5) sonnel. About 800 resident doctors assist the full-time physicians as a phase of their train-
ing in medicine and surgery while they acquire their specializations. The Mayo approach to treatment has been hailed for its almost miraculous patient recovery rate.

William Worral Mayo was born in Manchester, England, immigrated to the United States in 1845, and immediately began his medical training. In 1860, he took an active part
(10) in organizing the Minnesota Territory and accepted the position of an Army surgeon during a Sioux Indian outbreak. This appointment became a stepping stone for his advancement to the post of provost surgeon for the southern portion of the state in 1863. His personal dedication and courage became legendary when a cyclone struck Rochester, and he was placed in charge of an emergency hospital.

(15)   William Worral Mayo provided crucial assistance to his sons in launching their team practice in 1889, while they were holding positions at St. Mary's Hospital. William James became recognized for his surgical skill in gallstone, cancer, and abdominal operations. He and his brother, Charles Horace, founded the Mayo Graduate School of Medicine and do-
nated $1.5 million to establish the foundation for contributions. Charles William, the son
(20) of Charles Horace Mayo, became a member of the board of governors at the Mayo Graduate School and an alternate delegate to the United Nations General Assembly before retiring from the clinic in 1963.

William James Mayo presided in the American Medical Association and served in the Army military corps as a brigadier general in the medical reserve. Charles Horace was a pro-
(25) fessor of surgery and a health officer of Rochester subsequent to serving in the armed forces between 1914 and 1918. The Mayo practice became known far and wide for its success in surgical procedures. In 1914, the practice moved into its own medical center, and today the number of patients equals approximately 280,000 per annum. Since the clinic opened in 1907, 4.5 million patients have been treated there.

1. What is the best title for the passage?

   (A) A Welcome to the Mayo Clinic
   (B) Brilliant American Surgeons
   (C) The Contributions of the Mayo Family
   (D) The Start of a Successful Practice

2. In line 2, the word "integrated" is closest in meaning to

   (A) unified
   (B) goal-oriented
   (C) ready-made
   (D) unique

3. What can be inferred from the first paragraph?

   (A) Rochester, Minnesota is a city with a large population.
   (B) The Mayo Clinic employees have set many medical records.
   (C) The Mayo Clinic is a large specialized teaching hospital.
   (D) The clinic's physicians represent many medical specializations.

GO ON TO THE NEXT PAGE. ➡

4. According to the passage, William Worral Mayo was involved in caring for the patients affected by

(A) an outbreak of an epidemic
(B) a spread of disease among Indians
(C) a devastating natural disaster
(D) a brief military confrontation

5. In line 13, the word "dedication" is closest in meaning to

(A) dejection
(B) devotion
(C) deliberation
(D) delectation

6. According to the passage, who were the first physicians in the clinic?

(A) William Worral Mayo and Charles Horace Mayo
(B) William James Mayo and Charles Horace Mayo
(C) William Worral Mayo and William James Mayo
(D) William James Mayo and Charles William Mayo

7. In line 18, the word "founded" is closest in meaning to

(A) found
(B) established
(C) fortified
(D) articulated

8. In line 19, the word "contributions" is closest in meaning to

(A) contractions
(B) conventions
(C) gifts
(D) prizes

9. In addition to their medical expertise, what common characteristics distinguished the careers of the Mayo brothers?

(A) Funding of schools in Minnesota
(B) Positions on the board of directors
(C) Military and political service
(D) Donations for poor patients

10. In line 25, the phrase "subsequent to" is closest in meaning to

(A) because
(B) regardless of
(C) after
(D) contrary to

11. Where in the passage does the author state the principal reason for the expansion of the practice?

(A) Lines 5–6
(B) Lines 11–14
(C) Lines 17–22
(D) Lines 26–28

GO ON TO THE NEXT PAGE. ➡

Questions 12–23

Consumers are frequently unaware that about 30 percent of nationwide department stores are franchises with numerous outlets. Chain stores are a group of retail stores that are supervised or coordinated by centralized management. From a business perspective, chain *Line* stores have numerous advantages over independent stores, one of which is that the parent
(5) company almost always has the credit to purchase large quantities of goods to supply to its outlets and to receive a discount for placing such an order. Through the centralized system of distribution, chain stores can absorb the cost and price differential and attract consumers with various physical and psychological needs. They can also distribute their operating costs for accounting, advertising, marketing, merchandising, and transportation.

(10) In general, approximately 50 percent of gross product cost results from the associated marketing research and distribution. While research focuses on the probable market segments, it strongly considers consumer behavior and cognitive motives rather than the actual prices of goods. Similarly, the cost increase in the multiple channels of distribution accounts for about 23 percent of the unit price. By combining their marketing resources and
(15) distribution networks, franchise outlets can avoid performing whole stages of marketing studies and layers of distribution networks to reduce unit prices. It is the central company that conducts marketing and communicates with manufacturers, thus controlling production decisions and the pricing policy. Franchises operate according to their contracts with the parent company and pay it a fraction of their net gains. They symbolize a brand name
(20) and identify their goods with a particular range of quality that sets it apart from other, similar products. Essentially, chain stores convert consumer brand name loyalty into profit; this factor determines franchise proliferation and results in a relatively low degree of failure.

12. With what topic is the passage mainly concerned?

(A) The marketing of chain store products
(B) The business rationale for chain stores
(C) Pricing and distribution in franchises
(D) Brand name imaging of retail outlets

13. In line 2, the word "outlets" is closest in meaning to

(A) stock markets
(B) store rooms
(C) retailers
(D) outfits

14. In line 7, the word "absorb" is closest in meaning to

(A) absolve
(B) cushion
(C) hide
(D) advertise

15. It can be inferred from the passage that chain stores

(A) are more expensive than department stores
(B) can economize by controlling their operating costs
(C) have a greater consumer appeal than the parent company
(D) have power in identifying their market segments

16. According to the passage, what does marketing research include?

(A) The actual prices of goods
(B) Consumer segments and behavior
(C) Multiple channels of distribution
(D) The percentage of gross product cost

GO ON TO THE NEXT PAGE. ➡

17. In line 14, the phrase "accounts for" is closest in meaning to

 (A) sees as
 (B) counts on
 (C) adjusts
 (D) represents

18. Which of the following is NOT mentioned as a means through which chain stores control their prices?

 (A) Reducing distribution costs
 (B) Consolidating their finances
 (C) Dividing their purchase orders
 (D) Marketing a company brand name

19. Why does the author mention legally binding agreements between businesses?

 (A) To show feasible profitability of merchandising
 (B) To measure the value of consumer dependence on a product
 (C) To point out the means of parent company control
 (D) To exemplify the system of franchise operations

20. In line 19, the word "they" refers to

 (A) production decisions and the pricing policy
 (B) franchises
 (C) contracts
 (D) their net gains

21. It can be inferred from the passage that the parent company probably dictates

 (A) what sales personnel are employed
 (B) what profit an outlet makes
 (C) how goods are advertised
 (D) how products are packed

22. According to the passage, how do chain stores profit by being associated with the parent company?

 (A) They are not concerned about market instability.
 (B) They are not held accountable for a change in profits.
 (C) They put their needs ahead of those of the parent company.
 (D) They market consumer brand name recognition.

23. In line 21, the word "convert" is closest in meaning to

 (A) turn
 (B) nestle
 (C) antagonize
 (D) fit

GO ON TO THE NEXT PAGE. ➡

Questions 24–35

Because conducting censuses requires detailed planning, the organization conducting a census decides on and narrows the topics to be addressed and, more specifically, determines how to word the questions, tabulate the responses, and report the findings. Assimilating,
Line compiling, and statistically analyzing the information is a work-intensive process that may
(5) sometimes take up to a year. Censuses examine such issues as population size and density, employment and industrial affiliation, migration, formal education, income received, housing, marital status, relationship of each individual to the head of the family, and age. A detailed series of queries sample the data associated with the quality of housing, transportation, the level of industrial production, water and electricity consumption, or the
(10) functioning of the local government. Major censuses taken by the federal government are conducted every 10 years, in the years that end in zero. Surveys of agriculture take place every 5 years and cover the years ending in 4 and 9, manufacturing censuses in the years that end in 3 and 8, governmental units in the years ending in 2 and 7, and drainage and irrigation systems in the years ending in 9.
(15)   To ensure that the census information is complete, the organization conducting the census attempts to contact every individual residing or employed in a particular geographic area. To be consistent, information is gathered at approximately the same time. Because it is practically impossible to reach every person on the same day, censuses question the individual about conditions as they were on a certain date. Following the data gathering, the infor-
(20) mation is analyzed to determine the extent of social and economic change and problems, as well as the resources available to deal with them. During the years between censuses, the Census Bureau engages in monthly interviews and queries from a sample population to update its statistics. The issues of *Statistical Abstract of the United States* summarize all the information that is collected by 50 federal agencies and by private and public agencies.

24. With what aspect of conducting censuses is the passage mainly concerned?

(A) Content and timing
(B) Inquiring and analyzing
(C) Tallying and updating
(D) Reporting and publicizing

25. In line 2, the word "narrows" is closest in meaning to

(A) delimits
(B) declines
(C) defrays
(D) deflects

26. According to the passage, censuses take a great deal of

(A) funding
(B) publicity
(C) insight
(D) time

27. The author mentions that censuses gather data about all of the following EXCEPT

(A) household size
(B) agricultural production
(C) industrial output
(D) social networks

28. In line 8, the word "queries" is closest in meaning to

(A) entities
(B) terms
(C) quandaries
(D) questions

GO ON TO THE NEXT PAGE. ➡

29. It can be inferred from the passage that a census of industries took place in

(A) 1990
(B) 1994
(C) 1998
(D) 1997

30. In line 17, the word "consistent" is closest in meaning to

(A) constant
(B) uniform
(C) assorted
(D) conjectural

31. To gather complete information, the organization conducting the census contacts all people who

(A) speak at the same time
(B) have a similar economic status
(C) are involved in similar activities
(D) are concerned about a specific problem

32. Where in the passage does the author describe how census information is collected?

(A) Lines 1–3
(B) Lines 7–14
(C) Lines 15–19
(D) Lines 21–24

33. It can be inferred from the passage that census data are necessary to

(A) rebuild urban infrastructure
(B) determine arising needs
(C) analyze the electoral outlook
(D) identify sources of criminal activity

34. The author of the passage implies that most censuses are conducted by

(A) private agencies
(B) public organizations
(C) the central government
(D) the statistical bureau

35. In line 23, the word "statistics" is closest in meaning to

(A) equations
(B) solutions
(C) questionnaires
(D) data

GO ON TO THE NEXT PAGE. ➡

Questions 36-42

The body of the honey bee, like the bodies of all insects, is divided into three sections: the head, the thorax, and the abdomen. The bee's entire body is covered with fine hairs to which grains of pollen adhere as the bee moves from flower to flower, harvesting nectar and polli-
Line nating plants. The hairs on the antennae provide a means for tactile sensing without the
(5) ability to grasp extending objects. In pigmentation, bees range from black to shades of very pale brown, thus reflecting their wasplike ancestry. The queens are larger by far than both workers and drones, with the drones being bigger than workers.

A honey bee has five eyes—three secondary ones that form a triangle on top of its head and a large compound eye on either side of its head. The compound eyes center around thou-
(10) sands of lenses clustered closely to one another. Bees cannot focus their eyes, as many mammals do, because their eyes have no pupils. Bees were the first insects known to distinguish color, an ability due to the color sensitivity of their optic nerve particles. Their vision is especially receptive to hues of blue and yellow and to ultraviolet rays, unseen by humans. However, bees see red in the same way they see green but can distinguish geometrical patterns in
(15) the shapes of foliage and blossoms.

36. It can be inferred from the passage that the body of the bee

   (A) has a pronounced abdomen
   (B) has fine layers
   (C) is colored for protection
   (D) is typically compound

37. According to the passage, what do bees collect?

   (A) flowers
   (B) grains
   (C) nectar and pollen
   (D) extending objects

38. According to the passage, what purpose do the fine hairs on the body of the bee serve?

   (A) They identify the bees' ancestry.
   (B) They furnish a sense of touch.
   (C) They carry pollen to female blossoms.
   (D) They camouflage the insect.

39. How many classes of bees are mentioned in the passage?

   (A) Two
   (B) Three
   (C) Four
   (D) Five

40. In line 10, the word "clustered" is closest in meaning to

   (A) lined up
   (B) turned up
   (C) bunched
   (D) bundled

41. In line 13, the word "hues" is closest in meaning to

   (A) shades
   (B) layers
   (C) specks
   (D) circles

42. It can be inferred from the passage that bees are LEAST likely to distinguish

   (A) ultraviolet light
   (B) red flowers from foliage
   (C) shapes in their proximity
   (D) patterns of leaf veins

GO ON TO THE NEXT PAGE. ➡

Questions 43–50

The term "fixed star" refers to stars whose positions do not seem to change relative to other stars. As stars are constantly moving, their patterns alter gradually, but the difference may not appear significant over a period of 50 or 70 years, because, unlike planets, stars are
Line located at a great distance from the earth. Barnard's star, which is considered to move the
(5) fastest among the fixed stars, requires 200 years to noticeably alter its position by a distance equal to the moon's diameter. Compared to planets, which seem to be continuously shifting, stars appear stationary in their positions and relative distances from other bodies in a constellation. Astronomers employ spectrographs and photometers to keep track of perpetually shifting constellations. By using the spectrographs and photographs obtained over
(10) decades, scientists are able to detect changes in the proper motions of stars. By computing the differences in the spectra length, color, and shade of color, they can predict the direction of a star's movement in the near and distant future. A classical example is the cup of the Big Dipper, which is open quite a bit more widely now than it was 40,000 years ago. According to the spectrograph-based projections, 50,000 years from now the opening will be so expan-
(15) sive that the constellation will no longer resemble a dipper.

43. This passage is probably taken from an article discussing

(A) the uses of spectra for projections
(B) various fixed constellations and stars
(C) the classification of planets and stars
(D) the emergence and motions of stars

44. The author of the passage implies that stars

(A) seem to rotate differently than planets
(B) appear to retain their distances from other stars
(C) are presumed to be perpetually fixed and immobile
(D) alter their ray emissions gradually

45. The author mentions Barnard's star as

(A) an example of a very brilliant star
(B) a description of a constellation divide
(C) a point of reference for star mobility
(D) proof of star diameter and proximity

46. In line 7, the word "stationary" is closest in meaning to

(A) shining
(B) glimmering
(C) immobile
(D) immense

47. It can be inferred from the passage that

(A) stars revolve every 40,000 to 50,000 years
(B) stars alter their trajectories every 200 years
(C) planets are closer to the earth than stars
(D) planets do not appear to be as close as stars

48. In line 10, the word "detect" is closest in meaning to

(A) spy
(B) project
(C) trace
(D) compute

GO ON TO THE NEXT PAGE. ➡

49. The author of the passage implies that astronomers detect the movement of stars by

   (A) using photographs and mathematical reasoning
   (B) comparing the spectrum of each constellation
   (C) overlaying the spectrum images in succession
   (D) forecasting changes in the position of stars

50. The author of the passage conveys which of the following about fixed stars?

   (A) They are inspected by means of photometers.
   (B) They are comparatively simple to categorize.
   (C) Their movements are imperceptible.
   (D) Their spectra vary in intensity.

Practice TOEFL 6

Section 1
Listening Comprehension

In this section, you will demonstrate your skills in understanding spoken English. There are three parts in the Listening Section, with different tasks in each.

Part A

DIRECTIONS: In Part A you will hear short conversations between two speakers. At the end of each conversation, a third speaker will ask a question about what the first two speakers said. Each conversation and each question will be spoken only one time. Therefore, you must listen carefully to understand what each speaker says. After you hear a conversation and the question, read the four selections and choose the one that is the best answer to the question the speaker asked. Then, on your answer sheet, find the number of the question and blacken the space that corresponds to the letter for the answer you have chosen. Blacken the space completely so that the letter inside the space does not show.

Listen to the following example.

You will hear:

You will read:

(A) Mary bought some food.
(B) Mary had car trouble.
(C) Mary went shopping.
(D) Mary bought some gas.

Sample Answer
Ⓐ Ⓑ Ⓒ ●

From the conversation you learn that Mary stopped at the gas station on her way home. The best answer to the question "Does the car need to be filled?" is (D), "Mary bought some gas." Therefore, the correct answer is (D).

Now let us begin Part A with question number 1.

1. (A) She needs to check her room.
   (B) She should leave the key at the desk.
   (C) She can leave any time the front desk is open.
   (D) She doesn't need to return the key.

2. (A) He went to the movies yesterday.
   (B) He decided to go to the movies.
   (C) He was too tired to see the movie.
   (D) He stayed for the movie yesterday.

3. (A) The travel agent liked the book.
   (B) The book is about a travel agent.
   (C) The flight is full.
   (D) Travellers may have difficulty reading.

4. (A) She thinks that papers must be typed.
   (B) She believes that handwritten papers are acceptable.
   (C) Omitted words can be written in.
   (D) Typing skills are necessary for all students.

5. (A) He heard the noise.
   (B) He has decided already.
   (C) The man didn't like the noise.
   (D) The counsel will be noisy.

GO ON TO THE NEXT PAGE. ➡

6. (A) Do you have the chemistry assignment?
   (B) Will Frank come to the chemistry lab?
   (C) Does Frank teach chemistry?
   (D) Will Frank be willing to help us?

7. (A) Only two pieces of luggage can be checked in.
   (B) The boxes and the suitcases should be checked.
   (C) The suitcases belong to another passenger.
   (D) Suitcases cannot be checked in.

8. (A) Do you know where my coat is?
   (B) Have you been wearing my red coat?
   (C) Where is your coat?
   (D) Have you read it yet?

9. (A) He lives in the dorm.
   (B) He has a new apartment.
   (C) His apartment is north of campus.
   (D) He is moving soon.

10. (A) The wait is 15 minutes if you have a reservation.
    (B) Those who have to wait should make reservations.
    (C) The waiting room is on the fifth floor.
    (D) Without a reservation, you may wait for almost an hour.

11. (A) She thinks the food is excellent.
    (B) She feels that the price is reasonable.
    (C) She doesn't want to order the salad.
    (D) She thinks they should order dessert.

12. (A) Repair Jennifer's car.
    (B) Start driving to Jennifer's house.
    (C) Take Jennifer to the library.
    (D) Take Jennifer to the bank.

13. (A) He is excited about the show.
    (B) He has been to the museum many times.
    (C) He has seen the crafts displayed at the show.
    (D) He doesn't want to attend the craft show.

14. (A) Avoid traveling through the city.
    (B) Travel on a different day.
    (C) Stay away from highways.
    (D) Travel at 75 miles an hour.

15. (A) In the kitchen.
    (B) In a bookstore.
    (C) At a sports counter.
    (D) Near the outside door.

16. (A) She is the course advisor.
    (B) The man needs to take the history course.
    (C) The man is not taking a discussion course.
    (D) She cannot advise the man.

17. (A) It's around the corner.
    (B) It's in the next block.
    (C) It's on woman's right.
    (D) It's at the end of the block.

18. (A) At a packaging company.
    (B) In Seattle.
    (C) At a post office.
    (D) In a weight loss clinic.

19. (A) His wife does not like the man's brother.
    (B) He'll be busy on Saturday.
    (C) He'll be away for the weekend.
    (D) His wife will be away.

20. (A) A sales clerk.
    (B) A shoe-maker.
    (C) A receptionist.
    (D) A tailor.

21. (A) Go to the pool.
    (B) Make a phone call.
    (C) Correct the mistake.
    (D) Write a letter.

22. (A) It's been a great day.
    (B) We should do it all today.
    (C) We should stop for today.
    (D) Let's call Kay.

GO ON TO THE NEXT PAGE. ➡

23. (A) The lab is open every day.
    (B) The weather was terrible on Friday.
    (C) The test is at the end of the week.
    (D) The towels will be brought on Friday.

24. (A) In a garden
    (B) Near a pool
    (C) At an office
    (D) At a home

25. (A) Taking a class
    (B) Designing a building
    (C) Watching TV
    (D) Looking at pictures

26. (A) He doesn't know if the museum is
        open.
    (B) He has never been in a museum.
    (C) He thinks there is a museum nearby.
    (D) He doesn't have the directions.

27. (A) She has to take the boxes downstairs.
    (B) Would she mind helping him with the
        boxes?
    (C) The boxes downstairs are heavy.
    (D) Did the packers bring all the boxes?

28. (A) He has changed jobs.
    (B) He has two children.
    (C) He has two jobs.
    (D) He is looking for a job.

29. (A) Marsha is having a difficult time.
    (B) Marsha is not very practical.
    (C) Rob's jokes are difficult to understand.
    (D) Rob's jokes are not funny.

30. (A) The store is closing.
    (B) The store is near the bay.
    (C) The employees get a good salary.
    (D) The store offers part-time jobs.

GO ON TO THE NEXT PAGE. ➡

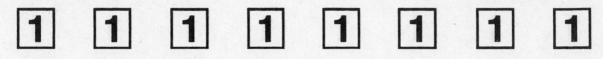

Part B

<u>DIRECTIONS</u>: In this part of the test, you will hear longer conversations. After each conversation, you will hear several questions. The conversations and questions will not be repeated.

After you hear a question, read the four possible answers in your test book and choose the best answer. Then, on your answer sheet, find the number of the question and fill in the space that corresponds to the letter of the answer you have chosen. Remember, you are not allowed to take notes or write in your test book.

31. (A) Various species of shark.
    (B) The oceans where sharks live.
    (C) Specific features of the shark's body.
    (D) Special characteristic of the shark's hearing.

32. (A) One or two
    (B) Approximately 45
    (C) About 100
    (D) More than 350

33. (A) Their attacks
    (B) Their teeth
    (C) Their hunting habits
    (D) Their electrical fields

34. (A) They move slowly and quietly.
    (B) They don't turn over on their backs.
    (C) Their tails and gills.
    (D) They have sharp senses of hearing and eyesight.

35. (A) He is new in the city.
    (B) He is sick.
    (C) His family needs to be treated.
    (D) His hospital doesn't provide the service.

36. (A) The man should go to the hospital.
    (B) The man needs to call the referral service.
    (C) The man's wife can make the phone calls.
    (D) The man needs to refer her to a physician.

37. (A) Whether a physician accepts new patients.
    (B) Whether patients like the physician.
    (C) Which doctors are employed by the referral service.
    (D) How often insurance claims need to be filed.

38. (A) Hospitals have dentists who require care.
    (B) She is not sure whether they are provided.
    (C) Dentists usually belong to an association.
    (D) Dental insurance is not accepted at hospitals.

GO ON TO THE NEXT PAGE. ➡

Part C

DIRECTIONS: In this part of the test, you will hear several short talks. After each talk, you will hear some questions. The talks and questions will be spoken only one time.

After you hear a question, read the four selections and choose the best answer. Then, on your answer sheet, find the number of the question and blacken the space that corresponds to the letter for the answer you have chosen.

Listen to this sample talk.

You will hear:

Now listen to the following example.

You will hear:

You will read:

(A) By cars and carriages.
(B) By bicycles, trains, and carriages.
(C) On foot and by boat.
(D) On board ships and trains.

Sample Answer

Ⓐ ● Ⓒ Ⓓ

The best answer to the question "According to the speaker, how did people travel before the invention of the automobile?" is (B), "By bicycles, trains, and carriages." Therefore, the correct answer is (B).

Now listen to another sample question.

You will read:

Sample Answer

Ⓐ Ⓑ ● Ⓓ

(A) One million
(B) Ten million
(C) Twelve million
(D) Ninety million

The best answer to the question "Approximately how many people are employed in the automobile service industry?" is (C), "Twelve million." Therefore, the correct answer is (C).

Remember, you are not allowed to take notes or write in your test book.

39. (A) To discuss the importance of expensive clothes.
    (B) To explain the purpose of interviews.
    (C) To prepare listeners for a job interview.
    (D) To emphasize the importance of being polite.

40. (A) It should be expensive.
    (B) It can bring good fortune.
    (C) It is required of all interviewers.
    (D) It should be clean.

41. (A) They don't care about their appearance.
    (B) They don't arrive on time?
    (C) They borrow other people's clothes.
    (D) They lose money if they are careless.

42. (A) To match that of the interviewer.
    (B) Increase it to save time.
    (C) Slow it down and think before responding.
    (D) To meet the interviewer's expectations.

GO ON TO THE NEXT PAGE. ➡

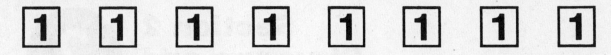

43. (A) A party in Boston.
    (B) A raid by American colonists.
    (C) Tea popularity in America.
    (D) The price of merchandise in Boston.

44. (A) In 1342
    (B) In 1660
    (C) In 1767
    (D) In 1773

45. (A) One
    (B) Two
    (C) Three
    (D) Four

46. (A) They wanted to profit from its sales.
    (B) They wanted to destroy it.
    (C) The tea was not fit for consumption.
    (D) The tea was too expensive to buy.

47. (A) 3 percent
    (B) 5 percent
    (C) 36 percent
    (D) 100 percent

48. (A) Events as they continue to occur.
    (B) Voters' attitudes at a particular time.
    (C) People's political beliefs in general.
    (D) Politician's views on current problems.

49. (A) They distributed the information.
    (B) They used a scientific method.
    (C) They reminded voters to go to the polls.
    (D) They made phone calls to ask for opinions.

50. (A) Roosevelt lost to Landon by a landslide.
    (B) The sample didn't include various groups of population.
    (C) Voters changed their minds.
    (D) The sample of the population was not large enough.

➤STOP◄

This is the end of the Listening Comprehension Section of the Test

The next part of the Test is Section 2.
Turn to the directions for Section 2, read them, and begin work.
Do not read or work on any other section of the test

Section 2
Structure and
Written Expression

2

Time: 25 minutes

Part A

This section is designed to test your ability to recognize language structures that are appropriate in standard written English. The questions in this section belong to two types, each of which has special directions.

DIRECTIONS: Questions 1–15 are partial sentences. Below each sentence you will see four words or phrases, marked (A), (B), (C), and (D). Select the <u>one</u> word or phrase that best completes the sentence. Then, on your answer sheet, find the number of the question you have selected. Blacken the space so that the letter inside the circle does not show.

Example I

Drying flowers is the best way _____ them.

(A) to preserve
(B) for preserving
(C) preserve
(D) preserved

Sample Answer

● Ⓑ Ⓒ Ⓓ

The sentence should state, "Drying flowers is the best way to preserve them." Therefore, the correct answer is (A).

Example II

Many American universities _____ as small, private colleges.

(A) begun
(B) beginning
(C) began
(D) for the beginning

Sample Answer

Ⓐ Ⓑ ● Ⓓ

The sentence should state, "Many American universities began as small, private colleges." Therefore, the correct answer is (C).

After you read the directions, begin work on the questions.

1. The red deer is a playful animal _____ the American elk.

(A) direct relationship
(B) relative to the direction
(C) directly related to
(D) relating it to the direct

2. Sally Ride participated in launching Canadian communication satellites and _____ pharmaceuticals.

(A) conduct experiments with
(B) experimented with conducting
(C) conducting experiments with
(D) experimental conduct with

GO ON TO THE NEXT PAGE. ➡

2   2   2   2   2   2   2   2

3. Various regions of North America _____ of European colonists, who spoke mostly English, Spanish, or French.

(A) have retained the languages
(B) retaining the languages
(C) the languages have retained
(D) the retaining of languages

4. Division means _____ into smaller equal groups.

(A) break up a number
(B) a number is a break up
(C) breaking up a number
(D) broken up is a number

5. Market research investigation is the formulation of a problem that a client _____.

(A) seeks solution
(B) to solve seeking
(C) solving to seek
(D) seeks to solve

6. In the early 18th century, Philadelphia and Boston were _____ New York, which continued to grow rapidly in the next century.

(A) largest and more prosperous than
(B) larger and more prosperous than
(C) prosperity and larger than
(D) than larger and more prosperous

7. Farmers grow oats to feed cattle _____.

(A) and sell to processing plants
(B) after they are being sold to processing plants
(C) and selling them to processing plants
(D) process and sold to them to plants

8. Pigment mixed with water does not dissolve but remains _____.

(A) suspending and forming paint
(B) suspend and form to paint
(C) suspended while painting
(D) suspended to form paint

9. Ralph De Palma, a pioneer American race driver, preferred matches against _____ to open competitions.

(A) other driver
(B) another driver
(C) drivers other
(D) driver, another

10. When one party arranges for a position in court, all involved _____.

(A) notified and must
(B) must be notified
(C) notifying them must be
(D) must be notifying

11. Alcohol, generally considered a depressant, decreases essential _____.

(A) functioning brain with
(B) functioning as a brain
(C) brain functions
(D) brain as a function of

12. Cooperatives, owned by the people who use their services, sell goods produced by their members or purchased _____.

(A) directly from farmers
(B) direct to the farmers
(C) farmers directly
(D) farmers with direct

GO ON TO THE NEXT PAGE. ➡

13. Marc Chagall's dreamlike paintings and _____ come from his recollections of childhood images and mementoes.

   (A) brilliantly colored
   (B) brilliant coloring
   (C) brilliant color
   (D) brilliantly and color

14. Rationalism as a philosophical trend was based on the idea _____.

   (A) reason is superior to experience that
   (B) that is reason superior to that experience
   (C) that reason is superior to experience
   (D) is that reason superior to experience

15. Rudolf Nureyev became recognized and admired for his stage activity and _____.

   (A) impressive dance technique
   (B) technique dance is impressive
   (C) technique in dance impressive
   (D) is impressive in dance technique

GO ON TO THE NEXT PAGE. ➡

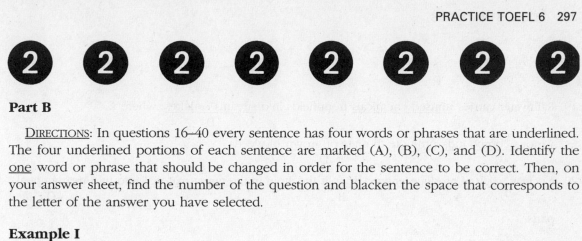

Part B

DIRECTIONS: In questions 16–40 every sentence has four words or phrases that are underlined. The four underlined portions of each sentence are marked (A), (B), (C), and (D). Identify the one word or phrase that should be changed in order for the sentence to be correct. Then, on your answer sheet, find the number of the question and blacken the space that corresponds to the letter of the answer you have selected.

Example I

Christopher Columbus <u>has sailed</u> from Europe in 1492 and
                          A

<u>discovered</u> a <u>new land</u> he <u>thought</u> to be India.
    B   C   D

Sample Answer

● Ⓑ Ⓒ Ⓓ

The sentence should state, "Christopher Columbus sailed from Europe in 1492 and discovered a new land he thought to be India." Therefore, you should choose answer (A).

Example II

<u>As the roles</u> of people in society change, <u>so does</u>
    A   B

the <u>rules of</u> conduct in certain <u>situations</u>.
        C   D

Sample Answer

Ⓐ ● Ⓒ Ⓓ

The sentence should state, "As the roles of people in society change, so do the rules of conduct in certain situations." Therefore, you should choose answer (B).

After you read the directions, begin work on the questions.

16. Balm which <u>grown in</u> damp <u>and shady</u> woodlands, is <u>a tall</u>, fragrant herb <u>of the mint</u> species.
                    A   B   C   D

17. Banks <u>store cash</u> in fireproof <u>safes insured</u> against fire, <u>robberies</u>, floods, theft, and
               A   B   C

<u>natural disaster</u>.
      D

18. During the Middle Ages, <u>riddles were</u> composed <u>of poets</u> and became <u>a form of</u> entertainment
                                  A   B   C

<u>and art</u>.
    D

GO ON TO THE NEXT PAGE. ➡

2 2 2 2 2 2 2 2

19. Rainwater carries <u>unused chemicals</u> from fields into <u>streams or lakes</u>, where

                          A   B

   <u>various compounds</u> promote the <u>rate of grown</u> of weeds.

        C   D

20. Nuclear <u>reactors produce</u> energy <u>by split</u> the atom in the <u>target material</u> into two <u>nearly equal</u>

                A   B   C   D

   parts.

21. Clifford Odets' play *Waiting for Lefty* <u>ranks among</u> <u>the most important</u> works <u>whom deal with</u>

                                       A   B   C

   the struggle of <u>the working</u> class.

                          D

22. <u>To enjoy</u> an opera fully, the listener <u>should be familiar</u> with the summary of the plot,

    A   B

   <u>particularly if</u> the opera <u>is singing</u> in a foreign language.

        C   D

23. In 1968, the U.S. <u>government effort</u> to <u>controls wages</u> and prices <u>to halt</u> inflation <u>had little</u>

                           A   B   C   D

   effect.

24. Annie Oakley <u>learned to</u> shoot <u>at the age</u> of eight and helped to <u>support her</u> family

                    A   B   C

   <u>for hunting</u> for a hotel restaurant.

       D

25. English is <u>the official</u> language of New Zealand and <u>when spoken</u> throughout

               A   B

   <u>the country while</u> Maoris <u>speak their own</u> language.

        C   D

26. Cumulative rhymes <u>repeat the informations</u> and <u>the wording</u> in earlier verses that <u>continue for</u>

                         A   B   C

   seven <u>to twelve cycles</u>.

           D

27. Animals <u>inhabiting the sea</u> bottom <u>can be carried</u> the <u>weight of the water</u> because

                A   B   C

   <u>it buoys them</u>.

       D

28. <u>Making a</u> photographic print <u>required paper</u> coated <u>with light-sensitive</u> chemicals that <u>react to</u>

   A   B   C   D

   special solutions.

GO ON TO THE NEXT PAGE. ➡

2 2 2 2 2 2 2 2

29. Cabbage and lettuce have <u>such a short</u> stems and <u>broad leaves</u> that they <u>appear to</u> have
          A   B   C

   <u>no stems at all</u>.
          D

30. Plowing reduces <u>the hard</u> of the <u>upper</u> 6 to 16 inches of the <u>earth's crust</u> and allows air move-
                        A   B   C

   ment into the gaps <u>between soil particles</u>.
                              D

31. In basic terms, all communication <u>is a process</u> of <u>exchange information</u>, imparting thoughts
                                            A   B

   and ideas, and attempting <u>to make</u> oneself <u>understood</u> by listeners or readers.
                                  C   D

32. Iron and steel are rigid <u>in their solid</u> state and <u>need to</u> be <u>melting when</u> they are to be
                                  A   B   C

   <u>reshaped into</u> new forms.
          D

33. Porous filters of charcoal <u>can remove</u> dust <u>particles from the</u> air if it is <u>directed through</u> them
                                    A   B   C

   in a <u>steadily stream</u>.
              D

34. The sender <u>places stamps</u> on packages <u>as proof</u> that postage <u>for mailing</u> an envelope or a
                    A   B   C

   package <u>has paid</u>.
                D

35. Potash <u>was originally</u> obtained <u>by running</u> water through wood ashes and <u>boiling the</u> solution
                  A   B   C

   in <u>cast-iron pot</u>.
          D

36. The earth's <u>gravitational force</u> for a given mass <u>accords matter</u> weight and <u>diminish</u> as an
                      A   B   C

   object <u>moves</u> away from the center of the earth.
              D

37. Allan Pinkerton organized <u>groups of armed</u> citizens <u>whose services</u> were available to
                                    A   B

   <u>employers for</u> a daily fee to <u>breaking labor</u> strikes.
          C   D

GO ON TO THE NEXT PAGE. ➡

38. The Bureau of Labor Statistics <u>found</u> that <u>few as</u> 14 percent of executives <u>write their own</u>
                                         A   B   C

    memos, <u>letters, and speeches</u>.
                      D

39. Real estate law holds that <u>not one</u> may legally plant or remove <u>plants of any kind</u>
                                        A   B

    <u>without permission</u> of the <u>land owner</u>.
              C   D

40. <u>National income</u> is defined as <u>the total</u> income earned, but <u>not necessarily</u> received by all
            A   B   C

    persons <u>lived in a</u> country during a period of time.
                    D

➤STOP◄

This is the end of Section 2

If you finish in less than 25 minutes, check your work on Section 2 only.
Do not read or work on any other section of the test.

Section 3
Reading Comprehension

Time: 55 minutes

<u>DIRECTIONS</u>: In the third part of this section you will read several passages. Each is followed by questions about it. For questions 1–50, you need to select the one best answer, (A), (B), (C), or (D), to each question. Then, on your answer sheet, find the number of the question and blacken the space that corresponds to the letter of the answer you have selected.

Answer all questions following a passage on the basis of what is stated or implied in the passage. Read the following passage:

> A tomahawk is a small ax used as a tool and a weapon by the North American Indian
> tribes. An average tomahawk was not very long and did not weigh a great deal. Originally,
> the head of the tomahawk was made of a shaped stone or an animal bone and was mounted on
Line a wooden handle. After the arrival of the European settlers, the Indians began to use toma-
(5) hawks with iron heads. Indian males and females of all ages used tomahawks to chop and cut
> wood, pound stakes into the ground to put up wigwams, and do many other chores. Indian
> warriors relied on tomahawks as weapons and even threw them at their enemies. Some types
> of tomahawks were used in religious ceremonies. Contemporary American idioms reflect
> this aspect of American heritage.

Example I

Early tomahawk heads were made of

Sample Answer

● Ⓑ Ⓒ Ⓓ

(A) stone or bone
(B) wood or sticks
(C) European iron
(D) religious weapons

According to the passage, the early tomahawk heads were made of stone or bone. Therefore, the correct answer is (A).

Example II

How has the Indian use of tomahawks affected American daily life today?

Sample Answer

Ⓐ Ⓑ ● Ⓓ

(A) Tomahawks are still used as weapons.
(B) Tomahawks are used as tools for certain jobs.
(C) Contemporary language refers to tomahawks.
(D) Indian tribes cherish them as heirlooms.

The passage states that "Contemporary American idioms reflect this aspect of American heritage." The correct answer is (C).

After you read the directions, begin work on the questions.

GO ON TO THE NEXT PAGE. ➡

Questions 1–10

Free-standing sculpture that is molded or carved is a type familiar to almost everyone. Although certain free-standing figures or groups of figures can have only a single side intended for viewing, others are completed on all sides. As with all other forms of art, the
Line ultimate shape of a sculpture reflects the artist's vision of individuals or experiences repre-
(5) sented by the work. Throughout history, people everywhere have discovered a need for sculpture as a record of events and feelings.

Materials which can be sculpted do much to contribute to the artist's imagination. Wood, stone, metal, and various types of plastic and synthetics are all used as sculpting media. When sculptures are made of stone, wood, ivory, or even ice, the sculptor carves or chips
(10) the substance to reduce it to the necessary shape. Developing a sculptured image on all sides represents a change from the older approach when artists left the back portion of the figure unfinished and rough. In fact, sculpture in relief is completely attached to the flat background material and appears to be a part of it. Relief, which is completed only on one side intended for viewing, was the first type of sculpture created by man, when ancient sculptors
(15) removed the background material in a side of a tree or a cave to make their drawing appear more realistic.

While creating a statue, the artist depends on the appropriate lighting to develop the figure because the quality of the final product relies on the interplay between light and shade. When the work is finished, the sculpture must be displayed in the same light as it was origi-
(20) nally created. If a light from a source is too weak or too strong, the effect that the sculptor intended may be lost. For example, in painting, the light and shade give the image shape and solidity that cannot be altered by an external light in which it is displayed. When a sculpture is exhibited, the artist's work is brought to life by light, and its character can be altered by the control of the light source. A fundamental difference between a painting and a sculp-
(25) ture is that when viewing a painting, the audience can only see the point of view that the painter had intended. A free-standing sculpture can be seen from practically any angle. The job of the sculptor is then to attain the quality and the volume of the image from any possible point of view.

In addition to carving a work, sculptures can be cast. In the process of casting, a sculpture
(30) can be reproduced in a mold when a liquefied medium is poured into a shape. After the material from which the sculpture is made hardens, the mold is removed, and the work is cleaned of the excess and polished. Casting allows the artist to produce as many replicas as needed. Most commercially sold sculptures are made in this way. Casting metals requires special care and skill. Bronze is the preferred metal because of its versatility and malleabil-
(35) ity. To make bronze sculpture, the space in a mold is filled with wax until it is melted by the heated metal. This process, sometimes called lost-wax, was favored by Benvenuto Cellini and was common among the artists in ancient China.

1. What is the main topic of this passage?

   (A) Differences between painting and sculpture
   (B) Sculpting techniques and media
   (C) Types of commercially produced sculptures
   (D) Reasons for enjoying sculpture

2. The word "ultimate" in line 4 is closest in meaning to

   (A) ulterior
   (B) final
   (C) formal
   (D) formidable

GO ON TO THE NEXT PAGE. ➡

3. According to the passage, the purpose of sculpture as a form of art is to

(A) Display a group of figures
(B) Reflect a human need for freedom
(C) Express an artistic vision
(D) Commemorate individuals and events

4. According to the passage, all of the following are true of sculpture EXCEPT that

(A) it can be found in all parts of the world
(B) it has undergone change since the early times
(C) it can be created from many substances
(D) it is no longer useful for people

5. The author of the passage implies that the most important factor in showing a sculpted work is

(A) the strength of the light source
(B) the development of the sculpted figure
(C) the shape of the material for sculpting
(D) the effect of light on the sculpted image

6. The word "audience" in line 25 is closest in meaning to

(A) listeners
(B) viewers
(C) public
(D) artists

7. What does the author mention as an important difference between a painting and a sculpture?

(A) A painting does not need shading to be displayed.
(B) A painting can be viewed from only one position.
(C) A sculpture needs to have proper light.
(D) A sculpture does not look good from all angles.

8. Which of the following is NOT mentioned as a sculpting medium?

(A) Ice
(B) Ivory
(C) Stone
(D) Wax

9. The word "replicas" in line 32 is closest in meaning to

(A) replacements
(B) molds
(C) reproductions
(D) monuments

10. According to the passage, what are the two basic methods for making sculptures?

(A) Carving and casting
(B) Free-standing and relief
(C) Hardening and melting
(D) Stone and metal

GO ON TO THE NEXT PAGE. ➡

Questions 11–21

The Beatles became the most popular group in rock music history. This quartet of extraordinarily talented musicians generated a phenomenal number of pieces that won gold records. They inspired a frenzy that transcended countries and economic strata. While all of
Line them sang, John Lennon and Paul McCartney wrote the majority of their songs. Originally,
(5) Lennon and five others formed a group called the Quarrymen in 1956, with McCartney joining them later that year. George Harrison, John Lennon, and Paul McCartney, together with Stuart Sutcliffe, who played the bass guitar, and Pete Best on the drums, performed together in several bands for a few years, until they finally settled on the Silver Beatles in 1960. American rock musicians, such as Chuck Berry and Elvis Presley, influenced Len-
(10) non's and McCartney's music, whose first hits consisted of simple tunes and lyrics about young love, "Love Me Do" and "Please, Please Me." The Beatles' U.S. tour propelled them to stardom and led to two movies *A Hard Day's Night* and *Help!*, filmed in 1964 and 1965. The so-called British invasion of the United States was in full swing when they took the top five spots on the singles charts, followed by the release of their first film.
(15) During the 1960s, their music matured and acquired a sense of melody. The lyrics of their songs became deeper and gained in both imagination and meaning. Their popularity continued to grow as the Beatles turned their attention to social problems and political issues in "Nowhere Man" and "Eleanor Rigby." Loneliness and nostalgia come through in their ballads "Michelle" and "Yesterday," which fully displayed the group's professional de-
(20) velopment and sophistication. Lennon's sardonic music with lyrics written in the first person, and McCartney's songs that created scenarios with off beat individuals, contributed to the character of the music produced by the group. In addition to their music, the Beatles set a social trend that popularized long hair, Indian music, and mod dress.

For a variety of reasons, the musicians began to drift apart, and their last concert took
(25) place in San Francisco in 1966. The newspapers and tabloids publicized their quarrels and lawsuits, and the much idolized group finally disbanded in 1970. However, their albums had outsold those of any other band in history. Although all of the Beatles continued to perform solo or form new rock groups, alone, none could achieve the recognition and success that they had been able to win together.

11. What does the passage mainly discuss?

(A) The history and music of the Beatles
(B) The history and milestones of rock music
(C) The fashion and music popular in the 1960s
(D) The creation and history of a music group

12. According to the passage, how many members were in the band, formed in 1956?

(A) Four
(B) Five
(C) Six
(D) Seven

13. According to the passage, which of the Beatles had the greatest musical talent?

(A) John Lennon and Paul McCartney
(B) George Harrison and John Lennon
(C) Stuart Sutcliffe and Pete Best
(D) John Lennon, Paul McCartney, and George Harrison

GO ON TO THE NEXT PAGE. ➡

14. The author of the passage implies that the Beatles

(A) competed with American musicians
(B) wrote their music as a group
(C) became popular relatively quickly
(D) were active in social movements

15. According to the passage, the Beatles' fame grew as a result of

(A) Chuck Berry's involvement
(B) their American tour
(C) two movies made in the U.S.
(D) their first two hits

16. The author of the passage implies that over time, the music and lyrics by the Beatles

(A) became more complex than at the beginning of their career
(B) declined in quality and political significance
(C) were dedicated to women named Eleanor and Michelle
(D) made them the richest musicians in the world

17. The word "acquired" in line 15 is closest in meaning to

(A) imparted
(B) attached
(C) imprinted
(D) attained

18. According to the passage, when did the Beatles experience their greatest success?

(A) In the late 1950s.
(B) After their break-up in 1970.
(C) During the early and mid-1960s.
(D) Throughout their lifetimes.

19. The word "scenarios" in line 21 is closest in meaning to

(A) sceneries
(B) situations
(C) life stories
(D) love themes

20. According to the passage, how did Lennon and McCartney enhance the music of the group?

(A) They struggled to reach stardom in the United States.
(B) They composed lyrics to scornful songs and ballads.
(C) Their music added distinctiveness to the Beatles' repertoire.
(D) Their loneliness and sadness made their music popular.

21. In line 26, the word "disbanded" is closest in meaning to

(A) separated
(B) slipped
(C) revelled
(D) bonded

GO ON TO THE NEXT PAGE. ➡

Questions 22–31

Like Europeans who arrived in the Americas, the first American Indians were immigrants. Because Indians were nomadic hunters and gatherers, they probably arrived in search of new hunting grounds from Asia when they crossed the ice-covered Bering Strait to Alaska. Anthro-
Line pologists estimate that the entire Indian population north of Mexico was slightly greater
(5) than 1,020,000 when the first settlers arrived from Europe. Although Native Americans belonged to one geographic race, their cultures and languages were only marginally similar, and by and large, they had different ways of life. Nomadic migrations required Indians to construct shelters that did not need to be transported, but could be easily erected from the materials found in their new location.

(10) Eastern Woodland Indian tribes lived in bark-covered wigwams that were shaped like cones or domes. The frame for the hut was made of young trees firmly driven into the ground, and then bent overhead to tie together with bark fibers or strings of animal hides. Sheets and slabs of bark were attached to the frame to construct the roof and walls, leaving an opening to serve as a door and to allow smoke to escape. The Iroquois in north eastern re-
(15) gions built longhouses that were more spacious than wigwams because five to a dozen families lived under one roof. During the winter, they plastered clay to the poles of the frame to protect the inhabitants from wind and rain.

Pueblo Indians who lived in the southwest portion of the United States in northern Arizona and New Mexico constructed elaborate housing with several stories and many rooms.
(20) Each family unit had only one room, and their ancestors dug shelters in the walls of cliffs and canyons. The ground story of a Pueblo dwelling had no doors or windows in order to prevent enemies from entering. The next level was set back the width of one room, and the row of rooms above it was set back once again, giving their houses the appearance of a terrace. Pueblos used ladders to climb to the upper levels and pulled them in when all family members re-
(25) turned for the night.

Indians living in deserts used sandstone and clay as construction materials. Those who lived in the valleys of rivers even made bricks of clay with wood chips to add strength and to prevent the clay from cracking. To make roofs, Pueblos tied logs together to make rafters and laid them across the two outside walls. On top of the rafters, layers of tree branches, sticks,
(30) grass, and brush created a solid roof to preclude the water from leaking inside. Pueblo dwellings were dark because windows were often not large enough to allow much light.

22. What does the passage mainly discuss?

(A) Different Indian tribes
(B) Types of households among Indians
(C) Types of shelters built by Indians
(D) Different Indian cultures

23. In line 6, the word "marginally" is closest in meaning to

(A) markedly
(B) minimally
(C) temporarily
(D) tentatively

24. In line 7, the phrase "by and large" is closest in meaning to

(A) mostly
(B) conversely
(C) occasionally
(D) notably

GO ON TO THE NEXT PAGE. ➡

25. The author of the passage implies that Indians

   (A) carried their construction materials to new locations
   (B) lived in settlements, similar to the Europeans
   (C) liked the climate in the Southwest
   (D) constructed shelters every time a tribe moved

26. According to the passage, what shape did the shelters of Woodland Indians have?

   (A) random
   (B) round
   (C) rectangular
   (D) convex

27. The author of the passage implies that Eastern Indians

   (A) constructed huts without roofs
   (B) planted trees to harvest crops
   (C) made fires inside their huts
   (D) used sheets and blankets as bedding

28. In line 16, the phrase "under one roof" is closest in meaning to

   (A) in separate sections
   (B) in several shelters
   (C) comfortably
   (D) together

29. What was the main difference between the dwellings of Pueblo and Woodland Indians?

   (A) The Pueblos lived in permanent structures, but the Woodland Indians lived in transient shelters.
   (B) The Pueblos used wood in their constructions, but the Woodland Indians relied mostly on animal hides.
   (C) The Woodland Indians lived on flat ground, but the Pueblos lived in canyons.
   (D) The Woodland Indians built small shelters, but the Pueblo rooms were large.

30. It can be inferred from the passage that Pueblo dwellings were designed to protect inhabitants from

   (A) attacks by enemies and cold winters
   (B) attacks by enemies and against rain water
   (C) wind storms and water from rain
   (D) wild animals, cold winters, and desert sands

31. The word "preclude" in line 30 is closest in meaning to

   (A) include
   (B) stop
   (C) preserve
   (D) conclude

GO ON TO THE NEXT PAGE. ➡

Questions 32–42

Continents and ocean basins represent the largest identifiable bodies on Earth. On the solid portions of the planet, the second most prominent features are flat plains, elevated plateaus, and large mountain ranges. In geography, the term "continent" refers to the surface of
Line continuous landmasses that together comprise about 29.2% of the planet's surface. On the
(5) other hand, another definition is prevalent in the general use of the term that deals with extensive mainlands, such as Europe or Asia, that actually represent one very large landmass. Although all continents are bounded by water bodies or high mountain ranges, isolated mainlands, such as Greenland and India-Pakistan areas are called subcontinents. In some circles, the distinction between continents and large islands lies almost exclusively in the
(10) size of a particular landmass.

The analysis of compression and tension in the earth's crust has determined that continental structures are composed of layers that underlie continental shelves. A great deal of disagreement among geologists surrounds the issue of exactly how many layers underlie each landmass because of their distinctive mineral and chemical composition. It is also quite
(15) possible that the ocean floor rests on the top of unknown continents that have not yet been explored. The continental crust is believed to have been formed by means of a chemical reaction when lighter materials separated from heavier ones, thus settling at various levels within the crust. Assisted by the measurements of the specifics within crust formations by means of monitoring earthquakes, geologists can speculate that a chemical split occurred to
(20) form the atmosphere, sea water, and the crust before it solidified many centuries ago.

Although each continent has its special features, all consist of various combinations of components that include shields, mountain belts, intracratonic basins, margins, volcanic plateaus, and blockvaulted belts. The basic differences among continents lie in the proportion and the composition of these features relative to the continent size. Climatic zones have
(25) a crucial effect on the weathering and formation of the surface features, soil erosion, soil deposition, land formation, vegetation, and human activities.

Mountain belts are elongated narrow zones that have a characteristic folded sedimentary organization of layers. They are typically produced during substantial crustal movements, which generate faulting and mountain building. When continental margins collide, the
(30) rise of a marginal edge leads to the formation of large mountain ranges, as explained by the plate tectonic theory. This process also accounts for the occurrence of mountain belts in ocean basins and produces evidence for the ongoing continental plate evolution.

32. What does this passage mainly discuss?

(A) Continental drift and division
(B) Various definitions of the term "continent"
(C) Continental structure and crust
(D) Scientific analyses of continental crusts

33. According to the passage, how do scientists define continents?

(A) As masses of land without divisions
(B) As extensive bodies of land
(C) As the largest identifiable features
(D) As surficial compositions and ranges

34. In line 7, the word "bounded" is closest in meaning to

(A) covered
(B) convened
(C) delimited
(D) dominated

GO ON TO THE NEXT PAGE. ➡

35. The author of the passage implies that the disagreement among scientists is based on the fact that

   (A) each continent has several planes and shelves
   (B) continents have various underlying layers of crust
   (C) continents undergo compression and experience tension
   (D) continents have different chemical makeup

36. The word "specifics" in line 18 is closest in meaning to

   (A) specialties
   (B) speculations
   (C) exact details
   (D) precise movements

37. The word "it" in line 20 refers to

   (A) a chemical split
   (B) the crust
   (C) the atmosphere
   (D) sea water

38. The author of the passage implies that

   (A) it is not known exactly how the continental crust was formed
   (B) geologists have neglected the exploration of the ocean floor
   (C) scientists have concentrated on monitoring earthquakes
   (D) the earth's atmosphere split into water and solids

39. According to the passage, what are the differences in the structure of continents?

   (A) The proportional size of continents to one another
   (B) Ratios of major components and their comparative size
   (C) The distinctive features of their elements
   (D) Climatic zones and their effect on the surface features

40. In line 31, the phrase "This process" refers to

   (A) continental collision
   (B) mountain ranges
   (C) the rise of margins
   (D) plate tectonic theory

41. The author of the passage implies that

   (A) the process of mountain formation has not been accounted for
   (B) mountain ranges on the ocean floor lead to surface mountain building
   (C) faulting and continental margins are parts of plate edges
   (D) the process of continent formation has not been completed

42. The word "evidence" in the last line is closest in meaning to

   (A) eventuality
   (B) confirmation
   (C) exemplification
   (D) challenge

GO ON TO THE NEXT PAGE. ➡

Questions 43–50

Chicago ranks as the leading industrial and urban center in North America. Carl Sandburg called it the "City of the Big Shoulders" primarily because in the 1930s, its population
contained a large segment of industrial workers, the largest agricultural market, and a huge
Line airport. This poetic phrase, however, does not do justice to the city's outstanding array of
(5) cultural institutions, such as the symphony orchestra and the museums of art and history.

The downtown business district on the shore of Lake Michigan is the hub of fashionable
and elegant boutiques, quaint restaurants, and high-rise office buildings. Lake Shore Drive
extends to both the north and south ends of the city, making it one of the most spectacular
roadways in the state of Illinois. The Old Water Tower, dwarfed by the John Hancock Cen-
(10) ter, is a must-see landmark frequented by thousands of tourists each year. Most of the Chicago lakefront is public, with spectacular beaches and wide lawns stretching along the shore
line.

Throughout its history, Europeans streamed into the city in search of jobs in steel mills
and factories. The large influx of population created tensions in various neighborhoods, and
(15) in the 1920s, Chicago gained a reputation for violence and crime that it never lived down.
Nonetheless, the booming industries continued to attract new residents into the thriving
city, despite its notoriety.

The Chicago metropolitan area has undergone dramatic changes since the 1940s when
the suburban population almost doubled, and the number of city residents fell. Today, most
(20) of the city's ethnic enclaves have faded away, but their rich heritage remains. The residents
take pride in impressive churches and blocks of homes constructed in the early 20th century
by industrious European immigrants who built the city. More than 85% of Chicagoans
were born in the United States, and access to Irish, Italian, Polish, and German community
institutions and businesses is not as important to them as it was to their grandparents. Ital-
(25) ian is no longer spoken in Little Italy, and Irish pubs have fewer Irish customers than those
of mixed, typically American origins.

43. What does the passage mainly discuss?

(A) Chicago's industrial and urban
   evolution
(B) Cultural and tourist attractions in
   Chicago
(C) The size of the city and its roadways
(D) The spectacular arrays of buildings in
   Chicago

44. According to the passage, Carl
Sandburg's phrase

(A) describes the city in the best light
(B) reflects the city in its entirety
(C) overlooks many of Chicago's
   attractive features
(D) gives an overview of Chicago's
   cultural life

45. The word "hub" in line 6 is closest in
meaning to

(A) hill
(B) center
(C) corner
(D) home

46. The author of the passage implies that

(A) the Old Water Tower is shorter than
   the John Hancock Center
(B) the John Hancock Center is probably
   the tallest building in the city
(C) the Old Water Tower and the John
   Hancock Center are located on the
   lake shore
(D) the Old Water Tower and the John
   Hancock Center are easy to reach by
   one of the Illinois roadways

GO ON TO THE NEXT PAGE. ➡

47. According to the passage, immigrants from Europe

(A) arrived in Chicago by ships and boats
(B) came to the city to enjoy its beaches
(C) arrived in large numbers
(D) came to Chicago to live in a large city

48. What changes have occurred in the city since the 1940s?

(A) Many residents moved out to neighboring towns.
(B) Its population grew rapidly.
(C) Many residents forgot their ethnic heritage.
(D) Its original builders moved back to Europe.

49. In line 22, the word "industrious" is the closest in meaning to

(A) employed in an industry
(B) hard-working
(C) ill-famed
(D) employed in construction

50. According to the passage, currently most residents of Chicago

(A) speak several languages
(B) do not shop in local stores
(C) do not have community institutions
(D) predominantly speak English

Practice TOEFL 7

Section 1
Listening Comprehension

In this section, you will demonstrate your skills in understanding spoken English. There are three parts in the Listening Section, with different tasks in each.

Part A

DIRECTIONS: In Part A you will hear short conversations between two speakers. At the end of each conversation, a third speaker will ask a question about what the first two speakers said. Each conversation and each question will be spoken only one time. Therefore, you must listen carefully to understand what each speaker says. After you hear a conversation and the question, read the four selections and choose the one that is the best answer to the question the speaker asked. Then, on your answer sheet, find the number of the question and blacken the space that corresponds to the letter for the answer you have chosen. Blacken the space completely so that the letter inside the space does not show.

Listen to the following example.

On the recording, you hear:

Sample Answer

Ⓐ Ⓑ Ⓒ ●

(Man)	Does the car need to be filled?
(Woman)	Mary stopped at the gas station on her way home.
(Narrator)	What does the woman mean?

In your test book, you will read:

(A) Mary bought some food.
(B) Mary had car trouble.
(C) Mary went shopping.
(D) Mary bought some gas.

From the conversation you learn that Mary stopped at the gas station on her way home. The best answer to the question "Does the car need to be filled?" is (D), "Mary bought some gas." Therefore, the correct answer is (D).

Now let us begin Part A with question number 1.

1. (A) He is happy to see the woman again.
   (B) He is glad the woman went running.
   (C) He is glad that he can return a favor.
   (D) He wants a piece of the cake she is baking.

2. (A) A hair stylist
   (B) An electrician
   (C) A die maker
   (D) A sales clerk

3. (A) A TV show
   (B) A newspaper
   (C) A newscast
   (D) A schedule

4. (A) The man is 20 minutes late.
   (B) The man came to the wrong place again.
   (C) The man has lost his pen several times.
   (D) It's too dark to look for the pen.

5. (A) In Seattle
   (B) In his office
   (C) On a plane
   (D) In San Francisco

GO ON TO THE NEXT PAGE. ➡

6. (A) Pay for new clothes
   (B) Exercise regularly
   (C) Have his clothes altered
   (D) Weigh himself every day

7. (A) She is a guest here.
   (B) She is still thinking.
   (C) She is finished ordering.
   (D) She is guessing.

8. (A) Tracey is very reliable.
   (B) Tracey doesn't mention Marsha.
   (C) Tracey is less dependable than Marsha.
   (D) Tracey is more striking than Marsha.

9. (A) He is joking.
   (B) He is not kidding.
   (C) He agrees with the woman.
   (D) He likes motorcycle races.

10. (A) Plan a vacation
    (B) Buy a camera
    (C) Take a trip
    (D) Leave the camera

11. (A) He is unloading the truck.
    (B) He has a good mind.
    (C) He is happy to help the woman.
    (D) He is also bothered by the noise.

12. (A) Cancel her appointment
    (B) Wait until June
    (C) See the doctor now
    (D) Make another appointment

13. (A) She doesn't like it when people look at her.
    (B) She doesn't intend to lend the man the money.
    (C) She works in the loan department at the bank.
    (D) Unlike the man, she has paid her tuition already.

14. (A) The cut should be made differently than was proposed.
    (B) There is ample time to analyze the data.
    (C) The time for data analysis may not be sufficient.
    (D) The market survey won't be completed in time.

15. (A) She knows about the road construction.
    (B) She can't find an alternate route home.
    (C) She wants more information about the traffic.
    (D) She wants the man to tell her about his problems.

16. (A) They should have stayed in their hotel.
    (B) They should have checked their route.
    (C) The stadium is difficult to find.
    (D) The map was lost while they were driving.

17. (A) Discuss buying the house
    (B) Talk to the buyer
    (C) Appraise the property
    (D) Play volleyball

18. (A) Looking for something else for the children to do
    (B) Finding other means of transportation
    (C) Canceling the trip to the newspaper
    (D) Taking the trip on another day of the week

19. (A) Playing cards
    (B) Writing letters
    (C) Playing a board game
    (D) Memorizing vocabulary

20. (A) She is surprised.
    (B) She is excited.
    (C) She is angry.
    (D) She is disgusted.

GO ON TO THE NEXT PAGE. ➡

21. (A) He cannot eat dinner alone.
    (B) He came in with two other people.
    (C) Three people will have dinner.
    (D) A table for two people is needed.

22. (A) The salesman was not helpful.
    (B) The salesman was excellent.
    (C) The man didn't need help.
    (D) The service was a whole lot better.

23. (A) The ball is in the front hall.
    (B) The light doesn't work.
    (C) She can smell something burning.
    (D) She cannot find the light.

24. (A) He is tired of sandwiches.
    (B) He's already had lunch.
    (C) He's gained weight.
    (D) It's too late for sandwiches.

25. (A) She couldn't hear the band.
    (B) The band was not very good.
    (C) She plays better than the band.
    (D) She liked it very much.

26. (A) He doesn't want to swim.
    (B) The pool is not in the city.
    (C) He is a city resident.
    (D) Nine years is a long time.

27. (A) They have an hour to spare.
    (B) The airport is not that far.
    (C) The clock should be repaired.
    (D) The clock is not accurate.

28. (A) The woman is a good guitar player.
    (B) The woman keeps changing her mind
        about hobbies.
    (C) He can teach the woman to take
        pictures and play guitar.
    (D) Photography is similar to playing guitar.

29. (A) She will drive the man.
    (B) Her car doesn't work.
    (C) The man can borrow her car.
    (D) She plans to go shopping.

30. (A) The instructor has a responsibility to
        help the man.
    (B) The assignments are unreasonably
        difficult.
    (C) The course is too advanced for the
        man.
    (D) Students are expected to do the
        assignments.

GO ON TO THE NEXT PAGE. ➡

Part B

DIRECTIONS: In this part of the test, you will hear longer conversations. After each conversation, you will hear several questions. The conversations and questions will not be repeated.

After you hear a question, read the four possible answers in your test book and choose the best answer. Then, on your answer sheet, find the number of the question and fill in the space that corresponds to the letter of the answer you have chosen.

Remember, you are not allowed to take notes or write in your test book.

Listen to the following example:

You will hear:

You will read:

Sample Answer

Ⓐ Ⓑ ● Ⓓ

(A) He has changed jobs.
(B) He has two children.
(C) He has two jobs.
(D) He is looking for a job.

From the conversation you learn that Tom has taken an additional job. The best answer to the question "Why is Tom tired?" is (C), "He has two jobs." Therefore the correct answer is (C).

31. (A) Gathering information about colleges
    (B) Choosing a good graduate school
    (C) Writing letters to apply for a job
    (D) Discovering essential facts

32. (A) Tuition and fees
    (B) Motivation
    (C) Job experience
    (D) Computers

33. (A) Going to college
    (B) Taking classes
    (C) Asking questions
    (D) Writing brochures

34. (A) Studying is similar to working.
    (B) They learn to work with computers.
    (C) In small classes, they prepare for jobs.
    (D) They take jobs available on campus.

35. (A) Mostly for herself
    (B) Primarily for her children
    (C) To guard the house
    (D) To take it to Scotland

36. (A) They are disciplined and reliable.
    (B) They cannot stay alone at home.
    (C) Children can take them to school.
    (D) Fifteen collies can herd cattle.

37. (A) Golden retrievers
    (B) Cocker spaniels
    (C) Terriers
    (D) Foxhounds

38. (A) Terriers have thick brown coats.
    (B) The family has little time to spend with it.
    (C) She should take of her children, instead of the dog.
    (D) Her children didn't like terriers as pets.

GO ON TO THE NEXT PAGE. ➡

Part C

DIRECTIONS: In this part of the test, you will hear several short talks. After each talk, you will hear some questions. The talks and questions will be spoken only one time.

After you hear a question, read the four selections and choose the best answer. Then, on your answer sheet, find the number of the question and blacken the space that corresponds to the letter for the answer you have chosen.

Remember, you are not allowed to take notes or write in your test book.

Now listen to the following example.

You will·read:

Sample Answer
Ⓐ ● Ⓒ Ⓓ

(A) By cars and carriages
(B) By bicycles, trains, and carriages
(C) On foot and by boat
(D) On board ships and trains

The best answer to the question "According to the speaker, how did people travel before the invention of the automobile?" is (B), "By bicycles, trains, and carriages." Therefore, the correct answer is (B).

Now listen to another sample question.

Sample Answer
Ⓐ Ⓑ ● Ⓓ

You·will read:

(A) One million
(B) Ten million
(C) Twelve million
(D) Ninety million

The best answer to the question "Approximately how many people are employed in the automobile service industry?" is (C), "Twelve million." Therefore, the correct answer is (C).

39. (A) Video rental business
    (B) Large motion picture studios
    (C) Vehicle rental agencies
    (D) Convenience and department stores

40. (A) Between 300 and 600
    (B) Between 5,000 and 7,000
    (C) Approximately 60,000
    (D) Over 90,000

41. (A) Rental space can be hard to find.
    (B) It's competitive and volatile.
    (C) Few stores in big cities rent videos.
    (D) It includes fast-food restaurants.

42. (A) Motion picture studios
    (B) Distribution networks
    (C) Convenience stores
    (D) Big chains of stores

43. (A) It extends the existing supply of minerals.
    (B) It contributes to pollution and waste.
    (C) Iron and aluminum are in short supply.
    (D) Mining aluminum costs a great deal.

GO ON TO THE NEXT PAGE. ➡

44. (A) 40 percent
    (B) 65 percent
    (C) One quarter
    (D) One half

45. (A) They have to pay taxes to recycle.
    (B) They are used to a throwaway lifestyle.
    (C) Environment is not a serious concern in the U.S.
    (D) Recycling does not provide many benefits.

46. (A) They encourage it.
    (B) They don't like it.
    (C) They make money from it.
    (D) They discuss it.

47. (A) A description of roses
    (B) The design of a colorful rose garden
    (C) Growing roses in various climates
    (D) Caring for shrubs and flowers

48. (A) The higher the rating, the fewer climates are suitable for a rose.
    (B) The higher the rating, the more areas are appropriate for growing a rose.
    (C) The highest rated rose is the most difficult to grow.
    (D) The highest rank is given to specially cultivated roses.

49. (A) Their flowers fail to open.
    (B) Their petals are limited in number and color.
    (C) Their flower production drops in summer heat.
    (D) They need to be watered frequently.

50. (A) Develop hardy varieties of roses.
    (B) Replace roses every spring.
    (C) Take a trip to a municipal garden.
    (D) Protect the shrubs from extreme cold.

➤STOP◄

This is the end of Section 1.

Read the directions for Section 2.
Do not read or work on any other section of the test.
Look at the time now before you begin work on Section 2.
Use exactly 25 minutes to work on Section 2.

Section 2
Structure and
Written Expression

2

Time: 25 minutes

This section is designed to test your ability to recognize language structures which are appropriate in standard written English. The questions in this section belong to two types, each of which has special directions.

DIRECTIONS: Questions 1–15 are partial sentences. Below each sentence you will see four words or phrases, marked (A), (B), (C), and (D). Select the <u>one</u> word or phrase that best completes the sentence. Then, on your answer sheet, find the number of the question you have selected. Blacken the space so that the letter inside the circle does not show.

Example I

Drying flowers is the best way - - - - - - - - them.

Sample Answer

● Ⓑ Ⓒ Ⓓ

(A) to preserve
(B) by preserving
(C) preserve
(D) preserved

The sentence should state, "Drying flowers is the best way to preserve them." Therefore, the correct answer is (A).

Example II

Many American universities - - - - - - - - as small, private colleges.

Sample Answer

Ⓐ Ⓑ ● Ⓓ

(A) begun
(B) beginning
(C) began
(D) for the beginning

The sentence should state, "Many American universities began as small, private colleges." Therefore, the correct answer is (C).

After you read the directions, begin work on the questions.

1. Beginning in the 1960s, national studies have surveyed changes in the values of college students to identify - - - - - - - - in college education.

   (A) that it is important to them
   (B) what is important to them
   (C) to them what is the importance
   (D) what importance to them

2. Bacteria that - - - - - - - - in ocean waters transport other organisms to new habitable environments and sources of nourishment.

   (A) free travel
   (B) traveling freely
   (C) travel freely
   (D) freely travels

GO ON TO THE NEXT PAGE. ➡

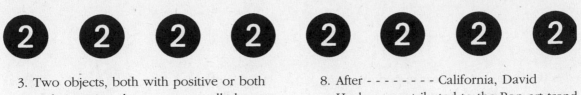

3. Two objects, both with positive or both with negative charges, are repelled, while objects with opposite charges - - - - - - - - .

(A) are attracting the other
(B) attracted to each other
(C) to each other attract them
(D) are attracted to each other

4. Roman law, one of - - - - - - - - with a continuous history, spread to many countries during the Roman conquest of Europe and Asia.

(A) the oldest existing systems
(B) systems, the oldest existing
(C) the existence, the oldest system
(D) existing the oldest system

5. Although the eucalyptus is native to Australia, - - - - - - - - in the U.S. belongs to the eucalyptus family, which comprises over 500 varieties.

(A) a large quantity of timber is harvested
(B) largely, a quantity of timber is harvested
(C) a large quantity of timber harvested
(D) a quantity of timber is large, harvested

6. Florida, mainly a peninsula jutting into the Atlantic Ocean, - - - - - - - - during the economic expansion of the 1990s.

(A) has been experienced, its fastest growth
(B) has experienced, it grows the fastest
(C) experienced its fastest growth
(D) its fastest growth has been experiencing

7. When an intersecting plane - - - - - - - - of a conical surface, the resulting curve is called the hyperbola.

(A) cuts both sides
(B) cutting both sides
(C) both sides are cut
(D) cut in both sides

8. After - - - - - - - - California, David Hockney contributed to the Pop art trend and developed his figurative style in painting portraits.

(A) he, moving to
(B) to moving
(C) moved to
(D) moving to

9. When the demand for merchandise exceeds capacity, customers - - - - - - - - , if no backup inventory is available.

(A) must turn away
(B) must turn them away
(C) must be turned away
(D) turn away and must be

10. Although - - - - - - - - to a public office, Robert Moses served as the New York secretary of state between 1927 and 1928 and led the state redevelopment program.

(A) he never elected
(B) electing never
(C) never electing
(D) never elected

11. Ostriches are flightless birds that can be - - - - - - - - 2.5 meters with exceptionally strong legs.

(A) as tall
(B) so tall as
(C) tall so as
(D) as tall as

12. Sandy beaches are popular recreational locations where people come - - - - - - .

(A) to swim, play sports, and sunbathe
(B) to swimming, playing sports, and sunbathing
(C) for a swim, playing sports and sunbathing
(D) swim, play sports, and sunbathe

GO ON TO THE NEXT PAGE. ➡

13. Ballet dancers appear to perform many movements - - - - - - - - .

   (A) that is unnatural in the body
   (B) that are unnatural for the body
   (C) where the body is unnatural
   (D) when the body is being unnatural

14. Export credit is a financial guarantee usually provided by a bank to enable companies - - - - - - - - when the payment is delayed or risky.

   (A) for the goods exported
   (B) to export goods
   (C) to exporting goods
   (D) exporting the goods to

15. Nightingales that can be heard at night as well as by day migrate to Africa in winters and Europe in summers - - - - - - in abundant supply.

   (A) when is food
   (B) when food is
   (C) their food is
   (D) there food is

GO ON TO THE NEXT PAGE. ➡

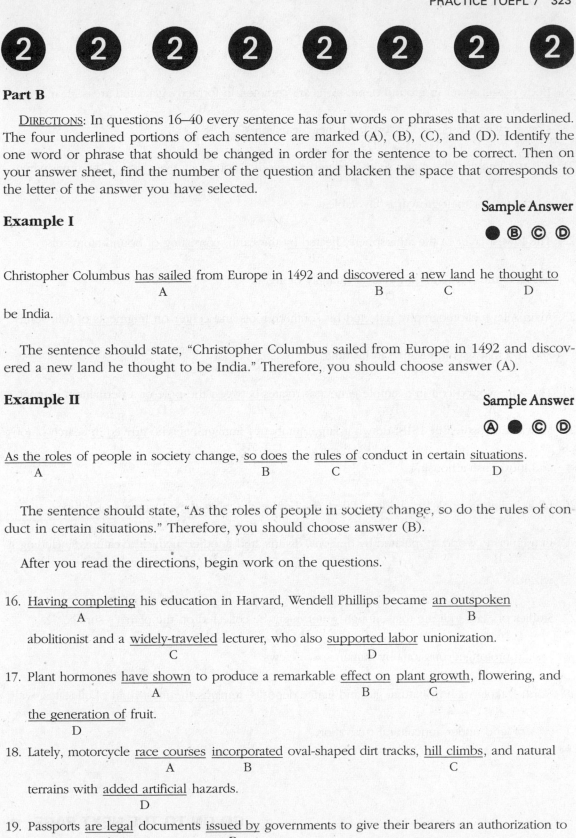

2 2 2 2 2 2 2 2

Part B

DIRECTIONS: In questions 16–40 every sentence has four words or phrases that are underlined. The four underlined portions of each sentence are marked (A), (B), (C), and (D). Identify the one word or phrase that should be changed in order for the sentence to be correct. Then on your answer sheet, find the number of the question and blacken the space that corresponds to the letter of the answer you have selected.

Example I

Sample Answer

● Ⓑ Ⓒ Ⓓ

Christopher Columbus <u>has sailed</u> from Europe in 1492 and <u>discovered a</u> <u>new land</u> he <u>thought to</u>
            A   B   C   D

be India.

  The sentence should state, "Christopher Columbus sailed from Europe in 1492 and discovered a new land he thought to be India." Therefore, you should choose answer (A).

Example II

Sample Answer

Ⓐ ● Ⓒ Ⓓ

<u>As the roles</u> of people in society change, <u>so does</u> the <u>rules of</u> conduct in certain <u>situations</u>.
  A   B   C   D

  The sentence should state, "As the roles of people in society change, so do the rules of conduct in certain situations." Therefore, you should choose answer (B).

  After you read the directions, begin work on the questions.

16. <u>Having completing</u> his education in Harvard, Wendell Phillips became <u>an outspoken</u>
        A   B

    abolitionist and a <u>widely-traveled</u> lecturer, who also <u>supported labor</u> unionization.
                            C   D

17. Plant hormones <u>have shown</u> to produce a remarkable <u>effect on</u> <u>plant growth</u>, flowering, and
                  A   B   C

    <u>the generation of</u> fruit.
        D

18. Lately, motorcycle <u>race courses</u> <u>incorporated</u> oval-shaped dirt tracks, <u>hill climbs</u>, and natural
                         A   B   C

    terrains with <u>added artificial</u> hazards.
                   D

19. Passports <u>are legal</u> documents <u>issued by</u> governments to give their bearers an authorization to
            A   B

    <u>cross nation</u> borders and <u>seek protection</u> in an emergency.
        C   D

GO ON TO THE NEXT PAGE. ➡

② ② ② ② ② ② ② ②

20. <u>Body of still</u> water in ground depressions are common <u>in formerly</u> glaciated areas, near
     A   B

    <u>slow-flowing</u> rivers, and <u>in low lands</u> near sea shores.
        C   D

21. It is <u>not known</u> why <u>many seeds undergo</u> a period of dormancy <u>even during</u> the times when
        A   B   C

    conditions for <u>their growth is</u> favorable.
                  D

22. <u>The lowest layer</u> of the atmosphere, <u>heated by</u> the Earth, <u>consisting of</u> bound atoms of
        A   B   C

    nitrogen and oxygen, <u>with a small</u> quantity of argon.
                        D

23. Alvin Ailey's choreography <u>reflected</u> his southern roots and <u>center</u> on <u>fragments of</u> folk songs
                           A   B   C

    and jazz that was <u>innovative</u> in his time.
                  D

24. The <u>wire-wound</u> coil <u>in a simple</u> generator <u>rotates between</u> the <u>pole of</u> a permanent magnet.
         A   B   C   D

25. Milwaukee, <u>settled in</u> 1818, <u>drawn a</u> large <u>number of</u> immigrants who <u>arrived in</u> search of jobs
             A   B   C   D

    and inexpensive housing.

26. J.R.R. Tolkien's book for children, titled *The Hobbit,* <u>describes the adventures</u> of Bilbo
                                               A

    <u>in a fantastic world</u>, populated by dragons, dwarfs, and <u>another mythical</u> creatures, <u>including</u> a
        B   C   D
    wizard.

27. Studies of Mars <u>indicate that</u> enough <u>water might</u> be collected on <u>the planet's</u> surface
                   A   B   C

    <u>sustain prolonged</u> missions by human space crews.
        D

28. North Dakota, <u>rich in</u> natural gas and lignite deposits, <u>remains</u> <u>the most rural</u> of all states, with
             A   B   C

    90% <u>of land</u> under agricultural cultivation.
        D

GO ON TO THE NEXT PAGE. ➡

2 2 2 2 2 2 2 2

29. Geological dating can be carried out <u>by measuring</u> how much radioactive <u>elements of a</u> rock
                                          A   B

    <u>have change</u> since the rock <u>was formed</u>.
       C   D

30. <u>Parallel beams</u> of light converge and <u>can be</u> eventually brought into focus <u>when pass</u> through
       A   B   C

    a convex lens <u>to produce</u> a real image on a screen.
                     D

31. If the air <u>temperature falls</u> below the <u>freezing point</u>, the dew <u>will freeze</u>, and the water vapor
                  A   B   C

    <u>can condenses</u> directly into ice.
       D

32. <u>Although different</u> in size and shape, most ferns are perennial and <u>spreading</u> by <u>low-growing</u>
       A   B   C

    root systems and spores <u>transported</u> by wind.
                                D

33. Walt Disney and his brother established <u>their animation</u> studio in Hollywood in 1923, and the
                                               A

    <u>first animation</u> cartoon with Mickey Mouse <u>appeared in</u> <u>black and white</u> in 1928.
       B   C   D

34. For centuries, philosophers and <u>artists alike</u> <u>have debated</u> the meaning of beauty and
                                        A   B

    questioned <u>whether it real</u> or <u>only perceived</u>.
                  C   D

35. In some musical compositions, regular <u>alternations</u> of the beat <u>are avoided</u> without repetition
                                             A   B

    <u>so that</u> the listener will not become <u>accustomed by</u> them.
       C   D

36. Margaret Mitchell, the author of *Gone with the Wind*, <u>had researched</u> the Civil War and then
                                                              A

    <u>had written</u> <u>the story about</u> Georgia and the period <u>that followed</u> the war.
       B   C   D

37. <u>As the sign</u> languages of <u>the deaf</u> show, <u>the sounds</u> of speech are not required <u>to expressing</u>
       A   B   C   D

    meaningful structures.

GO ON TO THE NEXT PAGE. ➡

38. In 1831, <u>English physicist</u>, Michael Faraday, discovered <u>the principle of</u> electromagnetic
         A   B

   induction, <u>which the</u> electric motor and the electric generator <u>are based</u>.
               C   D

39. <u>Aspiring to</u> eliminate slavery <u>entirely</u>, Francois Toussaint organized an army
     A   B

   <u>consisting mostly of</u> illiterate slaves into <u>a power</u> military force.
            C   D

40. <u>The human</u> rib cage protects the lungs and <u>the heart allows</u> the chest <u>to expand</u> and
        A   B   C

   <u>contract easily</u>.
        D

➤STOP◄

This is the end of Section 2.

Read the directions for Section 3.
Do not read or work on any other section of the test.
Look at the time now before you begin work on Section 3.
Use exactly 55 minutes to work on Section 3.

Section 3
Reading Comprehension

Time: 55 minutes

<u>DIRECTIONS</u>: In this section, you will read several passages. Each is followed by questions about it. For questions, 31–60, you need to select the <u>one</u> best answer, (A), (B), (C), or (D), to each question. Then, on your answer sheet, find the number of the question and blacken the space that corresponds to the letter of the answer you have selected.

Answer all questions following a passage on the basis of what is <u>stated</u> or <u>implied</u> in the passage.

Read the following passage:

> A tomahawk is a small ax used as a tool and a weapon by the North American Indian
> tribes. An average tomahawk was not very long and did not weigh a great deal. Originally,
> the head of the tomahawk was made of a shaped stone or an animal bone and was mounted on
Line a wooden handle. After the arrival of the European settlers, the Indians began to use toma-
(5) hawks with iron heads. Indian males and females of all ages used tomahawks to chop and cut
> wood, pound stakes into the ground to put up wigwams, and do many other chores. Indian
> warriors relied on tomahawks as weapons and even threw them at their enemies. Some types
> of tomahawks were used in religious ceremonies. Contemporary American idioms reflect
> this aspect of American heritage.

Example I

Early tomahawk heads were made of

(A) stone or bone
(B) wood or sticks
(C) European iron
(D) religious weapons

Sample Answer

● Ⓑ Ⓒ Ⓓ

According to the passage, the early tomahawk heads were made of stone or bone. Therefore, the correct answer is (A).

Example II

How has the Indian use of tomahawks affected American daily life today?

Sample Answer

Ⓐ Ⓑ ● Ⓓ

(A) Tomahawks are still used as weapons.
(B) Tomahawks are used as tools for certain jobs.
(C) Contemporary language refers to tomahawks.
(D) Indian tribes cherish them as heirlooms.

The passage states that "Contemporary American idioms reflect this aspect of American heritage." The correct answer is (C).

After you read the directions, begin work on the questions.

Questions 1–12

In the course of history, human inventions have dramatically increased the average amount of energy available for use per person. Primitive peoples in cold regions burned wood and animal dung to heat their caves, cook food, and drive off animals by fire. The first
Line step toward the developing of more efficient fuels was taken when people discovered that
(5) they could use vegetable oils and animal fats in lieu of gathered or cut wood. Charcoal gave off a more intensive heat than wood and was more easily obtainable than organic fats. The Greeks first began to use coal for metal smelting in the 4th century, but it did not come into extensive use until the Industrial Revolution.

In the 1700s, at the beginning of the Industrial Revolution, most energy used in the
(10) United States and other nations undergoing industrialization was obtained from perpetual and renewable sources, such as wood, water streams, domesticated animal labor, and wind. These were predominantly locally available supplies. By mid-1800s, 91 percent of all commercial energy consumed in the United States and European countries was obtained from wood. However, at the beginning of the 20th century, coal became a major energy source
(15) and replaced wood in industrializing countries. Although in most regions and climate zones wood was more readily accessible than coal, the latter represents a more concentrated source of energy. In 1910, natural gas and oil firmly replaced coal as the main source of fuel because they are lighter and, therefore, cheaper to transport. They burned more cleanly than coal and polluted less. Unlike coal, oil could be refined to manufacture liquid fuels for
(20) vehicles, a very important consideration in the early 1900s, when the automobile arrived on the scene.

By 1984, nonrenewable fossil fuels, such as oil, coal, and natural gas, provided over 82 percent of the commercial and industrial energy used in the world. Small amounts of energy were derived from nuclear fission, and the remaining 16 percent came from burning direct
(25) perpetual and renewable fuels, such as biomass. Between 1700 and 1986, a large number of countries shifted from the use of energy from local sources to a centralized generation of hydropower and solar energy converted to electricity. The energy derived from nonrenewable fossil fuels has been increasingly produced in one location and transported to another, as is the case with most automobile fuels. In countries with private, rather than public transpor-
(30) tation, the age of nonrenewable fuels has created a dependency on a finite resource that will have to be replaced.

Alternative fuel sources are numerous, and shale oil and hydrocarbons are just two examples. The extraction of shale oil from large deposits in Asian and European regions has proven to be labor consuming and costly. The resulting product is sulfur- and nitrogen-
(35) rich, and large-scale extractions are presently prohibitive. Similarly, the extraction of hydrocarbons from tar sands in Alberta and Utah is complex. Semi-solid hydrocarbons cannot be easily separated from the sandstone and limestone that carry them, and modern technology is not sufficiently versatile for a large-scale removal of the material. However, both sources of fuel may eventually be needed as petroleum prices continue to rise and limitations in
(40) fossil fuel availability make alternative deposits more attractive.

1. What is the main topic of the passage?

    (A) Applications of various fuels
    (B) Natural resources and fossil fuels
    (C) A history of energy use
    (D) A historical overview of energy rates

2. In line 2, the phrase "per person" is closest in meaning to

    (A) per capita
    (B) per year
    (C) per family
    (D) per day

GO ON TO THE NEXT PAGE. ➡

3. It can be inferred from the first paragraph that

   (A) coal mining was essential for primitive peoples
   (B) the Greeks used coal in industrial production
   (C) the development of efficient fuels was a gradual process
   (D) the discovery of efficient fuels was mostly accidental

4. In line 5, the phrase "in lieu" is closest in meaning to

   (A) in spite
   (B) in place
   (C) in every way
   (D) in charge

5. The author of the passage implies that in the 1700s, sources of energy were

   (A) used for commercial purposes
   (B) used in various combinations
   (C) not derived from mineral deposits
   (D) not always easy to locate

6. In line 16, the phrase "the latter" refers to

   (A) wood
   (B) coal
   (C) most regions
   (D) climate zones

7. In line 18, the word "They" refers to

   (A) coal and wood
   (B) main sources of fuel
   (C) natural gas and oil
   (D) industrializing countries

8. According to the passage, what was the greatest advantage of oil as fuel?

   (A) It was a concentrated source of energy.
   (B) It was lighter and cheaper than coal.
   (C) It replaced wood and coal and reduced pollution.
   (D) It could be converted to automobile fuel.

9. According to the passage, the sources of fossil fuels will have to be replaced because

   (A) they need to be transported
   (B) they are not efficient
   (C) their use is centralized
   (D) their supply is limited

10. It can be inferred from the passage that in the early 20th century, energy was obtained primarily from

   (A) fossil fuels
   (B) nuclear fission
   (C) hydraulic and solar sources
   (D) burning biomass

11. The author of the passage implies that alternative sources of fuel are currently

   (A) being explored
   (B) being used for consumption
   (C) available in few locations
   (D) examined on a large scale

12. In line 35, the word "prohibitive" is closest in meaning to

   (A) prohibited
   (B) provided
   (C) too expensive
   (D) too expedient

GO ON TO THE NEXT PAGE. ➡

Questions 13–23

Most forms of property are concrete and tangible, such as houses, cars, furniture, or anything else that is included in one's possessions. Other forms of property can be intangible, and copyright deals with intangible forms of property. Copyright is a legal protection ex-
Line tended to authors of creative works, for example, books, magazine articles, maps, films,
(5) plays, television shows, software, paintings, photographs, music, choreography in dance, and all other forms of intellectual or artistic property.

Although the purpose of artistic property is usually public use and enjoyment, copyright establishes the ownership of the creator. When a person buys a copyrighted magazine, it belongs to this individual as a tangible object. However, the authors of the magazine articles
(10) own the research and the writing that went into creating the articles. The right to make and sell or give away copies of books or articles belongs to the authors, publishers, or other individuals or organizations that hold the copyright. To copy an entire book or a part of it, permission must be received from the copyright owner, who will most likely expect to be paid.

Copyright law distinguishes between different types of intellectual property. Music may
(15) be played by anyone after it is published. However, if it is performed for profit, the performers need to pay a fee, called a royalty. A similar principle applies to performances of songs and plays. On the other hand, names, ideas, and book titles are excepted. Ideas do not become copyrighted property until they are published in a book, a painting, or a musical work. Almost all artistic work created before the 20th century is not copyrighted because it
(20) was created before the copyright law was passed.

The two common ways of infringing upon the copyright are plagiarism and piracy. Plagiarizing the work of another person means passing it off as one's own. The word *plagiarism* is derived from the Latin *plagiarus*, which means "abductor." Piracy may be an act of one person but, in many cases, it is a joint effort of several people who reproduce copyrighted mate-
(25) rial and sell it for profit without paying royalties to the creator. Technological innovations have made piracy easy, and anyone can duplicate a motion picture on videotape, a computer program, or a book. Video cassette recorders can be used by practically anyone to copy movies and television programs, and copying software has become almost as easy as copying a book. Large companies zealously monitor their copyrights for slogans, advertisements, and
(30) brand names, protected by a trademark.

13. What does the passage mainly discuss?

(A) Legal rights of property owners
(B) Legal ownership of creative work
(C) Examples of copyright piracy
(D) Copying creating work for profit

14. In lines 3 and 4, the word "extended" is closest in meaning to

(A) explicated
(B) exposed
(C) guaranteed
(D) granted

15. It can be inferred from the passage that copyright law is intended to protect

(A) the user's ability to enjoy an artistic work
(B) the creator's ability to profit from the work
(C) paintings and photographs from theft
(D) computer software and videos from being copied

GO ON TO THE NEXT PAGE. ➡

16. In line 16, the word "principle" is closest in meaning to

(A) crucial point
(B) cardinal role
(C) fundamental rule
(D) formidable force

17. Which of the following properties is <u>NOT</u> mentioned as protected by copyright?

(A) music and plays
(B) paintings and maps
(C) printed medium
(D) scientific discoveries

18. It can be inferred from the passage that it is legal if

(A) two songs, written by two different composers, have the same melody
(B) two books, written by two different authors, have the same titles
(C) two drawings, created by two different artists, have the same images
(D) two plays, created by two different playwrights, have the same plot and characters

19. With which of the following statements is the author most likely to agree?

(A) Teachers are not allowed to make copies of published materials for use by their students.
(B) Plays written in the 16th century cannot be performed in theaters without permission.
(C) Singers can publicly sing only the songs for which they wrote the music and the lyrics.
(D) It is illegal to make photographs when sightseeing or traveling.

20. In line 21, the phrase "infringing upon" is closest in meaning to

(A) impinging upon
(B) inducting for
(C) violating
(D) abhorring

21. The purpose of copyright law is most comparable with the purpose of which of the following?

(A) A law against theft
(B) A law against smoking
(C) A school policy
(D) A household rule

22. According to the passage, copyright law is

(A) meticulously observed
(B) routinely ignored
(C) frequently debated
(D) zealously enforced

23. In line 27, the word "practically" is closest in meaning to

(A) truthfully
(B) hardly
(C) clearly
(D) almost

GO ON TO THE NEXT PAGE. ➡

Questions 24–33

The official residence of the president of the United States is the White House, located at 1600 Pennsylvania Avenue, in Washington, D.C. The Commissioners of the District of Columbia held a meeting in 1792 and decided to hold a contest for the best design for the *Line* Presidential House. James Hoban, an architect born in Ireland, was the winner. His bid for (5) the construction of the mansion asked for $200,000, but the final cost of the building came to twice that amount. The work on the project began during the same year, and the grounds of approximately one and a half miles west of the Capitol Hill were chosen by Major Pierre-Charles L'Enfant, who was in charge of city planning. However, the construction continued for several more years, and George Washington had stepped down as president before the (10) building was habitable. When John Adams, the second president of the United States and his wife Abigail moved in in 1800, only six rooms had been completed.

The grey sandstone walls of the house were painted white during construction, and the color of the paint gave the building its name. The building was burned on August 24, 1814, and James Hoban reconstructed the house for President James Monroe and his family, who (15) moved there in 1817. The north portico was added to the building in 1829, water pipes were installed in 1833, gas lighting in 1848, and electricity in 1891. In 1948, inspectors announced that the building was so dilapidated that it was beyond repair and suggested that it was cheaper to construct a new one than repair the existing dwelling. However, the national sentiment was to keep the original form intact, and Congress appropriated $5.4 million dol-(20) lars for repairs. In 1961, Jacqueline Kennedy launched a program to redecorate the rooms and appointed a Fine Arts Committee to make choices of furnishing and colors.

The house of the president accords its residents a great deal of space. The living quarters contain 107 rooms, 40 corridors, and 19 baths. The White House contains a doctor's suite, a dentist's office, a large solarium, a broadcasting room, and a two-floor basement for storage (25) and service rooms. The office in which the president works is not located in the White House, but in a separate building called the West Wing. The White House stands on 16 acres of parklike land and overlooks a broad lawn, flower gardens, and wood groves.

24. In line 3, the word "contest" is closest in meaning to

(A) hearing
(B) concourse
(C) competition
(D) computation

25. What does the passage imply about the cost of the White House construction?

(A) It was proposed at the meeting of the commissioners.
(B) It did not adhere to the original estimate.
(C) It was not included in the architectural design.
(D) It was considered excessive for the presidential home.

26. In line 6, the word "grounds" is closest in meaning to

(A) high ground
(B) several lots
(C) site
(D) hills

27. It can be inferred from the passage that

(A) George Washington often used the White House steps
(B) George Washington contributed to the White House design
(C) George Washington never lived in the White House
(D) The White House was excluded from the city planning

GO ON TO THE NEXT PAGE. ➡

28. The author of the passage implies that the construction of the main White House building continued

   (A) up to 1800
   (B) after 1800
   (C) until 1814
   (D) until 1792

29. In line 17, the word "dilapidated" is closest in meaning to

   (A) ornate
   (B) run-down
   (C) old-fashioned
   (D) obscure

30. What can be inferred about the White House from the information in the second paragraph?

   (A) Few changes occurred in the structure in the first half of the 20th century.
   (B) The building was modernized extensively during one decade.
   (C) Running water was installed in the second half of the 19th century.
   (D) Each president added new features to the building's conveniences.

31. In line 19, the word "appropriated" is closest in meaning to

   (A) accumulated
   (B) accosted
   (C) authorized
   (D) aggrandized

32. In line 20, the word "launched" is closest in meaning to

   (A) lauded
   (B) lavished
   (C) began
   (D) requested

33. The passage mentions all of the following White House premises EXCEPT

   (A) hallways
   (B) kitchen
   (C) medical offices
   (D) storage rooms

GO ON TO THE NEXT PAGE. ➡

Questions 34–42

The organization of the family system in the United States emphasizes monogamy, neolocal residence, an extended family linkage, and a relatively free choice in the selection of mates. Compared to those in many other countries, American families are usually small and
Line isolated. Family and marital roles for men and women overlap considerably, with little dif-
(5) ferentiation. Marriage and divorce rates are high, and, according to demographic estimates, 95 percent or more of the adult population marry in the course of their lives. The rise in the divorce and remarriage rates has made definitions of family increasingly complex, although several basic patterns have remained stable.

The smallest family consists of two persons: a husband and a wife, a parent and a child, or
(10) a sister and a brother. Nuclear families include two or more persons who are related by marriage, blood, or adoption and who share a common household. A wide range of appropriate kinship patterns have developed in the past two decades, but marriage, an exclusive relationship between two people, is predominant. The only norm that is universally recognized by the society and by law permits a person to have only one spouse in a monogamous family.
(15) Serial monogamy has become ubiquitous, and it assumes that persons can have more than one spouse in the course of their lives, as long as there is only one spouse at a time.

Social norms pertaining to the choice of marriage partners prescribe appropriate and unacceptable characteristics. Most societies, including the U.S., grant acceptance to endogamous partners who marry within their own racial, ethnic, socioeconomic, educational,
(20) age, and religious groups. Traditionally, such norms are justified by common beliefs that those who share similar role expectations, values, attitudes, and customs are less likely to find themselves in conflict. On the other hand, an outcome of endogamous marriages may be that partners' similar socioeconomic levels tend to keep wealth and power within a group of the same class. Similarly, other unique benefits of such unions is that marrying within the
(25) same religious grouping may serve to retain the number of its members and, therefore, its political power and influence in the society as a whole.

34. According to the passage, a typical family unit in the U.S.

(A) has a free selection of mates
(B) shares a residence with other families
(C) lives close to other family members
(D) resides apart from its extended family

35. In line 4, the word "overlap" is closest in meaning to

(A) coincide
(B) consign
(C) collide
(D) concur

36. The author of the passage implies that American family relationships

(A) have remained stable
(B) have undergone changes
(C) have few disparities
(D) have little definition

37. What is the basis for the definition of a nuclear family in the U.S.?

(A) Blood relationships or adoption
(B) Two persons
(C) Households
(D) Marriage

GO ON TO THE NEXT PAGE. ➡

38. In line 12, the word "kinship" is closest in meaning to

(A) ownership
(B) sponsorship
(C) family connection
(D) family services

39. The author of the passage implies that the law in the U.S. permits a person to have

(A) one spouse in the course of a lifetime
(B) several spouses in sequential order
(C) a series of spouses at one time
(D) two spouses during their lifetime

40. In line 17, the word "prescribe" is closest in meaning to

(A) medicate
(B) limit
(C) determine
(D) legalize

41. According to the passage, what marriage partners are considered acceptable in most societies?

(A) Those that have similar social characteristics.
(B) Those that have a broad range of life experiences.
(C) Those that have a good socioeconomic foundation.
(D) Those that have similar attitudes to having children.

42. It can be inferred from the passage that endogamous marriages

(A) help to diversify the society
(B) help to preserve the existing social order
(C) increase social mobility of individuals
(D) decrease the number of conflicting signals

GO ON TO THE NEXT PAGE. ➡

Questions 43–50

For many people, mushrooms are strange, colorless, incomprehensible plants that should be avoided. Quaint tales and scary stories surround mushrooms because some are extremely poisonous. In reality, however, mushrooms are *fungi* that are simple plants without devel-
Line oped roots, leaves, stems, flowers, or seeds. They grow in wetlands, grassy meadows, and
(5) woods. Certain types of mushrooms are delicious and are included as ingredients in many recipes and trendy snacks. For example, morels are considered one of the choicest foods, and truffles, related to morels, are highly prized in Europe. Their shape is tubelike, and they remain entirely underground, a foot or more below the surface. In the old days, dogs and pigs were specially trained to hunt them by scent.

(10) Mushrooms stand out among other plants because they have no chlorophyll and cannot generate their own nourishment. The part of the fungus that rises above the ground is the fruiting body, and the vegetative part that produces growth is hidden under the ground. It can be usually dug up in the form of dense, white tangled filaments, which, depending on the food supply and moisture, can live for hundreds of years. In fact, mushrooms, as well as
(15) the rest of the fungus genus species, are one of the few remaining simple plants that are believed to be among the oldest living organisms. When their environment is not conducive to growth, filaments stop proliferating and can lie dormant for dozens of years.

Although mushrooms are rich in flavor and texture, they have little food value. Picking mushrooms requires a thorough knowledge of environments where they are most likely to
(20) grow and an ability to tell between edible and poisonous plants. Most mushrooms thrive in temperatures from 68° to 86° (F) with plenty of moisture, and nearly complete darkness produces the best crop. The entire mushroom should be picked, the stem, the cap, and whatever part that is underground. Brightly colored mushroom caps usually indicate that the plant is not fit for consumption, and the more the mushroom attracts attention, the more
(25) poisonous it is. Mushrooms with beautiful red or orange spotted caps that grow under large trees after a good rain are particularly poisonous. If milky or white juices seep from a break in the body of plant, chances are it should not be picked. Old mushrooms with brown caps are also not very safe.

43. In line 2, the word "quaint" is closest in meaning to

(A) convoluted
(B) fanciful
(C) irritating
(D) perfunctory

44. With which of the following statements is the author of the passage most likely to agree?

(A) In the old days, when food was scarce, people chose mushrooms as food.
(B) Mushrooms should be treated as all other plants.
(C) Because they are poisonous, people should stay away from mushrooms.
(D) Mushrooms have different forms of roots, stems, and leaves.

GO ON TO THE NEXT PAGE. ➡

45. In line 6, the word "trendy" is closest in meaning to

(A) tender
(B) experimental
(C) fashionable
(D) trusted

46. In line 7, the word "Their" refers to

(A) morels
(B) foods
(C) truffles
(D) morels and truffles

47. It can be inferred from the passage that mushrooms multiply mostly by means of

(A) moisture
(B) fruiting bodies
(C) nourishment
(D) root systems

48. The author of the passage implies that mushrooms

(A) have been known since ancient times
(B) are a relatively recent form of plants
(C) cannot survive without a good environment
(D) have been carefully analyzed

49. In line 20, the word "tell" is closest in meaning to

(A) narrate
(B) distinguish
(C) say
(D) see

50. What does the author of the passage imply about brightly colored mushrooms?

(A) They are beautiful.
(B) They should not be eaten.
(C) They attract attention.
(D) They should be destroyed.

Practice TOEFL 8

Section 1
Listening Comprehension

In this section, you will demonstrate your skills in understanding spoken English. There are three parts in the Listening Section, with different tasks in each.

Part A

DIRECTIONS: In Part A you will hear short conversations between two speakers. At the end of each conversation, a third speaker will ask a question about what the first two speakers said. Each conversation and each question will be spoken only one time. Therefore, you must listen carefully to understand what each speaker says. After you hear a conversation and the question, read the four selections and choose the one that is the best answer to the question the speaker asked. Then, on your answer sheet, find the number of the question and blacken the space that corresponds to the letter for the answer you have chosen. Blacken the space completely so that the letter inside the space does not show.

Listen to the following example.

On the recording, you hear:

Sample Answer

Ⓐ Ⓑ Ⓒ ●

(Man)   Does the car need to be filled?
(Woman)   Mary stopped at the gas station on her way home.
(Narrator)   What does the woman mean?

In your test book, you will read:

(A) Mary bought some food.
(B) Mary had car trouble.
(C) Mary went shopping.
(D) Mary bought some gas.

From the conversation you learn that Mary stopped at the gas station on her way home. The best answer to the question "Does the car need to be filled?" is (D), "Mary bought some gas." Therefore, the correct answer is (D).

Now let us begin Part A with question number 1.

1. (A) The soup is delicious.
   (B) The recipe is getting better.
   (C) The soup does not taste very good.
   (D) He decided to skip the soup.

2. (A) They have their troubles, and we have ours.
   (B) The man should write his own lab report.
   (C) They never tell us the correct hours.
   (D) The man needs to check the hours.

3. (A) Andy keeps track of advising and registration.
   (B) It is important to listen to Andy with skepticism.
   (C) It is not necessary to add salt to the dish.
   (D) Andy has already finished his registration.

GO ON TO THE NEXT PAGE. ➡

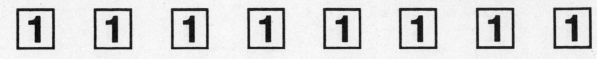

4. (A) The lettuce needs to be rinsed before it is used.
   (B) Let us wash up before we eat the sandwiches.
   (C) We like eating lettuce because it is healthy.
   (D) The lettuce is in the salad she is making.

5. (A) At the School of Business.
   (B) At a bookstore.
   (C) In a hardware shop.
   (D) In a grocery store.

6. (A) The sink has a bad odor.
   (B) It is too late to start looking at the puddle.
   (C) The man should not come at this hour.
   (D) The sink should be repaired.

7. (A) Mary is an author of a book.
   (B) Mary must have married a publisher.
   (C) The historian is getting married.
   (D) Historical novels are very popular.

8. (A) All customers get three pencils.
   (B) Those who take the test get a pencil.
   (C) All buyers receive a free gift.
   (D) Those who show their textbooks receive a free pencil.

9. (A) She has been looking for a cab for fifty minutes.
   (B) She has been looking for a taxi for a quarter of an hour.
   (C) She has been lost for fifteen minutes while wearing a light coat.
   (D) She has sized up the situation correctly and called a cab.

10. (A) People's recommendations are more effective than newspaper ads.
    (B) Most people do not pay attention to newspaper ads.
    (C) The new exhibit is promoted by the best advertising agency.
    (D) Words cannot describe the new exhibit effectively.

11. (A) The man needs to fill out the forms.
    (B) The man's car is out of gas and needs a fill-up.
    (C) The paint feels wet, and visitors should be careful.
    (D) The man is invited to go along.

12. (A) It is better to prepare before pouring it.
    (B) The batter contains four ingredients.
    (C) The mixture is poured on a hot surface.
    (D) The first pen is better than the next one.

13. (A) Julie and Michael plan to get married.
    (B) Julie and Michael decided to buy a new tie.
    (C) Julie's mother has not decided yet.
    (D) Julie's mother has no news to report.

14. (A) They cannot attend advising sessions.
    (B) An advisor is assigned to them.
    (C) They chose the wrong advising schedule.
    (D) An advisor shows them the correct schedule.

15. (A) It is a good idea to go jogging despite the hot weather.
    (B) It is important to stand up straight and exercise regularly.
    (C) The current weather is difficult to tolerate.
    (D) The weather has a long-standing pattern.

16. (A) They have little time for dancing these days.
    (B) They believe that gardening is serious business.
    (C) Their dancing classes have not started yet.
    (D) Their gardening business is off to a good start.

GO ON TO THE NEXT PAGE. ➡

17. (A) The color seems to be wrong.
    (B) She is not sure if she likes it.
    (C) She thinks that it is too short.
    (D) The man should not buy it.

18. (A) Renting a car
    (B) Going to the station
    (C) Planting a tree for children
    (D) Arriving late every day

19. (A) The search committee has filled out the applications.
    (B) The search for an office assistant has ended.
    (C) The hiring process has not been completed.
    (D) The applicants will still be reviewing the office.

20. (A) Come back on Tuesday.
    (B) Take the test.
    (C) Take the course.
    (D) Make a choice of a major.

21. (A) The dinner last week was a disaster.
    (B) She'll pay for the dinner.
    (C) She'll cook dinner this time.
    (D) She lives on Broadway.

22. (A) He finished the report already.
    (B) He wants to have another meeting.
    (C) He is tired of meetings.
    (D) He doesn't have time on Sunday.

23. (A) Making an appointment
    (B) Going out on a date
    (C) Discussing Peter
    (D) Scheduling a departure

24. (A) He will rest in the afternoon.
    (B) He has to keep working.
    (C) He needs to clean his desk.
    (D) He has missed the deadline.

25. (A) Fred is mysterious.
    (B) Fred's class is not difficult.
    (C) She doesn't know.
    (D) She is taking a different class.

26. (A) Roberta had misplaced her key before.
    (B) Roberta's husband is late again.
    (C) Roberta's husband does not treat her very well.
    (D) Roberta had returned from work.

27. (A) At a gift shop
    (B) In a bank
    (C) At a florist's
    (D) In a delivery office

28. (A) It takes an hour to get to the North Campus from here.
    (B) The shuttle comes twice an hour.
    (C) It'll be 15 minutes for the shuttle to get here.
    (D) The shuttle is 15 minutes behind the schedule.

29. (A) The man can't park there.
    (B) It's okay to leave the car only for a few minutes.
    (C) She doesn't live on this block.
    (D) The man should park in the driveway.

30. (A) The woman is more careful now than she used to be.
    (B) The woman is not very careful.
    (C) He will help the woman with the gate.
    (D) He wishes only the best for the woman.

GO ON TO THE NEXT PAGE. ➡

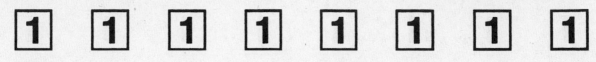

Part B

DIRECTIONS: In this part of the test, you will hear longer conversations. After each conversation, you will hear several questions. The conversations and questions will not be repeated.

After you hear a question, read the four possible answers in your test book and choose the best answer. Then, on your answer sheet, find the number of the question and fill in the space that corresponds to the letter of the answer you have chosen.

Remember, you are not allowed to take notes or write in your test book.

31. (A) Select trees that he can plant in his yard.
    (B) Suggest trees that do not require much care.
    (C) Figure out the best variety of trees.
    (D) Point out trees that are on sale.

32. (A) Fruit growth, shade, and appearance
    (B) Soil erosion, height, and slope orientation
    (C) Southern exposure, roots, and water
    (D) Soil density, light, and heat tolerance

33. (A) They do not do well in direct sunlight.
    (B) Their root systems need good drainage.
    (C) They improve the environment and shade.
    (D) Their height can become a problem.

34. (A) Buy a few short trees.
    (B) Prune more trees.
    (C) Learn more about trees.
    (D) Think a little longer.

35. (A) Talk to the violin maker.
    (B) Play the instrument.
    (C) Wait for the wood to dry.
    (D) Adjust the bow strings.

36. (A) It is a lengthy process.
    (B) It is a delightful hobby.
    (C) It is a musical endeavor.
    (D) It requires musical expertise.

37. (A) Music
    (B) Violin
    (C) Writing
    (D) Reading

38. (A) Glasses are less inconvenient.
    (B) Contacts can be more easily lost.
    (C) Contacts are more difficult to keep clean.
    (D) Glasses are less preferable.

39. (A) One
    (B) Two
    (C) Three
    (D) Four

40. (A) Researching lens plastics
    (B) Scheduling an eye exam
    (C) Locating an optometrist
    (D) Saving enough money

GO ON TO THE NEXT PAGE. ➡

Part C

<u>DIRECTIONS:</u> In this part of the test, you will hear several short talks. After each talk, you will hear some questions. The talks and questions will be spoken only one time.

After you hear a question, read the four selections and choose the best answer. Then, on your answer sheet, find the number of the question and blacken the space that corresponds to the letter for the answer you have chosen.

Remember, you are not allowed to take notes or write in your test book.

Now listen to the following talk.

You will hear:

You will read:

Sample Answer
Ⓐ ● Ⓒ Ⓓ

(A) By cars and carriages
(B) By bicycles, trains, and carriages
(C) On foot and by boat
(D) On board ships and trains

The best answer to the question "According to the speaker, how did people travel before the invention of the automobile?" is (B), "By bicycles, trains, and carriages." Therefore, the correct answer is (B).

Now listen to another sample question.

Sample Answer
Ⓐ Ⓑ ● Ⓓ

You will read:

(A) One million
(B) Ten million
(C) Twelve million
(D) Ninety million

The best answer to the question "Approximately how many people are employed in the automobile service industry?" is (C), "Twelve million." Therefore, the correct answer is (C).

41. (A) To assist international travelers with data and changes
    (B) To elaborate on the system calendars in various locations
    (C) To explain the conventions of marking and changing dates
    (D) To demonstrate the connections between meridians and air travel

42. (A) Travelers have to choose the best days and times for their cross-continental journeys.
    (B) The distance from Los Angeles to Asia is similar to that from New York to London.
    (C) Date changes occur some time when air travelers cross the Pacific.
    (D) A loss of several hours of sleep is possible during long cross-continental flights.

GO ON TO THE NEXT PAGE. ➡

43. (A) They should count the number of hours or add hours to the local time.
    (B) They need to add or subtract a day when crossing the date line.
    (C) They should buy a Western or Eastern calendar to match the local day count.
    (D) They need to count the beginnings of days from midnight to midnight.

44. (A) North-to-south standard time zones
    (B) Loose elliptical connections among longitudes
    (C) The line near the 24th hour on the local calendar
    (D) The area along the 180th meridian of longitude

45. (A) To describe the people who live on the island
    (B) To point out earth divisions similar to those in Alaska
    (C) To explain the rigidity of meridian lines
    (D) To illustrate the swerves in the date line

46. (A) The prehistoric northern settlements and the Northwestern Passage
    (B) The historical and economic significance of northern explorations
    (C) The Greek, English, and Spanish explorers of the northern seas
    (D) The connections between the English-Spanish war and northern explorers

47. (A) Together with the English, they defeated the Spanish fleet.
    (B) Unlike the Dutch, they looked for the Northern Passage.
    (C) Together with the Spanish, they controlled the southern seas.
    (D) Unlike other merchants, they did not trade in India.

48. (A) Those that are low in calories
    (B) Those that are high in protein
    (C) Those that are eaten on a usual basis
    (D) Those that are eaten at regular intervals

49. (A) Vitamins and minerals
    (B) Corn and potatoes
    (C) Bread and butter
    (D) Fish and beans

50. (A) Various kinds of fats
    (B) Different types of sugars
    (C) Half of all calories consumed by Americans
    (D) Half of all nutrients found in carbohydrates

➤STOP◀

This is the end of Section 1.

Read the directions for Section 2.
Do not read or work on any other section of the test.
Look at the time now before you begin work on Section 2.
Use exactly 25 minutes to work on Section 2.

Section 2 Structure and Written Expression

2

Time: 25 minutes

Part A

This section is designed to test your ability to recognize language structures which are appropriate in standard written English. The questions in this section belong to two types, each of which has special directions.

<u>DIRECTIONS</u>: Questions 1–15 are partial sentences. Below each sentence you will see four words or phrases, marked (A), (B), (C), and (D). Select the <u>one</u> word or phrase that best completes the sentence. Then, on your answer sheet, find the number of the question you have selected. Blacken the space so that the letter inside the circle does not show.

EXAMPLE I

Drying flowers is the best way - - - - - - - - them.

Sample Answer
● Ⓑ Ⓒ Ⓓ

(A) to preserve
(B) by preserving
(C) preserve
(D) preserved

The sentence should state, "Drying flowers is the best way to preserve them." Therefore, the correct answer is (A).

EXAMPLE II

Many American universities - - - - - - - - as small, private colleges.

Sample Answer
Ⓐ Ⓑ ● Ⓓ

(A) begun
(B) beginning
(C) began
(D) for the beginning

The sentence should state, "Many American universities began as small, private colleges." Therefore, the correct answer is (C).

After you read the directions, begin work on the questions.

GO ON TO THE NEXT PAGE. ➡

1. The Internet - - - - - - - - access to current news, political articles, business statistics, and software for practically any purpose.

   (A) can provide ready
   (B) can be provided readily
   (C) ready and can be providing
   (D) is ready and can provide

2. Descriptive analysis of language merely reflects - - - - - - - - used without concern for the social prestige of these structures.

   (A) it how grammar structures and vocabulary is
   (B) how are grammar structures and vocabulary
   (C) how grammar structures and vocabulary are
   (D) it is how grammar structures and vocabulary are

3. James Boswell was a Scottish author whose private journals - - - - - - - - personality and colorful experiences during his European journeys, meetings with renowned French philosophers, and adventures with Corsican rebels.

   (A) revelations of his fascinating
   (B) revealing his fascination
   (C) his revealing fascinations
   (D) reveal his fascinating

4. Originally, the first European colleges consisted of groups of individuals - - - - - - - - joined their efforts to study sciences, medicine, and law.

   (A) who lived together and
   (B) whose life together and
   (C) and who live together
   (D) whose living together and

5. Sedimentary rock represents geologically transformed minerals and small particles of - - - - - - - - deposited by the movement of water, wind, or glacial ice.

   (A) chemicals matter
   (B) chemical matter
   (C) matters of chemical
   (D) matters in chemicals

6. The buff pottery with red designs made by the Hohokam dessert dwellers in the Southwestern regions - - - - - - - - for its original construction and unique shape.

   (A) are highly prized
   (B) is a high price
   (C) is highly prized
   (D) are prized highly

7. Soap operas and day-time comedy serials were - - - - - - - - originated in Chicago in the 1930s, and most consisted of 15-minute episodes broadcast five times a week.

   (A) radio shows that
   (B) that radio showing
   (C) shown that radio
   (D) radio that is shown

8. Although food preferences vary a great deal from one individual to another, geographic location, traditional customs, and family socioeconomic position play a major role - - - - - - - -.

   (A) formational in dietary habits
   (B) informing dietary habits
   (C) in forming dietary habits
   (D) in forming dietary habitual

GO ON TO THE NEXT PAGE. ➡

9. Precipitation of microscopic marine organisms on the ocean floor results in the creation of limestone, - - - - - - - - parallel or discordant layers of deposited chemical material.

(A) characteristics in
(B) of the characteristic
(C) characterized by
(D) in the characterization of

10. Approximately 400 million to 250 million years ago, the ability of primitive plants to reproduce by seed - - - - - - - - to cope with harsher habitats than could the flora that reproduced by spores.

(A) has allowed for them
(B) was allowed by them
(C) have been allowed them
(D) allowed them

11. Some language experts might say - - - - - - - - to a person speaking a language one does not understand and still determine whether the speaker is excited or exhausted, angry, or pleased.

(A) that possibly it is to listen
(B) what is possible to listen to it
(C) that it is possible to listen
(D) whether is it a possibility to listen

12. David Smith, who welded metal sculptures and relied on his experience as a welder in a factory during World War II, opened new paths for - - - - - - - - to experiment with landscape art composed of objects.

(A) other artists
(B) another, artists
(C) others artists
(D) the others, artists

13. Exercise can be classified as active or passive with the former - - - - - - - - effort and the latter the use of machines or training assistants.

(A) involves physical
(B) physics is involved
(C) involving physical
(D) physically involved

14. The construction of the Alaska Highway - - - - - - - - in 1939 and led to a economic boom and population growth in Northern Territories.

(A) was beginning
(B) it began
(C) has been begun
(D) was begun

15. - - - - - - - - the perishable quality of organic fibers, it is not possible to trace early techniques associated with weaving and interlacing of twines and threads.

(A) Because
(B) Due to the fact that
(C) Because of
(D) Due to the fact

GO ON TO THE NEXT PAGE. ➡

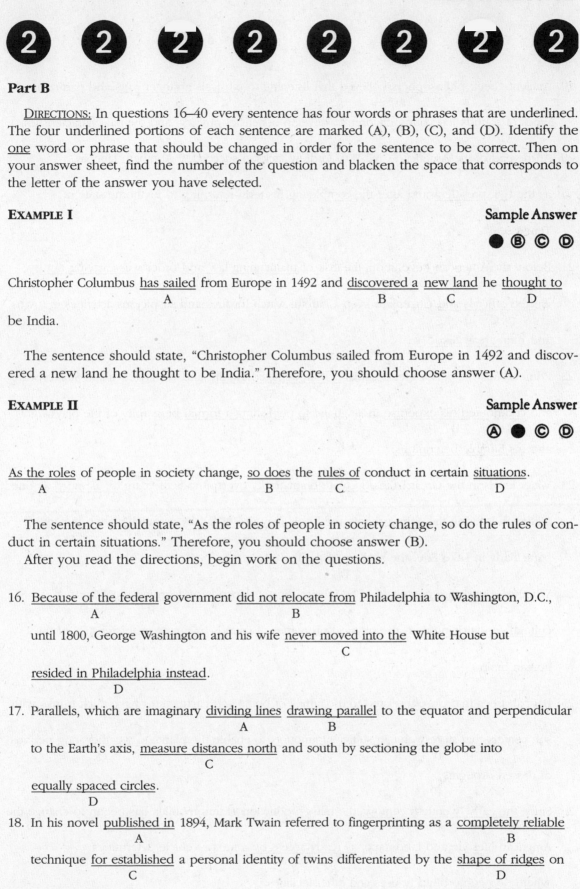

Part B

DIRECTIONS: In questions 16–40 every sentence has four words or phrases that are underlined. The four underlined portions of each sentence are marked (A), (B), (C), and (D). Identify the one word or phrase that should be changed in order for the sentence to be correct. Then on your answer sheet, find the number of the question and blacken the space that corresponds to the letter of the answer you have selected.

EXAMPLE I　　　　　　　　　　　　　　　　　　　　　**Sample Answer**

● Ⓑ Ⓒ Ⓓ

Christopher Columbus <u>has sailed</u> from Europe in 1492 and <u>discovered a</u> <u>new land</u> he <u>thought to</u>
　　　　　　　　　A　　　　　　　　　　　　　　B　　　　　　C　　　　　D

be India.

The sentence should state, "Christopher Columbus sailed from Europe in 1492 and discovered a new land he thought to be India." Therefore, you should choose answer (A).

EXAMPLE II　　　　　　　　　　　　　　　　　　　　**Sample Answer**

Ⓐ ● Ⓒ Ⓓ

<u>As the roles</u> of people in society change, <u>so does</u> the <u>rules of</u> conduct in certain <u>situations</u>.
　A　　　　　　　　　　　　　　　　　　　B　　　　　C　　　　　　　　　　D

The sentence should state, "As the roles of people in society change, so do the rules of conduct in certain situations." Therefore, you should choose answer (B).

After you read the directions, begin work on the questions.

16. <u>Because of the federal</u> government <u>did not relocate from</u> Philadelphia to Washington, D.C.,
　　　　　　A　　　　　　　　　　　　　　B

   until 1800, George Washington and his wife <u>never moved into the</u> White House but
   　　　　　　　　　　　　　　　　　　　　　　C

   <u>resided in Philadelphia instead</u>.
   　　　　D

17. Parallels, which are imaginary <u>dividing lines</u> <u>drawing parallel</u> to the equator and perpendicular
   　　　　　　　　　　　　　　　A　　　　　　B

   to the Earth's axis, <u>measure distances north</u> and south by sectioning the globe into
   　　　　　　　　　　C

   <u>equally spaced circles</u>.
   　　D

18. In his novel <u>published in</u> 1894, Mark Twain referred to fingerprinting as a <u>completely reliable</u>
   　　　　　　A　　　　　　　　　　　　　　　　　　　　　　　　　　　B

   technique <u>for established</u> a personal identity of twins differentiated by the <u>shape of ridges</u> on
   　　　　C　　　　　　　　　　　　　　　　　　　　　　　　　　　D

   their fingertips.

GO ON TO THE NEXT PAGE. ➡

2 2 2 2 2 2 2 2

19. Ancient Greek <u>philosophers believed</u> that listening to <u>musicals arrangements</u> and particular
                    A   B

    <u>types of sounds</u> led young children to develop beneficial <u>physical and mental</u> characteristics.
       C   D

20. At the end of the American Civil War, Andrew Jackson <u>succeeded</u> Abraham Lincoln
                                                 A

    <u>as the U.S. president</u> and after the <u>completing</u> his term <u>returning</u> to his home state of
          B   C   D

    Tennessee.

21. Before the American Revolution, the task of <u>maintaining law and</u> order <u>was carrying out</u> by
                                          A   B

    <u>elected officials and</u> citizens to keep a careful watch for fires and suspicious activities in towns
      C

    and <u>rural areas alike</u>.
          D

22. Edmund Malone was a great scholar <u>whom depicted the life</u> and work of William Shakespeare
                                      A

    and <u>contributed his expertise</u> in language <u>to publishing a formal</u> biography of the playwright
                  B   C

    and <u>his humble beginnings</u>.
            D

23. Water levels in the Great Lakes <u>fluctuate dramatically over</u> periods of years <u>by as much as</u> one
                                    A   B

    meter, and during the spring runoff, the levels <u>may rise or fall</u> by as much as two meters,
                                                C

    particularly in Lake Erie, <u>the shallow of the five</u>.
                                D

24. Whether <u>sounds are perceived</u> to be musical or not depends <u>on learning more</u> and
                   A   B

    <u>cultural conditioning than</u> the physical properties of sounds <u>or innate characteristics</u> of the
            C   D

    human brain.

25. Baobab trees <u>that closely related</u> to the family of bottle and cactus trees have thick trunks with
                   A

    soft centers <u>that store water</u> in <u>sufficient amounts</u> to enable the plants <u>to weather long</u> periods
                  B   C   D

    of dessert droughts.

26. Since <u>the early twentieth century</u>, the mass-production of automobiles <u>has begun to</u> change the
           A   B

    American lifestyle and landscape, <u>as ready access by</u> a motor vehicle determines
                                     C

    <u>where do people</u> build houses and other facilities.
      D

GO ON TO THE NEXT PAGE. ➡

2 2 2 2 2 2 2 2

27. Although radiocarbon dating of <u>archeological finds</u> can prove to be <u>fair reliable</u> for establishing
                                         A   B

    the age of prehistoric objects, additional techniques must <u>be employed</u> to date objects
                                                                      C

    <u>older than</u> 50,000 years.
        D

28. <u>Owing to</u> their superior skill, <u>highly competitive</u> athletes <u>have been known</u> to win contests and
        A   B   C

    break records even <u>when suffered</u> from injuries, physical disorders, and infections.
                            D

29. The keyboard <u>was invented</u> in medieval Europe during <u>the rise of</u> multipart musical composi-
                      A   B

    tions and <u>replacement the</u> mechanical dulcimer in <u>domestic uses</u> and public performances.
                    C   D

30. The Paleo-Indian tribes <u>were able to switch</u> from food gathering and nomadic way of life to
                                 A

    permanent settlements <u>only they</u> acquired <u>means of planting</u> and harvesting <u>more predictable</u>
                               B   C   D

    crops of grain and beans.

31. <u>Hand axes founded</u> in the high banks of the Thames River <u>have been identified</u> as much older
        A   B

    artifacts than pottery shards <u>excavated in the</u> lower flood planes <u>located in different</u> geological
                                        C   D

    strata.

32. In <u>stained-glass work</u>, cut pieces of colored glass <u>are positioned in</u> incremental frames made of
            A   B

    <u>shape metal strips</u> and soldered <u>to a large overall</u> frame.
        C   D

33. The colonies of settlers who <u>were called</u> the "Pennsylvania Dutch" actually <u>consisted from</u>
                                       A   B

    German, Swiss, and Moravian members of religious sects <u>who secluded</u> <u>themselves from</u>
                                                                C   D

    political and social affairs of their secular neighbors.

34. The price theory <u>that represents</u> the core of microeconomics <u>explained how</u> the variability of
                          A   B

    supply and demand <u>in competitive</u> <u>markets creates</u> an interplay of prices for goods and services.
                            C   D

35. Historians believe that Navajo tribes <u>migrated to the</u> south from the northwestern <u>coasts of</u>
                                                A   B

    Alaska and Canada <u>and populated the</u> Southwestern states <u>as recent as</u> 500 years ago.
                            C   D

GO ON TO THE NEXT PAGE. ➡

36. During his remarkable career, Paul Samuelson <u>served as</u> a magazine columnist, <u>consultant to</u>
                                                        A   B
research organizations, <u>advised two</u> presidents, and lecturer on mathematical analysis
                               C
<u>on levels of</u> employment.
        D

37. In 1838, Auguste Compte devised the term "sociology" <u>to refer</u> to a new science that
                                                                   A
<u>will discover</u> regularities of human society <u>similar to</u> laws of nature <u>by employing</u> investigative
        B   C   D
methods.

38. Although zebras are related to horses, <u>they are</u> size is closer <u>to that</u> of donkeys <u>whom they</u>
                                                   A   B   C
resemble in behavior and body form, <u>with short legs</u>, high shoulders, a stiff black mane, large
                                             D
ears, and a tufted tail.

39. <u>Influenced</u> by the advancements in behavioral sciences, George Mead <u>argued</u> that
         A   B
communication and interaction <u>with the environment</u> are the keys to <u>understand</u> an
                                       C   D
organism's self-consciousness.

40. Among the sixteenth-century Dutch painters, Peter Bruegel is <u>the most</u> notable <u>because of</u> his
                                                                       A   B
portrayal of peasant scenes and proverbial folktales that <u>have charmed</u> art aficionados
                                                                  C
<u>since more</u> than 400 years.
       C

►STOP◄

This is the end of Section 2.

Read the directions for Section 3.
Do not read or work on any other section of the test.
Look at the time now before you begin work on Section 3.
Use exactly 55 minutes to work on Section 3.

Section 3
Reading Comprehension

Time: 55 minutes

DIRECTIONS: In this section, you will read several passages. Each is followed by questions about it. For questions, 31–60, you need to select the <u>one</u> best answer, (A), (B), (C), or (D), to each question. Then, on your answer sheet, find the number of the question and blacken the space that corresponds to the letter of the answer you have selected.

Answer all questions following a passage on the basis of what is <u>stated</u> or <u>implied</u> in the passage.

Read the following passage:

> A tomahawk is a small ax used as a tool and a weapon by the North American Indian tribes. An average tomahawk was not very long and did not weigh a great deal. Originally, the head of the tomahawk was made of a shaped stone or an animal bone and was
> *Line* mounted on a wooden handle. After the arrival of the European settlers, the Indians began
> *(5)* to use tomahawks with iron heads. Indian males and females of all ages used tomahawks to chop and cut wood, pound stakes into the ground to put up wigwams, and do many other chores. Indian warriors relied on tomahawks as weapons and even threw them at their enemies. Some types of tomahawks were used in religious ceremonies. Contemporary American idioms reflect this aspect of American heritage.

EXAMPLE 1   **Sample Answer**

Early tomahawk heads were made of   ● Ⓑ Ⓒ Ⓓ

(A) stone or bone
(B) wood or sticks
(C) European iron
(D) religious weapons

According to the passage, the early tomahawk heads were made of stone or bone. Therefore, the correct answer is (A).

EXAMPLE II   **Sample Answer**

How has the Indian use of tomahawks affected American daily life today?   Ⓐ Ⓑ ● Ⓓ

(A) Tomahawks are still used as weapons.
(B) Tomahawks are used as tools for certain jobs.
(C) Contemporary language refers to tomahawks.
(D) Indian tribes cherish them as heirlooms.

The passage states that "Contemporary American idioms reflect this aspect of American heritage." The correct answer is (C).

After you read the directions, begin work on the questions.

GO ON TO THE NEXT PAGE. ➡

Questions 1-12

Architecture has social purposes and meets practical needs by means of combining art and technological innovations. In building construction, however, an emergence of new materials does not make its precursors obsolete, and architectural knowledge is cumulative.
Line The fact that today much is constructed from prefabricated concrete does not do away with
(5) brick. Furthermore, despite dramatic changes and increased technological sophistication of architectural design and construction, the essential apparatus of erecting a building has remained rooted in preindustrial traditional practices passed down during the millennia. The social and utilitarian expectations of structures are largely based on elemental demands of keeping out elements and enemies, ameliorating the extremes of heat, and avoiding the
(10) intrusion of wind, precipitation, and pests.

Gravity, air pressure, and earthquakes can induce tensions that have to be accounted for when constructing functional enclosed space. Vertical stacking of masonry materials causes compression that can lead to important problems when a structure is spanned to build a roof and connect walls. Arches, vaults, and domes were specifically developed to alleviate
(15) the compression by directing the spanning element along a curve rather than a straight line. Building suspension structures, dams, and tunnels became possible in the nineteenth century with the increased availability of steel that could reinforce structural frames and enable them to withstand natural forces previously believed to be insurmountable.

Functional evolutions of modern buildings create new demands on the analysis of struc-
(20) tural behavior and engineering. Few occupants of skyscrapers view elevators as elaborate systems of vertical transportation. Humidity and temperature control, forced ventilation, natural and artificial lighting, sanitation and disposal of waste, electrical wiring, and fire prevention make very tall constructions engineering marvels that also must be aesthetically pleasing and physically convenient.

(25)   Erecting a structure involves a great deal more than merely attending to the aesthetics and psychological experience of architectural space. The shape, size, and incombustibility of locally available construction materials fostered developments of specific technologies, and brick and stone masonry have evolved in response to the need for structural durability. Advances in civil engineering and knowledge associated with properties of building materials combine to lead to
(30) innovations in architectural design. Tools and skills required to exploit easily obtainable materials have continued to inform the development of modern industrialized technologies.

1. What is the main topic of the passage?

   (A) The modern art of architecture and social pressure
   (B) The profound importance of tradition in architecture
   (C) The mutual impact of architecture and technology
   (D) The great technological advances in building materials

2. The word "obsolete" in line 3 is closest in meaning to

   (A) obvious
   (B) obstinate
   (C) antiquarian
   (D) antiquated

3. The author mentions the word "brick" in line 5 as an example of which of the following?

   (A) How old techniques can continue to remain practical
   (B) How old buildings can coexist with modern architecture
   (C) How new knowledge can supplant traditional technology
   (D) How new design can improve traditional construction

GO ON TO THE NEXT PAGE. ➡

4. It can be inferred from the passage that pragmatic requirements of buildings

(A) retain essential sophistication
(B) hold constant over time
(C) stagnate over millennia
(D) stay rooted in the elements

5. What can be inferred from the passage about reducing the effects of material compacting?

(A) Masonry is stacked vertically by increasing compression.
(B) Downward pressure is dispersed by semicircular roofs.
(C) Buildings are spanned to account for the force of gravity.
(D) Vertical roofs are bent to counteract air pressure.

6. The word "withstand" in line 18 is closest in meaning to

(A) endure
(B) enlarge
(C) withdraw
(D) withhold

7. The purpose of paragraph 3 is to suggest that

(A) tall buildings require large amounts of wiring to make them functional
(B) architectural innovations pose new challenges for technological development
(C) skyscrapers need to be appealing and convenient for their occupants
(D) architects of modern buildings create a demand for engineering talent

8. The word "marvels" in line 23 is closest in meaning to

(A) miracle
(B) mirage
(C) conception
(D) construction

9. According to the passage, what is one of the important requirements of building materials?

(A) They need to be large and well shaped.
(B) They should be locally produced.
(C) They do not affect human psychology.
(D) They have to be inflammable.

10. The word "fostered" in line 27 is closest in meaning to

(A) founded
(B) focused
(C) encouraged
(D) enveloped

11. It can be inferred from the passage that architecture and engineering

(A) are at the opposite ends of the technological spectrum
(B) go hand in hand to promote art and science
(C) compete for technological advancements
(D) supercede aesthetic and experiential values

12. The word "inform" in line 31 is closest in meaning to

(A) insist on
(B) infringe on
(C) contrast with
(D) contribute to

GO ON TO THE NEXT PAGE. ➡

Questions 13–21

In the winter of 1848, James Marshall, a carpenter from New Jersey, was contracted by John Sutter to build a sawmill in Coloma in eastern California. On January 24, Marshall dis-covered gold on the mill grounds. He took his find to Sutter, who attempted to keep the
Line news a secret and made his hired hands promise not to divulge it. However, Samuel
(5) Brannan, a shrewd San Francisco businessman, who owned a general store in the vicinity of Sutter's mill, saw potential for profit. In the spring, after hearing the rumors from the storekeeper in Coloma, Brannan hastily traveled to the Sacramento Valley and on his return widely disseminated the news about the untold riches in the diggings.

The first new arrivals assumed that the story of the gold was a hoax, and many were idle
(10) curiosity seekers. However, within weeks, scores of city dwellers began to move by ships and boats to reach the Coloma fort, and in subsequent months, rumors spread further down the coast of California, across the Mexican border, and to Hawaii. In eastern states, the press published reports of miners who struck it rich overnight so vast were the California gold deposits. Between 1848 and 1851, in all, around half a million fortune-seekers from
(15) around the globe descended on California to pursue instant wealth and thus took part in one of the largest migrations in history.

The accounts of the Sutter Mill deposits were not entirely untruthful. In December of 1848, President James Polk confirmed the news about the California gold in a statement to Congress, and the message was picked up by press agencies worldwide. Not all Forty-
(20) Niners, as the prospectors came to be known, made their journey in vain. The swath of gold-bearing quartz ran 100 miles wide along the Sierra Nevada mountain range and stretched from La Porte to Mariposa. During the initial stages of the Gold Fever, yields of $300 to $400 a day were not infrequent, and by the end of 1849, nearly $10 million worth of deposits had been excavated. However, as competition for land claims increased, yields
(25) and profits began to drop off, and ore nuggets and dust began to disappear from dry streambeds and ravines. As mining operations became more laborious, individual prospec-tors were replaced by large commercial ventures, when groups of miners employed their penniless counterparts to divert and dry up rivers with strategically positioned dams and canals. The gold rush of 1849 was followed by the next wave of migrants headed to the
(30) Klondike region in Yukon Territory in mid-1897 to recover the gold at the conflation of two rivers.

13. The word "contracted" in line 1 is closest in meaning to

(A) empowered
(B) employed
(C) emboldened
(D) embodied

14. According to the passage, who was initially instrumental in diffusing accounts of Coloma gold?

(A) A carpenter
(B) A mill owner
(C) A merchant
(D) A business operator

GO ON TO THE NEXT PAGE. ➡

15. In line 5, the word "vicinity" is closest in meaning to

(A) proximity
(B) propensity
(C) propriety
(D) profundity

16. The purpose of paragraph 2 is to demonstrate

(A) the suspicions of curiosity seekers
(B) the significance of population resettlement
(C) the influence of published press reports
(D) the wealth of gold deposits

17. The word "scores" in line 10 is closest in meaning to

(A) a greater good
(B) a great stock
(C) a great many
(D) a greater evil

18. It can be inferred from the passage that California gold had a variety of

(A) polemical and ecological outcomes
(B) proclamations and denunciations in the White House
(C) proponents and opponents in Congress
(D) political and economic ramifications

19. In line 20, the word "prospectors" is closest in meaning to

(A) entrepreneurs
(B) enthusiasts
(C) miners
(D) minions

20. It can be inferred from the passage that many Forty Niners

(A) acquired great wealth
(B) infected many laborers
(C) attained great dispositions
(D) inflated many recounts

21. The author of the passage implies that the California Gold Fever

(A) was a unique event in North American history
(B) was a singular event in the succession of others
(C) presented a lone occurrence on the North American continent
(D) preserved a unique page in North American development

GO ON TO THE NEXT PAGE. ➡

Questions 22–31

During the late Middle Ages, oil paint took hold as the artistic medium of choice because it was effective, flexible, and resilient relative to the wax-based, watercolor, fresco, or tempera paints prevalent at the time. Although contemporary commercially prepared paints *Line* contain a mixture of pigments and linseed oil, poppy oil paints are also available to con-
(5) noisseurs. The original recipes developed in medieval European monasteries relied on fast-drying bases derived from various organic oils predominantly valued for their medicinal qualities. The pigments are insoluble, lightproof, and chemically inert powders ground in the base. Occasionally, varnish can be added to increase the paste's ability to reflect light and to cover pictures with a protective seal. The resulting stiff, resinous compounds are
(10) often packaged in flexible metal or plastic tubes. Historically, yellow pigments have been added to the oil, and then the paste was layered over tin foil to imitate the appearance of gold leaf.

Despite the numerous experiments to accelerate the drying process, oil paints dry comparatively slowly with little color alteration. An important advantage of color stability is that
(15) tones and undertones are easy to blend, match, transpose, and grade, and mistakes and smudges are simple to correct. Due to the creamy consistency of most mixtures, artists can exploit their viscosity in thick applications, sprays, thin trickles, and three-dimensional blobs. The purification by boiling and filtering and bleaching of oils can impart varied hues to powdered pigments, while drying time can be reduced by adding metallic oxides.
(20) Professional painters who mix their own medium usually have their own trademark methods of mixing materials that art experts recognize as a part of an artist's creative work.

The thickness of the paste also plays an important role in defining the stages of painting a picture. After the basic design is sketched in pencil or charcoal, the broad background or foreground areas of the canvas are covered with thin, diluted paint on top of the primer. A
(25) thicker paint, often with added varnish, is subsequently used to refine and outline the foundation. The width of the brush depends on the type of paint the artist chooses to use, and stiff bristles are usually found in narrow brushes for making sharp lines, while softer brushes of animal hair can be employed in broad strokes.

22. What does the passage mainly discuss?

(A) The evolution and history of oil paintings and media
(B) The technology and development of drying oils
(C) The recipes and ingredients for producing oil paints
(D) The composition and techniques for mixing oil paints

23. It can be inferred from the passage that oil paintings

(A) supplanted the use of tempera and fresco
(B) took hold of the artistic choices in the Middle Ages
(C) promoted artistic talent since the early times
(D) supported the usefulness of applying paints

GO ON TO THE NEXT PAGE. ➡

24. In lines 4 and 5, the word "connoisseurs" is closest in meaning to

   (A) explorers
   (B) experts
   (C) exporters
   (D) experimenters

25. According to the passage, medieval monks extracted oil

   (A) from minerals
   (B) in conjunction with pigments
   (C) from plants
   (D) in combination with medicines

26. In line 8, the phrase "the base" is closest in meaning to

   (A) paint
   (B) oil
   (C) chemicals
   (D) pestle

27. The purpose of paragraph 2 is to illustrate

   (A) the laboriousness of making oil paints
   (B) the durability of oil colors
   (C) the complexity of oil purification
   (D) the superiority of oil paints

28. In line 17, the word "viscosity" is closest in meaning to

   (A) stiffness
   (B) elasticity
   (C) stickiness
   (D) eloquence

29. Which of the following is NOT mentioned as components of oil paints?

   (A) accelerants
   (B) retarders
   (C) sealants
   (D) glosses

30. In line 20, the word "trademark" is closest in meaning to

   (A) signature
   (B) selection
   (C) significance
   (D) secret

31. The author of the passage implies that an oil painting

   (A) requires professional painters to mix their own paint
   (B) contains a layer of canvas and charcoal
   (C) thickens as the oil continues to dry in stages
   (D) requires multiple layers of brushwork

GO ON TO THE NEXT PAGE. ➡

Questions 32–41

Samuel Johnson's achievements in lexicography and writing have few rivals in English eighteenth-century literature. Johnson was born on September 18, 1709, in the family of a bookseller and stationer, and his education began informally among his father's books, as
Line Samuel was above all an insatiable reader. During his years at Pembroke College, Oxford,
(5) he acquired a reputation for prodigious learning and eccentricities that were as diverse as his reading. After being plagued by many ailments and emotional breakdowns, he was compelled to leave the college in poverty, and later in life, his despondency led him to a profound devotion to religion.

Following his father's death in 1731, Johnson tried his hand in teaching and attempted to
(10) run a school, but his early ventures met with rapid demise. When Johnson was twenty-six, he married Elizabeth Porter, a widow with a little fortune, who was twenty years his senior and who became the source of calm, support, and self-confidence in his life. In 1737 in London, Johnson began a life-long period of writing and lexicographic work that made him a figure of renown.

(15) To his contemporaries, Johnson was known as a man of large and unwieldy constitution and unpleasant manner. He recklessly dominated conversations, monopolized discussion topics, and boorishly overwhelmed opposing points of view. His antagonistic habits cost him many a friend. In 1747, burdened with extreme poverty, Johnson was commissioned to compile a dictionary by a consortium of booksellers who sought to raise their volume of
(20) sales. After eight years of obsessive and consuming labor, this monumental work with 40,000 entries with lucid, witty, occasionally spiteful, and idiosyncratic definitions, titled *Dictionary of the English Language*, saw the light of day in 1755. The remarkable, still-quoted lexicographic work with an enormous range of elucidating descriptions and illustrative exemplars became the imitable forerunner of how English language dictionaries are con-
(25) structed to this day.

During the nineteenth century, literary critics largely saw Johnson's literary contributions as slight with regard to their scholarly influence. It was perhaps Johnson's personal attributes that influenced the perspective through which he was portrayed. While his prose was viewed as dignified, vivid, and urbane, his vast body of work in poetry, novels, essays,
(30) tragedies, travelogues, biographies, diaries, and satire remained obscure until Joseph Krutch, an American critic, published a penetrating study *Samuel Johnson* in 1944. In 1978, Walter Bate won a Pulitzer Prize for his comprehensive psychological biography of Johnson that established him as rational, compassionate, and undaunted advocate of moral order and unceasing quest for truth.

32. What does the passage mainly discuss?

(A) The life, ailments, and dictionary of Samuel Johnson
(B) Samuel Johnson's controversial character and work
(C) Samuel Johnson's contradictory traits and publications
(D) The family, commissions, and biographies of Samuel Johnson

33. In line 5, the word "prodigious" is closest in meaning to

(A) immoral
(B) imminent
(C) immense
(D) immediate

GO ON TO THE NEXT PAGE. ➡

34. In line 6, the word "plagued" is closest in meaning to

 (A) diseased
 (B) disfigured
 (C) trampled
 (D) tormented

35. It can be inferred from the passage that Samuel Johnson

 (A) did not earn a college degree
 (B) did not enter a prestigious college
 (C) evaded unusual behaviors
 (D) avoided extremes of emotion

36. According to the passage, Johnson's marriage

 (A) was a miserable failure due to poverty
 (B) was motivated by convenience and money
 (C) provided him a safe haven
 (D) afforded him new writing venues

37. The word "antagonistic" in line 17 is closest in meaning to

 (A) hallow
 (B) heated
 (C) hospitable
 (D) hostile

38. According to the passage, the *Dictionary* descriptions of word meanings

 (A) are emulated by modern lexicographers
 (B) were not without peculiarities
 (C) are considered exemplary by linguists
 (D) were not consistently illustrated

39. The word "obscure" in line 30 is closest in meaning to

 (A) offensive
 (B) obtuse
 (C) irrelevant
 (D) irreverent

40. Which of the following is NOT mentioned among the genres of Johnson's writing?

 (A) Plays
 (B) Biographies
 (C) Quotations
 (D) Articles

41. The word "slight" in line 27 is closest in meaning to

 (A) trivial
 (B) triumphant
 (C) sinister
 (D) solemn

GO ON TO THE NEXT PAGE. ➡

Questions 42–50

Psychologists who work on motivation research a wide range of human traits and physiological characteristics that include the effects of hunger, reward, and punishment, as well as desires for power, tangible achievement, social acceptance, belongingness, self-esteem,
Line and self-actualization. A plethora of hypotheses developed in the nineteenth and twentieth
(5) centuries have the goal of identifying causes of an organism's behavior that can be both conscious and unconscious. The hierarchical organization of human needs is a theoretical model, originally established by an American psychologist, Abraham Maslow, in 1954. The needs located at the bottom of the pyramid are the essentials of physiological survival that encompass oxygen, water, nutrition, rest, and avoidance of pain. Maslow's theory, grounded
(10) in research, also stipulated that these are variable and, at least to some extent, may explain, for example, food gratification. The second tier is rooted in the human need for safety, stability, and protection.

In the human life cycle, the needs for belonging are manifested in the desires to marry, have a family, belong in a community or among similarly minded people. In part, the need
(15) to belong can also show up in a search for particular types of occupations or careers. The next level of the hierarchy in effect deals with two substrata, where the first presumes the need for status, prestige, recognition, appreciation, and dominance, and the higher division includes a conglomeration of emotionally centered traits that pivot on competence, confidence, mastery, achievement, independence, and freedom.

(20) The top tier is different from all others, and Maslow referred to it as growth motivation and self-actualization. At the highest level, individuals seek to realize and put to use their creativity, talent, leadership, curiosity, and understanding. At this level people can reach their full potentials and accurately perceive and accept reality, seek privacy and depth in personal relationships, resist enculturation, and develop social interests, compassion, and
(25) humanity. In many cases, self-actualizers do not lead ordinary lives, choose growth over safety, and cultivate peak experiences that leave their mark and change one for the better.

42. According to the passage, what does psychology of motivation attempt to uncover?

(A) Reactions to hunger and desires for power
(B) Developments of human physiology and mind
(C) Reasons for human conduct and moving forces
(D) Organization of human society and hierarchies

43. The word "plethora" in line 4 is closest in meaning to

(A) oversimplification
(B) overlap
(C) overreach
(D) overabundance

44. It can be inferred from the passage that in Maslow's hierarchy

(A) the first layer of needs dominates other tiers
(B) the highest level of the model supercedes the lower levels
(C) the second layer of needs is more urgent than the first
(D) the third level of the model is embedded in the fourth

45. The word "these" in line 10 refers to

(A) theory and research
(B) rest and avoidance of pain
(C) oxygen, water, nutrition, and rest
(D) the lowest set of factors

GO ON TO THE NEXT PAGE. ➡

46. The word "gratification" in line 11 is closest in meaning to

(A) gratitude
(B) pleasure
(C) gratuity
(D) pleasantry

47. It can be inferred from the passage that in modern-day terms, the second layer of needs can be reflected in people's desire for

(A) a house in an upscale neighborhood
(B) a protected existence and dependence
(C) a measure of job and financial security
(D) a degree of friendship and family life

48. The word "conglomeration" in line 18 is closest in meaning to

(A) complex
(B) congress
(C) conjunction
(D) connotation

49. Which of the following is NOT mentioned as a factor in human motivation?

(A) Esteem
(B) Participation
(C) Accomplishment
(D) Conformism

50. Which of the following conclusions is supported by the passage?

(A) Genuine self-actualizers may attain self-satisfaction.
(B) Sincere self-promoters can achieve full contentment.
(C) Real self-starters can achieve their lives' desires.
(D) True self-actualizers may lead complicated lives.

A. Tapescript for Chapter 4: Listening Comprehension

Exercise 1. Idioms and Two- or Three-Word Verbs

Part A

1. (Woman) How is Brian's mother doing?
   (Man) Brian hasn't heard from his mother since last month.
   (Narrator) What does the man mean? (12 seconds)

2. (Man) What did Professor White think about the study?
   (Woman) She pointed out the data's shortcomings that more or less affected the analysis of results.
   (Narrator) What can be said about Professor White? (12 seconds)

3. (Woman) In November, I'll need to find time to write the final exam.
   (Man) Because we'll be busy at the end of term, the final exam questions can be written ahead of time.
   (Narrator) What does the man mcan? (12 seconds)

4. (Man) Our product release date has been delayed again.
   (Woman) Could you let me know if you change your mind about taking time off next week?
   (Narrator) What does the woman mean? (12 seconds)

5. (Woman) Did Ann finish her wedding preparations?
   (Man) After the florist dropped off the samples of flower arrangements, Ann spent the whole day picking out the prettiest ones.
   (Narrator) What does the man say happened? (12 seconds)

6. (Man) William was late for the meeting.
   (Woman) It's no wonder. He had to walk for five blocks after he got off the bus at the wrong stop.
   (Narrator) What does the woman say about William? (12 seconds)

7. (Woman) How were Jane's grades?
   (Man) She dropped out of school before the grades were even posted.
   (Narrator) What does the man say about Jane? (12 seconds)

8. (Man) So Ellen finally got a new car?
   (Woman) She uses it every other day when she needs to go over to North Campus.
   (Narrator) What does the woman mean? (12 seconds)

9. (Woman) Can I talk to my agent about my house insurance policy?
   (Man)   Mr. Winters is about to leave for lunch and will not be able to check into your coverage until he comes back.
   (Narrator) What does the man mean? (12 seconds)

10. (Man)   How did Robert do on the writing test?
    (Woman) He left out part of the first sentence and didn't put a period after the second.
    (Narrator) What can be said about Robert? (12 seconds)

11. (Man)   Last month, I took on extra work and still couldn't save anything.
    (Woman) You could cut down on movies and the fancy dinners you like so much.
    (Narrator) What does the woman think the man should do? (12 seconds)

12. (Woman) I think it's about time the textbook in this class was replaced.
    (Man)   Why don't you bring it up at the meeting tomorrow?
    (Narrator) What does the man mean? (12 seconds)

13. (Man)   Yesterday, Bob ran into Sarah at the grocery store by the elementary school.
    (Woman) What was she doing there if she lives on Main Street?
    (Narrator) Where was Sarah yesterday? (12 seconds)

14. (Woman) You can come to Kansas with us. We are taking off next Friday, and we are going to drive through Illinois and Missouri.
    (Man)   It sounds like an interesting idea, but actually I was thinking of going to the ocean.
    (Narrator) What will the man probably do? (12 seconds)

15. (Man)   The Morrison Company turned down my application for their new position in the accounting department. I don't know how I can do without a job.
    (Woman) Well, don't take it so hard. Something else will turn up.
    (Narrator) What does the woman mean? (12 seconds)

16. (Woman) It's remarkable how quickly you finished paving the driveway. I'm impressed; it looks professionally done.
    (Man)   I had my brothers do some of it.
    (Narrator) What does the man mean? (12 seconds)

17. (Man)   How about a nice stroll by the river? We can look at the sunset, watch the water flow by, and listen to the birds sing.
    (Woman) To be honest, I'm not up to it. I feel a little out of sorts.
    (Narrator) What does the woman mean? (12 seconds)

18. (Man)   I wish Jack wouldn't mumble. Half of the time, I can't even make out what he is saying.
    (Woman) What he says is so unimportant that it wouldn't make any difference even if you did.
    (Narrator) What can be said of Jack? (12 seconds)

19. (Woman) I hear Chuck is not very well off even though he works day and night to make a living.
    (Man)   Well, he has his mother and two younger sisters to look after.
    (Narrator) What does the man mean? (12 seconds)

20. (Man)   It doesn't make sense for you to take the children to the dentist, go to the library, and then return downtown to pick them up.
    (Woman) Of course, you could stop by the library on your way home and check the book out for me.
    (Narrator) What is the woman suggesting? (12 seconds)

Part B

(Narrator) Questions 21 through 28 refer to the following dialogue.

(Woman) Hello, Harry. I thought it was you in the periodicals' section. I haven't seen you in ages.

(Man) Hello, Sue. The reason I haven't been around is that I've barely had the time to keep up with all things I have to do. I've been helping my brother remodel his house, and meanwhile my sister has arrived from San Diego. Well, you know how it is. We've been talking nonstop since she got here. And on top of it all, my mother's been under the weather, and I've also been visiting her quite a bit.

(Woman) It's a shame you've been so busy.

(Man) Well, how about you? What are you up to?

(Woman) Actually, an old friend I used to know in high school has talked me into going back to college this fall.

(Man) I can't believe it. Good for you. I'm glad you finally made up your mind to do it.

(Woman) To tell the truth, I don't have much confidence. It's been five years since I had to worry about homework. I'm here looking for a book so I can bone up on math before classes start.

(Man) I've got some old college texts that might help. You're welcome to them. Just come over any time. I'm positive you'll be in good shape before you know it.

(Woman) Thank you very much. I'll drop by sometime tomorrow if it's okay.

(Man) No problem. Well, I have to get going. See you then.

(Narrator)

21. Where is this conversation taking place? (12 seconds)
22. What can be said about the man's brother? (12 seconds)
23. What did the man say about his mother? (12 seconds)
24. How long has it been since the woman went to school? (12 seconds)
25. What does the woman plan to do? (12 seconds)
26. What does the man mean when he says "I can't believe it?" (12 seconds)
27. When is the woman going to review math? (12 seconds)
28. What does the man say to reassure the woman? (12 seconds)

Exercise 2. Implied Meanings

Part A

1. (Man) I'd like to make a reservation for next Friday. We'd like to sit by a window, if possible.
   (Woman) You'll need to call next Monday then.
   (Narrator) What does the woman imply? (12 seconds)

2. (Woman) I thought Molly would've called by now.
   (Man) If Molly could call you, I am sure she would.
   (Narrator) What does the man mean? (12 seconds)

3. (Man) What are you planning to do tomorrow?
   (Woman) Harold asked all his friends to pitch in with the packing before he rents the truck on Thursday.
   (Narrator) What does the woman mean? (12 seconds)

4. (Woman)   Can I take the composition course now?
   (Man)   Because our budget for this semester has been cut, it won't be offered until the spring term.
   (Narrator) What does the man imply? (12 seconds)

5. (Man)   How did Karen like her new clothes?
   (Woman)   She decided to return the skirt because it didn't match the blouse her mother gave her for her birthday.
   (Narrator) What does the woman mean? (12 seconds)

6. (Woman)   I wish Nancy could come with me to the welcome reception at the Athletic Club next Saturday.
   (Man)   She is invited, isn't she?
   (Narrator) What does the man ask? (12 seconds)

7. (Man)   I can't say that I am happy to be back.
   (Woman)   It's hard to believe that only a week ago we were swimming in the ocean and taking walks in the woods.
   (Narrator) What does the woman imply? (12 seconds)

8. (Woman)   I am going to try a new recipe for dinner tonight.
   (Man)   Cooking a meal every day has never been something I could either enjoy or become good at.
   (Narrator) What does the man mean? (12 seconds)

9. (Man)   Dr. Collins doesn't seem to be in his office.
   (Woman)   He doesn't hold regular office hours in the summer.
   (Narrator) What does the woman imply? (12 seconds)

10. (Woman) Look at this mess! I'll have to spend the rest of the day on it.
    (Man)   While you are cleaning the kitchen, I'll straighten up the living room and the play area in the basement. It won't take long if we both do the work.
    (Narrator) What does the man mean? (12 seconds)

11. (Man)   Had Fred told me he needed a hand, I would have fixed his faucet for him.
    (Woman) Well, you know how Fred is.
    (Narrator) What does the woman mean? (12 seconds)

12. (Man)   It looks like a new coat of paint will be necessary.
    (Woman) I can't guarantee that we can match the color on the hood and the passenger door.
    (Narrator) Where does this conversation take place? (12 seconds)

13. (Woman) They say that breakfast is the most important meal of the day.
    (Man)   Who has the time to eat breakfast?
    (Narrator) What does the man imply? (12 seconds)

14. (Man)   If this drought continues, farmers will lose half their crops.
    (Woman) They predict that the dry spell will end soon.
    (Narrator) What can be said about the weather outlook? (12 seconds)

15. (Man)   If you lose a library book, you have to buy a replacement. Another option is to pay the fine, but paying the fine usually is more expensive than buying the book.
    (Woman) In this case, I'll start looking for it in stores.
    (Narrator) What does the man mean? (12 seconds)

16. (Man)   Nobody by this name works here. The address on this letter is incorrect. What do you think I should do with it?
    (Woman)   Try calling the post office.
    (Narrator) What is the woman suggesting? (12 seconds)

17. (Woman)   I think it's terrific that Larry is going to stay with us for a week.
    (Man)   We'll see what you say next Tuesday.
    (Narrator) What does the man mean? (12 seconds)

18. (Woman)   I saw Steve with Carol at the air show a couple of days ago. But I thought he was dating Sally.
    (Man)   That was *last* week.
    (Narrator) What can be said about Steve? (12 seconds)

19. (Woman)   The election report has to be typed up right away, but Becky is busy copying right now.
    (Man)   Give the typing to Frank. He's been discussing his baseball game with Brian for the past twenty minutes.
    (Narrator) What is Frank's occupation? (12 seconds)

20. (Man)   My nephew bought an expensive new calculator, and he can't figure out how to operate it.
    (Woman)   An instruction booklet came with it, didn't it?
    (Narrator) What is the woman suggesting? (12 seconds)

Part B

(Narrator) Questions 21 through 28 refer to the following dialogue.

(Man)   I am sure you have some friends who are thin and others who are heavier. Everyone does. But it's really amazing to learn some of the reasons why people are the way they are. People's eating habits are formed by different pressures that they experience while growing up. Even in the same family, different children can form different habits as a result of their interactions with parents and brothers and sisters.

(Woman)   Really? Do you mean that a person's adult weight can be determined by childhood habits?

(Man)   Yes. Parents really have a strong influence on the development of children's attitudes and create habits that will last a lifetime. If food is used as a reward, for example, the daily snacks or sweets can lead to a dependence on food as a source of comfort. If parents tell children to clean their plates, children may eat more than they actually need. Over time, a few extra calories a day will add up to extra pounds. Adults who were overweight in childhood may have difficulty losing weight.

(Woman)   So, does the habit of overeating begin in childhood? It seems strange that adults are not able to change their behaviors.

(Man)   Well, it may not be so strange if you think about it. Every person has a self-image, that is, a mental picture of how he or she looks to others. People who are overweight often see themselves as unattractive. Those who see dealing with other people as threatening may overeat on purpose to make themselves less attractive. Being fat gives them an excuse for not having close friendships.

(Woman)   I can't believe that someone would become fat on purpose.

(Man)   Okay, let's take an example. Someone who is fat can say, "I don't have many friends because I am fat," although this may not be necessarily the only reason. Eating too much is a common way to feel better when people are frustrated and anxious. Some people eat too much when they are tired, worried, or scared. Psychologists say that the reasons for obesity are frequently related to emotional problems or difficulties.

(Narrator)

21. When are eating habits formed? (12 seconds)
22. Who has a major influence on the development of eating habits? (12 seconds)
23. Why do children often eat more than they need? (12 seconds)
24. How do children's wrong eating habits affect their lives as adults? (12 seconds)
25. Why is self-image important? (12 seconds)
26. How do some people use the fact that they are fat? (12 seconds)
27. How do some people cope with frustration and anxiety? (12 seconds)
28. How do psychologists describe the connection between emotional problems and obesity? (12 seconds)

Exercise 3. Specific Questions

Part C

(Narrator)   Questions 1 through 8 refer to the following lecture on telescopes.

(Woman)   Welcome to the University Observatory. We are very glad to have you here and hope that during your tour you will learn a great deal about how telescopes work and how they are constructed. To begin, telescopes are optical instruments that magnify objects located at a distance. Mostly, they are used to observe visible light given off by other objects. The refracting telescope, like this one to my right, is the simplest, containing a small eyepiece with two lenses that magnify the image. At the other end from the eyepiece, the object lens gathers light from the object that one is looking at. To focus the refracting telescope, the viewer must adjust the distance between the objective and the eyepiece. Today, the basic principle involved in the construction of the refracting telescope is used only in theater binoculars. It's considered too basic even for field binoculars, which produce a much sharper image.

The reflecting telescope is far more sophisticated than its refracting prototype. First of all, reflecting telescopes are usually much larger and have a substantially greater light-gathering capacity. Therefore, they allow an observer to see and photograph fainter objects than he or she could with refracting instruments. The main difference between them is that the reflecting telescope includes a curved mirror that serves as an objective. In addition, a smaller mirror is placed inside the tube near the eyepiece at a forty-five degree angle to the objective. When light waves enter the tube, the objective reflects them to the smaller mirror, which, in turn, reflects them into the eyepiece. As you can see, the eyepiece is located on the side of the telescope tube at a ninety-degree angle to it. In a combination refracting-reflecting telescope, the eyepiece is set behind the objective, which has a tiny opening in its center. When the light waves strike the objective, they are reflected back to a small mirror in front of the objective.

(Narrator)

1. Where does the lecture take place? (12 seconds)
2. What is the speaker's occupation? (12 seconds)
3. What is the main purpose of telescopes? (12 seconds)
4. How are images brought into focus in the refracting telescope? (12 seconds)
5. In what instruments is the refracting principle still used today? (12 seconds)
6. How many types of telescopes are mentioned in the lecture? (12 seconds)
7. What are the advantages of reflecting telescopes over refracting ones? (12 seconds)
8. What is the purpose of the mirrors in the reflecting telescope? (12 seconds)

Exercise 4. Emphasis, Stress, and Tone

Part A

1. (Woman) The door bell is ringing.
   (Man) Why is it always *my turn* to answer the door?
   (Narrator) What does the man imply? (12 seconds)

2. (Man) Did your husband put in the shrubs in just one day?
   (Woman) Dick not only planted *the hedge*, but he also trimmed *the trees*.
   (Narrator) What does the woman say about her husband? (12 seconds)

3. (Woman) Didn't Dennis take care of the parking ticket for you?
   (Man) Dennis remembered to pay his ticket, but he certainly forgot *mine*.
   (Narrator) What does the man mean? (12 seconds)

4. (Man) I can't believe Martha is having more food.
   (Woman) She won't be happy until she gets her *dessert*.
   (Narrator) What does the woman say about Martha? (12 seconds)

5. (Woman) I don't understand why you are so upset.
   (Man) How would *you* feel if you had to do all the chores around here?
   (Narrator) What does the man imply? (12 seconds)

6. (Man) Natalie is a polite and helpful child. We enjoyed having her over and would like her to visit again.
   (Woman) Are you talking about *my* daughter?
   (Narrator) What does the woman mean? (12 seconds)

7. (Woman) Before I take you to the airport, do you want to have a quick dinner at the Italian place near the Plaza?
   (Man) You can't have a *quick* dinner there.
   (Narrator) What does the man imply? (12 seconds)

8. (Woman) The light is still on in Emily's room. Do you suppose she is up at this hour?
   (Man) How should *I* know?
   (Narrator) What does the man mean? (12 seconds)

9. (Man) The new episode of your favorite show is on at 10 tonight. We can curl up on the couch and watch it together.
   (Woman) Not with the *manuscript* deadline coming up, we won't.
   (Narrator) What does the woman mean? (12 seconds)

10. (Woman) Now what's the problem?
    (Man) *This* time, I think it's the brakes.
    (Narrator) What does the man mean? (12 seconds)

Exercise 5. Sound Discrimination

Part A

1. (Man) This corn doesn't taste right.
   (Woman) Corn on the cob should be served with butter.
   (Narrator) What does the woman imply? (12 seconds)

2. (Woman) So, what did your family decide to do during the break?
   (Man)   Bill's idea of traveling to the shore resort won hands down.
   (Narrator) What does the man say about Bill? (12 seconds)

3. (Man)   How much do I owe you?
   (Woman) Let me pay for this drink, and you can pick up the tab for the next one.
   (Narrator) What does the woman mean? (12 seconds)

4. (Woman) What time does Andy need to get started?
   (Man)   He wound up the clock and set the alarm for three in the morning.
   (Narrator) What does the man say about Andy? (12 seconds)

5. (Man)   John has left for the airport.
   (Woman) How careless of him to leave his clothes and pills behind!
   (Narrator) What does the woman mean? (12 seconds)

6. (Man)   Why is there such a long line?
   (Woman) The bookstore is giving away free pencils to all those who purchase texts.
   (Narrator) What does the woman mean? (12 seconds)

7. (Man)   This area is so crowded that there is no room to work.
   (Woman) The files on the desk should be removed and put on the shelf.
   (Narrator) What is the woman suggesting? (12 seconds)

8. (Woman) I've heard that the director made an announcement. Do you know what the
             issue was?
   (Man)   He said that Arnold lacks the funds to complete his research.
   (Narrator) What was the announcement? (12 seconds)

9. (Man)   Marsha is tired of Rob's practical jokes. I think next time, she'll give him a
             piece of her mind.
   (Woman) Rob's humor can be hard to take.
   (Narrator) What will Marsha do? (12 seconds)

10. (Woman) Can I help you with something?
    (Man)   I've been trying to catch a cab for the past fifteen minutes, and there isn't one
              in sight.
    (Narrator) What does the man mean? (12 seconds)

Exercise 6. Comparisons

Part A

1. (Woman) Among your sons, Phil seems to have a particular talent for languages.
   (Man)   Phil writes better essays than George, but he speaks German less fluently than
             Sam.
   (Narrator) What does the man mean? (12 seconds)

2. (Man)   Are you a good typist?
   (Woman) I can type faster than Martin, but I also make more errors per page.
   (Narrator) What does the woman say about her typing? (12 seconds)

3. (Woman) The city council has approved the funding to add a turn lane to this road.
   (Man)   If the road is made wider, the sidewalk will have to be narrowed.
   (Narrator) What does the man mean? (12 seconds)

4. (Man)   Both Alex and Dan look fit.
(Woman) Although Alex weighs as much as Dan, he is five inches shorter.
(Narrator) What does the woman mean? (12 seconds)

5. (Woman) It gets dark early these days.
(Man)   In December, the days are shorter and the nights longer than in March.
(Narrator) What does the man mean? (12 seconds)

6. (Man)   If the blue dress is made of cheaper fabric than the red one, why is the blue one more expensive?
(Woman) It's more stylish.
(Narrator) How do the dresses compare? (12 seconds)

7. (Woman) Is the sales tally in yet?
(Man)   We sold more vehicles than in any one month in the past two years. The total comes to thirteen passenger cars, seven pick-up trucks, four vans, and just as many station wagons.
(Narrator) How many station wagons were sold? (12 seconds)

8. (Woman) According to the road atlas, the ride to Boston shouldn't have taken more than two and a half hours.
(Man)   The actual ride wouldn't have taken much more than that. It's the traffic jam that slowed us down for about an hour.
(Narrator) How long has the trip taken? (12 seconds)

9. (Man)   Five years ago, the gasoline tax was fifteen percent, then it was eight percent, and now it's close to twelve percent.
(Woman) If you crossed the state border, the tax would be twice as high.
(Narrator) About how much is the tax in the neighboring state? (12 seconds)

10. (Man)   Last time I wore this suit, it fit just fine. I think the suit coat has shrunk, and the pants have also become tighter.
(Woman) The suit isn't smaller. You've gotten fatter.
(Narrator) What has changed? (12 seconds)

Part B

<u>DIRECTIONS</u>: Choose the one sentence that is the best answer to the question you heard on the recording.

(Man)   We need to find a larger apartment. This one is too small. We have no room for storage, and the kitchen is not big enough for all of us.

(Woman) Although a bigger place would be nice, we can hardly afford to pay more than we are paying already.

(Man)   Well, we'll need to move out of the suburbs and closer to the city if we want a cheaper and larger place. Also, if we move, we can find an apartment that's closer to your office.

(Woman) A shorter drive is always a plus, but it's not as important to me as being able to pay the rent. The highway I take to work is not bad, and I don't mind the commute. Of course, taking the highway is the quickest way for me to get to work.

(Man)   Actually, I already called one place on Pine Street and made an appointment. We can go and look this afternoon if you have the time.

(Woman) I was planning to do some work on my status report, but it can wait. When do we need to leave?

(Narrator)

11. What is the main topic of this conversation? (12 seconds)
12. According to the conversation, where can they find cheaper rent? (12 seconds)
13. According to the woman, what is the most important consideration in their search? (12 seconds)
14. Where are the man and the woman going later in the day? (12 seconds)

B. Tapescripts for Practice TOEFL Tests 1–8

The Listening Comprehension section of the test is divided into three parts: Part A, Part B, and Part C. On the actual TOEFL test, you have twelve seconds to answer each question, and five seconds when you hear GO TO THE NEXT PAGE. You may need a stopwatch to time yourself while you are taking the Practice TOEFL tests in this book.

On the actual TOEFL test, you should mark your best choice for each answer because points are NOT taken off for wrong answers. The instructions for the Listening Comprehension sections of the practice TOEFL tests are given on the compact disc.

Read the directions in your book while you listen to the instructions on the recording.

Practice TOEFL 1

SECTION 1

LISTENING COMPREHENSION

(Narrator)   In this section, you will demonstrate your skills in understanding spoken English. There are three parts in the Listening Comprehension section, with different tasks in each.

Part A

DIRECTIONS: In Part A you will hear short conversations between two people. At the end of each conversation, a third person will ask a question about what the two people said. Each conversation and each question will be spoken only one time. For this reason, you must listen carefully to understand what each speaker says. After you hear a conversation and the question, read the four selections and choose the *one* that is the best answer to the question the speaker asked. Then, on your answer sheet, find the number of the question and blacken the space that corresponds to the letter for the answer you have chosen. Blacken the space completely so that the letter inside the space does not show.

Listen to the following example.

On the recording, you hear:
    (Man)   Does the car need to be filled?
    (Woman)   Mary stopped at the gas station on her way home.
    (Narrator) What does the woman mean?

In your test book, you will read:
           (A) Mary bought some food.
           (B) Mary had car trouble.
           (C) Mary went shopping.
           (D) Mary bought some gas.

From the conversation you learn that Mary stopped at the gas station on her way home. The best answer to the question "Does the car need to be filled?" is (D), "Mary bought some gas." Therefore, the correct answer is (D).

Now let us begin Part A with question number 1.

1. (Man)   Mike looks upset. He must have not done well on the test.
   (Woman) When he skips classes, he should at least borrow notes.
   (Narrator) What does the woman mean? (12 seconds)

2. (Woman) Hello. I'd like to make an appointment to have my blood pressure checked.
   (Man)   The office will reopen at 9 o'clock tomorrow morning.
   (Narrator) What does the man imply? (12 seconds)

3. (Man)   Here is your sandwich and coffee.
   (Woman) Excuse me, but I also ordered a salad.
   (Narrator) What does the woman mean? (12 seconds)

4. (Woman) Mr. Calvert had an appointment downtown.
   (Man)   Did he say when he is coming back?
   (Narrator) What does the man mean? (12 seconds)

5. (Man)   How will I know when my book's arrived?
   (Woman) After the library receives the book, we'll send you a postcard.
   (Narrator) What does the woman mean? (12 seconds)

6. (Woman) Where is Steve? He is usually here at 6.
   (Man)   He went out for dinner instead of cooking.
   (Narrator) What does the man say about Steve? (12 seconds)

7. (Man)   I don't need a parking sticker. I ride my bicycle every morning.
   (Woman) Students can purchase bike permits at the next counter.
   (Narrator) What does the woman imply? (12 seconds)

8. (Woman) This research paper has taken us almost two months already.
   (Man)   I wish they would tell us when the assignment is due.
   (Narrator) What does the man mean? (12 seconds)

9. (Man)   What was the terrible noise next door?
   (Woman) When the driver was backing out of the garage, he ran over the trash can.
   (Narrator) What does the woman mean? (12 seconds)

10. (Woman) What did Henry and Joan think about the commencement address?
   (Man)   Joan couldn't hear half of what the speaker said.
   (Narrator) What does the man mean? (12 seconds)

11. (Man)   My parents and I are very close, and I usually call them once or twice a week.
   (Woman) Once your phone is hooked up, you can call off campus.
   (Narrator) What does the woman mean? (12 seconds)

12. (Woman) Why didn't you get toothpaste while you were out?
   (Man)   The drugstore is sold out.
   (Narrator) What does the man mean? (12 seconds)

13. (Man)   I wish I could get around this slow-moving truck.
   (Woman) Don't try passing it on the right, you'll get a ticket.
   (Narrator) What does the woman imply? (12 seconds)

14. (Woman) Your parents' business has done very well. Does your father have an M.B.A.?
   (Man)   My father never went as far as college.
   (Narrator) What does the man say about his father? (12 seconds)

15. (Man)   I can't believe how many mistakes people make on the admission sheet.
   (Woman) Students seldom read instructions before filling out forms.
   (Narrator) What does the woman mean? (12 seconds)

16. (Woman) Excuse me, would you happen to know where the movie theater is?
   (Man)   Turn around, go back for about a mile, and you'll see it on your left.
   (Narrator) What did the man mean? (12 seconds)

17. (Man)   We never see Julie. During the summer, she came to visit Mary every week.
   (Woman) She is carrying a full course load this semester.
   (Narrator) What does the woman mean? (12 seconds)

18. (Woman)   You have many enjoyable activities scheduled for your geology students. I bet
              they are well-attended.
    (Man)   Hardly anyone went on the day trip to the falls.
    (Narrator) What does the man mean? (12 seconds)

19. (Man)   How did we do in St. Louis?
    (Woman)   The women's swim team lost, and so did the men's.
    (Narrator) What does the woman mean? (12 seconds)

20. (Woman)   I've heard that the sales have been pretty dismal this quarter.
    (Man)   Have you had a chance to look over the report yet?
    (Narrator) What does the man mean? (12 seconds)

21. (Man)   How come you brought your umbrella?
    (Woman)   One never knows about the weather this time of year.
    (Narrator) What does the woman mean? (12 seconds)

22. (Man)   You have to fill out the patient information form and the insurance form.
    (Woman)   Do I have to fill out both sides?
    (Narrator) Where is this conversation taking place? (12 seconds)

23. (Man)   I can't believe the sink is not draining again.
    (Woman)   It's time to call Acme Services.
    (Narrator) What is Acme Services? (12 seconds)

24. (Man)   Are you almost finished with your classes? When does the break start?
    (Woman)   I still have a research project to work on.
    (Narrator) What is the woman going to do next? (12 seconds)

25. (Man)   Where did you go last night?
    (Woman)   We found a nice little coffee shop at the end of the street.
    (Narrator) Where did the woman go? (12 seconds)

26. (Woman)   No sooner did we move in than the water heater stopped working.
    (Man)   How much did *that* cost you?
    (Narrator) What does the man mean? (12 seconds)

27. (Man)   I hear we will have new computers before the end of the month.
    (Woman)   It's about *time*.
    (Narrator) What does the woman mean? (12 seconds)

28. (Man)   Can we meet tomorrow? I need help preparing for my math test.
    (Woman)   Will Thursday be all right?
    (Narrator) What is the woman suggesting? (12 seconds)

29. (Man)   I need to break a dollar.
    (Woman)   Not *another* candy bar.
    (Narrator) What does the woman's response imply? (12 seconds)

30. (Man)   These pears are expensive.
    (Woman)   The strawberries are in season.
    (Man)   Let's get some then.
    (Narrator) Where is this conversation taking place? (12 seconds)

(Narrator)   This is the end of Part A.

Now read the directions for Part B while they are being read to you.

Part B

DIRECTIONS: In this part of the test, you will hear longer conversations. After each conversation, you will hear several questions. The conversations and questions will not be repeated.

After you hear a question, read the four possible answers in your test book and choose the best answer. Then, on your answer sheet, find the number of the question and fill in the space that corresponds to the letter of the answer you have chosen.

Remember, you are not allowed to take notes or write in your test book.

(Narrator) <u>Questions 31 through 35</u> refer to the following telephone conversation.

(Woman)   Hello, Jim. I hate to bother you so late.

(Man)   Hello, Gail. It's not *that* late.

(Woman)   I'm in a somewhat difficult situation and was wondering if you could give me some advice. I have to leave on business tomorrow, and my purse has ripped. Do you know what type of glue I can use for leather?

(Man)   Oh, there are many types of glue you can use. Epoxy, cement, and paste are easy to find and simple to use. I usually use epoxy to glue my children's shoes. Cement adhesive is better for porous materials, such as ceramics or porcelain, and paste is best for metal and other smooth surfaces.

(Woman)   You certainly sound like an expert. Where can I find epoxy?

(Man)   Any hardware store or even an office supply store would have it. If not, you could try a specialty store, but I'm sure it's pretty common.

(Woman)   Jim, thank you very much. I can always count on you when I'm in a jam.

(Man)   Glad to be of help. Have a nice trip. I'll see you after you get back.

(Narrator)

31. What is the main topic of this conversation? (12 seconds)
32. Why was the woman in a difficult situation? (12 seconds)
33. What did the woman ask the man to do? (12 seconds)
34. Why did the man mention his children's shoes? (12 seconds)
35. What is the man's attitude in this conversation? (12 seconds)

(Narrator) <u>Questions 36 through 38</u> refer to the following conversation about newspapers.

(Man)   I've always wanted to ask you why you read the *New York Times* instead of the *Seattle Post*. If we live in Seattle, don't you want to learn about the local news? For example, did the *Times* report the new developments in Vancouver?

(Woman)   Of course, I do, but the *Times* has a much better coverage of the international and national news. You are right, the *Post* covers the regional news in depth, but I learn more from the *Times*. And their movie reviews are the best. I read them every week. The Seattle news is covered in all radio reports, so I listen to the radio to find out what's happening in the city.

(Man)   So, you read the paper and listen to the radio. Now that I think about it, I do that, too. Yesterday, I heard that Portland is expanding its convention complex to bring more visitors to the city. Because Portland is not on the coast, not many tourists go there.

(Woman)   I read about it in the *Times*. They do have a very good coverage of developments throughout the country.

(Narrator)

36. Where do the man and the woman live? (12 seconds)
37. What does the woman do to keep up with the local news? (12 seconds)
38. How does the man stay up-to-date with the news? (12 seconds)

(Narrator)   This is the end of Part B.

Now read the directions for Part C while they are being read to you.

Part C

DIRECTIONS: In Part C you will hear short talks. At the end of each, you will be asked several questions. Each talk and each question will be spoken only one time. For this reason, you must listen carefully to understand what the speaker says. After you hear a question, read the four selections and choose the one that is the best answer to the question the speaker asked. Then, on your answer sheet, find the number of the question and blacken the space that corresponds to the letter for the answer you have chosen.

Listen to this sample talk.

You will hear:
(Man)   Before people used automobiles, they walked or rode bicycles for short distances and took trains, streetcars, or horse-drawn carriages for long-distance travel. When automobiles were first produced, only the rich could afford them. Today, almost every household in the United States owns at least one car, and ninety percent of American adults have drivers' licenses.

According to the yearly value of its output, the U.S. automobile industry exceeds all other manufacturing industries in the country. As a consumer, this industry also supports other major industries, such as steel, glass, and rubber. Furthermore, approximately twelve million Americans are employed in the auxiliary service industries consisting of repair shops and service stations.

(Narrator)   Now listen to the following question.

You will hear: According to the speaker, how did people travel before the invention of the automobile?

You will read:
(A) By cars and carriages
(B) By bicycles, trains, and carriages
(C) On foot and by boat
(D) On board ships and trains

The best answer to the question "According to the speaker, how did people travel before the invention of the automobile?" is (B), "By bicycles, trains, and carriages." Therefore, the correct answer is (B).
Now listen to another sample question.

(Narrator)   Approximately how many people are employed in the automobile service industry?

You will read:
(A) One million
(B) Ten million
(C) Twelve million
(D) Ninety million

The best answer to the question "Approximately how many people are employed in the automobile service industry?" is (C), "Twelve million." Therefore, the correct answer is (C).

(Narrator)   Questions 39 through 44 refer to the following lecture about mail.

(Woman)   In most airports, mail and other freight except the passengers' baggage is handled as cargo. In recent years, the number of tons of cargo processed by major airports has been growing twice as fast as the number of passengers. In small airports that have no separate cargo facilities, cargo is carried together with the passenger baggage. On the other hand, in large airports, cargo is directed to separate terminals that exclusively process cargo. After cargo is delivered to the airport, it is grouped by destination and, occasionally, by carrier company. Large postal outlets in airports sort mail to be delivered by various flights, depending on their scheduled departures and arrival times. Commercial cargo includes a wide range of articles, such as electronic goods, processed food items, machine parts, and even agricultural equipment. Airline economists claim that, because transporting goods doesn't require serving meals and drinks and employing stewards, companies make greater gains by carrying cargo than by carrying passengers.

(Narrator)

39. What is the main idea of this talk? (12 seconds)
40. What does the term "cargo" refer to? (12 seconds)
41. How is cargo processed at major airports? (12 seconds)
42. How is cargo carried from small airports? (12 seconds)
43. Where is mail sorted? (12 seconds)
44. What does commercial cargo include? (12 seconds)

(Narrator)   Questions 45 through 50 refer to the following lecture about apples.

(Man)   Among the thousands of varieties of apples, only a few account for most of the apples grown for commercial purposes and by individual gardeners. Three varieties, Delicious, Golden Delicious, and McIntosh, make up more than sixty percent of all apples sold. The apple varieties differ in the color of the peel, texture, size, and taste. The peel may be green, yellow, or red, and the flesh is usually white, cream, or yellow. The texture is classified as soft or firm, and the taste as tart or sweet. Sweet apples are eaten fresh, and the tart varieties are made into applesauce, cider, and vinegar. Apples are standard fare in most lunches that people either bag or buy. Apple juice factories and cider mills account for about thirty percent of the total consumption of processed apples, with the pulp being converted into cattle fodder. Crab apples belong to the wild varieties.

Because apple trees of all kinds require a cool climate to grow they don't do well in warmer areas. The trees are usually dormant during the winter and enjoy prolonged periods of cold weather. To produce a good crop, apple orchards also need high quantities of water during the winter when their root systems continue to extend. Although in Eurasia the fruit has been cultivated for thousands of years, it may not be common on other continents. Historically, the trees were scarce in Africa and Australia, where rains are limited to certain seasons that do not last longer than a couple of months. In these regions, as well as in South America, people first looked at apples as an exotic fruit even though they had been known for centuries.

(Narrator)

45. How many varieties of apples are grown for commercial purpose? (12 seconds)
46. What are possible colors for apple peels? (12 seconds)
47. How is the taste of apples classified? (12 seconds)
48. How are apples with high sugar content mostly used? (12 seconds)
49. According to the speaker, what do apple trees require to produce a good crop? (12 seconds)
50. In what regions were apple trees first cultivated? (12 seconds)

(Narrator)   STOP WORKING ON SECTION 1.

Practice TOEFL 2

SECTION 1

LISTENING COMPREHENSION

(Narrator) In this section, you will demonstrate your skills in understanding spoken English. There are three parts in the Listening Comprehension section, with different tasks in each.

Part A

DIRECTIONS: In Part A you will hear short conversations between two people. At the end of each conversation, a third person will ask a question about what the two people said. Each conversation and each question will be spoken only one time. For this reason, you must listen carefully to understand what each speaker says. After you hear a conversation and the question, read the four selections and choose the *one* that is the best answer to the question the speaker asked. Then, on your answer sheet, find the number of the question and blacken the space that corresponds to the letter for the answer you have chosen. Blacken the space completely so that the letter inside the space does not show.

Listen to the following example.

On the recording, you hear:
  (Man)   Does the car need to be filled?
  (Woman)   Mary stopped at the gas station on her way home.
  (Narrator) What does the woman mean?

In your test book, you will read:
            (A) Mary bought some food.
            (B) Mary had car trouble.
            (C) Mary went shopping.
            (D) Mary bought some gas.

From the conversation you learn that Mary stopped at the gas station on her way home. The best answer to the question "Does the car need to be filled?" is (D), "Mary bought some gas." Therefore, the correct answer is (D).

Now let us begin Part A with question number 1.

1. (Woman) The phone company called this morning, and there appears to be a problem with the bill.
   (Man)   This is the second time Peter forgot to pay it.
   (Narrator) What does the man mean? (12 seconds)

2. (Man)   I'd like to take Math three-o-five (305) this semester.
   (Woman) To register for the course, students must have the instructor's permission.
   (Narrator) What does the woman imply? (12 seconds)

3. (Woman)   Christie said you didn't have enough chairs last night.
   (Man)   We didn't expect forty people to attend the workshop.
   (Narrator) What does the man imply? (12 seconds)

4. (Man)   On Monday, Betty starts with the tool company.
   (Woman)   I am surprised she changed her mind about not taking that job.
   (Narrator) What does the woman mean? (12 seconds)

5. (Woman)   Today, I had a lot to do, with all the little things to take care of.
   (Man)   You dropped off my jacket at the cleaner's, didn't you?
   (Narrator) What does the man want to know? (12 seconds)

6. (Man)   The dean expected the entire staff to attend.
   (Woman)   Had the teachers known about the meeting, they would have attended it.
   (Narrator) What does the woman imply? (12 seconds)

7. (Woman)   We had a great time. And so many people came!
   (Man)   It was very nice of George to give me a party.
   (Narrator) What does the man say about George? (12 seconds)

8. (Man)   Do you have blank cards?
   (Woman)   Pharmacies seldom carry stationery.
   (Narrator) What does the woman mean? (12 seconds)

9. (Woman)   You said you'd be finished in an hour or two, but you've been working since noon.
   (Man)   This exam isn't as easy as it appears.
   (Narrator) What does the man mean? (12 seconds)

10. (Man)   A lot of my friends are out of work, and they don't seem to be able to get any job at all.
    (Woman)   In the past few years, unemployment has been climbing dramatically.
    (Narrator) What does the woman mean? (12 seconds)

11. (Woman)   How's Linda's report card this semester?
    (Man)   Her grades leave much to be desired.
    (Narrator) What does the man mean? (12 seconds)

12. (Man)   Are you looking for something to eat? There are apples and plums in the refrigerator.
    (Woman)   I'm thirsty after having that salty hamburger for dinner.
    (Narrator) What does the woman imply? (12 seconds)

13. (Woman)   It looks like you and Rebecca are going out. I have to stay here and finish the paper tonight.
    (Man)   We don't mind picking up a sandwich for you on our way home.
    (Narrator) What does the man mean? (12 seconds)

14. (Man)   Did Doug go with you to the precinct?
    (Woman)   Doug isn't old enough to vote.
    (Narrator) What does the woman mean? (12 seconds)

15. (Woman)   Carol tried to call Harry several times, but he is never home.
    (Man)   Harry works at a shoe store after school and on weekends.
    (Narrator) What does the man imply? (12 seconds)

16. (Man)   I am late for the presentation and can't find the conference room.
    (Woman)   Room four-o-seven (407) is not on the fourth floor but on the third.
    (Narrator) What does the woman imply? (12 seconds)

17. (Woman) Benjamin looks different somehow. Have you noticed?
    (Man)   Since he broke his glasses, he's had to use a spare pair.
    (Narrator) What does the man say about Benjamin? (12 seconds)

18. (Man)   I didn't know you come here to shop. Are you thinking of doing a little work on the house?
    (Woman) My brother suggested that we buy a set of tools for our father's birthday.
    (Narrator) What does the woman mean? (12 seconds)

19. (Woman) The area where Ann lives is great, but there seem to be few available units.
    (Man)   The apartment next door to Ann's has been vacant for twenty-one days.
    (Narrator) What does the man mean? (12 seconds)

20. (Man)   Can I help you find something? You seem to be having a bit of trouble.
    (Woman) Do you have a stain remover that can take grease out of this shirt?
    (Narrator) What does the woman want to know? (12 seconds)

21. (Man)   I've cleaned the entire house, and now I'm going for a game of tennis.
    (Woman) Good for you.
    (Narrator) What does the woman mean? (12 seconds)

22. (Woman) I bet you are glad the week is over. What are you going to do this weekend?
    (Man)   We have company coming from out of town.
    (Narrator) What does the man mean? (12 seconds)

23. (Man)   How big a tip should we leave?
    (Woman) Fifteen percent would be two dollars.
    (Narrator) Where is this conversation taking place? (12 seconds)

24. (Man)   Are you going to put in the cucumber seeds, too?
    (Woman) I think there's plenty of space to the right of the tomatoes.
    (Narrator) What are the man and woman probably doing? (12 seconds)

25. (Woman) Where should we go for lunch?
    (Man)   I don't know. What sounds good to you?
    (Narrator) What does the man mean? (12 seconds)

26. (Man)   It's only three o'clock, and we've already sold all the paperbacks and half of the hardback editions.
    (Woman) Maybe we should have ordered more hardback copies.
    (Narrator) Where is this conversation taking place? (12 seconds)

27. (Woman) Your super-unleaded grade is pretty expensive.
    (Man)   I don't think it's more expensive than at other places.
    (Narrator) What is the man's occupation? (12 seconds)

28. (Man)   You forgot to send a card to the Wilsons.
    (Woman) *I* forgot! Why didn't *you* send one?
    (Narrator) What does the woman mean? (12 seconds)

29. (Man)   It's time to go home, Karen. Dave and I are on our way to an Italian restaurant on High Street. Would you like to come to dinner with us?
    (Woman) Thanks, but I have the travel report to finish. I need to mail it first thing tomorrow morning.
    (Narrator) What is Karen going to do? (12 seconds)

30. (Woman)   Judy has given her notice to the manager, and she will be leaving the office in two weeks.
    (Man)   She made the right decision. I know she can use the better salary.
    (Narrator) What can be said about Judy? (12 seconds)

(Narrator)   This is the end of Part A.

Now read the directions for Part B while they are being read to you.

Part B

DIRECTIONS: In this part of the test, you will hear longer conversations. After each conversation, you will hear several questions. The conversations and questions will not be repeated.

After you hear a question, read the four possible answers in your test book and choose the best answer. Then, on your answer sheet, find the number of the question and fill in the space that corresponds to the letter of the answer you have chosen.

Remember, you are not allowed to take notes or write in your test book.

(Narrator)   Questions 31 through 34 refer to the following conversation about animation.

(Woman)   What movie are you going to see?
(Man)   I am taking my daughters to a matinee. We try to make it every Sunday. Unfortunately, they like cartoons, so I also have to watch them.
(Woman)   I like cartoons too. Last week, I saw an animated feature, and I really enjoyed it. Do you know how much work goes into making them? First, the story has to be written. Then an artist, or even a whole team of artists, draw the story, frame by frame. When that's done, the camera crew photographs the entire sequence. The dialogue and voice features add depth and specific dimensions to the animated characters to make the plot intriguing. The music and the dialogue are recorded to match the story and the action on film. Of course, special visual and sound effects are added to the basic layout. Without them, the final version of the feature wouldn't be nearly as much fun. I think cartoons are a form of art.
(Man)   I guess I will look at cartoons a little differently now than I used to. Where did you learn so much about how cartoons are made?

(Narrator)

31. Where is this conversation probably taking place? (12 seconds)
32. Why does the man say that it's unfortunate that his children like cartoons? (12 seconds)
33. What is the first step in making a cartoon? (12 seconds)
34. What is the purpose of special effects? (12 seconds)

(Narrator)   Questions 35 through 38 refer to the following conversation about autumn.

(Man)   I think after all the noise in the city, quiet walks in the woods can be very restful. Look, it's so pretty when the leaves are changing color. I am glad we decided to come here.
(Woman)   Seasonal changes always make things appear beautiful. In the spring, the green grass and leaves make everything seem new. In the autumn, when the leaves turn red, yellow, and brown, the woods are full of color. No wonder autumn is called *fall*. When leaves fall on the ground, they cover it like a blanket.
(Man)   Actually, the leaves turn color because in the autumn days are shorter than in the summer, and the number of daylight hours decreases. I'm sure this does not sound very romantic, but it's scientifically accurate.
(Woman)   Scientifically accurate or not, I just enjoy looking at the trees that can have a dozen different shades of color in their crowns.

(Narrator)

35. Where does this exchange probably take place? (12 seconds)
36. When does this conversation probably occur? (12 seconds)
37. Why do tree leaves change color? (12 seconds)
38. Why does the woman say "scientifically accurate or not"? (12 seconds)

(Narrator) This is the end of Part B.

Now read the directions for Part C while they are being read to you.

Part C

DIRECTIONS: In Part C you will hear short talks. At the end of each, you will be asked several questions. Each talk and each question will be spoken only one time. For this reason, you must listen carefully to understand what the speaker says. After you hear a question, read the four selections and choose the one that is the best answer to the question the speaker asked. Then, on your answer sheet, find the number of the question and blacken the space that corresponds to the letter for the answer you have chosen.

Listen to this sample talk.

You will hear:

(Man)   Before people used automobiles, they walked or rode bicycles for short distances and took trains, streetcars, or horse-drawn carriages for long-distance travel. When automobiles were first invented, only the rich could afford them. Today, almost every household in the United States owns at least one car, and ninety percent of American adults have drivers' licenses.

According to the yearly value of its output, the U.S. automobile industry exceeds all other manufacturing industries in the country. As a consumer, this industry also supports other major industries, such as steel, glass, and rubber. Furthermore, approximately twelve million Americans are employed in the auxiliary service industries consisting of repair shops and service stations.

(Narrator) Now listen to the following question.

You will hear: According to the speaker, how did people travel before the invention of the automobile?

You will read:

(A) By cars and carriages
(B) By bicycles, trains, and carriages
(C) On foot and by boat
(D) On board ships and trains

The best answer to the question "According to the speaker, how did people travel before the invention of the automobile?" is (B), "By bicycles, trains, and carriages." Therefore, the correct answer is (B).

Now listen to another sample question.

(Narrator) Approximately how many people are employed in the automobile service industry?

You will read:

(A) One million
(B) Ten million
(C) Twelve million
(D) Ninety million

The best answer to the question "Approximately how many people are employed in the automobile service industry?" is (C), "Twelve million." Therefore, the correct answer is (C).

(Narrator)   <u>Questions 39 through 43</u> refer to the following talk about air-conditioning.

(Man)   When it is hot and humid outside, most of us enjoy air-conditioning and some even consider it a necessity. Although many people believe that air-conditioning only cools the indoor air, it also controls its moisture content and cleanliness. Because human comfort depends on humidity to a large degree, air-conditioning can remove moisture from the air or add it as necessary. Air-conditioning devices also control air circulation in premises by bringing in fresh air and removing polluted or contaminated air. During winter, air-conditioning performs predominantly the same functions as it does in summer. It warms the air to a comfortable temperature and pumps clean, moist air into the quarters where people live and work. In business settings, air-conditioning improves the efficiency of workers. In air-conditioned offices, employees stay alert and become less tired than in offices without air-conditioning. They make fewer mistakes and have fewer accidents. The same can be said about drivers who may feel tired and sleepy while sitting in a warm vehicle, and insurance analysts have claimed that driving an air-conditioned car makes one less prone to accidents, particularly in the afternoon or evening. In Florida, where it's humid almost year round, the locals can't even imagine comfort without air-conditioning.

(Narrator)

39. What is the function of air-conditioning? (12 seconds)
40. How does air-conditioning affect the humidity in premises? (12 seconds)
41. Why is air removed from residential and working areas? (12 seconds)
42. How does air-conditioning work in winter? (12 seconds)
43. Why is air-conditioning beneficial for office workers? (12 seconds)

(Narrator)   <u>Questions 44 through 47</u> refer to the following talk about reporter career choices.

(Woman)   For those of you who dream of a career in the news profession, the opportunities are numerous. In the past decade, the job market for news reporters, editors, and investigators has been competitive, and as a general rule, there has been much demand for reporters in business and financial news. Unfortunately, opportunities for sports writers have not been as plentiful and are not likely to be so for a few more years. Before you set out to approach chief editors of specific papers, you should keep in mind that copy editors have been in far greater demand than either assignment reporters or professionals with skills in specialized areas, such as law and science. An important rule for all those who seek employment in the newspaper business is that your writing and reporting skills are never too good, and you need to work to improve them, even if you already have a job.

Jobs in magazine writing and journalism have not fared as well as those in the newspaper area because most magazines have cut their staffs. This means there may be an oversupply of trained and experienced magazine writers already, and magazines may be a difficult area for a new person to break into. Similarly, things are tight in broadcast journalism. Many radio and local T.V. stations have decided not to expand their reporting efforts, and the demand in radio and T.V. journalism has been sluggish. However, one new development in T.V. journalism is that currently many large-market stations have undertaken to run two-hour newscasts that have given prominence to local news on the national networks and stations. The expansion of the news format may translate into openings in this segment of the market.

(Narrator)

44. What areas of the newspaper business offer good employment opportunities? (12 seconds)
45. According to the speaker, what reporter skills need ongoing improvement? (12 seconds)
46. What is the situation in the magazine reporting business? (12 seconds)
47. What can be said about the future career opportunities in the newscast media? (12 seconds)

(Narrator) Questions 48 through 50 refer to the following talk on groundwater.

(Man) Groundwater is a vital source of drinking water and irrigation in the U.S. and other countries. Thousands of sources are found throughout the country. The economic forecasts show that its use will grow due to increased population, industrialization, and agricultural irrigation. Groundwater is not unlimited, and this essential form of the earth's resources may be depleted. Its supply cannot be renewed as quickly as that of rainwater, and some sources may disappear permanently. Another consideration to worry about is that contamination of groundwater has occurred in various places in the United States, so some of its sources are no longer potable. When groundwater is contaminated, it cannot be cleansed as simply as surface water because the flow of groundwater is slow and not turbulent, and contaminants cannot be dispersed and diluted by new water additions. Airborne bacteria that help cleanse surface water don't have access to groundwater flows. Because groundwater is not in contact with the oxygen in the atmosphere, only a small number among dozens of bacteria types can reach it to accelerate the cleansing processes. Once groundwater at a particular source is contaminated, it may take several hundred years to cleanse it of degradable wastes.

(Narrator)

48. According to the speaker, why is groundwater important? (12 seconds)
49. What are the causes of decrease in the groundwater supply? (12 seconds)
50. How long does it take to cleanse a groundwater supply? (12 seconds)

(Narrator) STOP WORKING ON SECTION 1.

Practice TOEFL 3

SECTION 1

LISTENING COMPREHENSION

(Narrator) In this section, you will demonstrate your skills in understanding spoken English. There are three parts in the Listening Comprehension section, with different tasks in each.

Part A

DIRECTIONS: In Part A you will hear short conversations between two people. At the end of each conversation, a third person will ask a question about what the two people said. Each conversation and each question will be spoken only one time. For this reason, you must listen carefully to understand what each speaker says. After you hear a conversation and the question, read the four selections and choose the *one* that is the best answer to the question the speaker asked. Then, on your answer sheet, find the number of the question and blacken the space that corresponds to the letter for the answer you have chosen. Blacken the space completely so that the letter inside the space does not show.

Listen to the following example.

On the recording, you hear:
(Man)   Does the car need to be filled?
(Woman)   Mary stopped at the gas station on her way home.
(Narrator)   What does the woman mean?

In your test book, you will read:
(A) Mary bought some food.
(B) Mary had car trouble.
(C) Mary went shopping.
(D) Mary bought some gas.

From the conversation you learn that Mary stopped at the gas station on her way home. The best answer to the question "Does the car need to be filled?" is (D), "Mary bought some gas." Therefore, the correct answer is (D).

Now let us begin Part A with question number 1.

1. (Man)   The medical license examination on June 22 was very difficult. Did Sandy pass?
   (Woman) She hasn't received a letter yet. But she says she sailed right through it.
   (Narrator) What does the woman say about Sandy? (12 seconds)

2. (Woman) The new sports complex is an excellent facility with all kinds of conveniences.
   (Man)   Last time we went, we drove around for forty minutes before we found a place to park.
   (Narrator) What does the man mean? (12 seconds)

3. (Man)   The stock market is up, but my son is losing money on his mutual funds.
   (Woman) If I were in his shoes, I would hire another broker to manage my investments.
   (Narrator) What does the woman imply? (12 seconds)

4. (Woman) The traffic is congested by Toledo, and it's getting close to the rush hour. I
              don't know what time I'll get there.
   (Man)   When you arrive at the house, just let yourself in.
   (Narrator) What does the man mean? (12 seconds)

5. (Man)   Chocolate must be an all-time favorite. We sell gallons of it.
   (Woman) Actually, vanilla ice cream accounts for seventy percent of all flavors sold in
              the past decade.
   (Narrator) What does the woman imply? (12 seconds)

6. (Woman) Did Liz get a used car?
   (Man)   She has already had to pay for new tires, and now it looks like she'll need a
              headlight.
   (Narrator) What does the man say about Liz? (12 seconds)

7. (Man)   I thought Joanna went to the art museum with Mark.
   (Woman) When Mark called at ten, Joanna had already gone canoeing with her brother.
   (Narrator) What does the woman mean? (12 seconds)

8. (Woman) Why did Bob and Lynn cancel their cruise? Is their company doing well?
   (Man)   Because of the change in revenue income, they had to take a cut in pay.
   (Narrator) What does the man mean? (12 seconds)

9. (Man)   Mrs. Bailey wants to be reimbursed. Do you know how much?
   (Woman) She was charged thirty-eight dollars for the flowers and another twelve for the
              delivery.
   (Narrator) What does the woman mean? (12 seconds)

10. (Woman) What changes are planned on the north side of the city?
    (Man)   The proposal to build a hospital in the area looks more promising than it did
              six years ago.
    (Narrator) What does the man imply? (12 seconds)

11. (Man)   Can I stay for just another minute? I really need to look something up.
    (Woman) Patrons are requested to leave the library when the closing bell is sounded.
    (Narrator) What does the woman mean? (12 seconds)

12. (Woman) The roads here seem very confusing to me. I am not sure I can find your
              house in time for us to make the performance.
    (Man)   Would you like to meet at the concert hall instead?
    (Narrator) What does the man suggest? (12 seconds)

13. (Man)   Is Rita ready with her data? We've got to make a good impression.
    (Woman) She made sure she checked the slides for the sales presentation.
    (Narrator) What does the woman say about Rita? (12 seconds)

14. (Woman) You bought twelve loaves of bread and five gallons of milk!
    (Man)   We've invited four couples to visit during the summer semester break.
    (Narrator) What does the man mean? (12 seconds)

15. (Man)   Isn't Margaret lonely? I know I would be.
    (Woman) Now that all her children are out of the house, she is thinking about going
              back to college.
    (Narrator) What does the woman say about Margaret? (12 seconds)

16. (Woman) Ralph doesn't seem to be worried about the boys.
    (Man) He doesn't let on what he is really thinking.
    (Narrator) What does the man mean? (12 seconds)

17. (Man) I swerved to avoid a dog and ran into a telephone pole.
    (Woman) No problem. We can have your car as good as new in a couple of days.
    (Narrator) What is the woman's occupation? (12 seconds)

18. (Woman) Arthur went grocery shopping at midnight. What an odd thing to do.
    (Man) The store *does* stay open.
    (Narrator) What does the man mean? (12 seconds)

19. (Man) You missed your flight! Was Ken angry?
    (Woman) Had he thought to pull over at that gas station we saw on Walnut Street, he wouldn't have run out.
    (Narrator) What does the woman imply about Ken? (12 seconds)

20. (Woman) We spent an entire week on words with primary and secondary stresses.
    (Man) Words that have two stressed syllables are not as common as those that have only one.
    (Narrator) What does the man mean? (12 seconds)

21. (Man) Do you know how this oven works? I can't figure it out.
    (Woman) Diane makes casseroles in it every week. She'd know.
    (Narrator) Where does this exchange occur? (12 seconds)

22. (Man) Carl didn't tell me his wife was away at her sister's in Bluffton.
    (Woman) Why is that such a big deal?
    (Man) She promised to baby-sit my children while I take my father-in-law shopping for a suit.
    (Narrator) Where is Carl's wife? (12 seconds)

23. (Woman) We've been waiting for the prescription for twenty-five minutes, and we still need to stop at the bank and pick up the sandwiches at the deli.
    (Man) We could've gone to the post office in the meantime.
    (Narrator) Where does this conversation take place? (12 seconds)

24. (Man) What time did they say your car would be ready?
    (Woman) They *said* it should be ready around three-thirty, but I'll be surprised if they finish before five.
    (Narrator) What can be concluded from the woman's statement? (12 seconds)

25. (Man) If I eat another bite, I won't be able to breathe.
    (Woman) You didn't have to have so much soup just an hour after you had half a watermelon.
    (Narrator) What can be said about the man? (12 seconds)

26. (Man) Not only did the Nixons come uninvited but they also brought their cousins.
    (Woman) It didn't bother *me*.
    (Narrator) What does the woman mean? (12 seconds)

27. (Man) Why didn't you go out with Nick? Didn't he say he wanted to take you out on the town?
    (Woman) All he ever talks about is tennis.
    (Narrator) What can be concluded from this exchange? (12 seconds)

28. (Man)   How many students do you have in your statistics class?

    (Woman) This year we restricted it to two hundred students, but there are probably just as many on the waiting list.

    (Narrator) What can be said about the statistics class? (12 seconds)

29. (Woman) I'm sorry, sir. Your coat isn't ready yet. I think we can have it for you in about an hour.

    (Man)   How long does it take to mend the sleeve lining?

    (Narrator) Where does this conversation take place? (12 seconds)

30. (Woman) May I have a glass of water? I'm thirsty, and I have a splitting headache.

    (Man)   I'll bring you some aspirin as soon as we get to a higher altitude.

    (Narrator) What is the man's occupation? (12 seconds)

(Narrator)   This is the end of Part A.

Now read the directions for Part B while they are being read to you.

Part B

DIRECTIONS: In this part of the test, you will hear longer conversations. After each conversation, you will hear several questions. The conversations and questions will not be repeated.

After you hear a question, read the four possible answers in your test book and choose the best answer. Then, on your answer sheet, find the number of the question and fill in the space that corresponds to the letter of the answer you have chosen.

Remember, you are not allowed to take notes or write in your test book.

(Narrator) Questions 31 through 34 refer to the following conversation about dolphins.

(Man)   Our next stop after the antelope and the deer area is the aquarium, where we keep our dolphins. We are very proud of the animals we have acquired, and we take very good care of them.

(Woman) I thought they were fish.

(Man)   Oh, no. Dolphins are mammals. They don't have gills, and they breathe by taking air into their lungs. Unlike fish, they can't remain under water for prolonged periods of time and need to come up for air. Mature dolphins eat fish, but they can also become prey for sharks. In fact, females nurse and protect their newborns for about a year till they become self-sufficient and can defend themselves.

(Woman) This is very interesting. I didn't know that.

(Man)   Here we are. Aren't they beautiful? You may also notice that these aquatic creatures don't have scales. They are the most sociable of the marine mammals. Here comes Violet, our oldest. She is almost twenty years old.

(Woman) What's their life span?

(Man)   It's hard to say because individuals are almost impossible to track. But on the average, I'd say about twenty-five years.

(Woman) Listen to them! They make so many noises.

(Man)   That's how they communicate with one another. Some scientists even think that dolphins have their own special language that allows them to warn one another, send messages, or signal the presence of a predator. Eventually, zoologists hope to learn specifically how dolphins transmit information.

(Woman) Thank you for taking the time. I've learned so much today.

(Narrator)

31. What is the main topic of this dialogue? (12 seconds)
32. Where does this conversation take place? (12 seconds)
33. How long do female dolphins stay with their young? (12 seconds)
34. How do dolphins communicate? (12 seconds)

(Narrator)   Questions 35 through 38 refer to the conversation about dictionaries.

(Man)   I always recommend that my students use a dictionary when they are working on a paper or a presentation. Dictionaries don't just give the meanings of words, but they also list information about word origins. They also point out which words are literary words, used in formal writing, and which words are colloquial or simply outdated.

(Woman)   That's right. Dictionaries can supply a wealth of information. Last semester, in my reading class, I encouraged students to look up idioms common in American English and foreign words borrowed from other languages. In that class, we had to use dictionaries all the time.

(Man)   Of course, one can't always rely on a dictionary, however good it is. When language learners acquire a sizable vocabulary, they may need to switch from a general dictionary to a specialized one that includes technical terms. No dictionary contains all the words of a language.

(Woman)   I must say, though, that using dictionaries can be tricky sometimes. If learners don't clearly understand how words are used but use them anyway, incorrect usage can make their speech or written assignments incomprehensible. In general, there are very few true synonyms, and although dictionaries cite words with similar meanings, these words may be used in completely different contexts.

(Narrator)

35. What is the main idea of this conversation? (12 seconds)
36. What types of dictionaries are mentioned in this talk? (12 seconds)
37. What did the woman say she did last semester? (12 seconds)
38. What can be a drawback in using a dictionary? (12 seconds)

(Narrator)   This is the end of Part B.

   Now read the directions for Part C while they are being read to you.

Part C

DIRECTIONS: In Part C you will hear short talks. At the end of each, you will be asked several questions. Each talk and each question will be spoken only one time. For this reason, you must listen carefully to understand what each speaker says. After you hear a question, read the four selections and choose the *one* that is the best answer to the sentence the speaker asked. Then, on your answer sheet, find the number of the question and blacken the space that corresponds to the letter for the answer you have chosen.

Answer all questions according to what is stated or implied in the lecture or conversation.

Listen to this sample talk.

You will hear:

(Man)   Before people used automobiles, they walked or rode bicycles for short distances and took trains, streetcars, or horse-drawn carriages for long-distance travel. When automobiles were first produced, only the rich could afford them. Today, almost every household in the United States owns at least one car, and ninety percent of American adults have drivers' licenses.

According to the yearly value of its output, the U.S. automobile industry exceeds all other manufacturing industries in the country. As a consumer, this industry also supports other major industries, such as steel, glass, and rubber. Furthermore, approximately twelve million Americans are employed in the auxiliary service industries consisting of repair shops and service stations.

(Narrator)   Now listen to the following question.

You will hear: According to the speaker, how did people travel before the invention of the automobile?

You will read:
  (A) By cars and carriages
  (B) By bicycles, trains, and carriages
  (C) On foot and by boat
  (D) On board ships and trains

The best answer to the question "According to the speaker, how did people travel before the invention of the automobile?" is (B), "By bicycles, trains, and carriages." Therefore, the correct answer is (B).

Now listen to another sample question.

(Narrator)   Approximately how many people are employed in the automobile service industry?

You will read:
  (A) One million
  (B) Ten million
  (C) Twelve million
  (D) Ninety million

The best answer to the question "Approximately how many people are employed in the automobile service industry?" is (C), "Twelve million." Therefore, the correct answer is (C).

(Narrator)   <u>Questions 39 through 42</u> refer to the following lecture about Lake Ontario.

(Man)   If you look out the window on the right side of the van, you will see Lake Ontario, the smallest and the most eastern of the five Great Lakes. Although the lake is navigable for large ships all year round, it is less traveled than the other Great Lakes. Lake Ontario borders the Canadian province of Ontario on its north side and the northwestern part of New York and forms a crucial link of the St. Lawrence Seaway.

The lake is about one hundred ninety-three miles long and fifty-three miles wide and covers an area of seven thousand five hundred square miles. The shore of the lake is approximately four hundred eighty miles around. Two-thirds of the lake waters lie below sea level and, because Lake Ontario is very deep, it does not freeze in the winter except near the shore where the water is shallow. A constant current carries the water from west to east at the rate of about one-third of a mile per hour.

Because of the capacity of large bodies of water to retain heat, the lake has a moderating effect on the climate of the areas that surround it. For example, while the eastern shore of the lake never has a really hot day, on its southern shore fruit trees grow both in the United States and Canada. The lake empties into the Atlantic Ocean through the St. Lawrence River, while the Niagara River and the Welland Canal connect it to Lake Erie in the southwest.

(Narrator)

39. How is Lake Ontario different from the other Great Lakes? (12 seconds)
40. What can be said about the traffic on Lake Ontario? (12 seconds)
41. How long is Lake Ontario's shore line? (12 seconds)
42. How does Lake Ontario affect the climate in its vicinity? (12 seconds)

(Narrator)   <u>Questions 43 through 47</u> refer to the following talk about Edgar Allan Poe.

(Woman)   Today, we move on in an overview of prominent figures in 19th-century American literature. We will begin with Edgar Allan Poe who, after more than a century since his death, remains among the most popular American authors of all time. He was born in Boston on January 19, 1809 to a family of traveling actors. About a year and a half later, his father, David Poe, left his wife and son and disappeared without a trace. Elizabeth Poe, who was an English-born actress, died in 1811 in Richmond, Virginia, during a tour, and her son was taken care of by the family of John Allan, a relatively wealthy tobacco exporter. The Allans had no children of their own, and Mrs. Allan became an affectionate mother for young Edgar. Because the Allans were well off, Edgar received a thorough education appropriate for a gentleman. The Allans traveled frequently on business, and young Poe lived with the family in England and Scotland between 1815 and 1820. There he attended a classical preparatory school at Stoke Newington for three years. When Poe turned eleven, the family moved back to Virginia, and he continued his education at a local academy. Later when Edgar entered the University of Virginia, he succeeded admirably in his academics. However, gambling led to the demise of his academic pursuits, and Allan removed Edgar from the university within a year.

(Narrator)

43. Where was Edgar Allan Poe born? (12 seconds)
44. What can be said about Poe's adoptive parents? (12 seconds)

45. How old was Edgar Allan Poe when his family moved back to Virginia? (12 seconds)
46. What can be said about Poe's study at the university? (12 seconds)
47. Why did John Allan remove Poe from the university? (12 seconds)

(Narrator)   Questions 48 through 50 refer to the following talk about advertising.

(Man)   To put it simply, advertising can be any form of presentation that promotes ideas, services, and goods that have a sponsor who pays for the advertising. All advertising is nonpersonal, and the information contained in it is directed toward a large group of people who have many different characteristics. What separates advertising from publicity is that advertising is paid for, while publicity cannot be bought. Sponsors such as hamburger and soft drink companies pay for the time and news media space that they use to get the information about their products to the public. In many cases, specifically indicating who the sponsor is for a particular advertisement can be the very purpose behind it. Political advertising is one of the prime examples of cases when identifying the sponsor is why the advertisement is made.

(Narrator)

48. What is one of the defining characteristics of advertising? (12 seconds)
49. Who is the audience for advertisements? (12 seconds)
50. What is the primary difference between publicity and advertising? (12 seconds)

(Narrator)   STOP WORKING ON SECTION 1.

Practice TOEFL 4

SECTION 1

LISTENING COMPREHENSION

(Narrator) In this section, you will demonstrate your skills in understanding spoken English. There are three parts in the Listening Comprehension section, with different tasks in each.

Part A

DIRECTIONS: In Part A you will hear short conversations between two people. At the end of each conversation, a third person will ask a question about what the two people said. Each conversation and each question will be spoken only one time. For this reason, you must listen carefully to understand what each speaker says. After you hear a conversation and the question, read the four selections and choose the *one* that is the best answer to the question the speaker asked. Then, on your answer sheet, find the number of the question and blacken the space that corresponds to the letter for the answer you have chosen. Blacken the space completely so that the letter inside the space does not show.

Listen to the following example.

On the recording, you hear:
  (Man)   Does the car need to be filled?
  (Woman)   Mary stopped at the gas station on her way home.
  (Narrator) What does the woman mean?

In your test book, you will read:
  (A) Mary bought some food.
  (B) Mary had car trouble.
  (C) Mary went shopping.
  (D) Mary bought some gas.

From the conversation you learn that Mary stopped at the gas station on her way home. The best answer to the question "Does the car need to be filled?" is (D), "Mary bought some gas." Therefore, the correct answer is (D).

Now let us begin Part A with question number 1.

1. (Woman) Professor White doesn't seem to be very patient with computers.
   (Man)   Well, regardless of her patience with computers, graduate students hold her in high regard.
   (Narrator) What can be said about Professor White? (12 seconds)

2. (Man)   The dinner was delicious. Thank you.
   (Woman) Would you like some cake and ice cream?
   (Narrator) What does the woman mean? (12 seconds)

3. (Woman) Can't Eric lend you some money?
   (Man)   He is out of cash.
   (Narrator) What does the man say about Eric? (12 seconds)

4. (Man)   I am still trying to finish copying this stack of papers.
   (Woman)   When you leave, be sure that the copying machine is turned off.
   (Narrator) What does the woman mean? (12 seconds)

5. (Woman)   Tom got a C in Mrs. Walker's class.
   (Man)   It's surprising that he passed his Latin at all.
   (Narrator) What does the man imply? (12 seconds)

6. (Man)   I'd be curious to find out what Janet's bills came to.
   (Woman)   She paid sixty dollars for a pair of shoes and one hundred fifty dollars for a dress.
   (Narrator) What does the woman say about Janet? (12 seconds)

7. (Woman)   The construction of the Science Complex is finally over. Have you seen it yet?
   (Man)   The new engineering building is far from what I expected.
   (Narrator) What does the man mean? (12 seconds)

8. (Man)   I got my teeth cleaned today.
   (Woman)   So, you *have* gone to a dentist.
   (Narrator) What does the woman mean? (12 seconds)

9. (Woman)   Have Nick and Sally made all the arrangements for the reception?
   (Man)   It appears that one hundred and thirty guests are coming to the wedding, and the hall they rented is not nearly large enough.
   (Narrator) What does the man imply? (12 seconds)

10. (Man)   I'd like to cash a traveler's check for a thousand dollars.
    (Woman)   The manager can help you.
    (Narrator) What does the woman imply? (12 seconds)

11. (Woman)   The people across the street are getting their house ready for sale.
    (Man)   I know. Last week, they had the windows washed and the carpets steamed.
    (Narrator) What does the man mean? (12 seconds)

12. (Man)   Kate should be proud of her accomplishment. How did she react to the news?
    (Woman)   When she learned that she won the first prize, she was at a loss for words.
    (Narrator) What can be said about Kate? (12 seconds)

13. (Woman)   How about a cup of coffee? You look tired.
    (Man)   Every morning I promise myself that I'll go to bed early but I end up staying up anyway.
    (Narrator) What does the man mean? (12 seconds)

14. (Man)   Is Ronald going to Iowa to see his parents?
    (Woman)   He wants to travel abroad this summer.
    (Narrator) What does the woman mean? (12 seconds)

15. (Woman)   Why don't her roommates forward the package to her?
    (Man)   They don't have her address, and they don't know how to get in touch with her.
    (Narrator) What does the man mean? (12 seconds)

16. (Man)   We've been driving for forty-five minutes already, and I expected the trip to take no longer than half an hour.
    (Woman)   If you hadn't missed the turn-off, we could've made it there on time.
    (Narrator) What does the woman mean? (12 seconds)

17. (Woman)   The number of incoming undergraduates is high this fall.
    (Man)   The business school enrollment is only a third of the predicted figures.
    (Narrator) What does the man mean? (12 seconds)

18. (Man)   What's Henry been up to? I've seen him at the school of music several times in the past month.
    (Woman)   Can you believe that he has taken up singing at *his* age.
    (Narrator) What does the woman mean? (12 seconds)

19. (Woman)   You seem upset. Is something wrong?
    (Man)   I'm sick and tired of explaining the same thing just because someone is not listening.
    (Narrator) What does the man mean? (12 seconds)

20. (Woman)   I've been trying to find you. Where have you and your sister been?
    (Man)   We took a path down to the river.
    (Narrator) What does the woman mean? (12 seconds)

21. (Woman)   Did you get tickets for the game?
    (Man)   The line was too long, and I had little time. Maybe we can call the box office and try our luck there.
    (Narrator) What are the man and woman probably going to do next? (12 seconds)

22. (Man)   I think we need to have another phone line installed. The one we have is always busy.
    (Woman)   Not on *our* budget we don't.
    (Narrator) What does the woman mean? (12 seconds)

23. (Man)   You can sign up for the placement test in room 208 (two-oh-eight).
    (Woman)   I don't think I should be required to take the placement test. I passed my math class in my other school.
    (Man)   All transfer students have to take the test.
    (Narrator) What can be concluded from this conversation? (12 seconds)

24. (Man)   The flower bed in the front is so full of weeds that you can barely see the tulips. The hedges need to be trimmed, and the grass could use some work.
    (Woman)   Mr. Smith could take care of all of these problems.
    (Narrator) What is Mr. Smith's job? (12 seconds)

25. (Woman)   The battery is getting low, and we'll probably miss the second half of the press conference.
    (Man)   If you adjust the volume, we will hear better.
    (Narrator) What are the man and woman probably doing? (12 seconds)

26. (Man)   The actual fee for a compact is one hundred dollars per week. The other charges come from the insurance and mileage fees.
    (Woman)   I didn't realize these were extra.
    (Narrator) Where is this conversation probably taking place? (12 seconds)

27. (Man)   I have such a bad ear infection that I won't be able to come to the final exam this afternoon.
    (Woman) Only your instructor can tell you what to do in this situation.
    (Narrator) What did the woman mean? (12 seconds)

28. (Man)   I hate to say it, but I didn't get much out of this course on urban economics.
    (Woman) What you get out of it depends on what you put into it.
    (Narrator) What can be said about the woman? (12 seconds)

29. (Man)   Do you carry books on early American crafts?
    (Woman) Well, we used to, but we couldn't sell many. If you need a specific text, you could write directly to the publisher.
    (Narrator) Where is this conversation taking place? (12 seconds)

30. (Man)   Despite his age, Edward is the best cross-country skier I have ever seen.
    (Woman) Oh, he really is. Last year, he came in first in a ten-mile race.
    (Narrator) What can be said about Edward? (12 seconds)

(Narrator)   This is the end of Part A.

Now read the directions for Part B while they are being read to you.

Part B

DIRECTIONS: In this part of the test, you will hear longer conversations. After each conversation, you will hear several questions. The conversations and questions will not be repeated.

After you hear a question, read the four possible answers in your test book and choose the best answer. Then, on your answer sheet, find the number of the question and fill in the space that corresponds to the letter of the answer you have chosen.

Remember, you are not allowed to take notes or write in your test book.

(Narrator)   Questions 31 through 37 refer to the following dialogue about popcorn.

(Man)   Even if we are going to stay home to watch the movie, we should still make popcorn. That way, we can have it like we would in a movie theater without having to bother with driving, parking, and paying the outrageous ticket prices.
(Woman) What a great idea! But we don't have a popcorn popper.
(Man)   No problem. All we need is a cooking pot and a little oil. You can pop popcorn in anything that you can heat up to four hundred degrees. That's how the settlers did it before poppers even existed. Actually air corn poppers are best, and they don't cost much.
(Woman) Oil adds calories. Without oil, you can have as much of it as you want. Not only does it taste good, it's also good for you.
(Man)   We can't do without oil. We'll have burned corn kernels, not popped. Oil heats the corn kernel and makes the moisture turn to steam and burst.
(Woman) All right, but don't add a lot of it. It's amazing how much bigger the popped corn is compared to the kernel. I read somewhere that popped corn is thirty to forty times larger. Just imagine that!
(Man)   Here, have some. And you said we needed a corn popper.

(Narrator)

31. Where is this conversation taking place? (12 seconds)
32. What is necessary to make popcorn? (12 seconds)
33. What can be said about air corn poppers? (12 seconds)
34. What does the woman say about oil? (12 seconds)
35. Why is oil necessary for popping corn? (12 seconds)
36. What will happen if oil is not used for popping corn? (12 seconds)
37. How can the size of the popped corn be compared to that of the kernel? (12 seconds)

(Narrator)   This is the end of Part B.

Now read the directions for Part C while they are being read to you.

Part C

DIRECTIONS: In Part C you will hear short talks. At the end of each, you will be asked several questions. Each talk and each question will be spoken only one time. For this reason, you must listen carefully to understand what each speaker says. After you hear a question, read the four selections and choose the *one* that is the best answer to the question the speaker asked. Then, on your answer sheet, find the number of the question and blacken the space that corresponds to the letter for the answer you have chosen.

Listen to this sample talk.

You will hear:
  (Man)   Before people used automobiles, they walked or rode bicycles for short distances and took trains, streetcars, or horse-drawn carriages for long-distance travel. When automobiles were first invented, only the rich could afford them. Today, almost every household in the United States owns at least one car, and ninety percent of American adults have drivers' licenses.

According to the yearly value of its output, the U.S. automobile industry exceeds all other manufacturing industries in the country. As a consumer, this industry also supports other major industries, such as steel, glass, and rubber. Furthermore, approximately twelve million Americans are employed in the auxiliary service industries consisting of repair shops and service stations.

(Narrator)   Now listen to the following sample question.

You will hear: According to the speaker, how did people travel before the invention of the automobile?

You will read:
          (A) By cars and carriages
          (B) By bicycles, trains, and carriages
          (C) On foot and by boat
          (D) On board ships and trains

The best answer to the question "According to the speaker, how did people travel before the invention of the automobile?" is (B), "By bicycles, trains, and carriages." Therefore, the correct answer is (B).

Now listen to another sample question.

(Narrator)   Approximately how many people are employed in the automobile service industry?

You will read:

     (A) One million
     (B) Ten million
     (C) Twelve million
     (D) Ninety million

The best answer to the question "Approximately how many people are employed in the automobile service industry?" is (C), "Twelve million." Therefore, the correct answer is (C).

(Narrator)   Questions 38 through 42 refer to the following talk about school policy.

(Woman)   First of all, I would like to explain the course policies to you. The class meets three times a week for twelve weeks. In addition to the weekly written assignments, there are reading materials which must be covered before the end of the term. The written projects must be handed in on certain days of the week, but you are free to complete your readings at any time during the week when they are assigned.

Attendance in this class is taken at roll time. If you miss more than five class sessions, I will submit a written absence report to your adviser. If you must miss a class because you are ill or have an urgent matter to attend to, you need to inform me in order to avoid an unexcused absence. It is your responsibility to make up the work if you miss classes for any reason whatsoever. If you hand in your assignment after the due date, your grade will be lowered.

(Narrator)

38. What is the main topic of this talk? (12 seconds)
39. When must the weekly readings be completed? (12 seconds)
40. What would the speaker do if students miss more than five classes? (12 seconds)
41. How can students avoid unexcused absences? (12 seconds)
42. Why should written work be turned in on time? (12 seconds)

(Narrator)   Questions 43 through 46 refer to the following talk.

(Man)   As most of you already know, a flu epidemic has invaded not only our city but also the entire state. To decrease your chances of catching flu, you must have a clear understanding of how viral diseases spread.

Flus are viral, communicable diseases that spread from person to person through contact. Coughing and sneezing are the most common ways in which a virus travels from one person to another. When someone coughs or sneezes, the tiny droplets containing viruses are expelled into the air. If a person nearby breathes in these droplets, the virus travels from a sick person to a healthy one. After a virus invades a healthy cell, it multiplies rapidly and eventually damages or destroys the cell. If the number of contaminated cells is large, the person becomes ill.

You should note that colds spread in the same fashion as viral diseases. Touching door and faucet handles, shaking hands, and sharing towels can easily help transmit contagious diseases. One more complication needs to be mentioned. Some people who carry the infectious organisms within their bodies do not show any symptoms and are not even aware of being contagious but are, nevertheless, capable of transmitting viruses. Frequently, carriers of infections spread diseases unknowingly to themselves and others.

(Narrator)

43. What is the main idea of this talk? (12 seconds)
44. What is the most common cause of flu transmission? (12 seconds)
45. How do colds spread? (12 seconds)
46. Who are the carriers of viral diseases? (12 seconds)

(Narrator)   Questions 47 through 50 refer to the following talk about American values.

(Woman)   Did you know that we live in times of not only great technological but also social changes that affect our society daily? American cultural and social values are undergoing major modifications, as has been repeatedly pointed out in studies dealing with opinion research in the past ten or fifteen years.

Unlike in the 1960s and 1970s, currently only twenty percent of the American public cites traditional values of hard work, family, and sacrifice as important to them. Polling firms throughout the country have found that leisure activities have come to occupy a prominent place in people's lives. As a result, time has already become and will continue to be a scarce and valuable commodity. Manufacturers of time-saving products and suppliers of services, such as fast-food restaurants, prepared foods sold in stores, microwave ovens, disposable paper and fiber goods, fast-drying paints, and professional lawn services have shown a remarkable gain in revenue. A drive for self-fulfillment is also now looked at as an intrinsic American cultural value, although it was not commonly discussed even twenty years ago. The public seems to display an unprecedented desire to spend money and effort on improving looks and feeling healthy, vigorous, and energetic. People's desire to satisfy personal creativity has given a boost to purchases of hobby products, weight-reducing services, and even whirlpool baths.

(Narrator)

47. Who first noted a change in American social and cultural values? (12 seconds)
48. What does the speaker say has become a scarce commodity? (12 seconds)
49. What does the public seem to be willing to spend effort on? (12 seconds)
50. According to the speaker, why do people purchase hobby-related goods? (12 seconds)

(Narrator)   STOP WORKING ON SECTION 1.

Practice TOEFL 5

SECTION 1

LISTENING COMPREHENSION

(Narrator)   In this section, you will demonstrate your skills in understanding spoken English. There are three parts in the Listening Comprehension section, with different tasks in each.

Part A

Directions: In Part A you will hear short conversations between two people. At the end of each conversation, a third person will ask a question about what the two people said. Each conversation and each question will be spoken only one time. Therefore, you must listen carefully to understand what each speaker says. After you hear a conversation and the question, read the four selections and choose the *one* that is the best answer to the question the speaker asked. Then, on your answer sheet, find the number of the question and blacken the space that corresponds to the letter for the answer you have chosen. Blacken the space completely so that the letter inside the space does not show.

Listen to the following example.

On the recording, you hear:
  (Man)   Does the car need to be filled?
  (Woman)   Mary stopped at the gas station on her way home.
  (Narrator)   What does the woman mean?

In your test book, you will read:
          (A) Mary bought some food.
          (B) Mary had car trouble.
          (C) Mary went shopping.
          (D) Mary bought some gas.

From the conversation you learn that Mary stopped at the gas station on her way home. The best answer to the question "Does the car need to be filled?" is (D), "Mary bought some gas." Therefore, the correct answer is (D).

Now let us begin Part A with question number 1.

1. (Woman) I feel a draft. Is the window shut?
   (Man)   When they left, they didn't close the door.
   (Narrator) What does the man mean? (12 seconds)

2. (Man)   Rich surely spends a lot of time studying.
   (Woman) Had he known that the math class requires so much work, he would have taken it *next* year.
   (Narrator) What does the woman mean? (12 seconds)

3. (Woman)   What were those people asking you?
   (Man)   They were wondering if the picture is for sale.
   (Narrator) What does the man mean? (12 seconds)

4. (Man)   Jim was excited about *something*.
   (Woman)   He spent fifteen minutes telling me about a magazine article he found very
               interesting.
   (Narrator) What does the woman say about Jim? (12 seconds)

5. (Woman)   What do you mean you're moving? Your car is falling apart.
   (Man)   Once I figured out that I couldn't afford a new car, I decided to find a better
               apartment.
   (Narrator) What does the man mean? (12 seconds)

6. (Man)   Slow down! You are passing every car on the road.
   (Woman)   Most drivers don't observe the speed limit unless they think the police will
               stop them.
   (Narrator) What does the woman imply? (12 seconds)

7. (Woman)   I like that woman's outfit. I think black is always a practical color for office
               clothes.
   (Man)   Now that shades of pink are in fashion again, black looks outdated.
   (Narrator) What does the man mean? (12 seconds)

8. (Man)   When I came from work at 5:30, the bank was closed already.
   (Woman)   Why don't they keep the banks open longer hours?
   (Narrator) What does the woman mean? (12 seconds)

9. (Woman)   These students don't even know what the grading policy is.
   (Man)   When the teacher explained the course requirements, they were probably day-
               dreaming.
   (Narrator) What does the man mean? (12 seconds)

10. (Man)   Why are you going back?
    (Woman) I can't remember whether or not I locked the door.
    (Narrator) What does the woman mean? (12 seconds)

11. (Woman) Nancy told me she is angry at you.
    (Man)   Nancy may be angry at me, but she's not half as angry at me as I am at her.
    (Narrator) What does the man mean? (12 seconds)

12. (Man)   How did the interview go? What did you think of Paul?
    (Woman) He was so ill at ease that I felt sorry for him.
    (Narrator) What does the woman imply? (12 seconds)

13. (Woman) Don and Katherine took their luggage to the airport tonight instead of tomor-
               row morning.
    (Man)   They'll never make it back in time for the show.
    (Narrator) What does the man say about Don and Katherine? (12 seconds)

14. (Man)   Won't you have some more turkey?
    (Woman) Thank you, but I've had two helpings already.
    (Narrator) What does the woman imply? (12 seconds)

15. (Woman) Excuse me, is this a new rule?
    (Man)   In light of numerous complaints, the management no longer allows smoking
               in the lounge.
    (Narrator) What does the man mean? (12 seconds)

16. (Man)   You don't think we need a new copier, do you?
    (Woman) It was jammed six times last week and five times this week.
    (Narrator) What does the woman imply? (12 seconds)

17. (Woman) Maybe we should invite the Johnsons to come with us.
    (Man)   The Johnsons stopped going to the club because they don't like the service.
    (Narrator) What does the man imply? (12 seconds)

18. (Man)   They did a great job, but it looks like you'd need to take some time off.
    (Woman) It took them two days to paint the house and another day to clean up.
    (Narrator) What does the woman imply? (12 seconds)

19. (Woman) What would it cost me to mail this package?
    (Man)   To send it by first-class mail costs two dollars and ninety cents, and second-class postage is one dollar and forty cents.
    (Narrator) What does the man imply? (12 seconds)

20. (Man)   What's wrong with him? He seems irritable this morning.
    (Woman) Mike didn't get much sleep because his neighbor's dog was barking all night.
    (Narrator) What does the woman mean? (12 seconds)

21. (Woman) I want to change my clothes. Where are our suitcases?
    (Man)   I took them down to the front desk.
    (Narrator) Where does this conversation take place? (12 seconds)

22. (Man)   It's snowing pretty hard, and the roads will be slippery. Will you call me when you get home?
    (Woman) Don't worry. I'll be fine.
    (Narrator) What does the woman mean? (12 seconds)

23. (Man)   Do you mind giving me a ride to work?
    (Woman) Not at all. It's on my way to school.
    (Narrator) What does the woman agree to do? (12 seconds)

24. (Woman) I ordered these books six weeks ago, and they still haven't arrived.
    (Man)   Personally, I will never do business with that distributor again.
    (Narrator) What can be said about the man? (12 seconds)

25. (Man)   What do you think this word is?
    (Woman) I don't know. I can't read Greg's handwriting. In my opinion, if he bothers to write at all, he should make it legible.
    (Narrator) What are the man and woman probably looking at? (12 seconds)

26. (Man)   I don't think Joe is going to pass French.
    (Woman) Not the way *he* is going.
    (Narrator) What does the woman mean? (12 seconds)

27. (Man)   In this conference room, we can be more comfortable than in 217 (two-seventeen). I'm sure we can seat over thirty people here.
    (Woman) You're right. We can put a note on the door to let people know that the meeting has been moved to the conference room.
    (Narrator) Where does this conversation take place? (12 seconds)

28. (Woman) Can you go down to the store on the corner? We need to get some milk for breakfast in the morning.
    (Man)   At *this* hour?
    (Narrator) What does the man mean? (12 seconds)

29. (Woman) I love the apple pie. It tastes just like my mother's. You couldn't buy one like this at any bakery.
    (Man)   Your husband is really good at it, isn't he?
    (Narrator) Who made the pie? (12 seconds)

30. (Woman) The Stevensons are taking their entire family to Hawaii for the summer.
    (Man)   How can they afford something like that?
    (Narrator) What does the man mean? (12 seconds)

(Narrator) This is the end of Part A.

Now read the directions for Part B while they are being read to you.

Part B

DIRECTIONS: In this part of the test, you will hear longer conversations. After each conversation, you will hear several questions. The conversations and questions will not be repeated.

After you hear a question, read the four possible answers in your test book and choose the best answer, Then, on your answer sheet, find the number of the question and fill in the space that corresponds to the letter of the answer you have chosen.

Remember, you are not allowed to take notes or write in your test book.

(Narrator) Questions 31 through 34 refer to the following conversation about shoes.

(Woman) Your shoes are dirty. You need to clean them off before you go inside.
(Man)   Okay. I'll wash them with water from the hose.
(Woman) You can't wash leather shoes with water. You'll ruin them. Shoes are actually pretty complicated these days. We are so used to wearing shoes that few of us even think about them, apart from the times when we put them on and take them off.
(Man)   If I could, I'd go barefoot.
(Woman) Well, you were born a few thousand years too late. People didn't always wear shoes. No one knows when people first began to use them, but archaeologists say that the first shoes that covered feet were wrappings of animal skins worn in cold climates. Sandals appeared later in southern regions and were most likely made of wood, with leather or cloth attaching the soles to the upper part of the foot. I think they were probably pretty uncomfortable.
(Man)   You know all this about shoes. So, why did they change from sandals to the types of shoes we wear now?
(Woman) Over time, shoes began to be used not only for protection but also for decoration. Elaborate buckles, buttons, and embroidery covered most shoe uppers for royalty and commoners in France and in Spain. For example, high heels came into fashion in the 1600s and were worn by men. However uncomfortable they are, people have continued to wear them for more than 300 years.
(Man)   The history of shoes sounds pretty elaborate.
(Woman) It is, and that's not all. Silk, satin, velvet, and lizard skins are still used for making dress shoes for special occasions. Today's shoes are relatively cheap because most models are designed by computer, and their components are cut by laser and sewn together by programmed machinery.
(Man)   It's hard to imagine how much technology has affected everything we do, use, and wear. Even something seemingly as simple as shoes!

(Narrator)

31. What was the earliest footwear made of? (12 seconds)
32. Which of these words probably best describes the first shoes? (12 seconds)
33. Approximately how long have high-heeled shoes been worn? (12 seconds)
34. Why are shoes comparatively cheap today? (12 seconds)

(Narrator)   Questions 35 through 38 refer to the following conversation about life's changes.

(Woman)   Imagine meeting you at the terminal after all these years.

(Man)   My bus for Baltimore is leaving in about twenty minutes. And where are you going?

(Woman)   My brother is getting married in New York on Tuesday. Maybe you remember him; he was about eight years old when you saw him last.

(Man)   Of course I remember him. He used to watch birds from the window in his room.

(Woman)   Well, he moved to Philadelphia about five years ago, but now he works for a telephone company and commutes from the suburbs.

(Man)   I suppose we all have grown older. Last time I saw you, you were still in high school.

(Woman)   Those days are over. My daughter's in high school now. I'm sure your children are probably getting ready to graduate from college.

(Man)   You're right. Ken is twenty-three and lives in Chicago, and Elizabeth is twenty-one.

(Woman)   I'm sorry but I think this is my boarding announcement. It looks like it's time for me to go.

(Narrator)

35. Where does this conversation occur? (12 seconds)
36. Where is the woman going? (12 seconds)
37. When did the man and the woman meet last? (12 seconds)
38. How many children does the man have? (12 seconds)

(Narrator)   This is the end of Part B.

Now read the directions for Part C while they are being read to you.

Part C

DIRECTIONS: In Part C you will hear short talks. At the end of each, you will be asked several questions. Each talk and each question will be spoken only one time. For this reason, you must listen carefully to understand what the speaker says. After you hear a question, read the four selections and choose the *one* that is the best answer to the question the speaker asked. Then, on your answer sheet, find the number of the question and blacken the space that corresponds to the letter for the answer you have chosen.

Listen to this sample talk.

You will hear:

(Man)   Before people used automobiles, they walked or rode bicycles for short distances and took trains, streetcars, or horse-drawn carriages for long-distance travel. When automobiles were first produced, only the rich could afford them. Today, almost every household in the United States owns at least one car, and ninety percent of American adults have drivers' licenses.

According to the yearly value of its output, the U.S. automobile industry exceeds all other manufacturing industries in the country. As a consumer, this industry also supports other major industries, such as steel, glass, and rubber. Furthermore, approximately twelve million Americans are employed in the auxiliary service industries consisting of repair shops and service stations.

(Narrator)   Now listen to the following question.

You will hear: According to the speaker, how did people travel before the invention of the automobile?

You will read:

        (A) By cars and carriages
        (B) By bicycles, trains and carriages
        (C) On foot and by boat
        (D) On board ships and trains

The best answer to the question "According to the speaker, how did people travel before the invention of the automobile?" is (B), "By bicycles, trains, and carriages." Therefore, the correct answer is (B).

Now listen to another sample question.

(Narrator)   Approximately how many people are employed in the automobile service industry?

You will read:

        (A) One million
        (B) Ten million
        (C) Twelve million
        (D) Ninety million

The best answer to the question "Approximately how many people are employed in the automobile service industry?" is (C), "Twelve million." Therefore, the correct answer is (C).

(Narrator)   <u>Questions 39 through 43</u> refer to the following talk.

(Woman)   Those of you who aspire to enter the police force have the idea that being a police officer is exciting. Your training in the academy will teach you skills you've never even thought of. Whereas some aspects of the job can be interesting, the daily tasks that police officers perform are unexciting. Patrolling streets and assisting people with various problems are not the most interesting aspects of the job. On the city streets, traffic officers in charge of public safety direct traffic, enforce parking and speed laws, and verify the licensing of vehicles. Most police officers consider such assignments as walking the beat tedious. Because they are always watching for signs of trouble or disturbance, officers may be under a great deal of stress. Occasionally, highway police officers have to change tires for motorists who can't do the job themselves, and sometimes they do it in the pouring rain or during a blizzard. When officers are called upon to resolve disputes or protect victims of crime, their personal safety can't always be guaranteed. Writing police reports and memos is another necessary part of police officers' work. Few officers enjoy it, but all of them have to do it.

(Narrator)

39. What is the main idea of this talk? (12 seconds)
40. How did the speaker describe the daily tasks of a police officer? (12 seconds)
41. Which aspects of police work can be dangerous? (12 seconds)
42. According to the speaker, which aspect of police work has to be performed by all officers? (12 seconds)
43. What can be said about the majority of police activity? (12 seconds)

(Narrator)   <u>Questions 44 through 50</u> refer to the following talk about American literature.

(Woman)   Most people don't know that when settlers first arrived in America and during their first century in their new country, they produced an enormous amount of writing. They described their adventures in the wilderness, settlements, nature, and their encounters with strange people. They kept detailed chronicles of their lives, and some produced literally volumes. The colonial writing became a very large body of material that served as inspiration for the writers even in the 19th century. Today, for readers it provides insight and understanding of the experiences that helped shape the American national character and legal institutions.

Contrary to what most Americans believe, the first permanent American settlement was a result of commercial, rather than religious, interests. The Virginia Company established the Jamestown colony in 1607 and expected that it would attract the trade from the English who traveled through the area. However, their expectations were unrealistic, and only several tailors came to the town during its first year. Nonetheless, the records from the colony, epidemic fevers, Indian raids, and property conflicts with Indian tribes provide us with rich heritage from which to study and learn.

A large number of settlers in New England, specifically at Massachusetts Bay, were highly educated, especially clergymen and government officials. They produced a considerable body of writing, although they were not writers in the professional sense. They were primarily concerned about building a new civil society on which their lives and fortunes depended. The governor of the Massachusetts Bay Company, John Winthrop, moved the office of his company from London to Boston Bay. This move allowed the colony to become a powerful center based on self-government. As all governments do, the Puritans also documented their procedures and decisions and created large amounts of writing. Salem and Plymouth were prospering cities, and Harvard, the first colonial university, was established in Massachusetts.

In the Middle Colonies, the Quaker city of Philadelphia had become the colonial center by 1750. Attracted by the volume of the commercial activity in the city, many settlers moved there and established schools and libraries. Of course, all Americans know that both the Declaration of Independence and the Constitution were signed in Philadelphia. Actual literary work was also created at that time and included observations of natural history and collections of essays, such as William Penn's famous *Some Fruits of Solitude*, published in 1693.

(Narrator)

44. What is the main topic of this talk? (12 seconds)
45. Why did early settlers write? (12 seconds)
46. According to the speaker, why do readers today need to read these early accounts? (12 seconds)
47. Who established the first American settlement? (12 seconds)
48. Where did American self-government first begin? (12 seconds)
49. In what city was the Constitution written? (12 seconds)
50. What did first American literary work include? (12 seconds)

(Narrator)   STOP WORKING ON SECTION 1.

Practice TOEFL 6

SECTION 1

LISTENING COMPREHENSION

(Narrator)   In this section, you will demonstrate your skills in understanding spoken English. There are three parts in the Listening Comprehension section, with different tasks in each.

Part A

DIRECTIONS: In Part A you will hear short conversations between two people. At the end of each conversation, a third person will ask a question about what the first two people said. Each conversation and each question will be spoken only one time. For this reason, you must listen carefully to understand what each speaker says. After you hear a conversation and the question, read the four selections and choose the *one* that is the best answer to the question the speaker asked. Then, on your answer sheet, find the number of the question and blacken the space that corresponds to the letter for the answer you have chosen. Blacken the space completely so that the letter inside the space does not show.

Listen to the following example.

   On the recording, you hear:
       (Man)   Does the car need to be filled?
       (Woman)   Mary stopped at the gas station on her way home.
       (Narrator)   What does the woman mean?

   In your test book, you will read:
               (A) Mary bought some food.
               (B) Mary had car trouble.
               (C) Mary went shopping.
               (D) Mary bought some gas.

From the conversation you learn that Mary stopped at the gas station on her way home. The best answer to the question "Does the car need to be filled?" is (D), "Mary bought some gas." Therefore, the correct answer is (D).

Now let us begin Part A with question number 1.

You will hear:

1. (Woman) What should I do with the key?
    (Man)   When you check out, you can return it at the front desk.
    (Narrator) What does the man mean? (12 seconds)

2. (Man)   What did John see last night?
   (Woman) He was so tired yesterday that he decided to stay home instead of going to the
            movies.
   (Narrator) What does the woman say about John? (12 seconds)

3. (Woman) Couldn't you get a seat on the next flight?
   (Man)   The travel agent said that it's completely booked.
   (Narrator) What does the man mean? (12 seconds)

4. (Man)   Is it okay to submit a handwritten paper instead of typewritten?
   (Woman) As far as I know.
   (Narrator) What does the woman imply? (12 seconds)

5. (Woman) Hopefully, we didn't disturb you. Students were trying to decide who would
            attend the President's counsel and they were very enthusiastic.
   (Man)   They *were* noisy.
   (Narrator) What does the man imply? (12 seconds)

6. (Woman) I don't understand what we are supposed to do in this chemistry assignment.
   (Man)   Do you think Frank can help us?
   (Narrator) What does the man ask? (12 seconds)

7. (Man)   I'd like to check in these boxes and the three suitcases.
   (Woman) The limit is two pieces per passenger.
   (Narrator) What does the woman mean? (12 seconds)

8. (Woman) What are you looking for?
   (Man)   Have you seen my red coat anywhere?
   (Narrator) What does the man mean? (12 seconds)

9. (Man)   Are you and Paul still neighbors?
   (Woman) Paul has moved to an apartment near the North Campus dorms.
   (Narrator) What does the woman say about Paul? (12 seconds)

10. (Woman) Do you have a table available?
    (Man)   If you don't have a reservation, you may have to wait about fifty minutes.
    (Narrator) What does the man mean? (12 seconds)

11. (Man)   I can't believe they charge fifteen dollars for a chicken dinner.
    (Woman) But the salad and the dessert are included.
    (Narrator) What does the woman mean? (12 seconds)

12. (Woman) Jennifer's car wouldn't start, and she needs a ride to the library.
    (Man)   It's on my way to the bank.
    (Narrator) What did the man imply he would do? (12 seconds)

13. (Woman) Did you hear about the new crafts show at the City Center?
    (Man)   I think I've seen more craft shows than I've ever wanted to.
    (Narrator) What does the man mean? (12 seconds)

14. (Man)   The road construction in Detroit always creates traffic jams on the highways.
    (Woman) You could take two-seventy-five (275) around the city.
    (Narrator) What does the woman suggest? (12 seconds)

15. (Woman) Do you carry books on outdoor cooking?
    (Man)   We used to, but we don't any longer.
    (Narrator) Where does this conversation take place? (12 seconds)

16. (Man)   I don't think I need to take another history course.
    (Woman) You should discuss that with your advisor.
    (Narrator) What does the woman imply? (12 seconds)

17. (Woman) Can you tell me where the conference center is located?
    (Man)   Go straight to the light at the end of the block and turn right.
    (Narrator) Where is the conference site located? (12 seconds)

18. (Man)   How much does it cost to mail a package overnight to Seattle?
    (Woman) It depends on its weight.
    (Narrator) Where does this conversation take place? (12 seconds)

19. (Woman) My brother is coming to spend the weekend with us, and we wanted to have you and your wife for dinner on Saturday.
    (Man)   She'll be out of town.
    (Narrator) What does the man mean? (12 seconds)

20. (Woman) I'd like to return the shoes and the shirt.
    (Man)   No problem. May I see your receipt?
    (Narrator) What is the man's occupation? (12 seconds)

21. (Man)   We're on our way to the pool. Would you like to come with us?
    (Woman) I have to write a letter to the phone company to clear up the mistake on my bill.
    (Narrator) What will the woman do next? (12 seconds)

22. (Man)   It's already nine. I wonder how much more we can get done today.
    (Woman) Well, let's call it a day.
    (Narrator) What does the woman mean? (12 seconds)

23. (Man)   I couldn't finish the assignment because during the summer the lab hours are restricted.
    (Woman) Whether the lab is open or not, the test on vowels will be given on Friday.
    (Narrator) What does the woman mean? (12 seconds)

24. (Woman) The ribbons and the balloons make the room look so cheerful.
    (Man)   Laura went out of her way to decorate the house for the occasion.
    (Narrator) Where is this conversation taking place? (12 seconds)

25. (Man)   Do you mind if I change the channel?
    (Woman) Actually, I think this program looks interesting.
    (Narrator) What are the man and the woman probably doing? (12 seconds)

26. (Woman) Excuse me, do you know where the museum is?
    (Man)   I didn't even know there was one here.
    (Narrator) What does the man mean? (12 seconds)

27. (Woman) It looks like you've finished packing.
    (Man)   Could you help me take these boxes downstairs?
    (Narrator) What does the man mean? (12 seconds)

28. (Man)   Has Tom been tired lately?
    (Woman) He's taken a second job.
    (Narrator) What does the woman say about Tom? (12 seconds)

29. (Woman) Marsha is getting tired of Rob's practical jokes.
    (Man)   Rob's humor can be difficult to take sometimes.
    (Narrator) What does the man mean? (12 seconds)

30. (Man)   I've been looking for a part-time job, but haven't had much luck.
    (Woman) The clothing store on the corner pays its employees well.
    (Narrator) What does the woman mean? (12 seconds)

(Narrator)   This is the end of Part A.

Now read the directions for Part B while they are being read to you.

Part B

DIRECTIONS: In this part of the test, you will hear longer conversations. After each conversation, you will hear several questions. The conversations and questions will not be repeated.

After you hear a question, read the four possible answers in your test book and choose the best answer. Then, on your answer sheet, find the number of the question and fill in the space that corresponds to the letter of the answer you have chosen.

Remember, you are not allowed to take notes or write in your test book.

(Narrator)   Questions 31 through 34 refer to the following conversation about sharks.

(Woman)   Sharks are meat-eating fish and are the most feared of sea creatures. Although no one knows exactly how many species of sharks exist, over 350 have been identified. Sharks vary greatly in size and behavior, and most species are found in warm waters of the Atlantic and Indian Oceans. People frequently believe that sharks have few rivals, but a shark's greatest enemy is a bigger shark.

(Man)   Do they eat people?

(Woman)   Contrary to a popular belief that sharks virtually feed on people, fewer than 100 shark attacks are reported each year. I'd like to point out that this number includes all attacks in the world.

(Man)   How fast can sharks swim? If a shark attacks you, do you have a chance to escape?

(Woman)   Well, an escape can be difficult. Usually, sharks are not very fast, but when necessary, they can move at bursts of up to forty-five miles an hour. Their tails help sharks gain speed; however, they cannot maintain it for long periods of time.

(Man)   Their teeth *do* look pretty frightening.

(Woman)   The most amazing feature of sharks is their teeth. First of all, sharks have several rows of teeth, and second, their teeth can be replaced as often as every week or two. Some people believe that before sharks bite, they have to turn over on their backs, but that is a myth. Sharks can bite in any position.

(Man)   In all the movies about sharks, I've seen that they can hear movement in the water from great distances. Is that also a myth?

(Woman)   No, it isn't. Sharks have a keen sense of hearing and excellent eyesight that make them excellent hunters. Also, their bodies can sense movement of water, which allows them to identify the presence of another live creature. Sharks can detect even the smallest electrical fields emitted by fish that move their gills. This ability also permits sharks to navigate their way through the ocean.

(Narrator)

31. What is the main topic of this conversation? (12 seconds)
32. How many shark attacks occur annually? (12 seconds)
33. What does the man say is frightening about sharks? (12 seconds)
34. What makes sharks good hunters? (12 seconds)

(Narrator)   <u>Questions 35 through 38</u> refer to the following conversation about looking for a physician.

(Man)   When I lived in Los Angeles, I had a great family doctor. Since we moved, I haven't been able to find a physician. I am not even sure how to go about looking for one.

(Woman)   It's really not that difficult. Most hospitals have a physician-referral service. You could call one.

(Man)   That's a great idea. But there are so many hospitals.

(Woman)   I'm sure there is a hospital in the area where you live. If you call, you can ask for a referral to a family physician close to your house.

(Man)   But what if they refer me to a doctor who doesn't accept new patients?

(Woman)   Usually, hospitals have this information and won't refer you to someone who doesn't. However, to be on the safe side, you can ask for two or three referrals. You can also tell them if you are looking for a family doctor who is associated with a particular hospital. Another thing to bring to their attention is whether the doctor files claims with your insurance company.

(Man)   It sounds like a great service. Do they also recommend dentists?

(Woman)   I don't know about dentists. You can ask them when you call.

(Narrator)

35. Why is the man looking for a physician? (12 seconds)
36. What does the woman suggest? (12 seconds)
37. According to the woman, what information do hospitals usually have? (12 seconds)
38. What does the woman say about dentist referrals? (12 seconds)

(Narrator)   This is the end of Part B.

Now read the directions for Part C while they are being read to you.

Part C

<u>DIRECTIONS</u>: In Part C you will hear short talks. At the end of each, you will be asked several questions. Each talk and each question will be spoken only one time. For this reason, you must listen carefully to understand what the speaker says. After you hear a question, read the four selections and choose the *one* that is the best answer to the question the speaker asked. Then, on your answer sheet, find the number of the question and blacken the space that corresponds to the letter for the answer you have chosen.

Listen to this sample talk.

You will hear:
   (Man)   Before people used automobiles, they walked or rode bicycles for short distances and took trains, streetcars, or horse-drawn carriages for long-distance travel. When automobiles were first produced, only the rich could afford them. Today, almost every household in the United States owns at least one car, and ninety percent of American adults have drivers' licenses.

   According to the yearly value of its output, the U.S. automobile industry exceeds all other manufacturing industries in the country. As a consumer, this industry also supports other major industries, such as steel, glass, and rubber. Furthermore, approximately twelve million Americans are employed in the auxiliary service industries consisting of repair shops and service stations.

(Narrator)   Now listen to the following question.

You will hear: According to the speaker, how did people travel before the invention of the automobile?·

You will read:
  (A) By cars and carriages
  (B) By bicycles, trains, and carriages
  (C) On foot and by boat
  (D) On board ships and trains

The best answer to the question "According to the speaker, how did people travel before the invention of the automobile?" is (B), "By bicycles, trains, and carriages." Therefore, the correct answer is (B).

Now listen to another sample question.

(Narrator)   Approximately how many people are employed in the automobile service industry?

You will read:
  (A) One million
  (B) Ten million
  (C) Twelve million
  (D) Ninety million

The best answer to the question "Approximately how many people are employed in the automobile service industry?" is (C), "Twelve million." Therefore, the correct answer is (C).

(Narrator)   Questions 39 through 42 refer to a talk about job interviews.

(Man)   During a job interview, your behavior, clothes, and speech are important. It's important that you arrive on time and be polite, sincere, and organized. Most people don't realize that the way one dresses for an interview is also important. If your clothes are wrinkled or mismatched, the interviewer may think that you really don't care about your appearance and even about the quality of your work. Your outfit doesn't have to cost a fortune, but it should be neat and clean to make a good impression on the interviewer. And please, please don't arrive at the interview in clothes that have stains or rips. Don't borrow your friend's clothes if they don't fit well. This is one of the common mistakes that job seekers make: they don't want to spend the money and end up losing a chance to get an offer.

It's important to remember that if you don't make a good first impression, you may not get a chance to make another one. When you speak, you need to adjust your speech rate. If the interviewer speaks fast, you have to speak just as fast. If the person in charge speaks slowly, you'll have to slow down. Research has shown that most (people) like those individuals who speak at the same speed as they do.

(Narrator)

39. What is the main purpose of this talk? (12 seconds)
40. What does the speaker say about an interview outfit? (12 seconds)
41. What is a common mistake people make when they go for an interview? (12 seconds)
42. How should interviewees adjust their speech rate? (12 seconds)

(Narrator)　<u>Questions 43 through 46</u> refer to a talk about the Boston Tea Party.

(Woman)　In 1767, the British imposed heavy taxes on goods sold in America. The taxation caused a public uproar, and eventually, all but one of the taxes were repealed. The tax that remained in effect had to do with the sale of tea imported from Britain or other colonies. In addition to this tax, the British government allowed one company to sell tea at lower prices, and American merchants were afraid that they could not compete fairly. At first, when tea arrived in Boston Harbor, the local merchants protested and attempted to have the tea returned to England. This attempt failed, but on December 16, 1773, about 100 colonists raided three British merchant vessels anchored in Boston Harbor and threw 342 containers of tea overboard into the waters of the Atlantic Ocean. This raid was called the Boston Tea Party by the Boston newspapers.

(Narrator)

43. What is the main idea of this talk? (12 seconds)
44. When did the Boston Tea Party take place? (12 seconds)
45. How many British ships did colonists raid? (12 seconds)
46. Why did colonists throw the tea overboard? (12 seconds)

(Narrator)　<u>Questions 47 through 50</u> refer to a talk on political polling.

(Man)　In political polling, the purpose of any sample is to produce results that can be useful. Therefore, the findings have to be valid and reliable, and a sample has to be large enough to represent the voters' opinions. Of course, we all understand that political polls cannot be one hundred percent accurate, but still, the margin of error cannot exceed two or three percent. If poll results exceed that, they may not be valid. Even five percent is excessive.

As a rule, political polls are not completely reliable. Any pollster will tell you that they cannot scientifically predict outcomes. They describe people's attitudes at a certain moment in time, but people's attitudes obviously change as events continue to occur.

The sample of the population has to include various groups of people that represent all voters and not just a selected minority. Let me give you an example. In 1936, *Literary Digest*, a popular publication at the time, decided to conduct a political poll. They used the telephone to obtain their sample and tried to predict if Alf Landon would be the next president. I'd like to remind you that Landon was defeated by a landslide and lost to Franklin Roosevelt. His defeat by the majority of the electorate was one of the worst in history. Although the *Literary Digest* poll predicted that Landon would win, the prediction was clearly off the mark. So, what went wrong? Well, in 1936, only wealthy people could afford to have a telephone. And the wealthy strongly supported Landon. However, they did not represent the majority opinion, even though their number was large enough for the sample size to be valid. So, it's not that polls simply have to be large enough, but they have to represent the entire voting population. Otherwise, their results won't be valid.

(Narrator)

47. According to the speaker, what is an acceptable margin of error in political polls? (12 seconds)
48. What do political polls describe? (12 seconds)
49. How did *Literary Digest* obtain their sample? (12 seconds)
50. Why were the results of the poll invalid? (12 seconds)

(Narrator)　STOP WORKING ON SECTION 1.

Practice TOEFL 7

SECTION 1
LISTENING COMPREHENSION

(Narrator)   In this section, you will demonstrate your skills in understanding spoken English. There are three parts in the Listening Comprehension section, with different tasks in each.

Part A

DIRECTIONS: In Part A you will hear short conversations between two people. At the end of each conversation, a third person will ask a question about what the two people said. Each conversation and each question will be spoken only one time. For this reason, you must listen carefully to understand what each speaker says. After you hear a conversation and the question, read the four selections and choose the *one* that is the best answer to the question the speaker asked. Then, on your answer sheet, find the number of the question and blacken the space that corresponds to the letter for the answer you have chosen. Blacken the space completely so that the letter inside the space does not show.

Listen to the following example.

On the recording, you hear:
(Man)   Does the car need to be filled?
(Woman)   Mary stopped at the gas station on her way home.
(Narrator)   What does the woman mean?

In your test book, you will read:
(A) Mary bought some food.
(B) Mary had car trouble.
(C) Mary went shopping.
(D) Mary bought some gas.

From the conversation you learn that Mary stopped at the gas station on her way home. The best answer to the question "Does the car need to be filled?" is (D), "Mary bought some gas." Therefore, the correct answer is (D).

Now let us begin Part A with question number 1.

1. (Woman) I was wondering if I could borrow a cup of sugar. I'm baking a cake, and I ran out.
   (Man)   I'm glad it's *your* turn to ask for something.
   (Narrator) What does the man mean? (12 seconds)

2. (Woman) I bought this tie for my husband, but he doesn't like the color.
   (Man)   Would you like to take another look at our selection?
   (Woman) I'd rather have a refund.
   (Narrator) What is the man's job? (12 seconds)

3. (Woman) I'm afraid there is no Sunday edition. It comes out only on weekdays.
   (Man)   Isn't there news on Sunday?
   (Narrator) What are the man and the woman talking about? (12 seconds)

4. (Man)   Have you seen a thick, dark-blue pen? I've looked for twenty minutes, and I can't find it anywhere.
   (Woman) Did you misplace it *again*? You'll find it. You always do.
   (Narrator) What conclusion can be drawn from the woman's statement? (12 seconds)

5. (Woman) Because of the fog in Seattle, Mr. Black's flight has been delayed, and it looks like he's still waiting for the departure.
   (Man)   Oh, thank you for calling. Is he going to be in his office tomorrow, or is he going directly to San Francisco?
   (Narrator) Where is Mr. Black today? (12 seconds)

6. (Man)   I've gained weight. If I don't start exercising every day, none of my clothes will fit.
   (Woman) I could've *told* you that.
   (Narrator) What does the woman suggest to the man? (12 seconds)

7. (Woman) I'd like a pound of your chicken salad and a half a pound of roast beef.
   (Man)   Will that be all?
   (Woman) I guess so.
   (Narrator) What does the woman mean? (12 seconds)

8. (Man)   Marsha strikes me as an unreliable person. She has lost more papers than I care to mention.
   (Woman) She is not half as bad as Tracey.
   (Narrator) What does the woman say about Tracey? (12 seconds)

9. (Woman) Motorcycle races can be very dangerous if you don't know what you are doing.
   (Man)   No kidding.
   (Narrator) What can be concluded from the man's response? (12 seconds)

10. (Woman) I am looking forward to this trip. Don't forget the camera. Last time we went on a tour, you left it behind.
    (Man)   *You* carry it then.
    (Narrator) What are the man and the woman going to do next? (12 seconds)

11. (Woman) Do you mind closing the door? When they unload the truck, they are very noisy.
    (Man)   Do *I* mind? I'd be happy to.
    (Narrator) What does the man mean? (12 seconds)

12. (Man)   Peggy wanted to cancel her appointment with Dr. Robinson this afternoon.
    (Woman) She can certainly do that, but the doctor is leaving tomorrow, and he won't be back until June.
    (Man)   In this case, I think she'd better keep it.
    (Narrator) What did the man say Peggy will do? (12 seconds)

13. (Man)   The bank has turned down my application for a loan. I need $500 to pay my tuition.
    (Woman) Don't look at *me*.
    (Narrator) What does the woman mean? (12 seconds)

14. (Woman) The deadline for the market survey is the fifteenth of December. To analyze the data, we have to finish collecting it by the first of November.
    (Man)   This may be cutting it a little too close.
    (Narrator) What does the man mean? (12 seconds)

15. (Man)   The road construction on route seventy-one (71) is creating terrible traffic backups.
    (Woman)   *Tell* me about it. That's the road I have to take home.
    (Narrator) What can be said about the woman? (12 seconds)

16. (Man)   They got so lost driving from the stadium that it took them almost two hours to find their way back to the hotel.
    (Woman)   Didn't they have a map?
    (Narrator) What does the woman mean? (12 seconds)

17. (Man)   This house has four bedrooms, three bathrooms, a spacious living room, and a volleyball court in the backyard.
    (Woman)   Do you suppose we could schedule an appointment with the owner?
    (Narrator) What would the woman like to do? (12 seconds)

18. (Man)   Mrs. Cook's class is going to visit the newspaper on Tuesday, and we are asking for volunteers to help with transportation.
    (Woman)   Thirty-five children would require *eight* passenger cars. What else can we do?
    (Narrator) What does the woman suggest? (12 seconds)

19. (Woman)   This game can be fun, and it also helps you expand your vocabulary. It's easy to learn. You put together words in a sequence, using the letters on these cards. See?
    (Man)   Where did you put the letter cards?
    (Narrator) What are the man and the woman doing? (12 seconds)

20. (Man)   I heard Matthew followed Jenny to her new job. And their house is up for sale.
    (Woman)   Is *that* so?
    (Narrator) What does the woman mean? (12 seconds)

21. (Woman)   Two for dinner tonight?
    (Man)   Another person is going to join us.
    (Narrator) What does the woman mean? (12 seconds)

22. (Woman)   I don't think the salesman helped us a whole lot.
    (Man)   I agree.
    (Narrator) What does the man mean? (12 seconds)

23. (Man)   It's dark in the front hall.
    (Woman)   The bulb's burned out.
    (Narrator) What does the woman imply? (12 seconds)

24. (Woman)   How about some sandwiches and chips for lunch?
    (Man)   What, *again*?
    (Narrator) What does the man mean? (12 seconds)

25. (Man)   I thought the band played really well. How did you like it?
    (Woman)   I've heard better.
    (Narrator) What does the woman mean? (12 seconds)

26. (Woman)   Only city residents are allowed to swim in the pool.
    (Man)   I've lived here for the past nine years.
    (Narrator) What does the man imply? (12 seconds)

27. (Man)   It's a quarter to twelve. Your flight is at 1:15, and it'll take us a good hour to get to the airport.
    (Woman)   The clock is ten minutes fast.
    (Narrator) What does the woman mean? (12 seconds)

28. (Woman) Photography is an exciting hobby. I'd like to learn how to take good pictures.
    (Man) Last year, you wanted to take guitar lessons.
    (Narrator) What does the man imply? (12 seconds)

29. (Man) I have to see my accountant tomorrow, and my car is in the shop. Could you take me?
    (Woman) Sorry. I have to work all day tomorrow. But you are welcome to use my car.
    (Narrator) What does the woman mean? (12 seconds)

30. (Man) My math instructor doesn't want to help me with the course assignments. She seems to think that we are all mathematicians.
    (Woman) Keeping up with the assignments is your responsibility.
    (Narrator) What does the woman imply? (12 seconds)

(Narrator) This is the end of Part A.

Now read the directions for Part B while they are being read to you.

Part B

DIRECTIONS: In this part of the test, you will hear longer conversations. After each conversation, you will hear several questions. The conversations and questions will not be repeated.

After you hear a question, read the four possible answers in your test book and choose the best answer. Then, on your answer sheet, find the number of the question and fill in the space that corresponds to the letter of the answer you have chosen.

Remember, you are not allowed to take notes or write in your test book.

(Narrator) Questions 31 through 34 refer to a conversation about selecting a college.

(Woman) When I graduated from high school, I never had a chance to go to college, but now I may be able to. So, I've been trying to decide what college to apply to and thought you could help me.

(Man) I'd be glad to talk to you about it. There are many things to consider. When you think of going to college, you need to be prepared to work hard. Studying takes up a lot of time, and students who are not motivated usually don't succeed.

(Woman) I can easily see how motivation can affect success in learning. Taking college classes may not be very different from doing many other things. If you like what you do, you do a better job.

(Man) And when you are trying to figure out which college to attend, there are many questions one should ask. Asking for information can help you discover many facts about the school, what courses it offers, and what kinds of facilities it provides for students.

(Woman) Should I ask for a brochure? Maybe I need to write letters to several schools to find out about their libraries, laboratories, computers, and other facilities.

(Man) That sounds like a good start. In addition, asking about their teaching methods and the average class size may give you the information you need to decide.

(Woman) These are essential facts. So, if I'm going to write to them for information, what else do I need to find out?

(Man) Okay, other key questions are about their tuition, fees, and assistance available for students. For example, can the college help students get a job? Many colleges hire their students to work in offices, mail rooms, food services, and dorms. Not only do students earn money, but also they acquire work experience that they need to get jobs when they graduate.

(Narrator)

31. What is the main topic of this conversation? (12 seconds)
32. What is important for success in college? (12 seconds)
33. What does the man suggest to the woman? (12 seconds)
34. How do students get job experience at college? (12 seconds)

(Narrator) Questions 35 through 38 refer to a conversation about dogs.

(Man)   You bought a dog! I can't believe it. Why did you buy a dog?
(Woman)   It's not just a dog. It's a bearded collie. They were known for being guards of cat-
           tle and sheep in Scotland in the fifteenth century. I bought it because I thought it
           would be good for the children to have. They'll have to take care of it and feed it.
           And they will learn responsibility by caring for another living creature.
(Man)   Why did you buy a collie?
(Woman)   Collies are disciplined and reliable. They are highly intelligent. They can help their
           owners by guarding the house. They don't require a lot of attention and can be
           left alone for long periods of time. When we both go to work and the children go
           to school, it'll have to stay alone and take care of itself.
(Man)   Sounds like you've given this a lot of thought.
(Woman)   Yes, I have. Besides collies, I also studied up on terriers, golden retrievers, cocker
           spaniels, and foxhounds. Terriers are good dogs, and they are beautiful. They have
           clean, smooth coats, square heads, and big brown eyes. Terriers like people, and
           they are good pets because they like affection. Terriers are smaller than collies, and
           they are very playful.
(Man)   So, why didn't you get a terrier then?
(Woman)   I didn't because they seem to be strongly attached to people. I'm in the office from
           eight to four, and the children are at school from 7:30 to 3:30. So, if we are out of
           the house all day, who is going to take care of the dog? Collies seem to be a bet-
           ter choice. We need a dog that doesn't need a lot of attention. It seems that a ter-
           rier wouldn't fit in because it likes to be around people and we spend a lot of time
           out of the house.

(Narrator)

35. Why did the woman buy a dog? (12 seconds)
36. What does the woman say about collies? (12 seconds)
37. What are the other types of dogs the woman liked? (12 seconds)
38. Why didn't the woman buy a terrier? (12 seconds)

(Narrator) This is the end of Part B.

Now read the directions for Part C while they are being read to you.

Part C

DIRECTIONS: In Part C you will hear short talks. At the end of each, you will be asked several questions. Each talk and each question will be spoken only one time. For this reason, you must listen carefully to understand what the speaker says. After you hear a question, read the four selections and choose the *one* that is the best answer to the question the speaker asked. Then, on your answer sheet, find the number of the question and blacken the space that corresponds to the letter for the answer you have chosen.

Listen to this sample talk.

You will hear:

(Man)   Before people used automobiles, they walked or rode bicycles for short distances and took trains, streetcars, or horse-drawn carriages for long-distance travel. When automobiles were first produced, only the rich could afford them. Today, almost every household in the United States owns at least one car, and ninety percent of American adults have drivers' licenses.

According to the yearly value of its output, the U.S. automobile industry exceeds all other manufacturing industries in the country. As a consumer, this industry also supports other major industries, such as steel, glass, and rubber. Furthermore, approximately twelve million Americans are employed in the auxiliary service industries consisting of repair shops and service stations.

(Narrator)   Now listen to the following question.

You will hear: According to the speaker, how did people travel before the invention of the automobile?

You will read:

    (A) By cars and carriages
    (B) By bicycles, trains, and carriages
    (C) On foot and by boat
    (D) On board ships and trains

The best answer to the question "According to the speaker, how did people travel before the invention of the automobile?" is (B), "By bicycles, trains, and carriages." Therefore, the correct answer is (B).

Now listen to another sample question.

(Narrator)   Approximately how many people are employed in the automobile service industry?

You will read:

    (A) One million
    (B) Ten million
    (C) Twelve million
    (D) Ninety million

The best answer to the question "Approximately how many people are employed in the automobile service industry?" is (C), "Twelve million." Therefore, the correct answer is (C).

(Narrator)   Questions 39 through 42 refer to the following talk about video rentals.

(Woman)   Like most other businesses, home video consists of three segments. They are first, production, second, distribution, and finally, retail. When companies produce prerecorded cassettes and DVDs, that's production. Most of the home-video market consists of sales of movies, and almost all motion picture studios dominate the production of cassettes and DVDs. Just as an example, two thirds of video-cassette and DVD sales come from the ten largest studios, and 20th Century Fox and Columbia occupy the first and the second place.

Studios do not sell directly to retailers, distributors do. And more than ninety distribution firms in the U.S. have become the bridge between production and retail. Cassette and DVD distributors make it easy for retail stores to become a video-rental outlet. These days, more than 60,000 convenience stores rent videos. And that's in addition to the 30,000 video rental stores. The retail business is volatile, and it's very competitive. A retail store can carry about 5,000 to 7,000 movies, which include current and old titles. On the other hand, convenience and grocery stores usually have about 300 to 500 titles that are current pictures. The video-rental business these days is almost like fast-food restaurants, and a store covers a certain area of about three miles in each direction. Independently owned stores have a tough time competing with large chains that dominate the business. The largest one has about 2,700 franchises, and the second largest, about 800.

(Narrator)

39. What is the main topic of this talk? (12 seconds)
40. Approximately how many retail outlets rent videos? (12 seconds)
41. What does the speaker say about the video-rental business? (12 seconds)
42. Who dominates the video-rental business? (12 seconds)

(Narrator)   Questions 43 through 46 refer to the following talk about recycling.

(Man)   Iron and aluminum represent ninety-four percent of all metal use. Recycling items that contain these metals extends the supply of mineral resources because it reduces the use of virgin materials mined from the earth's crust. Using recycled iron, or scrap iron as it is also called, not only conserves iron ore and coal, but it also requires sixty-five percent less energy and forty-two percent less water to process. In addition, recycling produces eighty-five percent less air pollution. It is somewhat surprising that only about one fourth of all iron and aluminum used in the world today comes from recycling efforts. For example, beverage cans are one of the largest sources of recycled aluminum, but almost half of all cans produced each year are thrown away.

There are several factors that negatively affect metal recycling in the U.S. The fact that the U.S. metal industry has not modified its equipment to process recycled metals is one of them. Another is that most Americans have a "throwaway" mentality; they have been conditioned to throw things away.

Manufacturers promote this lifestyle through advertising because it increases short-term consumption, but they neglect to take into account the long-term environmental costs. Consumers pay for these costs in the form of taxes and have no easily identifiable reason to recycle. American consumers often think that returning beverage cans is too much trouble. They would rather toss them away and have someone else deal with them. Merchants don't like having returned metal cans in their stores. Labor unions worry that workers in the can manufacturing industry will lose their jobs. A national law requiring the return of beverage cans would reduce the processing of virgin aluminum ore by fifty-five to seventy-five percent. Urban solid waste would also fall by one percent and save taxpayers twenty-five to fifty million dollars a year.

(Narrator)

43. Why is the recycling of metals desirable? (12 seconds)
44. What is the proportion of iron and aluminum that comes from recycling? (12 seconds)
45. According to the speaker, why do American consumers often fail to recycle? (12 seconds)
46. What does the speaker say about merchants' attitudes toward recycling beverage containers? (12 seconds)

(Narrator)   Questions 47 through 50 refer to the following talk about roses.

(Woman)   There is little doubt that roses are one of the most preferred and best-loved flowers in almost all climate zones. Most lose their leaves in the fall, but some can be evergreen in very mild climates. Centuries of cultivation have created an amazing array of flowers of every form and color. The smallest are a foot high, with flowers as small as a thumbnail. The largest bloom with flowers as big as a salad plate. Red, pink, and white are the traditional colors, but orange, yellow, black, and purple also can be found in the gardens of devoted growers.

Growing these shrubs is not complicated if their type and variety are suitable for the climate zone. Each year, the American Rose Society publishes ratings of roses on the scale from one to ten, and the higher the rating, the better the rose. The highest-rated roses grow in most climates, but those with low ratings do well only in certain regions of the country. In areas with cool summers, roses with a great number of petals should be avoided because they often fail to open. Also dark-colored roses don't do well because they do not develop their full color. In hot-summer areas, roses can grow in any garden, but their flowers open soon after they bud, and the color of their petals fades quickly. Roses bloom best during the spring and fall, and flower production falls during intensely hot summers.

In areas with cold winters, some of the marketed roses are not hardy enough, and special protection is needed to assure that they survive from winter to winter. To determine which roses are best suited for a particular climate, a novice gardener may want to take a trip to a municipal garden or an established private rose garden. Obviously, the varieties of shrubs found there will perform well in that climate zone.

(Narrator)

47. What is the main topic of this talk? (12 seconds)
48. How does the American Rose Society rate roses? (12 seconds)
49. What does the speaker say about growing roses in very hot climates? (12 seconds)
50. What does a rose gardener need to do in climates with cold winters? (12 seconds)

(Narrator)   STOP WORKING ON SECTION 1.

Practice TOEFL 8

SECTION 1

LISTENING COMPREHENSION

(Narrator)   In this section, you will demonstrate your skills in understanding spoken English. There are three parts in the Listening Comprehension section, with different tasks in each.

Part A

DIRECTIONS: In Part A you will hear short conversations between two people. At the end of each conversation, a third person will ask a question about what the two people said. Each conversation and each question will be spoken only one time. For this reason, you must listen carefully to understand what each speaker says. After you hear a conversation and the question, read the four selections and choose the *one* that is the best answer to the question the speaker asked. Then, on your answer sheet, find the number of the question and blacken the space that corresponds to the letter for the answer you have chosen. Blacken the space completely so that the letter inside the space does not show.

Listen to the following example.

On the recording, you hear:
    (Man)   Does the car need to be filled?
    (Woman)   Mary stopped at the gas station on her way home.
    (Narrator) What does the woman mean?

In your test book, you will read:
        (A) Mary bought some food.
        (B) Mary had car trouble.
        (C) Mary went shopping.
        (D) Mary bought some gas.

From the conversation you learn that Mary stopped at the gas station on her way home. The best answer to the question "Does the car need to be filled?" is (D), "Mary bought some gas." Therefore, the correct answer is (D).

Now let us begin Part A with question number 1.

1. (Woman) So, you've decided to try the new soup recipe. How has it turned out?
    (Man)   I've had better.
    (Narrator) What does the man imply? (12 seconds)

2. (Man)   I seem to be having trouble with this lab report. Do you know when Dr. Hill will be in today?
    (Woman) Her office hours are posted on the door.
    (Narrator) What does the woman mean? (12 seconds)

3. (Woman) Andy seems to think that we will get a few days' extension to finish advising and registration for the fall.
    (Man)   Andy's information should be taken with a grain of salt.
    (Narrator) What does the man imply? (12 seconds)

4. (Man)   Are you making sandwiches?
   (Woman) Almost done, but the lettuce should be washed before we eat it.
   (Narrator) What does the woman mean? (12 seconds)

5. (Woman) Your total comes to $187.15.
   (Man)   Business courses like to require these expensive hardbacks.
   (Narrator) Where does this conversation take place? (12 seconds)

6. (Man)   Why is there a puddle on the floor?
   (Woman) The sink is leaking again. I'll call to see if we can get somebody to come and
            take a look.
   (Narrator) What does the woman suggest? (12 seconds)

7. (Woman) Is there a big reception going on in the lobby of the Moss Hall?
   (Man)   Mary's finally published her historical novel.
   (Narrator) What does the man imply? (12 seconds)

8. (Man)   Look at this long line! It'll take us an hour to get out of here.
   (Woman) The bookstore is giving away free pencils to all those who purchase their
            texts.
   (Narrator) What does the woman mean? (12 seconds)

9. (Man)   We should be able to make it to the airport on time. I am not worried.
   (Woman) I've been trying to find a cab for the past 15 minutes, and there isn't one in
            sight.
   (Narrator) What does the woman mean? (12 seconds)

10. (Woman) A large newspaper ad is a good way to promote the new exhibit.
    (Man)   Word of mouth is the best advertising.
    (Narrator) What does the man assume? (12 seconds)

11. (Man)   I am tired of working on this painting, and I really need a break.
    (Woman) If you feel up to it, you can come with us.
    (Narrator) What does the woman suggest? (12 seconds)

12. (Woman) Your pancakes always look wonderful.
    (Man)   First, pour the batter on a hot pan and then flip it over.
    (Narrator) What does the man say? (12 seconds)

13. (Man)   Julie's mother has been making a lot of phone calls today.
    (Woman) The big news is that Julie and Michael have finally decided to tie the knot.
    (Narrator) What does the woman mean? (12 seconds)

14. (Woman) I'd rather talk to Dr. Mills than Professor Ellis.
    (Man)   First-year students don't choose their own advisors.
    (Narrator) What does the man say about first-year students? (12 seconds)

15. (Man)   A little exercise will do me good, and I think I'll go for a run.
    (Woman) How can you stand jogging in this humidity?
    (Narrator) What does the woman mean? (12 seconds)

16. (Woman) Bob and Margaret are so serious about their dancing classes.
    (Man)   Well, they used to be until they started their gardening business.
    (Narrator) What does the man say about Bob and Margaret? (12 seconds)

17. (Man)   I've been trying to decide whether to buy this shirt. What do you think?
    (Woman) It seems a bit long, doesn't it?
    (Narrator) What does the woman imply? (12 seconds)

18. (Woman) Look at this daily rate! We should get a compact instead of a station wagon.
    (Man) With three children?
    (Narrator) What are they probably discussing? (12 seconds)

19. (Man) Could you tell me if the position of the office assistant has been filled?
    (Woman) The search committee will start interviewing applicants next week.
    (Narrator) What does the woman imply? (12 seconds)

20. (Woman) I'd like to take Math 118 (one eighteen) or Math 124 (one twenty four) next term, and I don't know which one is required for my major. What exactly is the difference between the two courses?
    (Man) The choice between the two depends on your score on the placement test. Would you like to sign up for the one on Tuesday?
    (Narrator) What does the man suggest that the woman do? (12 seconds)

21. (Man) After the movie, we can have dinner at the new place that just opened on Broadway and Union. Everyone's raving about it.
    (Woman) This one is on me. I owe you one from last week.
    (Narrator) What does the woman mean? (12 seconds)

22. (Woman) So, we don't have to rush. If we don't finish the lab report this afternoon, we can meet again tomorrow and get it done before the deadline.
    (Man) Just what we all need. . . . Another meeting.
    (Narrator) What does the man imply? (12 seconds)

23. (Man) We can leave on the twenty-fifth of October or the third of November. These days are the most convenient.
    (Woman) Either date is okay with me. It's up to Peter.
    (Narrator) What are the man and the woman probably doing? (12 seconds)

24. (Woman) It's great to see a little sun, isn't it? A perfect day for a little walk.
    (Man) I plan to stay chained to my desk this afternoon. My proposal is due by the end of the day.
    (Narrator) What does the man mean? (12 seconds)

25. (Man) How did Fred manage to pass his social psychology class?
    (Woman) It's a mystery to me.
    (Narrator) What does the woman mean? (12 seconds)

26. (Woman) Roberta has lost her house key, and she has to wait for her husband to return from work to let her in.
    (Man) What else is new.
    (Narrator) What does the man imply? (12 seconds)

27. (Man) I'd like to order these delivered. Also, a gift note would be nice to include.
    (Woman) They are free with bouquets or potted plants of $50 or more.
    (Narrator) Where is this conversation taking place? (12 seconds)

28. (Woman) Can you tell me when the North Campus shuttle gets here?
    (Man) At 15 after the hour and 15 before the hour.
    (Narrator) What does the man mean? (12 seconds)

29. (Man) Is it okay for me to leave my car here for just a few minutes?
    (Woman) You are blocking the driveway.
    (Narrator) What does the woman say? (12 seconds)

30. (Woman) What a day! First, I scratched my arm while I was trying to close the gate, and then I slipped on the ice and almost twisted my ankle.
    (Man) I wish you'd be more careful.
    (Narrator) What does the man mean? (12 seconds)

(Narrator) This is the end of Part A.

Now read the directions for Part B while they are being read to you.

Part B

DIRECTIONS: In this part of the test, you will hear longer conversations. After each conversation, you will hear several questions. The conversations and questions will not be repeated.

After you hear a question, read the four possible answers in your test book and choose the best answer. Then, on your answer sheet, find the number of the question and fill in the space that corresponds to the letter of the answer you have chosen.

Remember, you are not allowed to take notes or write in your test book.

(Narrator) Questions 31 through 34 refer to the following conversation about trees.

(Man) Hi! I need to buy a tree for my yard, and I can't figure out what would be the best variety. There are so many available for sale that I don't know where to start. Could you recommend two or three that are easy to grow?

(Woman) I'd be happy to. First, you need to tell me whether you'd like to plant for shade, ornament, or fruit. Then it's important to consider the type of soil and exposure you have in your yard.

(Man) Well, I'd like to get a tall tree to put on the sunny slope on the south side of my property. Actually, I think the soil is eroding on that ridge, and maybe, the tree roots can slow the erosion down.

(Woman) In this case, I think that a walnut may be quite suitable. On the south side, there is usually a good deal of sun exposure and heat, and for example, sycamores or cottonwoods do not do well in such environments. It's also important to think about drainage because if the soil is heavy and compact, swampy areas are not a favorable match for walnuts. Walnuts and pines thrive in direct sun and loose sandy soils, where they can spread their shallow roots.

(Man) Walnuts grow to be enormous, don't they? Cedars or another type of evergreen seem to be a bit shorter. Do you think that a very tall tree may become a problem on an uneven slope?

(Woman) The pine family is medium-size, even fully grown, and walnuts are certainly much taller when they reach their maximum height. However, pruning either walnuts or evergreens is not recommended. Besides, it will take decades for trees to reach such a height that their tops become inaccessible.

(Man) Thank you very much for your help. This definitely gives me food for thought. To be honest, it may be a good idea for me to buy a book on trees and read up a little before I actually buy a real tree.

(Narrator)

31. What does the man ask the woman to do? (12 seconds)
32. What are the important considerations when planting a tree? (12 seconds)
33. What do evergreens need to grow well? (12 seconds)
34. What does the man say he should probably do next? (12 seconds)

(Narrator)   <u>Questions 35 through 37</u> refer to the following conversation between a professor and a student.

(Woman)   I was looking over the class roster yesterday and noticed that you major in violin. I've always been fond of violin music. I even took lessons for several years, but didn't think that I had enough talent or skill to become a professional musician.

(Man)   Well, my father is a violin maker, and as a child, I was surrounded by violins and violin music. His workshop always used to smell like drying wood and lacquer, and I spent days watching him create instruments that musicians admired. When they came to get their orders, they had to try out the sound, singing tones, rapid figurations, and melodies, and I just couldn't get enough. I used to sit quietly in the corner and watch them adjust the strings and the bow. So, I guess I got so interested that when it was time to go to college, I already knew I wanted to be a violinist.

(Woman)   You have a delightful story here. Have you considered submitting it as a final term paper? Our final assignment will be a short story, and you don't need to look very far to come up with one. What you just told me makes for a terrific exposition or a descriptive narrative. As a devotee of violin music, I'd love to read about a violin maker and his son who falls in love with music by watching his father work.

(Man)   Thank you. I could write a book about making sound boxes out of plain pieces of wood and bows out of long, hard, narrow planks of brazilwood. My father is the real expert.

(Narrator)

35. What do musicians do to test a violin? (12 seconds)
36. What can be inferred about violin making? (12 seconds)
37. What does the professor probably teach? (12 seconds)

(Narrator)   <u>Questions 38 through 40</u> refer to the following conversation about contact lenses.

(Man)   How do you like your new contact lenses? I am debating whether to get a pair, but they seem to be awfully expensive.

(Woman)   Who can compare cumbersome and inconvenient glasses to contacts? You don't need to worry about breaking them or having them fall off your nose. Eyeglass lenses are easy to scratch when wiping them, and sometimes, they even fall out of the frame. Today's contact lens plastics are a miracle of modern technology. If you get an eye exam and a precise fitting, then your contacts can be customized to cover only the cornea of the eye and precisely fit over its curvature to reduce eye irritation. Contacts are so convenient, particularly if you play sports. You can run, jump, and kick without worrying whether your eyeglasses will come off.

(Man)   Well, how long does it take to get used to wearing them? I've worn glasses all my life and don't know a thing about wearing contacts.

(Woman)   No time at all. My optometrist told me that soft lenses are much better than hard ones. Hard ones do take a bit of practice, but soft lenses are made of a malleable material that forms itself to the shape of your cornea. Best of all, though, are the extended-wear lenses that my friend Sally has. She doesn't even have to take hers off or clean them. She wears them for a week and then throws them out. Compared to glasses, the extended-wear lenses are expensive. They cost several hundred dollars a year, but I am sure that if you have the money, the convenience can't be beat.

(Man)   You surely do sound like you like yours. Where did you buy them?

(Woman)   I'd be happy to give you my doctor's name and phone number, but to start, you
            need to have your eyes checked and the lenses fitted, and then it may take a week
            or two for your pair to be made at the lab. When they are ready, the doctor will
            call you in for another appointment to see if they fit. If they are not comfortable,
            the doctor or the lab may have to adjust them.

(Man)   Boy, this sounds more complicated than buying a bike!

(Narrator)

38. What is the woman's opinion about eyeglasses and contacts? (12 seconds)
39. How many types of contact lenses are mentioned in the conversation? (12 seconds)
40. According to the woman, what is the first step in buying contacts? (12 seconds)

(Narrator)   This is the end of Part B.

Now read the directions for Part C while they are being read to you.

Part C

DIRECTIONS: In Part C you will hear short talks. At the end of each, you will be asked several
questions. Each talk and each question will be spoken only one time. For this reason, you must
listen carefully to understand what the speaker says. After you hear a question, read the four
selections and choose the one that is the best answer to the question the speaker asked. Then,
on your answer sheet, find the number of the question and blacken the space that corresponds
to the letter for the answer you have chosen.

Listen to this sample talk.

You will hear:
    (Man)   Before people used automobiles, they walked or rode bicycles for short dis-
                tances and took trains, streetcars, or horse-drawn carriages for long-distance
                travel. When automobiles were first produced, only the rich could afford
                them. Today, almost every household in the United States owns at least one
                car, and ninety percent of American adults have drivers' licenses.

                According to the yearly value of its output, the U.S. automobile industry
                exceeds all other manufacturing industries in the country. As a consumer, this
                industry also supports other major industries, such as steel, glass, and rubber.
                Furthermore, approximately twelve million Americans are employed in the
                auxiliary service industries consisting of repair shops and service stations.

(Narrator)   Now listen to the following question.

You will hear: According to the speaker, how did people travel before the invention of the
                automobile?

You will read:
                (A) By cars and carriages
                (B) By bicycles, trains, and carriages
                (C) On foot and by boat
                (D) On board ships and trains

The best answer to the question "According to the speaker, how did people travel before
the invention of the automobile?" is (B), "By bicycles, trains, and carriages." Therefore, the correct answer is (B).

Now listen to another sample question.

(Narrator)   Approximately how many people are employed in the automobile service industry?

You will read:
        (A) One million
        (B) Ten million
        (C) Twelve million
        (D) Ninety million

The best answer to the question "Approximately how many people are employed in the automobile service industry?" is (C), "Twelve million." Therefore, the correct answer is (C).

(Narrator)   <u>Questions 41 through 45</u>. Listen to the talk about the international date line.

(Woman)   Those of you who have traveled from the U.S. to Europe or Asia or across continents know that during the journey, one can gain or lose time while being transported from one point on the earth's surface to another. When passengers are traveling eastward, for example, from New York to London, the time of day is an hour later with each time zone they cross. Heading westward, for example from Los Angeles to Asia, passengers notice that the time of day is an hour earlier with each time zone. However, an imaginary line that runs through the Pacific Ocean called the International Date Line changes the current date, and in Los Angeles, the calendar date is one day earlier than it would be in Asia. According to the conventions of measuring time across the globe, a calendar day runs from midnight to midnight in any locality. To simplify date divisions, in the modern time of air travel, international stock markets, Internet, and satellites, the Earth is divided into twenty-four north-to-south standard time zones, and somewhere in the world, a new date begins every hour, when the time on the meridian that marks the date change is midnight.

The International Date Line falls loosely along the 180th meridian of longitude that actually forms an ellipsis and connects with the prime meridian at zero degrees longitude. I say loosely because the date line is not rigid, but it deviates east or west of the meridian to allow small groups of islands and the people who populate them to have the same calendar as New Zealand. In other cases, date line divisions can be somewhat more political, for example when the Aleutian Islands have the same date as Alaska but not the Bering Strait.

(Narrator)

41. What is the main purpose of the lecture? (12 seconds)
42. What does the lecturer say about travel east and west? (12 seconds)
43. According to the lecturer, how should airplane passengers adjust their day counts? (12 seconds)
44. Based on the lecture, what is the approximate marker of the date change? (12 seconds)
45. Why does the lecturer mention New Zealand? (12 seconds)

(Narrator)   <u>Questions 46 and 47</u>. Listen to the talk given by a history professor.

(Man)   Today we will begin our examination of the first polar explorations. To start, I'd like to present a brief overview and then we can discuss the interesting points in greater detail. The first explorers of the northern regions two thousand years ago were Greeks from Massilia who discovered a new territory hundreds of miles north of the British Isles, which the Greek record keeper called "Thule." Based on the records of that exploratory voyage led by Pytheas, it is not possible to tell with certainty whether the newly discovered landmass was today's Iceland or any number of small islands near the coast of Norway. Following the initial voyage, polar expeditions did not resume until more than a thousand years later, when a ship sailed around the northern tip of Norway in what is now known as the White Sea. During the ninth and tenth centuries, Viking settlements emerged in Iceland and the southern coast of Greenland. However, no archeological evidence has been found that the Viking settlers moved further north, toward the enormous ice-covered regions near or around the North Pole.

Many centuries later, the Spanish and the Portuguese came to dominate the Indian trade and southern sea routes, thus precluding the passage of English and Dutch marine merchants. So, in fact, it was the English and the Dutch who undertook the first explorations of the northern seas in an attempt to find alternate navigable routes along the north coast of Asia or North America. In their search for the Northwest Passage, the English were also the first to determine that their sailing ships were no match for the ice in the Arctic Ocean. Around the end of the sixteenth century, after the English fleet defeated the Spanish Armada, the southern sea routes became open to all merchants, and the need for the explorations of the Arctic was greatly reduced.

(Narrator)

46. What is the main topic of the lecture? (12 seconds)
47. What does the professor say about the Portuguese? (12 seconds)

(Narrator)   Questions 48 through 50. Listen to the lecture on food and nutrition.

(Man)   The study of food and nutrition is a science that encompasses all aspects of food processing that the human body needs to live, grow, function, fight diseases, and heal. The foods someone eats regularly or often are called a diet. Contrary to a popular belief, a diet does not refer to reductions in food intake in order to lose weight. Energy represents one of the body's most fundamental needs, and to obtain energy, it converts food into fuel that is burned in the presence of oxygen. I should point out that all activity of the body requires energy, including breathing and blinking, as well as chopping wood and running up the stairs. Similarly, energy is required to repair damaged tissue, grow new cells, and regulate such essential systems as blood flow and temperature maintenance. The functioning of the body systems requires appropriate supplies of nutrients, which are divided into six major categories: water, proteins, carbohydrates, fats, vitamins, and minerals. Proteins are small units of amino acids requisite for rebuilding and growing tissue. It is widely known that a human body consists mostly of water, and proteins are the second greatest substance in body composition, or possibly third, with the inclusion of fat. Good sources of protein can be found in meat, poultry, fish, milk, and eggs. For vegetarians, beans, peas, whole-grain bread, cereals, and nuts can also do an excellent job. On the other hand, carbohydrates supply a little over half of all calories consumed by Americans. Starches found in potatoes, corn, wheat, and rice, as well as various types of sugars, provide most carbohydrates that are converted into energy. Sugars are not necessary for the functioning of the body, and they provide energy without nutrition. These are sometimes referred to as empty calories. Foods rich in carbohydrates, such as grains, are also the crucial sources of protein in most countries of the world where meat, fish, and legumes are relatively scarce.

(Narrator)

48. According to the lecture, what types of foods are included in a diet? (12 seconds)
49. Based on the lecture, what can be excellent sources of protein? (12 seconds)
50. According to the lecture, what food sources are NOT essential for the human body? (12 seconds)

(Narrator)   STOP WORKING ON SECTION 1.

C. Scoring Practice Tests

ETS uses complex statistical procedures to score the TOEFL. In addition, because each test question has a different measure of difficulty, the exact formula for computing the final test score differs from test to test.

The score for each section of the test is computed separately based on a specific mathematical formula. Below, you will find scoring guidelines that can give an approximate indication of your actual TOEFL score and percentile ranking.

To compute your approximate score use the following steps.

1. Compare your answers on a practice test to the answer key and count the number of correct answers *in each section separately*.
2. Then determine the converted score that corresponds to the number of the correct answers for each section. Use Table 1 to determine your converted score. In the leftmost column, headed Number Correct, find the number of questions that you answered correctly; and then locate the converted score for Section 1 in the next column to the right. Do the same for Sections 2 and 3. For example, if you answered 40 questions correctly in the Listening Comprehension section, your converted score is 55; 30 correct answers in the Structure and Written Expression section equal a converted score of 54, and so on.
3. Figure out your approximate total score.
   a. Add your three converted scores from Section 1, Section 2, and Section 3.
   b. Multiply the sum by 10.
   c. Divide by 3.

For example, if your converted score on Section 1 is 54, on Section 2 is 56, and on Section 3 is 53:

$$50 + 56 + 53 = 159$$
$$159 \times 10 = 1590$$
$$1590 \div 3 = 530$$

Your approximate TOEFL score would be 530.

IT IS IMPORTANT TO REMEMBER, HOWEVER, THAT CONVERSION TABLES VARY FOR EACH TEST AND CAN SHOW ONLY AN APPROXIMATION OF YOUR ACTUAL TOEFL SCORE.

TABLE 1. SCORE CONVERSION TABLE FOR PRACTICE TESTS 1–8

	Section		
Number Correct	Listening Comprehension	Structure and Written Expression	Vocabulary and Reading Comprehension
59–60			65–67
57–58			62–63
54–56			60–61
51–53			58–59
48–50	65–68		56–57
46–47	62–64		54–55
44–45	59–61		52–53
41–43	56–58		51–50
38–40	54–55	63–68	48–49
35–37	52–53	59–62	46–47
33–34	50–51	57–58	44–45
30–32	48–49	54–56	42–43
27–29	46–47	51–53	40–41
24–26	44–45	48–50	38–39
21–23	42–43	45–47	36–37
18–20	40–41	42–43	34–35
15–17	38–39	39–41	32–33
12–14	36–37	37–38	29–31
9–11	34–35	33–36	27–28
6–8	32–33	29–31	25–26
4–5	29–31	25–28	23–24
0–3	25–27	20–24	21–22

Source: *2003–04 TOEFL Information Bulletin for Computer-Based and Paper-Based Testing.*
Princeton, N.J.: Educational Testing Service.

The Score Conversion Table also shows that the score values of the three TOEFL sections are not equal. For example, in most tests the maximum converted score on each section ranges between 65 and 68. To obtain the maximum score, you need to answer 50 questions correctly in the Listening Comprehension section, 40 in Structure and Written Expression, and 60 in Vocabulary and Reading Comprehension. Although the computation of score points per question in each section is not as straightforward as simple division, it follows that the score value of each question is somewhat greater in Section 2 than in either Section 1 or Section 3.

You may also notice that an increase of 1 in the number of correct answers does not always mean an increase in the converted score.

For example, if the number of correct answers in the Listening Comprehension section is increased from 31 to 32, the converted score does not increase. It is impossible to predict where the value of correct answers changes because converted score tables vary for each section and test.

TOEFL Percentile Ranks

After you receive your official TOEFL score, you can use your converted scores for each section to figure out the percentile rankings that correspond to your converted score. The data provided in Table 2 are obtained from ETS results to show how your scores compare to those of other test-takers.

TABLE 2. TOEFL PERCENTILE RANKS BY SECTION

Converted Score	Listening Comprehension	Structure and Written Expression	Vocabulary and Reading Comprehension
68	—	97	—
66	99	82	96
64	97	71	89
62	93	61	79
60	87	52	66
58	79	42	53
56	68	33	41
54	56	26	30
52	44	20	22
50	31	14	15
48	21	10	10
46	12	7	7
44	7	4	4
42	4	3	3
40	2	1	2
38	1	1	1
36	1		1
34			
32			

Source: *2003–04 TOEFL Information Bulletin for Computer-Based and Paper-Based Testing.* Princeton, N.J.: Educational Testing Service.

To determine how your converted scores compare to those of others, find your converted score for each section of the TOEFL in the leftmost column. The value in the column corresponding to the section of the TOEFL you are checking tells you the percent of the test-takers whose scores were lower than yours. For example, if your converted score for the Listening Comprehension section is 60, you can see in the Listening Comprehension column that 87 percent of all test-takers received lower scores in that section. If your converted score for the Structure and Written Expression section is 50, you scored higher in that section than 14 percent of test-takers did, and so on.

ETS also provides similar information for the TOEFL total score. Table 3 allows you to compare your total converted score to the scores of others.

TABLE 3. TOEFL TOTAL PERCENTILE RANKS

Total Converted Score	Percentile Rank
660	99
640	94
620	84
600	71
580	57
560	44
540	33
520	24
500	16
480	11
460	7
440	4
420	2
400	1
380	
320–360	

Source: *2003–04 TOEFL Information Bulletin for Computer-Based and Paper-Based Testing*. Princeton, N.J.: Educational Testing Service.

Again, find your total converted score in the left column. The value in the right column corresponds to the percentage of people whose total TOEFL scores are lower than yours. For example, if your total converted score is 480, 11 percent received scores lower than you. However, if the institution in which you would like to enroll requires a total score of 550 and your score is 540, the fact that 33 percent of the test-takers received scores lower than yours may be of little help. The most important purpose that Table 3 can serve is that, as you study and your English skills improve, you can see the improvement in your own score.

Percentile rank tables for undergraduates, graduates, applicants for medical licenses, men, women, and test-takers from each country can be obtained directly from ETS. You can write to the ETS TOEFL Services at the address given on page 1.

Comparing Your TWE Scores

TWE is scored on a 6-point scale, moving upward from 1 to 6. To compare your TWE score to the scores of other test-takers, use Table 4. The data in this table provide the most up-to-date information published by ETS on the TWE percentile ranks.

TABLE 4. TWE PERCENTILE RANKS

TWE Score	Percentile Rank	TWE Score	Percentile Rank
6.0	—	3.0	14
5.5	99	2.5	4
5.0	94	2.0	2
4.5	85	1.5	1
4.0	57	1.0	—

Source: *2003–04 TOEFL Information Bulletin for Computer-Based and Paper-Based Testing.* Princeton, N.J.: Educational Testing Service.

If your TWE score is 4.5, it is higher than the scores of 85 percent of those who took the TWE between July 2001 and June 2002. In this case, as with other TOEFL scores, it is the institution in which you would like to enroll that determines the acceptable TWE score.

D. Answer Keys

Practice for Listening Comprehension (Chapter 4)

Exercise 1. Idioms

PART A

1. B	5. C	9. C	13. A	17. C
2. C	6. B	10. B	14. C	18. A
3. B	7. B	11. C	15. C	19. B
4. C	8. D	12. B	16. C	20. D

PART B

21. C	23. D	25. D	27. C
22. C	24. A	26. D	28. B

Exercise 2. Implied meanings

PART A

1. B	5. C	9. B	13. C	17. D
2. B	6. A	10. D	14. A	18. A
3. A	7. D	11. C	15. B	19. B
4. B	8. C	12. B	16. C	20. D

PART B

21. C	23. C	25. B	27. D
22. B	24. C	26. A	28. B

Exercise 3. Specific content questions (tested only in Part C)

1. C	3. B	5. D	7. A
2. B	4. B	6. B	8. D

Exercise 4. Emphasis, stress, and tone (tested only in Part A)

PART A

1. A	3. C	5. C	7. A	9. C
2. D	4. B	6. D	8. B	10. D

Exercise 5. Sound discrimination (tested only in Part A)

PART A

1. B	3. B	5. B	7. B	9. C
2. D	4. D	6. C	8. B	10. C

Exercise 6. Comparisons

PART A

1. C	3. C	5. B	7. A	9. C
2. B	4. D	6. C	8. D	10. D

PART B

11. B	12. A	13. C	14. C

Practice for Structure and Written Expression (Chapter 6)

Exercise 1. Nouns and noun phrases

PART A

1. A	3. B	5. B	7. D	9. A
2. C	4. D	6. A	8. D	10. B

PART B

1. C	3. A	5. B	7. C	9. D
2. D	4. C	6. B	8. A	10. C

Exercise 2. Verbs and verb phrases

PART A

1. B	3. D	5. C	7. B	9. D
2. D	4. A	6. D	8. B	10. B

PART B

1. B	3. B	5. D	7. C	9. D
2. B	4. D	6. A	8. D	10. C

Exercise 3. Adjectives and adjective phrases

PART A

1. C	3. A	5. B	7. C	9. B
2. C	4. D	6. B	8. B	10. B

PART B

1. B	3. B	5. A	7. D	9. A
2. C	4. D	6. A	8. B	10. B

Exercise 4. Pronouns

PART A

1. B	3. D	5. D	7. B	9. C
2. B	4. C	6. A	8. C	10. B

PART B

1. D	3. B	5. C	7. D	9. B
2. B	4. D	6. B	8. A	10. D

Exercise 5. Function and placement of adverbs

PART A

1. A	3. B	5. B	7. A	9. C
2. B	4. A	6. D	8. B	10. C

PART B

1. B	3. A	5. B	7. C	9. D
2. B	4. A	6. A	8. B	10. B

Exercise 6. Parallel structure

PART A

1. D	3. B	5. B	7. B	9. A
2. C	4. D	6. D	8. C	10. A

PART B

1. C	3. B	5. B	7. A	9. C
2. D	4. C	6. D	8. D	10. D

Exercise 7. Subordinate clauses

PART A

1. A	3. C	5. C	7. B	9. B
2. D	4. C	6. B	8. A	10. C

PART B

1. C	3. A	5. C	7. A	9. A
2. C	4. B	6. C	8. B	10. C

Exercise 8. Subject/verb presence and agreement; repeated subject

PART A

1. B	3. C	5. C	7. B	9. A
2. B	4. D	6. C	8. C	10. D

PART B

1. B	3. D	5. B	7. C	9. B
2. B	4. B	6. C	8. B	10. A

Exercise 9. Active/passive voice

PART A

1. B	3. B	5. C	7. C	9. D
2. C	4. B	6. A	8. C	10. B

PART B

1. D	3. B	5. B	7. A	9. A
2. D	4. B	6. B	8. C	10. C

Exercise 10. Gerunds/infinitives

PART A

1. B	3. B	5. D	7. C	9. B
2. C	4. C	6. A	8. C	10. A

PART B

1. A	3. D	5. C	7. D	9. D
2. C	4. C	6. D	8. B	10. D

Exercise 11. Prepositions and prepositional phrases

PART A

1. B	2. C	3. C	4. C	5. C

PART B

1. D	2. D	3. C	4. C	5. A

Exercise 12. Repeated meaning (tested only in Part B)

1. D	3. B	5. C	7. C	9. B
2. A	4. B	6. A	8. A	10. B

Exercise 13. Verb tense/inversion

PART A

1. B	2. C	3. C	4. C	5. A

PART B

1. D	2. A	3. B	4. C	5. C

Exercise 14. Main clause structure; partial and complete main clauses

PART A

1. D	2. C	3. D	4. B	5. C

PART B

1. B	2. A	3. B	4. C	5. A

Practice for Reading Comprehension (Chapter 8)

PART A. Vocabulary practice

EXERCISE 1

1. B	7. B	13. B	19. B	25. D
2. C	8. B	14. C	20. B	26. C
3. C	9. D	15. B	21. B	27. B
4. B	10. C	16. B	22. A	28. C
5. B	11. D	17. A	23. D	29. B
6. D	12. A	18. D	24. B	30. D

EXERCISE 2

1. A	7. A	13. C	19. B	25. B
2. D	8. C	14. B	20. D	26. C
3. A	9. A	15. B	21. D	27. C
4. B	10. C	16. B	22. D	28. A
5. C	11. A	17. A	23. C	29. B
6. C	12. A	18. A	24. A	30. C

EXERCISE 3

1. A	4. A	7. C	10. C
2. A	5. C	8. B	11. D
3. C	6. B	9. B	12. C

EXERCISE 4

1. A	4. B	7. D	10. C
2. C	5. B	8. B	11. B
3. B	6. C	9. A	12. C

EXERCISE 5

1. D	3. B	5. A	7. A	9. A
2. D	4. C	6. D	8. C	10. A

EXERCISE 6

1. C	4. D	7. D	10. D
2. B	5. C	8. A	11. D
3. B	6. C	9. B	

EXERCISE 7

1. A	4. C	7. C	10. B
2. C	5. A	8. B	11. C
3. B	6. B	9. B	12. C

EXERCISE 8

1. C	3. C	5. C	7. B
2. C	4. C	6. C	8. C

EXERCISE 9

1. A	3. D	5. A	7. B	9. A
2. A	4. C	6. B	8. B	10. D

EXERCISE 10

1. C	4. B	7. D	10. C
2. B	5. B	8. A	11. C
3. D	6. C	9. C	12. A

EXERCISE 11

1. A	3. C	5. D	7. C	9. B
2. B	4. A	6. C	8. B	10. B

EXERCISE 12

1. D	3. A	5. A	7. C
2. C	4. C	6. B	8. D

Practice TOEFL 1

Section 1. Listening comprehension

PART A

1. D	7. C	13. C	19. A	25. C
2. A	8. A	14. B	20. D	26. C
3. B	9. D	15. C	21. A	27. C
4. B	10. D	16. C	22. B	28. A
5. D	11. C	17. D	23. B	29. A
6. B	12. C	18. B	24. C	30. D

PART B

31. C	33. C	35. B	37. C
32. C	34. D	36. B	38. A

PART C

39. D	42. B	45. B	48. A
40. B	43. B	46. A	49. B
41. A	44. A	47. B	50. D

Section 2. Structure and written expression

PART A

1. B	4. C	7. A	10. C	13. C
2. B	5. B	8. D	11. A	14. C
3. A	6. C	9. D	12. C	15. B

PART B

16. C	21. D	26. A	31. B	36. A
17. D	22. A	27. C	32. D	37. A
18. B	23. D	28. D	33. C	38. D
19. D	24. D	29. D	34. D	39. C
20. D	25. C	30. A	35. B	40. B

Section 3. Reading comprehension

PART A

1. B	11. C	21. B	31. A	41. B
2. A	12. C	22. A	32. C	42. B
3. C	13. B	23. C	33. B	43. D
4. D	14. B	24. C	34. A	44. C
5. C	15. C	25. C	35. B	45. A
6. C	16. D	26. C	36. B	46. C
7. A	17. C	27. A	37. D	47. A
8. A	18. A	28. D	38. C	48. C
9. D	19. B	29. C	39. C	49. A
10. B	20. C	30. B	40. A	50. B

Practice TOEFL 2

Section 1. Listening comprehension

PART A

1. B	7. B	13. C	19. B	25. C
2. B	8. B	14. D	20. A	26. B
3. C	9. D	15. C	21. A	27. A
4. B	10. A	16. C	22. B	28. B
5. B	11. C	17. D	23. B	29. D
6. A	12. C	18. A	24. B	30. D

PART B

31. D	33. B	35. B	37. B
32. D	34. B	36. C	38. A

PART C

39. B	42. C	45. C	48. A
40. C	43. C	46. B	49. B
41. A	44. A	47. C	50. B

Section 2. Structure and written expression

PART A

1. A	4. C	7. C	10. D	13. A
2. B	5. B	8. B	11. B	14. D
3. C	6. A	9. B	12. C	15. B

PART B

16. C	21. A	26. A	31. D	36. C
17. D	22. C	27. A	32. B	37. A
18. A	23. B	28. D	33. A	38. C
19. C	24. C	29. B	34. C	39. B
20. D	25. D	30. A	35. A	40. C

Section 3. Reading comprehension

1. C	11. A	21. A	31. B	41. C
2. B	12. B	22. D	32. C	42. D
3. B	13. B	23. D	33. A	43. C
4. C	14. C	24. D	34. C	44. A
5. D	15. A	25. C	35. A	45. A
6. A	16. C	26. C	36. B	46. B
7. D	17. D	27. D	37. B	47. C
8. B	18. B	28. C	38. B	48. C
9. C	19. A	29. B	39. A	49. C
10. B	20. A	30. D	40. B	50. D

Practice TOEFL 3

Section 1. Listening comprehension

PART A

1. A	7. A	13. A	19. B	25. B
2. C	8. B	14. D	20. D	26. C
3. B	9. D	15. B	21. A	27. D
4. A	10. D	16. A	22. B	28. B
5. B	11. C	17. A	23. C	29. D
6. C	12. A	18. C	24. C	30. B

PART B

31. B	33. B	35. B	37. D
32. D	34. B	36. B	38. C

PART C

39. D	42. B	45. B	48. B
40. C	43. D	46. A	49. B
41. C	44. A	47. B	50. A

Section 2. Structure and written expression

PART A

1. B	4. C	7. B	10. B	13. C
2. A	5. B	8. A	11. C	14. D
3. C	6. D	9. B	12. B	15. B

PART B

16. D	21. B	26. D	31. D	36. D
17. D	22. C	27. D	32. B	37. C
18. A	23. B	28. B	33. C	38. D
19. D	24. B	29. D	34. B	39. B
20. D	25. C	30. B	35. B	40. C

Section 3. Reading comprehension

1. B	11. B	21. B	31. C	41. D
2. C	12. B	22. C	32. B	42. B
3. C	13. B	23. D	33. C	43. C
4. A	14. A	24. B	34. C	44. B
5. C	15. C	25. D	35. B	45. B
6. C	16. B	26. C	36. C	46. C
7. B	17. C	27. A	37. B	47. C
8. B	18. B	28. D	38. C	48. B
9. C	19. B	29. D	39. D	49. D
10. D	20. C	30. D	40. C	50. A

Practice TOEFL 4

Section 1. Listening comprehension

PART A

1. C	7. B	13. B	19. C	25. A
2. C	8. A	14. D	20. B	26. B
3. B	9. C	15. B	21. B	27. D
4. A	10. B	16. B	22. C	28. C
5. B	11. C	17. D	23. C	29. A
6. C	12. B	18. C	24. B	30. C

PART B

31. C	33. B	35. C	37. A
32. C	34. B	36. B	

PART C

38. B	41. A	44. B	47. B	50. D
39. D	42. C	45. C	48. A	
40. D	43. A	46. D	49. C	

Section 2. Structure and written expression

PART A

1. B	4. C	7. D	10. C	13. C
2. B	5. C	8. B	11. D	14. B
3. C	6. B	9. B	12. B	15. D

PART B

16. D	21. A	26. B	31. D	36. D
17. C	22. A	27. C	32. A	37. D
18. C	23. A	28. A	33. B	38. C
19. B	24. C	29. D	34. B	39. C
20. D	25. D	30. C	35. C	40. B

Section 3. Reading comprehension

PART A

1. D	11. D	21. B	31. D	41. C
2. C	12. B	22. B	32. B	42. B
3. A	13. A	23. C	33. C	43. C
4. D	14. D	24. A	34. C	44. C
5. A	15. B	25. A	35. D	45. A
6. B	16. D	26. A	36. D	46. D
7. A	17. B	27. B	37. A	47. C
8. D	18. B	28. D	38. C	48. C
9. D	19. B	29. B	39. D	49. B
10. B	20. C	30. B	40. C	50. B

Practice TOEFL 5

Section 1. Listening comprehension

PART A

1. D	7. B	13. B	19. C	25. C
2. C	8. D	14. C	20. A	26. D
3. A	9. D	15. B	21. B	27. C
4. D	10. C	16. B	22. D	28. D
5. A	11. C	17. C	23. B	29. C
6. D	12. D	18. B	24. A	30. D

PART B

31. C	33. B	35. B	37. D
32. B	34. C	36. D	38. B

PART C

39. C	42. D	45. A	48. C
40. C	43. C	46. A	49. A
41. D	44. B	47. B	50. B

Section 2. Structure and written expression

PART A

1. B	4. D	7. B	10. A	13. B
2. C	5. B	8. A	11. D	14. A
3. A	6. D	9. C	12. C	15. C

PART B

16. B	21. C	26. D	31. C	36. C
17. D	22. C	27. D	32. A	37. D
18. A	23. B	28. C	33. A	38. D
19. A	24. B	29. D	34. D	39. C
20. C	25. B	30. C	35. D	40. C

Section 3. Reading comprehension

1. C	11. D	21. C	31. C	41. A
2. A	12. B	22. D	32. C	42. B
3. D	13. C	23. A	33. B	43. B
4. C	14. B	24. A	34. C	44. B
5. B	15. B	25. A	35. D	45. C
6. B	16. B	26. D	36. D	46. C
7. B	17. D	27. D	37. C	47. C
8. C	18. C	28. D	38. B	48. C
9. C	19. C	29. C	39. B	49. A
10. C	20. B	30. B	40. C	50. C

Practice TOEFL 6

Section 1. Listening comprehension

PART A

1. B	7. A	13. D	19. D	25. C
2. C	8. A	14. A	20. A	26. D
3. C	9. B	15. B	21. D	27. B
4. B	10. D	16. D	22. C	28. C
5. C	11. B	17. A	23. C	29. D
6. D	12. C	18. C	24. D	30. C

PART B

31. C	33. B	35. A	37. A
32. C	34. D	36. B	38. B

PART C

39. C	42. A	45. C	48. B
40. D	43. B	46. B	49. D
41. C	44. D	47. A	50. B

Section 2. Structure and written expression

PART A

1. C	4. C	7. A	10. B	13. B
2. C	5. D	8. D	11. C	14. C
3. A	6. B	9. B	12. A	15. A

PART B

16. A	21. C	26. A	31. B	36. C
17. D	22. D	27. B	32. C	37. D
18. B	23. B	28. B	33. D	38. B
19. D	24. D	29. A	34. D	39. A
20. B	25. B	30. A	35. D	40. D

Section 3. Reading comprehension

PART A

1. B	11. A	21. A	31. B	41. D
2. B	12. D	22. C	32. C	42. B
3. C	13. A	23. B	33. A	43. A
4. D	14. C	24. A	34. C	44. C
5. D	15. B	25. D	35. D	45. B
6. B	16. A	26. B	36. C	46. A
7. B	17. D	27. C	37. B	47. C
8. D	18. C	28. D	38. A	48. A
9. C	19. B	29. A	39. B	49. B
10. A	20. C	30. B	40. A	50. D

Practice TOEFL 7

Section 1. Listening comprehension

PART A

1. C	7. C	13. B	19. C	25. B
2. D	8. C	14. C	20. A	26. C
3. B	9. C	15. A	21. C	27. D
4. C	10. C	16. B	22. A	28. B
5. A	11. D	17. A	23. B	29. C
6. B	12. C	18. B	24. A	30. D

PART B

31. A	33. C	35. B	37. C
32. B	34. D	36. A	38. B

PART C

39. A	42. D	45. B	48. B
40. D	43. A	46. B	49. C
41. B	44. C	47. C	50. D

Section 2. Structure and written expression

PART A

1. B	4. A	7. A	10. D	13. B
2. C	5. C	8. D	11. D	14. B
3. D	6. C	9. C	12. A	15. B

PART B

16. A	21. D	26. C	31. D	36. B
17. A	22. C	27. D	32. B	37. D
18. B	23. B	28. D	33. B	38. C
19. C	24. D	29. C	34. C	39. D
20. A	25. B	30. C	35. D	40. B

Section 3. Reading comprehension

1. C	11. A	21. A	31. C	41. A
2. A	12. C	22. B	32. C	42. B
3. C	13. B	23. D	33. B	43. B
4. B	14. D	24. C	34. D	44. B
5. C	15. B	25. B	35. A	45. C
6. B	16. C	26. C	36. A	46. C
7. C	17. D	27. C	37. A	47. D
8. D	18. B	28. B	38. C	48. A
9. D	19. A	29. B	39. B	49. B
10. A	20. C	30. A	40. C	50. B

Practice TOEFL 8

Section 1. Listening comprehension

PART A

1. C	7. A	13. A	19. C	25. C
2. D	8. C	14. B	20. B	26. A
3. B	9. B	15. C	21. B	27. C
4. A	10. A	16. A	22. C	28. B
5. B	11. D	17. D	23. D	29. A
6. D	12. C	18. A	24. B	30. B

PART B

31. B	33. B	35. B	37. C	39. C
32. D	34. C	36. A	38. D	40. B

PART C

41. C	43. B	45. D	47. C	49. D
42. C	44. D	46. B	48. C	50. B

Section 2. Structure and written expression

PART A

1. A	4. A	7. A	10. D	13. C
2. C	5. B	8. C	11. C	14. D
3. D	6. C	9. C	12. A	15. C

PART B

16. A	21. B	26. D	31. A	36. C
17. B	22. A	27. B	32. C	37. B
18. C	23. D	28. D	33. B	38. A
19. B	24. B	29. C	34. B	39. D
20. D	25. A	30. B	35. D	40. D

Section 3. Reading comprehension

1. C	11. B	21. B	31. D	41. A
2. B	12. D	22. D	32. B	42. C
3. A	13. B	23. A	33. C	43. D
4. B	14. C	24. B	34. D	44. A
5. B	15. A	25. C	35. A	45. D
6. A	16. B	26. B	36. C	46. B
7. B	17. C	27. D	37. D	47. C
8. A	18. D	28. C	38. B	48. A
9. D	19. C	29. B	39. C	49. D
10. C	20. A	30. A	40. C	50. D

E. Answer Sheets

PRACTICE TOEFL 1   ANSWER SHEET

SAMPLE

SIDE 2		Choose only one answer for each question. Carefully and completely fill in the oval corresponding to the answer you choose so that the letter inside the oval cannot be seen. Completely erase any other marks you may have made. Choose only one answer for each question.

FORM

TEST BOOK SERIAL NUMBER

CORRECT   WRONG   WRONG   WRONG   WRONG
Ⓐ Ⓑ ● Ⓓ   Ⓐ Ⓑ ⊘ Ⓓ   Ⓐ Ⓑ ⊗ Ⓓ   Ⓐ Ⓑ Ⓒ Ⓓ   Ⓐ Ⓑ ● Ⓓ

SEAT NUMBER

NAME (Print) _____
FAMILY NAME (SURNAME)   GIVEN (FIRST NAME)   MIDDLE NAME

REGISTRATION NUMBER   **SIGNATURE**

SEX	DATE OF BIRTH
☐ MALE ☐ FEMALE	MO / DAY / YEAR

SECTION 1

1 Ⓐ Ⓑ Ⓒ Ⓓ
2 Ⓐ Ⓑ Ⓒ Ⓓ
3 Ⓐ Ⓑ Ⓒ Ⓓ
4 Ⓐ Ⓑ Ⓒ Ⓓ
5 Ⓐ Ⓑ Ⓒ Ⓓ
6 Ⓐ Ⓑ Ⓒ Ⓓ
7 Ⓐ Ⓑ Ⓒ Ⓓ
8 Ⓐ Ⓑ Ⓒ Ⓓ
9 Ⓐ Ⓑ Ⓒ Ⓓ
10 Ⓐ Ⓑ Ⓒ Ⓓ
11 Ⓐ Ⓑ Ⓒ Ⓓ
12 Ⓐ Ⓑ Ⓒ Ⓓ
13 Ⓐ Ⓑ Ⓒ Ⓓ
14 Ⓐ Ⓑ Ⓒ Ⓓ
15 Ⓐ Ⓑ Ⓒ Ⓓ
16 Ⓐ Ⓑ Ⓒ Ⓓ
17 Ⓐ Ⓑ Ⓒ Ⓓ
18 Ⓐ Ⓑ Ⓒ Ⓓ
19 Ⓐ Ⓑ Ⓒ Ⓓ
20 Ⓐ Ⓑ Ⓒ Ⓓ
21 Ⓐ Ⓑ Ⓒ Ⓓ
22 Ⓐ Ⓑ Ⓒ Ⓓ
23 Ⓐ Ⓑ Ⓒ Ⓓ
24 Ⓐ Ⓑ Ⓒ Ⓓ
25 Ⓐ Ⓑ Ⓒ Ⓓ
26 Ⓐ Ⓑ Ⓒ Ⓓ
27 Ⓐ Ⓑ Ⓒ Ⓓ
28 Ⓐ Ⓑ Ⓒ Ⓓ
29 Ⓐ Ⓑ Ⓒ Ⓓ
30 Ⓐ Ⓑ Ⓒ Ⓓ
31 Ⓐ Ⓑ Ⓒ Ⓓ
32 Ⓐ Ⓑ Ⓒ Ⓓ
33 Ⓐ Ⓑ Ⓒ Ⓓ
34 Ⓐ Ⓑ Ⓒ Ⓓ
35 Ⓐ Ⓑ Ⓒ Ⓓ
36 Ⓐ Ⓑ Ⓒ Ⓓ
37 Ⓐ Ⓑ Ⓒ Ⓓ
38 Ⓐ Ⓑ Ⓒ Ⓓ
39 Ⓐ Ⓑ Ⓒ Ⓓ
40 Ⓐ Ⓑ Ⓒ Ⓓ
41 Ⓐ Ⓑ Ⓒ Ⓓ
42 Ⓐ Ⓑ Ⓒ Ⓓ
43 Ⓐ Ⓑ Ⓒ Ⓓ
44 Ⓐ Ⓑ Ⓒ Ⓓ
45 Ⓐ Ⓑ Ⓒ Ⓓ
46 Ⓐ Ⓑ Ⓒ Ⓓ
47 Ⓐ Ⓑ Ⓒ Ⓓ
48 Ⓐ Ⓑ Ⓒ Ⓓ
49 Ⓐ Ⓑ Ⓒ Ⓓ
50 Ⓐ Ⓑ Ⓒ Ⓓ

SECTION 2

1 Ⓐ Ⓑ Ⓒ Ⓓ
2 Ⓐ Ⓑ Ⓒ Ⓓ
3 Ⓐ Ⓑ Ⓒ Ⓓ
4 Ⓐ Ⓑ Ⓒ Ⓓ
5 Ⓐ Ⓑ Ⓒ Ⓓ
6 Ⓐ Ⓑ Ⓒ Ⓓ
7 Ⓐ Ⓑ Ⓒ Ⓓ
8 Ⓐ Ⓑ Ⓒ Ⓓ
9 Ⓐ Ⓑ Ⓒ Ⓓ
10 Ⓐ Ⓑ Ⓒ Ⓓ
11 Ⓐ Ⓑ Ⓒ Ⓓ
12 Ⓐ Ⓑ Ⓒ Ⓓ
13 Ⓐ Ⓑ Ⓒ Ⓓ
14 Ⓐ Ⓑ Ⓒ Ⓓ
15 Ⓐ Ⓑ Ⓒ Ⓓ
16 Ⓐ Ⓑ Ⓒ Ⓓ
17 Ⓐ Ⓑ Ⓒ Ⓓ
18 Ⓐ Ⓑ Ⓒ Ⓓ
19 Ⓐ Ⓑ Ⓒ Ⓓ
20 Ⓐ Ⓑ Ⓒ Ⓓ
21 Ⓐ Ⓑ Ⓒ Ⓓ
22 Ⓐ Ⓑ Ⓒ Ⓓ
23 Ⓐ Ⓑ Ⓒ Ⓓ
24 Ⓐ Ⓑ Ⓒ Ⓓ
25 Ⓐ Ⓑ Ⓒ Ⓓ
26 Ⓐ Ⓑ Ⓒ Ⓓ
27 Ⓐ Ⓑ Ⓒ Ⓓ
28 Ⓐ Ⓑ Ⓒ Ⓓ
29 Ⓐ Ⓑ Ⓒ Ⓓ
30 Ⓐ Ⓑ Ⓒ Ⓓ
31 Ⓐ Ⓑ Ⓒ Ⓓ
32 Ⓐ Ⓑ Ⓒ Ⓓ
33 Ⓐ Ⓑ Ⓒ Ⓓ
34 Ⓐ Ⓑ Ⓒ Ⓓ
35 Ⓐ Ⓑ Ⓒ Ⓓ
36 Ⓐ Ⓑ Ⓒ Ⓓ
37 Ⓐ Ⓑ Ⓒ Ⓓ
38 Ⓐ Ⓑ Ⓒ Ⓓ
39 Ⓐ Ⓑ Ⓒ Ⓓ
40 Ⓐ Ⓑ Ⓒ Ⓓ

SECTION 3

1 Ⓐ Ⓑ Ⓒ Ⓓ   31 Ⓐ Ⓑ Ⓒ Ⓓ
2 Ⓐ Ⓑ Ⓒ Ⓓ   32 Ⓐ Ⓑ Ⓒ Ⓓ
3 Ⓐ Ⓑ Ⓒ Ⓓ   33 Ⓐ Ⓑ Ⓒ Ⓓ
4 Ⓐ Ⓑ Ⓒ Ⓓ   34 Ⓐ Ⓑ Ⓒ Ⓓ
5 Ⓐ Ⓑ Ⓒ Ⓓ   35 Ⓐ Ⓑ Ⓒ Ⓓ
6 Ⓐ Ⓑ Ⓒ Ⓓ   36 Ⓐ Ⓑ Ⓒ Ⓓ
7 Ⓐ Ⓑ Ⓒ Ⓓ   37 Ⓐ Ⓑ Ⓒ Ⓓ
8 Ⓐ Ⓑ Ⓒ Ⓓ   38 Ⓐ Ⓑ Ⓒ Ⓓ
9 Ⓐ Ⓑ Ⓒ Ⓓ   39 Ⓐ Ⓑ Ⓒ Ⓓ
10 Ⓐ Ⓑ Ⓒ Ⓓ   40 Ⓐ Ⓑ Ⓒ Ⓓ
11 Ⓐ Ⓑ Ⓒ Ⓓ   41 Ⓐ Ⓑ Ⓒ Ⓓ
12 Ⓐ Ⓑ Ⓒ Ⓓ   42 Ⓐ Ⓑ Ⓒ Ⓓ
13 Ⓐ Ⓑ Ⓒ Ⓓ   43 Ⓐ Ⓑ Ⓒ Ⓓ
14 Ⓐ Ⓑ Ⓒ Ⓓ   44 Ⓐ Ⓑ Ⓒ Ⓓ
15 Ⓐ Ⓑ Ⓒ Ⓓ   45 Ⓐ Ⓑ Ⓒ Ⓓ
16 Ⓐ Ⓑ Ⓒ Ⓓ   46 Ⓐ Ⓑ Ⓒ Ⓓ
17 Ⓐ Ⓑ Ⓒ Ⓓ   47 Ⓐ Ⓑ Ⓒ Ⓓ
18 Ⓐ Ⓑ Ⓒ Ⓓ   48 Ⓐ Ⓑ Ⓒ Ⓓ
19 Ⓐ Ⓑ Ⓒ Ⓓ   49 Ⓐ Ⓑ Ⓒ Ⓓ
20 Ⓐ Ⓑ Ⓒ Ⓓ   50 Ⓐ Ⓑ Ⓒ Ⓓ
21 Ⓐ Ⓑ Ⓒ Ⓓ
22 Ⓐ Ⓑ Ⓒ Ⓓ
23 Ⓐ Ⓑ Ⓒ Ⓓ
24 Ⓐ Ⓑ Ⓒ Ⓓ
25 Ⓐ Ⓑ Ⓒ Ⓓ
26 Ⓐ Ⓑ Ⓒ Ⓓ
27 Ⓐ Ⓑ Ⓒ Ⓓ
28 Ⓐ Ⓑ Ⓒ Ⓓ
29 Ⓐ Ⓑ Ⓒ Ⓓ
30 Ⓐ Ⓑ Ⓒ Ⓓ

SCORE CANCELLATION

If you want to cancel your scores from this administration, complete A and B below. The scores will not be sent to you or your designated recipients, and they will be deleted from your permanent record. To cancel your scores from this test administration, you must

A. fill in both ovals here   and B. sign your name in full below

◯ — ◯

ONCE A SCORE HAS BEEN CANCELED, IT CANNOT BE REINSTATED ON YOUR PERMANENT RECORD

1R	2R	3R	TCS	FOR ETS USE ONLY	F
1CS	2CS	3CS			

PRACTICE TOEFL 2   ANSWER SHEET

SAMPLE

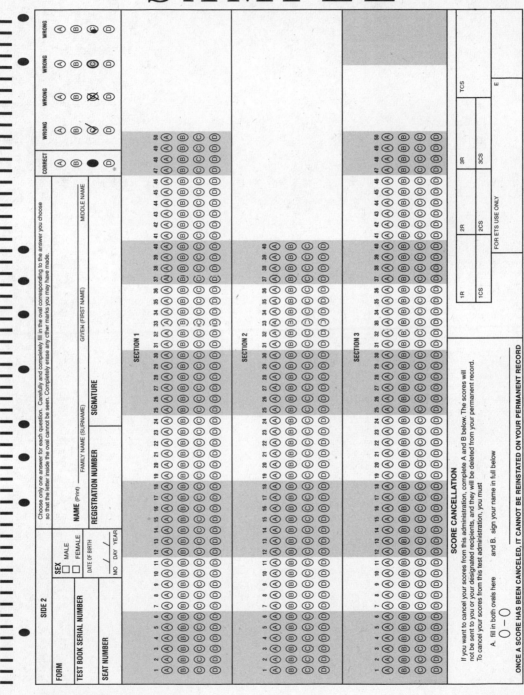

PRACTICE TOEFL 3   ANSWER SHEET

SAMPLE

SIDE 2		

FORM

TEST BOOK SERIAL NUMBER

SEAT NUMBER

SEX	DATE OF BIRTH	
☐ MALE ☐ FEMALE	MO / DAY / YEAR	

Choose only one answer for each question. Carefully and completely fill in the oval corresponding to the answer you choose so that the letter inside the oval cannot be seen. Completely erase any other marks you may have made. Choose only one answer for each question.

CORRECT	WRONG	WRONG	WRONG	WRONG
Ⓐ Ⓑ ● Ⓓ	Ⓐ Ⓑ Ⓥ Ⓓ	Ⓐ Ⓑ Ⓧ Ⓓ	Ⓐ Ⓑ Ⓒ Ⓓ	Ⓐ Ⓑ Ⓒ Ⓓ

NAME (Print)
FAMILY NAME (SURNAME)   GIVEN (FIRST NAME)   MIDDLE NAME

REGISTRATION NUMBER   **SIGNATURE**

SECTION 1	SECTION 2	SECTION 3

SCORE CANCELLATION

If you want to cancel your scores from this administration, complete A and B below. The scores will not be sent to you or your designated recipients, and they will be deleted from your permanent record. To cancel your scores from this test administration, you must

A. fill in both ovals here   and B. sign your name in full below

◯ — ◯

ONCE A SCORE HAS BEEN CANCELED, IT CANNOT BE REINSTATED ON YOUR PERMANENT RECORD

1R	2R	3R	TCS	FOR ETS USE ONLY	F
1CS	2CS	3CS			

SAMPLE

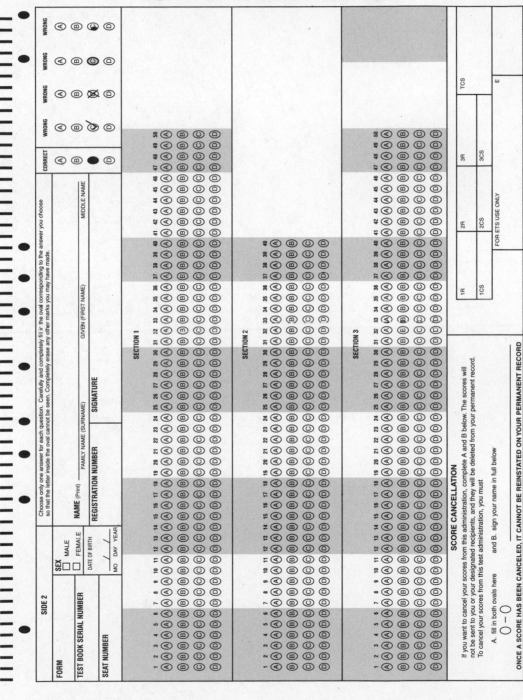

PRACTICE TOEFL 5   ANSWER SHEET

SAMPLE

SIDE 2	Choose only one answer for each question. Carefully and completely fill in the oval corresponding to the answer you choose so that the letter inside the oval cannot be seen. Completely erase any other marks you may have made. Choose only one answer for each question.

FORM

TEST BOOK SERIAL NUMBER

CORRECT	WRONG	WRONG	WRONG	WRONG
Ⓐ Ⓑ ● Ⓓ	Ⓐ Ⓥ Ⓒ Ⓓ	Ⓐ Ⓑ Ⓧ Ⓓ	Ⓐ Ⓑ Ⓒ Ⓓ	Ⓐ Ⓑ ● Ⓓ

SEAT NUMBER

NAME (Print) _____

FAMILY NAME (SURNAME)   GIVEN (FIRST NAME)   MIDDLE NAME

SEX	DATE OF BIRTH		
☐ MALE ☐ FEMALE	MO / DAY / YEAR		

REGISTRATION NUMBER   **SIGNATURE**

SECTION 1 / SECTION 2 / SECTION 3

SECTION 1

1–50 Ⓐ Ⓑ Ⓒ Ⓓ

SECTION 2

1–40 Ⓐ Ⓑ Ⓒ Ⓓ

SECTION 3

1–30 Ⓐ Ⓑ Ⓒ Ⓓ   31–50 Ⓐ Ⓑ Ⓒ Ⓓ

SCORE CANCELLATION

If you want to cancel your scores from this administration, complete A and B below. The scores will not be sent to you or your designated recipients, and they will be deleted from your permanent record. To cancel your scores from this test administration, you must

A. fill in both ovals here   and B. sign your name in full below

◯ — ◯

ONCE A SCORE HAS BEEN CANCELED, IT CANNOT BE REINSTATED ON YOUR PERMANENT RECORD

1R	2R	3R	TCS	FOR ETS USE ONLY	F
1CS	2CS	3CS			

PRACTICE TOEFL 6 ANSWER SHEET

SAMPLE

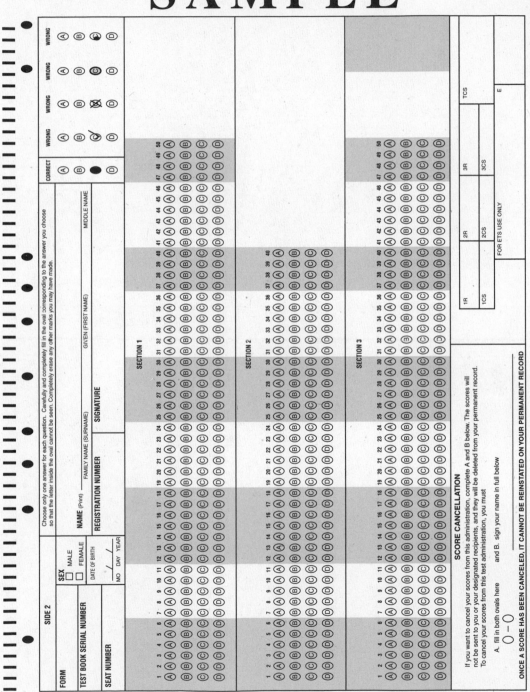

PRACTICE TOEFL 7   ANSWER SHEET

SAMPLE

SIDE 2
FORM
TEST BOOK SERIAL NUMBER
SEAT NUMBER

Choose only one answer for each question. Carefully and completely fill in the oval corresponding to the answer you choose so that the letter inside the oval cannot be seen. Completely erase any other marks you may have made. Choose only one answer for each question.

CORRECT	WRONG	WRONG	WRONG	WRONG
Ⓐ Ⓑ ● Ⓓ	Ⓐ Ⓑ Ⓥ Ⓓ	Ⓐ Ⓧ Ⓧ Ⓓ	Ⓐ Ⓑ Ⓒ Ⓓ	Ⓐ Ⓑ Ⓒ Ⓓ

NAME (Print)

FAMILY NAME (SURNAME)   GIVEN (FIRST NAME)   MIDDLE NAME

REGISTRATION NUMBER   **SIGNATURE**

SEX	DATE OF BIRTH
☐ MALE ☐ FEMALE	MO / DAY / YEAR

SECTION 1

1 Ⓐ Ⓑ Ⓒ Ⓓ
2 Ⓐ Ⓑ Ⓒ Ⓓ
3 Ⓐ Ⓑ Ⓒ Ⓓ
4 Ⓐ Ⓑ Ⓒ Ⓓ
5 Ⓐ Ⓑ Ⓒ Ⓓ
6 Ⓐ Ⓑ Ⓒ Ⓓ
7 Ⓐ Ⓑ Ⓒ Ⓓ
8 Ⓐ Ⓑ Ⓒ Ⓓ
9 Ⓐ Ⓑ Ⓒ Ⓓ
10 Ⓐ Ⓑ Ⓒ Ⓓ
11 Ⓐ Ⓑ Ⓒ Ⓓ
12 Ⓐ Ⓑ Ⓒ Ⓓ
13 Ⓐ Ⓑ Ⓒ Ⓓ
14 Ⓐ Ⓑ Ⓒ Ⓓ
15 Ⓐ Ⓑ Ⓒ Ⓓ
16 Ⓐ Ⓑ Ⓒ Ⓓ
17 Ⓐ Ⓑ Ⓒ Ⓓ
18 Ⓐ Ⓑ Ⓒ Ⓓ
19 Ⓐ Ⓑ Ⓒ Ⓓ
20 Ⓐ Ⓑ Ⓒ Ⓓ
21 Ⓐ Ⓑ Ⓒ Ⓓ
22 Ⓐ Ⓑ Ⓒ Ⓓ
23 Ⓐ Ⓑ Ⓒ Ⓓ
24 Ⓐ Ⓑ Ⓒ Ⓓ
25 Ⓐ Ⓑ Ⓒ Ⓓ
26 Ⓐ Ⓑ Ⓒ Ⓓ
27 Ⓐ Ⓑ Ⓒ Ⓓ
28 Ⓐ Ⓑ Ⓒ Ⓓ
29 Ⓐ Ⓑ Ⓒ Ⓓ
30 Ⓐ Ⓑ Ⓒ Ⓓ
31 Ⓐ Ⓑ Ⓒ Ⓓ
32 Ⓐ Ⓑ Ⓒ Ⓓ
33 Ⓐ Ⓑ Ⓒ Ⓓ
34 Ⓐ Ⓑ Ⓒ Ⓓ
35 Ⓐ Ⓑ Ⓒ Ⓓ
36 Ⓐ Ⓑ Ⓒ Ⓓ
37 Ⓐ Ⓑ Ⓒ Ⓓ
38 Ⓐ Ⓑ Ⓒ Ⓓ
39 Ⓐ Ⓑ Ⓒ Ⓓ
40 Ⓐ Ⓑ Ⓒ Ⓓ
41 Ⓐ Ⓑ Ⓒ Ⓓ
42 Ⓐ Ⓑ Ⓒ Ⓓ
43 Ⓐ Ⓑ Ⓒ Ⓓ
44 Ⓐ Ⓑ Ⓒ Ⓓ
45 Ⓐ Ⓑ Ⓒ Ⓓ
46 Ⓐ Ⓑ Ⓒ Ⓓ
47 Ⓐ Ⓑ Ⓒ Ⓓ
48 Ⓐ Ⓑ Ⓒ Ⓓ
49 Ⓐ Ⓑ Ⓒ Ⓓ
50 Ⓐ Ⓑ Ⓒ Ⓓ

SECTION 2

1 Ⓐ Ⓑ Ⓒ Ⓓ
2 Ⓐ Ⓑ Ⓒ Ⓓ
3 Ⓐ Ⓑ Ⓒ Ⓓ
4 Ⓐ Ⓑ Ⓒ Ⓓ
5 Ⓐ Ⓑ Ⓒ Ⓓ
6 Ⓐ Ⓑ Ⓒ Ⓓ
7 Ⓐ Ⓑ Ⓒ Ⓓ
8 Ⓐ Ⓑ Ⓒ Ⓓ
9 Ⓐ Ⓑ Ⓒ Ⓓ
10 Ⓐ Ⓑ Ⓒ Ⓓ
11 Ⓐ Ⓑ Ⓒ Ⓓ
12 Ⓐ Ⓑ Ⓒ Ⓓ
13 Ⓐ Ⓑ Ⓒ Ⓓ
14 Ⓐ Ⓑ Ⓒ Ⓓ
15 Ⓐ Ⓑ Ⓒ Ⓓ
16 Ⓐ Ⓑ Ⓒ Ⓓ
17 Ⓐ Ⓑ Ⓒ Ⓓ
18 Ⓐ Ⓑ Ⓒ Ⓓ
19 Ⓐ Ⓑ Ⓒ Ⓓ
20 Ⓐ Ⓑ Ⓒ Ⓓ
21 Ⓐ Ⓑ Ⓒ Ⓓ
22 Ⓐ Ⓑ Ⓒ Ⓓ
23 Ⓐ Ⓑ Ⓒ Ⓓ
24 Ⓐ Ⓑ Ⓒ Ⓓ
25 Ⓐ Ⓑ Ⓒ Ⓓ
26 Ⓐ Ⓑ Ⓒ Ⓓ
27 Ⓐ Ⓑ Ⓒ Ⓓ
28 Ⓐ Ⓑ Ⓒ Ⓓ
29 Ⓐ Ⓑ Ⓒ Ⓓ
30 Ⓐ Ⓑ Ⓒ Ⓓ
31 Ⓐ Ⓑ Ⓒ Ⓓ
32 Ⓐ Ⓑ Ⓒ Ⓓ
33 Ⓐ Ⓑ Ⓒ Ⓓ
34 Ⓐ Ⓑ Ⓒ Ⓓ
35 Ⓐ Ⓑ Ⓒ Ⓓ
36 Ⓐ Ⓑ Ⓒ Ⓓ
37 Ⓐ Ⓑ Ⓒ Ⓓ
38 Ⓐ Ⓑ Ⓒ Ⓓ
39 Ⓐ Ⓑ Ⓒ Ⓓ
40 Ⓐ Ⓑ Ⓒ Ⓓ

SECTION 3

1 Ⓐ Ⓑ Ⓒ Ⓓ   31 Ⓐ Ⓑ Ⓒ Ⓓ
2 Ⓐ Ⓑ Ⓒ Ⓓ   32 Ⓐ Ⓑ Ⓒ Ⓓ
3 Ⓐ Ⓑ Ⓒ Ⓓ   33 Ⓐ Ⓑ Ⓒ Ⓓ
4 Ⓐ Ⓑ Ⓒ Ⓓ   34 Ⓐ Ⓑ Ⓒ Ⓓ
5 Ⓐ Ⓑ Ⓒ Ⓓ   35 Ⓐ Ⓑ Ⓒ Ⓓ
6 Ⓐ Ⓑ Ⓒ Ⓓ   36 Ⓐ Ⓑ Ⓒ Ⓓ
7 Ⓐ Ⓑ Ⓒ Ⓓ   37 Ⓐ Ⓑ Ⓒ Ⓓ
8 Ⓐ Ⓑ Ⓒ Ⓓ   38 Ⓐ Ⓑ Ⓒ Ⓓ
9 Ⓐ Ⓑ Ⓒ Ⓓ   39 Ⓐ Ⓑ Ⓒ Ⓓ
10 Ⓐ Ⓑ Ⓒ Ⓓ   40 Ⓐ Ⓑ Ⓒ Ⓓ
11 Ⓐ Ⓑ Ⓒ Ⓓ   41 Ⓐ Ⓑ Ⓒ Ⓓ
12 Ⓐ Ⓑ Ⓒ Ⓓ   42 Ⓐ Ⓑ Ⓒ Ⓓ
13 Ⓐ Ⓑ Ⓒ Ⓓ   43 Ⓐ Ⓑ Ⓒ Ⓓ
14 Ⓐ Ⓑ Ⓒ Ⓓ   44 Ⓐ Ⓑ Ⓒ Ⓓ
15 Ⓐ Ⓑ Ⓒ Ⓓ   45 Ⓐ Ⓑ Ⓒ Ⓓ
16 Ⓐ Ⓑ Ⓒ Ⓓ   46 Ⓐ Ⓑ Ⓒ Ⓓ
17 Ⓐ Ⓑ Ⓒ Ⓓ   47 Ⓐ Ⓑ Ⓒ Ⓓ
18 Ⓐ Ⓑ Ⓒ Ⓓ   48 Ⓐ Ⓑ Ⓒ Ⓓ
19 Ⓐ Ⓑ Ⓒ Ⓓ   49 Ⓐ Ⓑ Ⓒ Ⓓ
20 Ⓐ Ⓑ Ⓒ Ⓓ   50 Ⓐ Ⓑ Ⓒ Ⓓ
21 Ⓐ Ⓑ Ⓒ Ⓓ
22 Ⓐ Ⓑ Ⓒ Ⓓ
23 Ⓐ Ⓑ Ⓒ Ⓓ
24 Ⓐ Ⓑ Ⓒ Ⓓ
25 Ⓐ Ⓑ Ⓒ Ⓓ
26 Ⓐ Ⓑ Ⓒ Ⓓ
27 Ⓐ Ⓑ Ⓒ Ⓓ
28 Ⓐ Ⓑ Ⓒ Ⓓ
29 Ⓐ Ⓑ Ⓒ Ⓓ
30 Ⓐ Ⓑ Ⓒ Ⓓ

SCORE CANCELLATION

If you want to cancel your scores from this administration, complete A and B below. The scores will not be sent to you or your designated recipients, and they will be deleted from your permanent record. To cancel your scores from this test administration, you must

A. fill in both ovals here   and B. sign your name in full below

◯ — ◯

ONCE A SCORE HAS BEEN CANCELED, IT CANNOT BE REINSTATED ON YOUR PERMANENT RECORD

1R	2R	3R	TCS	FOR ETS USE ONLY	F
1CS	2CS	3CS			

PRACTICE TOEFL 8   ANSWER SHEET

SAMPLE

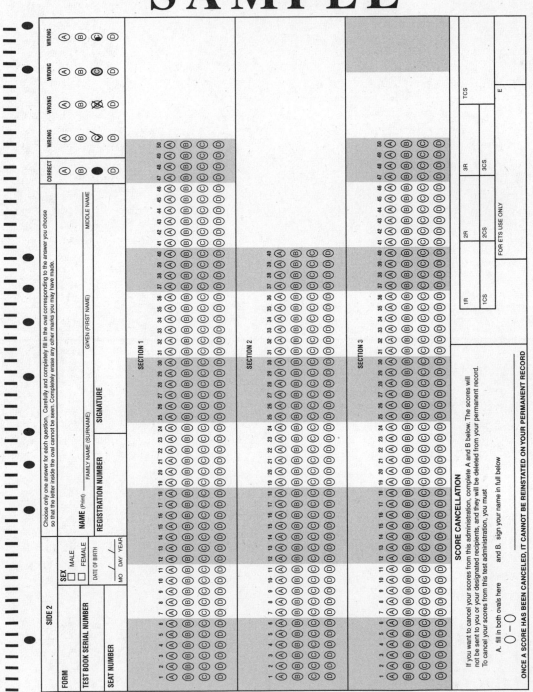

NOTES

NOTES

NOTES